TREASURY *of* PRECIOUS QUALITIES

A COMMENTARY ON THE ROOT TEXT
OF JIGME LINGPA

~~~~

༄༅། །ཡོན་ཏན་རིན་པོ་ཆེའི་མཛོད་ཀྱི་མཆན་འགྲེལ་
ཐེག་གསུམ་བདུད་རྩིའི་ཉིང་ཁུ་
ཞེས་བྱ་བ་བཞུགས་སོ། །

པདྨ་ཀུ་རའི་སྒྲ་བསྒྱུར་མ་ཕྱུན་ཚོགས་ནས་
སྒྲ་བསྒྱུར་ཤུས། །

The Padmakara Translation Group gratefully acknowledges the generous support of the Tsadra Foundation in sponsoring the translation of this book.

TREASURY *of* PRECIOUS QUALITIES

A COMMENTARY ON THE ROOT TEXT
OF JIGME LINGPA
ENTITLED

The Quintessence of the Three Paths

by Longchen Yeshe Dorje, Kangyur Rinpoche
Translated by the Padmakara Translation Group
Forewords by H. H. the Dalai Lama
and Jigme Khyentse Rinpoche

SHAMBHALA
BOSTON & LONDON
2001

Shambhala Publications, Inc.
Horticultural Hall
300 Massachusetts Avenue
Boston, Massachusetts 02115
www.shambhala.com

9 8 7 6 5 4 3 2 1

First Edition
Printed in the United States of America

⊗ This edition is printed on acid-free paper that meets the
American National Standards Institute z39.48 Standard.
Distributed in the United States by Random House, Inc.,
and in Canada by Random House of Canada Ltd

Library of Congress Cataloging-in-Publication Data
Klong-chen Ye-shes-rdo-rje, Bka'-'gyur Rin-po-che
[Yon tan rin po che'i mdzod kyi mchan 'grel theg gsum bdud rtsi'i
nying khu. English]
Treasury of Precious Qualities : a commentary on the root text of
Jigme Lingpa / by Longchen Yeshe Dorje Kangyur Rinpoche.
p. cm.
ISBN 1-57062-598-0
1. 'Jigs-med-gling-pa Rang-byung-rdo-rje, 1729 or 1730–1798. Yon tan
rin po che'i mdzod. 2. Rdzogs-chen (Nying-ma-pa) I. 'Jigs-med-
gling-pa Rang-byung-rdo-rje, 1729 or 1730–1978. Yon tan rin po che'i
mdzod dga' ba'i char. II. Title
BQ7662.4.J573 K59 2001
294.3'420423—dc21
00-067961

Contents ⌒〜

Foreword ❧

by HIS HOLINESS THE DALAI LAMA

The view of the Great Perfection (Dzogchen) is difficult and profound. The main texts that explain it are Longchen Rabjampa's *Treasury of the Supreme Vehicle*, which is itself quite difficult, and the *Treasury of the Expanse of Reality*. It is my advice that people who are interested in the Nyingma path in general and the Great Perfection teachings in particular should study Rigdzin Jigme Lingpa's more accessible *Treasury of Precious Qualities*. The work translated here is the first volume of a commentary to that book by Kangyur Rinpoche, Longchen Yeshe Dorje.

The *Treasury of Precious Qualities* is a text belonging to the stages of the path (*lam rim*) genre that covers all the stages of the path to enlightenment according to the Nyingma tradition up to and including the teachings of Dzogchen. The present volume covers the sutra section that presents a detailed exposition of the path from the perspective of the three kinds of beings, classified according to their aspirations. It opens with an account of the four thoughts that turn the mind toward the Dharma, the nature of the cycle of existence, the four noble truths, and the twelve links of dependent arising. On this basis, it explains how to take refuge in the Buddha, his teaching, and the spiritual community; the significance of doing so; and how to generate within oneself the awakening mind of bodhichitta. The presentation of the six perfections—generosity, ethics, patience, effort, meditation, and wisdom—includes a discussion of the three vows (the vow of individual emancipation, the Bodhisattva vow, and the tantric vow) as a guide to conduct, and an exposition of the Middle Way (Madhyamika) as a guide to the correct view.

Thorough and complete in every way, this commentary is comprehensive, fairly brief, and easy to read. I believe the members of the Padmakara Translation Group have taken great pains to render a clear, accessible English translation that readers will find illuminating. I pray that they will take great inspiration from it in their own practice of the path to enlightenment.

Foreword ⌖⌁

The *Treasury of Precious Qualities* by Rigdzin Jigme Lingpa, and the commentary on it composed by Kangyur Rinpoche, are the works of genuine masters who were utterly free from the concerns of this world and the desire for wealth and renown. The great value of these texts lies in the fact that they present the Buddhadharma in a way that is truly grounded in the words of the Buddha himself. Their lineage is pure and their teachings are authentic. It is amazing that these teachings still exist. They arose solely thanks to the unspeakable kindness of the Buddha Shakyamuni, the source of the tradition, without whom neither the Dharma that we study and practice, nor the Sangha, to which we think we belong, would exist.

These teachings were brought to Tibet and preserved for us through the enlightened power of Padmasambhava, the Lotus-Born Guru, through the learning and authority of the Bodhisattva abbot Shantarakshita, and through the protective, nurturing patronage of the Dharma king Trisong Detsen. It is mainly thanks to their sublime compassion and the compassion of those who followed them—the twenty-five great disciples of Guru Rinpoche, the Indian panditas, and the Tibetan translators, together with all the other masters of the lineage—that we can still receive the teachings of the Buddha and put them into practice. Kyabje Kangyur Rinpoche's commentary on the *Treasury of Precious Qualities* translated here is a distillation and a key to the vast array of teachings that the great beings of Tibet and India have set forth and brought to fruition. It really is an indispensable and trustworthy guide to anyone who has even the slightest interest in Buddhism. For it expounds what the Dharma actually is. It throws light upon our lives, on where we stand, and on our practice. For those who read it, may it prove a rich treasure of genuine information and a constant source of inspiration and encouragement.

JIGME KHYENTSE RINPOCHE

Introduction ⟳

This book is a translation of the first part of a commentary on the *Treasury of Precious Qualities*, the celebrated work of Rigdzin Jigme Lingpa (1730–1798), which, in a slender volume of elegant verses, presents the entire Buddhist path according to the Nyingma or Ancient school of Tibetan Buddhism. The text, both root and commentary, is structured gradually and shows how all the Buddha's teachings, from the basic essentials to the most advanced practices of the Great Perfection, converge without contradiction into a single path to enlightenment. As such, the *Treasury of Precious Qualities* is a universally respected text and is studied in all Nyingma establishments, usually as a completing résumé, rounding off the long course of advanced study. Translated into English, it is an indispensable manual for those drawn to the Nyingma teachings.

JIGME LINGPA*

Although he came to be regarded as one of the most important figures in the Nyingma lineage and an incarnation of both the great master Vimalamitra and the Dharma king Trisong Detsen, Jigme Lingpa was born and grew up in a situation of simple obscurity. At the age of six, he was placed in the monastery of Palri in south Tibet, where, after taking the vows of preliminary ordination, he imbibed a basic monastic education. Seven years later, at the age of thirteen, he met his teacher, the great tertön Rigdzin Thukchok Dorje, from whom he received many transmissions and instructions. His youth was marked by unusual spiritual precocity, and visions of Guru Padmasambhava, the dakini Yeshe Tsogyal, and other enlightened beings became a regular feature of his experience. A visionary encounter with Manjushrimitra, one of the patriarchs of the Dzogchen lineage, proved a turning point in his

---

* This account is adapted from the biography of Jigme Lingpa. See also *Masters of Meditation and Miracles* by Tulku Thondup.

Rigdzin Jigme Lingpa (1730–1798).

life, and he decided to lay aside his monastic robe in preference for the white shawl and the long hair of a yogi. He was temperamentally drawn to a life of solitary practice and, while still a young man, completed two three-year retreats. In the course of the first, he became a tertön, a discoverer of hidden Dharma treasures, and he revealed the important cycle of teachings and practices known as the *Longchen Nyingthik.** It was, however, during his second retreat, which he began at the age of thirty-one at Samye Chimphu, that his most profound experiences began to manifest. For it was then that he directly beheld the great master Longchen Rabjam in three successive visions. In the first, he received the transmission of the entire range of Longchenpa's teachings; in the second, he was granted the authorization to uphold and propagate them; and finally, in the course of the third vision, the minds of the two masters mingled ineffably so that the realization of Longchenpa arose instantaneously in the mind of Jigme Lingpa. The two masters, historically separated by five centuries, became henceforth identical in terms of knowledge and accomplishment.

Later, after concluding his second retreat, Jigme Lingpa began to expound, now seven years after its discovery, his Dharma treasure, the *Longchen Nyingthik*, transmitting it to his close disciples, Jigme Trinle Özer (the first Dodrupchen Rinpoche) and Jigme Gyalwa'i Nyugu (who passed it on to his disciple Patrul Rinpoche). The *Longchen Nyingthik* subsequently spread throughout Tibet and remains to this day one of the most important systems of meditative and yogic practice in the Nyingma school.

The latter part of Jigme Lingpa's life was spent at Tsering Jong, a small hermitage and meditation center, which he founded in the south of Tibet. He lived there in great simplicity, receiving and instructing his many disciples and using the gifts of patrons in all sorts of compassionate and religious activities. It was, for instance, his lifelong habit to save the lives of animals by buying them from butchers and hunters, and setting them free. His life, in short, was that of a great Bodhisattva, the personification of the qualities and ideals described in the scriptures

---

* A full description of this discovery can be found in the introduction to *The Wish-Fulfilling Jewel* by Dilgo Khyentse Rinpoche.

and set forth in his own writings. He composed an autobiography in which we may catch a glimpse of a warm, affectionate character, clear-sighted, utterly fearless, and without guile, marked by the compassion and clarity of supreme attainment:

> My perceptions have become like those of a little boy, and I take pleasure in playing with children. But when I come across people with important faults of character, I don't hesitate to confront them directly with their shortcomings—even if they are important religious leaders or generous sponsors. . . . Whatever I am doing, whether sitting still or walking around, whether eating or sleeping, my mind is in a state that is never separate from the clarity of the ultimate nature. In whatever I do for the Dharma, I pledge myself to complete it, however impossible it may seem.

Simple as his lifestyle may have been, Jigme Lingpa was nevertheless a scholar of prodigious learning. It is said that he was "born wise," with an understanding and a capacity to assimilate the teachings without much need for study. As he himself said, it was profound visionary experience, rather than intellectual application, that released the immense flood of knowledge latent in the nature of his mind, with the result that the impounded waters of his wisdom "burst forth" from within. He compiled the twenty-five-volume collection of the Nyingma tantras and composed a history of them, and at his death he left behind nine volumes of original treatises and discovered treasure texts. Of these, the *Longchen Nyingthik* collection is certainly the most important and well known, while the *Treasury of Precious Qualities*, together with its two-volume autocommentary, is his most celebrated work of scholarship.

THE TEXT ITSELF

The *Treasury of Precious Qualities* consists of two main sections devoted respectively to the sutras and the tantras. The sutra section, which is the subject of the present volume of the commentary, covers the ethical,

Jamyang Khyentse Wangpo (1820–1892).
An incarnation of Jigme Lingpa and one of the principal founders of the Rimé, or nonsectarian movement. He was one of the main holders of the lineage of the Treasury of Precious Qualities, *through whom the transmission was passed down to Kangyur Rinpoche.*

psychological, and philosophical teachings, which are embodied in the Tripitaka and shared by all schools of Tibetan Buddhism. The essential thrust is toward the Mahayana, but the text naturally subsumes and exhaustively covers questions more associated with the Hinayana perspective, such as the fundamental issues of karma and ethics, the four noble truths, and the twelvefold chain of dependent arising. And it is noteworthy that considerable attention is given to the subject of the Pratimoksha, or the vows of Individual Liberation, which, as the commentary itself explains, was not discussed at length in Gyalwa Longchenpa's own work *The Great Chariot*, to which the *Treasury of Precious Qualities* may, in this respect, be regarded as a supplement.

In the manner of most Buddhist "root texts," the *Treasury of Precious Qualities* is comprehensive but concise, a distillation in fact that is practically impenetrable to all but experts already seasoned in the Buddhist teachings. It is, moreover, composed in verse and makes use of elaborate poetic language, rich in metaphor. A commentary is indispensable, and, in addition to Jigme Lingpa's own exposition, several have been composed over the last two centuries.

Traditionally, scriptures and religious texts may be explained in different ways, thus giving rise to a variety of commentarial styles. A *spyi 'grel*, or general commentary, gives a comprehensive overview of a text. A *don 'grel*, or "meaning commentary," expounds and discusses the text's essential meaning and purpose. By contrast, the *mchan 'grel* and the *tshig 'grel* (respectively, a commentary in the form of footnotes and a commentary of every word) painstakingly gloss the actual wording of the original, in the first case partially, in the second case entirely. In both *mchan 'grel* and *tshig 'grel*, the words of the original work are woven into the text of the commentary, where they are indicated (in the Tibetan) by small circles placed beneath the letters, the words being interpreted briefly, at length, or not at all, as the case may be. Finally, there exists a kind of commentary known as *dka' gnad*, the purpose of which is to elucidate only difficult or controversial points. The size of these commentaries varies a great deal, ranging from full-length treatises to concise guides, the latter being virtually memory aids for readers already well versed in the material.

As already said, Jigme Lingpa produced a lengthy, two-volume "meaning commentary" of his own, namely, the *Two Chariots* or *shing rta rnam gnyis*. This of course must remain the ultimate reference, but it is well known for being as difficult as it is profound. Jigme Lingpa's disciple Dodrupchen Jigme Trinle Özer (1745–1821) wrote a shorter commentary, as did the latter's Gelugpa disciple Alak Sogpo Ngawang Tendar (b. 1759). Patrul Rinpoche, Orgyen Jigme Chökyi Wangpo (1808–1887), composed a guide for teaching the *Treasury of Precious Qualities*, as well as several outlines and a clarification of difficult points. Later, around the turn of the twentieth century, Khenpo Yönten Gyamtso, belonging to Gemang, a branch of Dzogchen monastery, composed an exhaustive, accessible, and very popular commentary in two books: *zla ba'i 'od zer* (Radiance of the Moon) and *nyi ma'i 'od zer* (Refulgence of the Sun).

The text that we have chosen for translation is the single-volume commentary, *The Quintessence of the Three Paths*, by Kyabje Kangyur Rinpoche, Longchen Yeshe Dorje. Although this is itself a mighty tome of six hundred pages, it is comparatively short, similar in size to the commentaries of the first Dodrupchen Rinpoche and Alak Sogpo Ngawang Tendar. The essence of Kangyur Rinpoche's work consists of footnotes to the *Treasury of Precious Qualities*, which he composed with reference to the studies he had made earlier at the feet of his principal teacher Jedrung Trinle Jampa Jungne of Riwoche (1856–1922). The text was completed in 1983 by Kyabje Dilgo Khyentse Rinpoche (1910–1991), who wrote the introductory verses and the conclusion. Jedrung Rinpoche himself received the transmission of the *Treasury of Precious Qualities* from Jamyang Khyentse Wangpo, who received it in turn from Jigme Lingpa's disciple Jigme Gyalwa'i Nyugu. Kangyur Rinpoche also studied the text with his uncle, Khenpo Dawö Zhonnu, abbot of Kathog monastery, whose transmission lineage is traced through the first Dodrupchen Rinpoche, Gyalse Zhenpen Thaye, Patrul Rinpoche, Orgyen Tendzin Norbu, and the khenpos Yönten Gyamtso and Samten Gyamtso.

While covering the whole of Jigme Lingpa's text, this commentary focuses on certain specific aspects, which it explains in detail. On the whole, it presupposes that the reader is already familiar with the whole range of scholastic terms and categories belonging to the Abhidharma literature, as well as with the broad sweep of the sutra and tantra teachings. As we have already said, the *Treasury of Precious Qualities* is often expounded at the end of a comprehensive course of study, as a kind of concluding recapitulation in which many essential details are mentioned only briefly and in passing, it being assumed that the reader is already conversant with them. For this reason, Kangyur Rinpoche's commentary, as it stands, is in many places probably beyond the reach of the kind of reader for whom this translation is intended, namely, Western Buddhists eager to enlarge and deepen their understanding of the Dharma. As a solution to this problem, it seemed desirable to supply, as much as possible, the elements necessary for a ready understanding of the commentary without the need for extensive research in other books, some of which are, in any case, still unavailable in translation. We have therefore supplied lengthy notes and a series of appendixes, borrowing freely from the *mkhas 'jug* of Ju Mipham Rinpoche, the commentary of Khenpo Yönten Gyamtso mentioned above, and the *sdom gsum* of Kyabje Dudjom Rinpoche. We hope that this will facilitate the reader's appreciation of Kangyur Rinpoche's commentary, which, while of a manageable size, is itself an inestimable mine of precious instruction.

KYABJE KANGYUR RINPOCHE

Aside from the merely practical considerations of brevity and accessibility, there are deeper, more personal reasons for working on this commentary and attempting to share it with others—namely, that its author was and remains one of the most significant sources of inspiration for the transmission of Buddhadharma to the West. As recorded in a devotional poem of Dilgo Khyentse Rinpoche, Kangyur Rinpoche (1897–1975) was born in Kham in the east of Tibet and, like Jigme Lingpa before him, exhibited astonishing spiritual qualities and abilities even from his earliest childhood. While still very young, he met and delighted the heart of Mipham Rinpoche, who was renowned as being Manjushri himself. In due course, he entered the monastery of Riwoche, where he was accepted by his root guru, the incomparable tertön Jedrung Rinpoche, Trinle Jampa Jungne. Riwoche was an important center of the Rimé, or nonsectarian tradition, and comprised two main colleges, one belonging to the Nyingma tradition and one to the tradition of Taklung Kagyu. Kangyur Rinpoche studied there for many years, eventually occupying the position of vajra master.

In due course, he withdrew from the monastery and the positions of importance that he held there and took up the life of a wandering hermit, living in mountain caves and visiting places of pilgrimage all over Tibet and the Himalayan region—in every sense following in the footsteps of Patrul Rinpoche (the author of *The Words of My Perfect Teacher*), in whose tradition he is most certainly to be located. To magisterial learning were thus added many years of meditative retreat and yogic practice, resulting in supreme accomplishment. Many stories are told about him: of his meditative experiences, his visits to hidden lands, and his discovery of Dharma treasures. Once, for example, while on pilgrimage to Lhasa, he went to visit and pay his respects to the great monastic university of Sera. While he was there, he was challenged to debate by some of the monks, avid to test their dialectical skills on an unknown newcomer. Accepting the challenge, Kangyur Rinpoche acquitted himself with such brilliance, defeating more than ten geshes in succession, that the word went round that he must be a manifestation of Je Tsongkhapa himself, who is said to pay anonymous visits to his disciples from time to time, in order to check the quality of their debate!

Kangyur Rinpoche was, as we have just indicated, a tertön, a revealer of Dharma treasures, and was regarded as an emanation of Namkha'i Nyingpo, one of the foremost disciples of Guru Padmasambhava, the Indian master who established Buddhism in Tibet in the eighth century. In the course of his life, Kangyur Rinpoche experienced many pure visions of great masters of the past—Vimalamitra, So Yeshe Wangchuk, Taksham Samten Lingpa, and others—from whom he received numerous teachings and transmissions, becoming thus the holder of many rare and prized "short lineages." A notable feature of his innumerable activities was the reading transmission of the Kangyur, the canon of Buddhist scriptures consisting of over a hundred volumes. And it was from the fact that he completed this immense undertaking no fewer

Jedrung Rinpoche, Trinley Jampa Jungne (1856–1922).
A disciple of Jamyang Khyentse Wangpo and the root teacher of Kangyur Rinpoche. He presided over the monastery of Kham Riwoche, where the traditions of both the Ancient Translation school and that of Taklung Kagyu were taught and practiced. He was a celebrated tertön, or revealer of treasure teachings. It was from him that Kangyur Rinpoche received the transmission of the Treasury of Precious Qualities.

than twenty-four times that the name Kangyur Rinpoche came to be applied to him.

Foreseeing the disaster to come, he left Tibet some time before 1959 and traveled to India with a large collection of books and precious manuscripts, thereby preserving many texts which would otherwise have been lost forever. He eventually settled in Darjeeling with his family and founded a monastery there. It was here, in the late sixties and early seventies, that he encountered the spiritual aspirations of Westerners and was one of the first Tibetan masters to accept them as disciples. Thus, while the destruction of Tibet continued apace, Kangyur Rinpoche labored not only for the preservation of the Dharma in exile, but with great kindness laid the foundations for its propagation in Western lands. Willing as he may have been to accept Westerners as his students, Kangyur Rinpoche's approach was always profoundly traditional, and it was his wish that his disciples should be trained, as far as they were able and without shortcuts, in all the successive stages of the path. He never in fact traveled to the West, but after his death and in accordance with his wishes, his eldest son, Taklung Tsetrul Rinpoche, Pema Wangyal, came to France (soon to be followed by the rest of his family) and established several traditional three-year retreat centers in Dordogne. Here a sizable number of Western students have had the good fortune to practice according to the Nyingma tradition, receiving instructions and transmissions from such great masters as Dudjom Rinpoche, Dilgo Khyentse Rinpoche, Dodrupchen Rinpoche, and Nyoshul Khen Rinpoche. Subsequently, some of the students who had completed long retreats began the work of making Buddhist texts available in translation. It was thus that the Padmakara Translation Group came into being, the natural outcome of the original impetus set in motion by Kangyur Rinpoche, who, as its first and abiding inspiration, may be regarded in every sense as its founding father. To make his work available in English and other languages is an attempt to repay in some measure our debt of gratitude, as well as to be of some service to the Western Buddhist community.

THE TRANSLATION

In covering the general sweep of sutra teachings, this commentary naturally contains a wealth of technical vocabulary covering not only the metaphysical, psychological, and epistemological categories of the Abhidharma, but also of the Prajnaparamita sutras and the philosophical teachings of the four Buddhist tenet systems, particularly that of the Madhyamika. This has implied a certain amount of research, and a good deal of inventiveness, on the part of the translators, who have gratefully adopted the terminology already used by other translators as this came to hand and seemed appropriate. Nevertheless, the fact that so much Buddhist literature in English has appeared in recent years should not be allowed to conceal the fact that the translation of Buddhist texts into Western languages is still in its infancy, and that it is vain to suppose that we are anywhere near establishing a universally accepted (or acceptable) vocabulary in translation. This is the unfortunate consequence of translating into a language that is closely associated with a specific culture equipped with its own native, non-Buddhist philosophical and religious traditions. English, rich in synonyms as it may be, and patient of accretion from other languages, does not yet possess a generally accepted vocabulary able to express with ease the subtleties of Buddhist psychology and metaphysics. In the present case, the translators were often at a loss to find the right word and frequently have been called upon to press words into a service for which they were not originally conceived, with the inevitable consequence of often ill-sounding approximations. Examples of this abound, and one need only consider such basic terms as "merit," "emotion," "monk," "compassion," "patience," "nature," and "essence" to appreciate the difficulty. However, we hope that the present work will contribute usefully to a future and more perfect translation of the Buddhist sutra teachings into English. The names of the scriptures cited in the commentary posed something of a problem. For obvious reasons, it was desirable to refer to them by their Sanskrit titles. In the case of the sutras and shastras, this was not difficult, since the titles of these texts are easy to find—in, for instance, the indexes of the Kangyur and Tengyur published by Tarthang Rinpoche. The situation was different in the case of the tantras. With the exception of well-known texts like the *Guhyagarbha, Guhyasamaja,* and *Kalachakra* (the names of which are given in Sanskrit), most of the tantras referred to were difficult for us to locate. Therefore,

Kangyur Rinpoche (1897–1975).

rather than hazard a translation of our own, we decided to preserve a clear reference by leaving the titles in Tibetan.

ACKNOWLEDGMENTS

The translation of *The Quintessence of the Three Paths* was begun at the behest and under the supervision of Kangyur Rinpoche's youngest son, Jigme Khyentse Rinpoche. One of the main factors that helped in the completion of the work was the cycle of teachings centered on the *Treasury of Precious Qualities* that Khyentse Rinpoche set in motion in 1995 and which continued until the summer of 1999. This enterprise involved numerous lamas' visits to Dordogne. The first transmissions and explanations were given by Rabjam Rinpoche and Khenpo Gyurme Tsultrim of Shechen monastery in Nepal, followed by Khenchen Pema Sherab Rinpoche of Peyul monastery in India, who visited France on three successive occasions. To all these lamas we wish to express our profound appreciation and gratitude. We wish to thank most particularly Alak Zenkar Rinpoche, who visited Dordogne at Christmas 1996 and gave unsparingly of his time and scholarship to help us with many difficult points. From beginning to end, the entire work has been sustained by the kindness and enthusiasm of Jigme Khyentse Rinpoche, who at the end of the project patiently read through the entire text with us. Of course, any imperfections in the finished product remain entirely the responsibility of the translators.

The Quintessence of the Three Paths was translated by the Padmakara Translation Group, which on this occasion consisted of Helena Blankleder and Wulstan Fletcher, who would like to express their gratitude to their readers, Pamela Law, Adrian Gunther, and Jenny Kane, for their invaluable and much appreciated assistance.

Padmakara,
Dordogne,
Anniversary of Rigdzin Jigme Lingpa, 1999

TREASURY *of*
PRECIOUS QUALITIES

A COMMENTARY ON THE ROOT TEXT
OF JIGME LINGPA

~~~~

Streaming through the clouds of the five kayas
In the Infinite Expanse of Dharma-space,
The lotus garden of the Highest Vehicle
Lies open in myriad rays of Love and Knowledge.
I pay homage to the Father and Son[1]
United in the sphere of my own faith.

Here I will unfold a feast of limpid words,
A nectar-light, a treatise well explained[2]
And able to reveal the meaning of
The Treasury of Precious Qualities,
A unique text that perfectly displays
The Buddha's Doctrine in its full extent.

Prologue ෙ~

T he *Treasury of Precious Qualities* is a work of major importance setting forth in its entirety the profound path of the Vajra Essence[3]
according to the tradition of the Ancient Translation school. It is a key
to innumerable crucial points of doctrine and lays before the reader a
complete and infallible path to enlightenment—the distilled essence of
the entire ocean of sutra and mantra.

THE TITLE

As a preamble to the commentary on this text, it is necessary to reflect
upon the meaning of its title, and this will be done according to the
system of five elements:[4] the purpose of a title, the title itself, a word-
for-word explanation, the overall meaning, and responses to possible
objections.

As soon as they have grasped the sense of a book's title, people of
high intelligence will know exactly what the treatise contains; those
of moderate capacity will understand whether the text belongs to the
Mahayana or Hinayana; while those of only modest ability will have no
difficulty in locating the volume concerned.

A doctrinal exposition traditionally begins with an introduction, and
this normally opens with an explanation of the title. There are three
reasons why titles are given in Sanskrit. The first is to reassure the
reader of the authenticity of the teaching, the second is to inculcate a
predisposition toward the sacred tongue, while the third is that the
Sanskrit language acts as a vehicle of blessings.

The Sanskrit title is *Guna Kosha Ratna Pramoda Brishti Nama*. This is
rendered into Tibetan as *yon tan rin po che'i mdzod dga' ba'i char zhes bya ba*,
and means *The Rain of Joy, the Treasury of Precious Qualities*. The verbal

equivalence is as follows: *guna/yon tan*/quality; *kosha/mdzod*/treasure; *ratna/rin po che*/precious; *pramoda brishti/dga' ba'i char*/rain of joy; *nama/ zhes bya ba*/named.

The word "Qualities" appears in the title because this text is a source of all the qualities that derive from a correct following of the stages of the paths associated with the three classes of spiritual practitioners.[5] These qualities are "Precious" because it is through the practice of these paths that all the desirable aspects of the twofold aim* are achieved. Furthermore, this text is such a mine of excellent teachings and expressions that it may properly be called a "Treasury." Finally, since it is like a pleasant shower for those who wish to cultivate in their hearts a harvest of virtuous activities, the text is called a "Rain of Joy." The terms *nama* in Sanskrit and *zhes bya ba* in Tibetan are the conventional indications of a title.

In sum, the *Treasury of Precious Qualities* is like a rich thesaurus productive of all the qualities of the path and its fruit.

It may be objected that joy is not a particular attribute of rain. After all, there is a rain of burning coals in the realms of hell, and a rain of scorching sand in the worlds of the nagas and pretas. But this is not a valid objection, since in this context the image of rain is taken from the phenomenon occurring in the higher realms of gods and humans, where it is productive of delight. It is not a reference to the rain that falls in the lower realms.

Homage to the Three Jewels

The Three Jewels of Buddha, Dharma, and Sangha are the rarest and most sublime objects in the universe. Therefore, from now until he attains enlightenment, the author of the treatise pays heartfelt respect to them in thought, word, and deed, his aim being to protect beings who wander in samsara, afflicted by many evils.

The Three Jewels may be explained according to their essential characteristics, the etymology of the Tibetan term, their various subsidiary aspects, and an explanation of the Sanskrit term. Essentially, buddha-

---

* Buddhahood for oneself and the temporary and ultimate fulfillment of other beings.

hood is the perfection of all the qualities of "elimination" and "realization."* According to the Tibetan expression *sangs rgyas*, a Buddha is one
who has awoken (*sangs*) from the deep sleep of ignorance and whose
mind has blossomed (*rgyas*) like a lotus flower with the knowledge of
all things. Buddhahood in turn has three aspects: (a) the *kayas*, which
act like containers for (b) the wisdoms contained therein, together with
(c) the enlightened activities that flow from these. Finally, the Sanskrit
word *Buddha* means "one who perfectly comprehends," one whose mind
encompasses all objects of cognition and thoroughly understands them.

Essentially, the Dharma is characterized by the elimination of one or
both of the twin veils of defiled emotion and cognitive obscuration, or
the means to this elimination. The Tibetan word *chos* is so used because
the Dharma purges (*'chos*) the mind of negative emotion, in the same
way that medicine cures someone who is sick. As to its aspects, the
Dharma may be classified in two ways: on the one hand, as the Dharma
of transmission and the Dharma of realization, and on the other, as the
third and fourth of the four noble truths, the truth of cessation and the
truth of path. In Sanskrit, the word *dharma* means "to hold." In other
words, the Dharma is what holds beings to the perfect path and keeps
them from the ways of samsara and the lower realms.

Essentially, the Jewel of the Sangha is characterized by the possession
of two qualities: knowledge of the truth and freedom from defilements.
The Tibetan term *dge 'dun* refers to those who have a keen interest (*'dun*)
in the path of perfect virtue (*dge*). Such practitioners may be divided
into those belonging to the Hinayana Sangha of Shravakas and Pratyekabuddhas, and those belonging to the Mahayana Sangha of Bodhisattvas. The Sanskrit word has the meaning of "assembly" and refers to
the community of those who are not distracted from the path by anyone, even the gods.

The words "I prostrate" express a perfect salutation to the Three
Jewels. This may be made on three levels: first, by realizing the view;†
then, by proficiency in meditation; and finally, by an act of devout
veneration.

---

* The former are so called because they refer to the removal of the emotional and cognitive
  veils. The latter are qualities acquired as the positive result of progress on the path. See
  chapter 6.
† The recognition of the true nature of the mind and of all phenomena.

The "Precious Three" of the root verse is a reference to the Three Jewels and indicates that the Body, Speech, Mind, Qualities, and Activities of the Buddha are renowned throughout the three worlds. Jigme Lingpa gives an elegant illustration of this by referring to the story of how the Buddha once sent a message to the princess Vine-of-Pearls in the form of a picture of himself together with some verses, printed on a piece of white cloth. When the girl saw the image, the joy she experienced was so intense that it was like a samadhi devoid of even the subtlest kind of discursive thought. And as she reflected on the meaning of the message, the one hundred and twelve obscurations* that are hindrances to liberation, and which are discarded on the path of seeing, fell away. The root text compares these obscurations to the deceitful faces of Mara's daughters, which are like the lilies of the night, opening in darkness and blasted by the sun of wisdom cultivated on the path of seeing. As a result, Vine-of-Pearls was prepared for the dissipation of what is to be eliminated on the path of meditation. And all this came about through the power of the Buddha's compassion. All such religious stories that tell of the effects of the Three Jewels are worthy of universal consideration, for they powerfully counteract the mental distraction and defiled emotion that are the very nature of samsaric existence.

Commitment to Compose the Text

The boundless collections of sutra and tantra teachings were propounded by the Buddha, master of the supreme wisdom of omniscience, who set them forth by means of the five excellences.[6] His followers, the noble Bodhisattvas, composed commentaries beautiful in word and meaning, on the basis of the system of five major elements, compiling them according to the "fourfold interrelated purpose."[7] These scriptures and commentaries are as vast and profound as a great ocean; they are a veritable treasure of purifying waters. Thanks to them the Doctrine of the Conqueror has remained for a long time. Maitreya has said:

> All Dharma is contained in Word and Commentary,
> The perfectly expressed and its interpretation.

---

* See chapter 6, p. 125.

These two ensure that Shakyamuni's Doctrine
Will remain for long within the world.

The Buddha's teaching, so profound and hard to fathom, and the commentaries upon it, have not yet faded from the world, and are here condensed into a single treatise. But Jigme Lingpa says that he lacks the three qualifications for composition[8] and that his treatise is the rough work of an ignorant gossip. He says that his book is destitute of the two qualities of healing defilements and protecting from the sufferings of samsara. It lacks the three characteristics of a Buddhist composition and is quite possibly tainted with the six faults of non-Buddhist writings.[9] It is, he says, a cacophonous din, like a "wave-garlanded torrent" cascading into a deep ravine in a dense jungle. But even though he considers his treatise to be an ugly and inelegant thing, he says nevertheless that it is based on the perfect utterances of the Sacred Teaching and is therefore worthy of attention. Of course, this verse is just an expression of the author's modesty.

The presentation of the *Treasury of Precious Qualities* is made under five important headings:[10] a note about the author, the scriptural sources of the treatise, its general tendency, its condensed meaning, and finally its purpose.

1. The author of the *Treasury of Precious Qualities* was Jigme Lingpa, a master who had direct experience of the ultimate truth of the sublime path, the natural state of Great Perfection. Due to this, he was at one with the primordial Buddha Samantabhadra,* the all-embracing sovereign of an oceanlike infinity of mandalas. He perfected the sheer virtuosity of all-discerning primal wisdom and the creative power of awareness. As a result, the immensity of twofold knowledge† surged forth in him, and he displayed a mastery of the five great sciences and other topics, entirely without the need for study—a fact that was widely perceived by others. It was thus that he gained the three qualifications for composing commentaries. Indeed, it is recorded that while he was immersed in the quintessential practice of a three-year retreat in the

---

* *kun tu bzang po*, the personification of primordial awareness that is forever free from delusion.
† This refers to the knowledge of the nature of things (*ji lta ba'i mkhyen pa*) and the knowledge of all things in their multiplicity (*ji snyed pa'i mkhyen pa*).

forest charnel ground of Samye Chimphu, the omniscient Drimé Özer, the glorious Ngaki Wangchuk, appeared to him three times in his wisdom body. Through the transmission of the blessings of Body, Speech, and Mind, their minds mingled, and from that moment onward, the author of this treatise, Jigme Lingpa, the Vidyadhara Pema Wangchen Yeshe Rolpa'i Dorje, became a great lord of the supreme vehicle.

2. This treatise is a distillation of the Tripitaka and the four tantra classes as spoken by the Buddha, together with the commentaries that were written to elucidate their meaning.

3. Of the two vehicles of Hinayana and Mahayana, this treatise tends to the Mahayana; of the sutra and mantra sections of the Mahayana, it tends toward mantra; of the outer and inner sections of the Mantrayana, it tends toward the innermost, unsurpassable tantras.

4. All the stages of the paths peculiar to the three kinds of beings are explained as steps on the way to the Natural Great Perfection. Thus the different goals of persons of fundamental, medium, and great capacity are harmonized into a single and final path.

5. When, on the occasion already mentioned, Jigme Lingpa beheld Gyalwa Longchenpa for the second time, the omniscient Lord of Dharma gave him a book, telling him that it clearly explained all the hidden meanings of his work *The Great Chariot*. This was the permission authorizing Jigme Lingpa to compose his treatise. Focusing on the paths of Individual Liberation and the general Mantrayana, together with the sections on the ground, path, and fruit of the Great Perfection (which are not discussed in detail in *The Great Chariot*), the present text represents the quintessence of the whole of Longchenpa's *Seven Treasures*. It was composed for the sake of future disciples, so that they might grasp the entire Doctrine without error. It brings together without contradiction all the teachings of the Victorious Ones, blending them into a path to buddhahood suitable to be followed by a single individual and providing everything necessary for the practice.

These five headings thus give a clear idea of the contents of this treatise. They are meant to inform readers so that they will have confidence and thus become suitable vessels for the teachings contained.

From time without beginning until this present moment, we have suffered through our defilements and clinging to self. We have labored long beneath the scourge of the different forms of birth,[11] the sufferings of age that overthrows our youth, of sickness that destroys our health, and of death that robs us of our life. For all these ills there is one great remedy: the sacred Dharma flavored with the sweetness of ambrosia. At first, at the time of hearing and studying it, it is a nectar for the ear, inspiring faith where previously there had been no faith. Later, at the stage of reflection, it is an antidote for the distracted mind, bringing joy where no joy had been before. Finally, at the stage of meditation, it gives rise to the wisdom of supreme knowledge, completely liberating the mind and bringing freedom where previously there had only been enslavement. Yet, like dogs before a pile of grass, foolish beings ignore the sacred teachings, though they be spread out before them like an open meadow—even placed directly in the palms of their hands! They plunge themselves into evil. How is one to teach such people, giving them an instruction that distills into a single book the whole meaning of the nine vehicles? It is indeed a formidable task. Yet moved by his love for beings and unable to turn away from them, Jigme Lingpa promises to compose his text.

Part One

Turning the Mind to the Dharma

CHAPTER I

The Value of Human Existence

SAMSARIC EXISTENCE

For ages we have lingered in samsara, unaware of its defects, believing that it is a wholesome, beneficial place. And yet it is a state in which suffering and its causes abound and where the qualities of liberation languish and wither. It is a desolate wilderness in which many times in the past our bodies and minds have burned in agony and have endured the pains of mutilation and decapitation. Moreover, latent within us, there are still many karmic seeds that will provoke such sufferings in the future. Human beings generally do not see this and are thus not only without regret for their condition but actually crave the transient and futile pleasures of the higher realms. Totally unaware that they should engage in virtue and refrain from evil, they pass their lives sunk in negativity. Theirs is what is called a "mere human existence." By their negative actions of thought and deed, they destroy themselves and render meaningless the freedoms and advantages of their human condition.[12] From their lofty position in samsara they plunge again into evil circumstances. Thus they wander in the three lower realms, in the heavens of the insensate gods without perception, or in barbarous regions (where the Dharma is not heard); they are born physically or mentally handicapped, have wrong views, and take birth in places where no Buddha has appeared.

EIGHT CONDITIONS IN WHICH THERE IS NO FREEDOM TO PRACTICE THE DHARMA

On the ground of burning iron, without a single moment of relief, beings are slain again and again by the henchmen of the Lord of Death, who brandish frightful weapons, swords, and hammers and inflict terrible pain. Until their evil karma has been exhausted, these beings in hell are unable to die, and, due to karmic effects resembling the cause*—in other words, their compulsive tendency to negativity—they are caught in a web of evil karma inspired by hatred, and their infernal life span is measureless.

Pretas generally are completely deprived of food and drink; they do not find even the slightest filthy fragment of pus, blood, or excrement to eat. No need to say, then, that they are tormented by hunger and thirst. The cooling effect of the moon in summer and the warming effect of the sun in winter are all reversed; rain and hail are misperceived as lightning and thunderbolts; and the rivers are filled with pus and blood. For pretas that are afflicted outwardly, streams and orchards dry up as soon as they look at them. Those afflicted inwardly have heads that are not in proportion to their bodies: their mouths are as small as the eye of a needle, while their bellies are the size of an entire country. If they swallow a little food and drink, it scorches their intestines and they suffer intolerable pain. Their life span is uncertain, depending on the strength of obscurations due to former avarice. Generally speaking, one of their days is equal to a month by human reckoning, and they live for five hundred of their own years.

In the depths of the great oceans, fish and sea monsters devour each other, the bigger ones gulping down the smaller. Animals scattered over the surface of the earth, wild and unclaimed, are the prey of hunters with their nets and traps, their poisoned arrows and their snares, and they die cruel deaths. Animals domesticated by man are slaves to their masters. They are tamed and subjugated with saddles, bridles, and nose-ropes. Their masters ride on them, tether them, and place burdens on their backs. They herd and castrate them, shear off their hair, and bleed them while still alive. And through such treatment, animals are reduced to every extremity of suffering. Being without intelligence, they cannot recite even a single *mani*.† When beings are born in such a condition they are helpless, and we are told that the life span of animals ranges

---

* See chapter 3, p. 57.
† In other words, the six-syllable mantra of Avalokiteshvara, OM MANI PADME HUNG.

from the momentary existence of insects to that of nagas and such-like that can live for a *kalpa*.

Since the unwavering action[13] that sustains their life-principle is extremely protracted, and their lives are therefore very long, lasting for twenty intermediate kalpas, the gods of the formless realm have no occasion to cultivate a sense of disgust for samsara and a desire to leave it. Moreover, the consciousness of the insensate gods, who are without perception, does not operate throughout the duration of their existence. They are therefore deprived of any basis for hearing and reflecting on the Dharma. Their abode is far removed from that of the gods of the fourth samadhi, just as a solitary place is remote from a populous city. These divine beings[14] have no notion of Dharma, and thus when their thoughts begin to stir at the end of their existence, they conceive the false view that there is no path to liberation, and as a consequence they fall into the lower realms. To be born in these states is to be deprived of freedom to practice Dharma.

The inhabitants of so-called barbarous lands do indeed have a human aspect, walking upright on their two feet. But they live practically like animals and are utterly ignorant of the Doctrine. Virtue is foreign to their minds, and they are given over to negativity. They live immersed in various kinds of evil activity such as wounding others with poisoned arrows, and even make it a tenet of their religion. They wander in the undergrowth of false views and, worse than animals, turn upside down the moral principles of what is to be adopted and what is to be rejected. The way of liberation is unknown to them.

Those whose faculties are impaired, who lack, for instance, the ability to speak, and especially those who are mentally handicapped, may encounter a spiritual guide who is on the supreme level of accomplishment, and they may even hear his or her teaching. But what is said is unintelligible to them, like the booming of an echo. The sense of the teaching is lost on them, and they fail to grasp the vital point of what actions are to be adopted and what should be forsaken. Thus their fortune is marred and they suffer greatly in this desolate and fearful wasteland of samsara.

To be born in samsara through the effect of karma and defilements is like being adrift upon a vast ocean, unfathomable and shoreless. To obtain a human form is like having a great boat with which to cross this ocean and reach the island of liberation. But though people may possess all their faculties, and though they may have intelligence, like a sail to propel them in the direction of freedom, this excellent support is wasted when the mind is clouded by false beliefs. As a result, such people fail to enter the Dharma and do not undertake the path to liberation so pleasing to the Buddha, who appeared in the world to set it forth. Denying the karmic principle of cause and effect, and claiming that there is no afterlife and so forth, they are beset by demons hindering them from the path of liberation. They fall under their power and lose their freedom.

To take a human birth during a dark kalpa is once again of no avail, for these are periods when the light of Dharma does not shine, when no Buddhas appear in the world from the time of its formation until its destruction. To take such a birth is to be like a man who has fallen into a pitch-dark crevasse and has broken his legs. However much he tries to get out, he can neither see the way nor even move, for his legs are shattered. In just the same way, without the light of the path of freedom, people are unaware of the three trainings that could lead them to liberation. They constantly pursue false paths because of their ignorance and defilements. Not only have they fallen into a dreadful place from which they cannot escape, but by degrees they fall deeper and deeper, from the states of animals and pretas down to the infernal realms. The freedom to practice Dharma is totally absent.

In all such terrible circumstances, in which evil actions bring forth their results in manifold suffering, whirling like the all-destroying hurricane at the end of time, the body is worn away with pain, and fear is the natural condition of the mind. Beings indulge in negative habits; they turn their backs on the sacred teaching. Thus we are advised to reflect again and again on how we might avoid being born in the eight conditions in which there is no freedom to practice the Dharma. Jigme Lingpa calls on us to follow the path of liberation with diligence, so that by relying on the teacher and his profound instructions, we might make meaningful the opportunity that we now possess.

FIVE INDIVIDUAL AND FIVE CIRCUMSTANTIAL ADVANTAGES

To have taken birth in a "central" land where the Dharma is proclaimed is like being a sapling planted in pure soil. To have fully functioning sense faculties and healthy limbs, and thus to have the basis for the reception, meditation, and practice of the teachings, is to be like a healthy tree in leaf and branch. To have confidence in the Doctrine of the Victorious One; to have the karma of one's body, speech, and mind in perfect flower, undamaged by the hail of evil actions contrary to the Dharma (sins of immediate effect and false views concerning the Three Jewels); to have been born a human being able to uphold the Dharma and acquire the qualities of liberation: all this is like a miraculous, wish-fulfilling tree. It is exceedingly rare and significant, and to put these five individual advantages to good effect is of the highest importance.

The fact that a Buddha has appeared in our world, an occurrence that is as rare as the flowering of the udumbara;* the fact that he proclaimed the Doctrine and that the three turnings of the Dharma wheel have blossomed into flower; the fact that through explanation and practice this Doctrine in both transmission and realization still exists in our day without decline; the fact that there are still teachers who have perfectly embraced the Dharma; and finally the fact that we have been welcomed into the "cool shade" of a virtuous friend, a perfect guide on the path to liberation: these five circumstantial advantages are even rarer than the five individual ones.

THE RARITY OF A PRECIOUS HUMAN EXISTENCE

Why is it so necessary to tread the path with diligence and without delay? As we have said, the five individual advantages are as rare as the wish-fulfilling tree, while the five circumstantial advantages are like the udumbara flower, even rarer than the earlier five. These ten taken to-

---

* The udumbara flower is said to blossom only once in a kalpa.

gether form the special characteristics, and the eight freedoms form the basis, of what we call a precious human existence.[15] If we do not take advantage of it now, an opportunity such as this will not be found again. The reason for saying this may be illustrated with examples. One could imagine, for instance, an ocean, vast as the three-thousandfold universe. In the depths of this ocean lives a blind turtle that rises to the surface only once every century. To attain a human birth is rarer than the chance occurrence of the turtle surfacing to find its head inside a yoke drifting at random on the water's surface. Or again, one could suggest the difficulty of attaining a precious human existence by using numerical illustrations. Compared with the number of beings in the animal kingdom, humans are like stars seen during the day as compared with stars seen at night. And the same ratio may be applied between animals and pretas, and again between pretas and the denizens of the realms of hell.

This precious human existence is thus most rare and extremely meaningful. If those who journey on the pathways of the Dharma with liberation as their goal, who now have in their possession the great ship of freedom and advantage, and who have met with a holy teacher who is the guide and, as it were, the navigator of such a ship—if such people fail to cross the ocean of the boundless and unfathomable sufferings of samsara to the dry land of liberation, their opportunity will have been completely squandered. All this should be a subject of reflection and a spur to greater exertion.

Part Two

An Incentive for the Practice

CHAPTER 2

Impermanence

THE IMPERMANENCE OF THE OUTER WORLD

It is written in the *Condensed Prajnaparamita-sutra*:

> Wind arises grounded upon space.
> On this the mass of water stands,
> And thereupon, the earth, the ground of living beings.

Phenomenal existence, as this appears to deluded perception, consists of the three-thousandfold universe: an inanimate basis or vessel together with the beings that are its animate contents. This universe passes through a sequence of formation, duration, destruction, and voidness.* Each of these phases lasts for twenty intermediate kalpas, and the eighty taken together make up one great kalpa. A single universe, which is the impermanent environment of living beings, comprises four continents situated around a Mount Meru with its celestial abodes of the desire realm and the pure form realms. A thousand of such universes make up a so-called thousandfold universe. A thousand of these form an intermediary universe, and these yet again multiplied by a thousand comprise what is known as the "great three-thousandfold universe." In Tibetan, the word for universe (*'jig rten*) is a pejorative term, since it means "basis of decay." It is so called because, from the moment it comes into being, decay and death are intrinsic to it. One could almost say that the world and its inhabitants are tormented and punished by these four phases of formation, duration, destruction, and voidness. Indeed, the root verse specifies that there will be seven destructions by fire and one by water. As the *Anityartha-parikatha* says:

---

* See appendix 1, p. 269.

Then the earth will be destroyed,
Then the mountains will collapse in dust,
And all the waters of the seas run dry—
No need to mention, then, the fate of living beings.

The impermanence of living beings

Because they see that ordinary beings entertain false views, imputing permanent existence to what is composite and fleeting, the Buddhas, foremost among the living, and teachers of gods and humankind, display their joyful passing into nirvana, even though they possess the supreme and adamantine form, the Dharmakaya, that is immune to decay. They relinquish their capacity to remain forever, untouched and unmarred by the passage of time. Therefore, if Buddhas themselves are impermanent, is there any need to doubt the transience of ordinary beings whose lives are as fragile as bubbles?

Some beings perfect the four worldly samadhis and the different levels of absorption. As a result, they can sustain the burden of a life span ranging from an intermediate kalpa in the heaven of the Pure, up to eighty thousand great kalpas at the Peak of Existence. But even this falls short of the goal of permanent happiness. Even beings like these must follow the effects of their white and black actions and without a doubt will come to die. Brahma, Ishvara, Shiva, Vishnu, and the other gods who possess supernatural knowledge and miraculous powers, together with all the Chakravartins—even they are disappointed in their bliss, for they know of no way to escape the demon Lord of Death. What need is there to speak of people like ourselves?

To enjoy perfect happiness and pleasure in the higher realms of samsara is to be like the deer roaming wild and free for the three months of summer in a landscape filled with wholesome plants and flowers. But just as the hunter lies in wait, hidden from sight in a gully on the mountainside, thinking constantly of how to kill them, the robber Lord of Death, with his deadly club in his hand, thinks of one thing only: how he might draw beings into the snare of death and steal away their lives. As Ashvaghosha has written:

Of all those born upon this earth
Or in the upper realms,
Did you see, or hear, or even doubt,
That some were born and have not died?

People are tormented by the heat of early summer and cannot bear to go out in the sun. They long for the cool light of the autumn moon, but they do not worry, in fact the thought never crosses their minds, that with the arrival of autumn, a hundred days of their lives will have passed and brought them nearer to their deaths.

People also mourn at the deaths of others, without reflecting that the Lord of Death is advancing upon them as well. They spend their time immersed in the hopes and fears of life as though they were going to live forever. This is so foolish!

As it is said in the *Anityartha-parikatha*:

To enter on the path of life
Adds nothing to your length of days,
And death is not a flaw within the scheme of things.
Why therefore do you sorrow at it so?

Imagine that four giants, tremendously strong, stand back to back and each shoots an arrow directly in front of him; it would be a quick man indeed who could run round and catch them all before they fell to earth! Yet even quicker are the pretas that move over the earth, propelled by the miraculous force that is the fruit of their karma. Faster than the earthbound pretas are the pretas that move through the air, and even faster are the chariots of the sun and moon, while the swiftest of all are the divine beings who move miraculously through the strength of their merit. Yet quicker than all of these is the passing of this human life!

The body of a man or woman still growing to early adulthood is magnificent and strong. But in due course, their constitution begins to falter, and it is as if they are being punished by the scourge of old age. When the four elements[16] are balanced, all is well, but then illness strikes and torments both body and mind. It may be that, for the moment, thanks to positive actions done in the past and the coincidental effect of favorable conditions, people experience great happiness and the pleasure of companions, wealth, fame, and so forth. But "since all that meets must separate, and all that is accumulated drains away," all of this will decline. When the momentum of this life is lost, or when certain untimely circumstances occur, death in all its dreadfulness will throw itself upon them without delay. This is described with many examples in the *Rajavavadaka-sutra*.

When the time of death comes, our much-cherished bodies are overthrown in the struggle with the Lord of Death. Even Vajrapani can give us no protection, and we plunge into the abyss of hopeless suffering. At that time, the provisions of this life mean nothing anymore, and the glow of youth fades and withers like a flower in the frost. The five sense faculties fail and cease to function, like a flame blown out by the wind. No medicine can soothe the pain of the cutting of the thread of life. Even if the universal remedy were to hand, it would be to no avail; and even doctors as skillful as Jivakakumara* must turn away from such patients who look at them with eyes wide and staring with terror. There is nothing to be done. When the energy that imparts movement to the body begins to decline, there comes complete exhaustion and paralysis, and as it begins to flow abnormally, the limbs shudder and twitch. Respiration is difficult, and the rattling of the breath is short and feeble. All around the family stands—father, mother, friends, and kin. Everyone is sobbing and lamenting, pleading with their loved one not to leave them. But the hook of their prayers can find no purchase. The dying person starts to gasp as respiration becomes increasingly shallow, fine like a strand of horsehair. And then the ruthless Lord of Death severs it with the edge of his sharp ax. In that instant, the bloom and beauty of life vanishes, the face becomes livid, the eyes fill with tears, and as the skin of the face is stretched toward the back of the skull, the mouth opens and the teeth become visible in the grinning rictus of death. The thick darkness of the bardo of becoming comes to meet the dying, and they are driven from behind by the cyclonic wind of karma. They must

* *'tsho byed gzhon nu*, the most celebrated physician in the time of the Buddha.

pass through many terrifying hallucinations. Six uncertainties will come about: those of location, resting place, behavior, sustenance, companions, and mental state. Then there will be the three dreadful abysses of hatred, desire, and confusion, white as ash, dark red, and black. Four dreadful sounds will occur. As the energy of the earth element reemerges, a roar will be heard as of collapsing mountains; as the energy of the fire element reemerges, there will be the sound of blazing forests; as the energy of the water element reemerges, there will be the crashing of tumultuous seas; and as the energy of the wind element reemerges, there will be the shrieking of a gale like the winds of the end of time.*

From now on, may the thought of our impermanence spur us on!

---

* For a detailed description of the bardo state, see appendix 2, p. 279, and *The Mirror of Mindfulness* by Tsele Natsok Rangdrol.

Part Three

The Gradual Path of the Three Kinds of Beings

THE PATH OF BEINGS OF LESSER SCOPE

Ethical Teachings in Relation to the Karmic Law of Cause and Effect

CHAPTER 3

The Law of Karma

THE KARMIC PROCESS IN GENERAL

There is absolutely no doubt that when we die, we must go where we are propelled. Like fish caught on a hook, we are entangled in the strings of our karma and pulled into one or other of the six realms, high or low. This is nothing but the effect of actions, positive or negative. It is true that, ultimately speaking, there is no such thing as origination, but on the level of relative truth, the karmic principle of cause and effect is inescapable. It is like a gardener planting two kinds of seed, the bitter aloe or the sweet grape. The resulting crops will have a corresponding taste. In the same way, the existential quality of our present lives, whether fortunate or otherwise, is but the product of positive or negative actions to which we have become accustomed in our previous existences.

Actions never fail to produce an effect

The shadow of a bird soaring in the sky may be temporarily invisible, but it is still there and will always appear when the bird comes to earth. In the same way, when attendant causes coincide with the factors of Craving and Grasping,* karma comes to fruition and results in a life situation that is either favorable or unfavorable. As the sutra says, "The karma that living beings gather is never worn away even after a hundred kalpas. When the moment comes and the appropriate conditions gather, the fruit of action will come to maturity."

---

* See *The twelve links of dependent arising*, chapter 4, p. 86.

The karmic process is irresistible

For as long as phenomena are apprehended as truly existent, even small negative actions are liable to have immense consequences. They are likened in the root verse to a monstrous fire-vomiting mare—a reference to the volcanoes that encircle the ocean of brine on the rim of the world.* The fire of these volcanoes is able to dry up the countless waves of the sea that here symbolize happy incarnations, the fruit of positive action. It is important to study sutras such as the *Saddharmasmrityupasthana, Karmashataka, Lalitavistara,* and *Karmavibhanga,* for they describe how our human condition, which is like a ship in which we can sail to the precious isle of Omniscience, may be wrecked and brought to utter ruin.

The results of evil deeds, namely, the lower realms so full of dreadful and inescapable misery, are said in the root text to have been unable, for the moment, to overwhelm our strength, our army of ten "virtues tending to happiness"[17]—in other words, our fortunate existence in higher states. These virtues are like heroes whose land is not yet overrun by the legions of suffering. And yet if our determination weakens, we shall fall into the ten evil actions and thence into lower existences. There are many ways in which this might happen. Some people, aspiring to liberation, receive the vows of pure discipline from their abbots or preceptors. But tempted by desire or other evil thoughts, they break their commitments and fall, defeated in their monastic resolve. Again, some people kill animals for the sake of gain, thereby shortening their own lives.† Some, out of aggression, go off to war only to be killed themselves. Some, inspired by virtue, embrace an ascetic discipline, becoming indifferent even to food and clothing. But later, victims of their desire, they settle down to married life. Some devote themselves with great effort to study and reflection, but they are unable to free themselves of the eight worldly concerns and are carried away by mundane preoccupations. Some, instead of offering their wealth to the Three Jewels, lavish it on their relatives or squander it in lawsuits.

---

* See Jamgon Kongtrul Lodro Tayé, *Myriad Worlds,* p. 111.
† One of the karmic results of killing is a shortening of the killer's own life.

On the whole, a moral conscience with regard to oneself and one's religious values, and a sense of shame in respect of the opinions of others, are two factors that work in tandem to put a brake on evil behavior. Some people, however, abandon both their conscience and their sense of shame.* They disregard virtuous conduct and in one way or other indulge in evil, succumbing to habits they have grown accustomed to from time without beginning. This is how people fall into the lower realms and stay there.

Karmic effects are not transferable from one mindstream to another

The perpetrator of an act is always the one who experiences its karmic consequences. In any case, negative actions done for the sake of others, whether in the name of the Three Jewels, on behalf of relatives, friends, or dependents, or in the defense of one's country, will be found upon careful examination to spring from self-centred motives. Thus, gravely negative behavior, such as aggression motivated by an evil intention, will always ripen upon the perpetrator, not upon those on behalf of whom the action is performed. The latter will be untouched by the negativity of the agent, who, as the root text says, plunges into evil, unleashing the elephant of wickedness from the restraining harness of self-control—an image used to illustrate the magnitude of the evil involved.

An explanation of the eight worldly concerns and thirteen influential factors

Ordinary beings, who are naive and behave like children, are led astray by the eight worldly concerns. They wish for gain, crave physical and mental comforts, bask in the indirect pleasures of good reputation, and are exhilarated when they are openly praised. On the other hand, they are depressed and humiliated when the opposite occurs: loss, discomfort, bad reputation, and blame.

* *ngo tsha* and *khrel yod*, respectively.

In addition to these eight worldly concerns, there are thirteen other factors that exert a profound influence over human behavior. Of these, the first five are concerned with personal prestige and result in arrogance. They are: (1) social status; (2) a tall and handsome appearance; (3) wealth and influence; (4) extensive knowledge of secular and religious matters; and (5) youth. In addition to these, there is (6) indifference, or rather indolence. This is the reverse of enthusiastic endeavor and makes people appear spineless and incapable. Then there is (7) conceit—when people wrongly think that they are fine and talented—a pride that will itself prevent the growth of such qualities in the mind. After this come the two enemies of the glorious but arduous practices of the sacred Dharma, namely, (8) desire and (9) resentment. These are like demons that sap whatever qualities have been developed in the past and hinder their cultivation in the future. Then there is (10) miserly attachment to wealth, the very antithesis of generosity, as a result of which people become increasingly (11) centered upon themselves and their possessions. Because of this, their hearts are invaded by the creeping plant of (12) cunning and (13) duplicity, the source of faithless and deceitful attitudes. Influenced by all these factors, people trick and mislead each other in the interests of their own advancement. But such behavior is like eating poison—calamitous in both this life and the next. These thirteen factors should be rejected for the enemies that they are.

The proliferating tendency of karmic results

The positive and negative behavior from which samsara is compounded produces fruits of happiness and suffering that are of a disproportionate magnitude. And this is so on a far greater scale than may be observed in the causal relationships of ordinary experience, such as seeds giving rise to plants. The slightest action can have immense consequences. This is illustrated by the story of the king Mandhata who, in a previous existence, had, as a small boy, cast a handful of peas in offering to the Buddha Vipashyin.* Four of these peas fell into the Buddha's begging

---

* The first Buddha of this Fortunate Kalpa.

bowl; two struck his body at the level of his heart; and one got caught in his robe. Because of this action of offering the peas, Mandhata subsequently became a Chakravartin who through his golden wheel held sway over the four cosmic continents. He then became a powerful ruler in the celestial realm of the Four Great Kings and finally was born in the heaven of the Thirty-three, where he shared the position of the thirty-two divine sovereigns.[18] Likewise, Shariputra offered a piece of cloth to an Arhat and as a result attained great wisdom. By contrast, there is a story that a certain monk abused one of his confreres, telling him to eat excrement. As a result, he was later born as an intrauterine parasite, and later as a worm living in a latrine.

Therefore, as it says in the rhyme:

> Little virtues do not shun
> Thinking that no gain is won.
> For drops of rain from cloud and sky
> Will fill an ocean by and by.
> And little faults do not ignore
> And think there is no ill in store.
> For tiny though the spark may burn
> A mountain of dry grass to ash will turn.

And as it is written in the *Bodhicharyavatara*:

> And those who harbor evil in their minds
> Against such lords of generosity, the Buddha's heirs,
> Will stay in hell, the Mighty One has said,
> For ages equal to the moments of their malice.
> (I, 34)

A tiny seed, no bigger than a mustard grain, can give rise to an *ashota* tree, which when it is fully grown has branches measuring a league in length. But even this example gives no idea of how, in the karmic process, positive and negative effects increase out of all proportion to their causes.

Assessing the gravity of positive and negative actions

Phenomena, whether animate or inanimate, are neither the product of *prakriti* nor the handiwork of some kind of divine creator;[19] neither do they arise spontaneously from themselves. They are the product of the mind and mental factors: positive and negative thoughts. A piece of cloth is colored differently according to the dyes employed. In the same way, a positive or negative action may appear insignificant in itself, but due to its underlying motive, its effect may be very considerable in terms of resultant happiness or suffering. If an action is performed unintentionally and without long forethought, and if the agent has a strong feeling of remorse afterward, the effect of the action will be greatly reduced because the two crucial factors of premeditation and satisfaction are lacking. If the root of a plant is medicinal, the stem and fruit will also be medicinal; if the root is poisonous, there is no doubt that the shoot will be poisonous as well. In the same way, the effect of an action depends not so much on the apparent goodness or badness of the act itself, but rather on the character of its root: the positive or negative intention that propelled it. It is said in one of the sutras:

> With good intention
> One man placed
> His boots
> On Buddha's head.
> Another, well-intentioned,
> Took them off.
> And both
> Were later born as kings.

In the desire realm, the importance of actions, positive or negative, depends on the presence or absence of five factors. The first is the factor of constancy, namely, a continuous intention to perform the action. The second is the factor of determination, by virtue of which the agent is not distracted from his or her purpose by some other interest. The third factor is the absence of any countermanding force whereby the intention is attenuated by opposing considerations. The fourth and fifth factors consist in whether the action has as its object the "field of ex-alted qualities" or the "field of benefits," respectively. The field of ex-alted qualities is a technical term for the Three Jewels. The field of benefits refers to the parents of the agent and those to whom a debt of gratitude is owed, as well as all objects of compassion, such as the chronically sick, road-weary travelers, and poor beggars. The assessment of the gravity of a positive or negative action thus depends on whether the action is directed at one or the other of these two fields and whether the first, second, and third motivating factors are present.

The basis of the karmic phenomenon

The fundamental basis upon which karma manifests is the so-called *alaya*, the indeterminate "ground of all," which veils the uncompounded nature of the mind. This alaya is a neutral and undifferentiated state and underlies all habitual predispositions. Its nature is coemergent igno-rance, but out of it arise, nevertheless, the factors of clarity and knowing which are comparable to the limpid surface of a mirror. This is the *alayavijnana*, the fundamental level of consciousness, the working envi-ronment for the ebb and flow of the seven consciousnesses arising from it. Of these, the mental consciousness cognizes objects in the most gen-eral sense. The "defiled emotional consciousness" inwardly grasps at the ego or self, on the basis of which outer experience is divided up into "wanted" and "unwanted." The visual consciousness perceives shapes by means of the organ of sight, and the other sense consciousnesses function similarly, in their different ways, up to and including tactility, which experiences physical sensation throughout the body. The six consciousnesses (five of sense and one of mind) do not in themselves generate karma, even though karma is accumulated when these con-sciousnesses manifest. The latter are, however, permeated by the igno-rance of apprehending the personal and phenomenal self, and this ignorance is the root of all delusion and sorrow. It is a great demon nurturing the three poisons of the afflictions, due to which beings either perform negative actions and fall into the lower realms, or accumulate positive actions "tending to happiness," which propel them into the higher states of existence but do not lead to liberation, being still within the sphere of ignorance.[20] Actions producing rebirth in the upper realms are tinged with pride or envy. In the first case, they produce birth among the gods and humans; in the second, they tend to birth among the asuras. It is in this way that the different levels of samsara come about.

Propelling and completing actions

Two kinds of action (which can be either positive or negative) play a part in this process. First there is "propelling action," which projects into a specific samsaric state, followed by "completing action," which generates the circumstances experienced within that state. These two kinds of action are interrelated according to four possible permutations.

1. When the propelling and completing actions are both positive, birth in the realms of gods or humans is attained, together with the enjoyment of every kind of excellence such as good family, physical strength and beauty, high renown, and great prosperity.

2. When positive propelling action is complemented by negative completing action, birth in a higher realm occurs, but this is marred by the possession of impaired faculties and other handicaps or else by the domination of others.

3. When both propelling and completing actions are negative, the result is birth in the lower realms, where nothing but suffering is experienced.

4. When negative propelling action is accompanied by positive completing action, situations arise like those of certain animals or pretas, which despite their unfortunate condition enjoy great beauty, strength, magnificence, and wealth.[21]

According to the Sautrantika, Chittamatra, and Madhyamika schools, a single action may give rise to one or many existences. An example of the first case is the story of the woman who was reborn in the heaven of the Pure because of the compassion she had for her daughter. The second case is illustrated by the words of Arya Aniruddha, who proclaimed that through the ripening of a single good action, he was born seven times as a god in the heaven of the Thirty-three and afterward as a wealthy member of the Shakya tribe. It is claimed, moreover, that several actions can combine to give rise to a single life, as in the case of Devadatta, who, due to actions accumulated over a series of lives, was both a monk and an evildoer. On the other hand, several actions can produce several existences, as happened to Arya Upasena, who experienced a series of lives that were the result of numerous individual acts. In the *Abhidharmakosha*,[22] however, it is said, "One propelling action produces one birth, while the circumstantial character of that birth is the result of several completing actions." This shows that the Vaibhashikas hold that one propelling action brings about only one birth and several propelling actions result in several existences.

The performed and stored aspects of actions

An action propels into a specific birth depending on its gravity and intensity. This in turn is assessed according to the action's "performed" and "stored" aspects, which, according to their four permutations, are as follows:

1. An action is both performed and stored when, for example, a person wishes to inflict harm on another, does so, and is subsequently satisfied at the resulting situation.

2. An action is performed but not stored when, for example, one is obliged, against one's wish, to harm enemies or deprive people of their possessions, in order to save life or to prevent lawless people from ruling the country unjustly and in violation of the Dharma.

3. An action is stored but not performed when, for example, a person has long nourished the wish to deceive another but in the event fails to do so.

4. Finally, there are indeterminate actions that are neither performed nor stored, in other words, chance and unintentional actions that have no ripened effect at all.

By weighing these four permutations and discerning the presence or absence of the five factors of constancy, determination, and the rest, as explained above, the intensity of good or evil deeds, in their two aspects of being performed and stored, may be evaluated—as also the extent of their specific results.[23]

Negative actions

Negative actions regarding the Three Jewels

When a house is burning down, the only thing that can counteract the fire is water. But if the water is contained in a vessel and the fire evaporates it, there is obviously nothing to counteract the blaze. In the same way, if we destroy the representations of the Body, Speech, and Mind of the Buddhas; if we revile and spurn the Sacred Dharma; if we criticize and despoil the noble Sangha; if out of malice we forsake the Three Jewels and turn away from them and their protection, there is no remedy, no means of rectifying so great an evil.[24] Consequently, no other action is as negative as this.

The crucial role of intention

It should be added to what has just been said that the six consciousnesses and their associated sense faculties, as found in ordinary beings and therefore characterized by the dualistic apprehension of subject and object, are the doors or media through which karma is accumulated. The agent of this accumulation is intention, virtuous, nonvirtuous, or neutral. Intention arises in association with other mental factors (for example, the three types of feeling and the three types of perception).[25] Thus good and bad karmas are accumulated and stored in the alaya. It is, however, impossible for the ordinary mind to pinpoint how, and how many, subtle karmas are created* by the eighty-four thousand kinds of discursive thought. Nevertheless, it is a fact that through them karma is generated.

The ten negative actions

There are ten ways of behaving, related to body, speech, and mind, that are to be abandoned.

To begin with, there are three physical acts: killing, taking what is

---

* "This means that it is impossible to say which thought has generated which action giving rise to which result." [YG I, 254] (For a key to abbreviations used in notes, see p. 349.)

not given, and sexual misconduct. These are followed by four negative actions of speech: lying, divisive speech, worthless chatter, and harsh words. Finally, there are three negative actions of mind: covetousness, evil intent, and wrong views.

1. *Killing*

A complete act of killing takes place according to five criteria.

    a. A living being must be the object of the action.
    b. There must be no mistaking the intended victim.
    c. There must be the specific intention to kill.
    d. The act must be performed knowingly.
    e. The death of the being must ensue.

Similar to this are all acts of aggression when death occurs, through beating and so forth, even when death is not actually intended.

2. *Theft*

The act of taking what is not freely given is fully accomplished when four elements are present.

    a. The object concerned must be the possession of another.
    b. The agent knows that this is the case.
    c. The agent knowingly appropriates it.
    d. The object moves its location and becomes the agent's property.

Related to theft are acts whereby things are acquired by deceit, for instance, in commercial transactions, or by extortion, or through the imposition of unjust fines, confiscation, and so on.

3. *Sexual Misconduct*

Sexual misconduct takes place when three elements are present.

    a. It is known that the object of desire is the partner of another, or else a person engaged by someone else. One is aware that one is in the presence of a representation of the Buddha, or of persons with pratimoksha ordination (clerical or lay). One has intercourse with someone judged inappropriate in terms of custom, time, or any other criterion.*

b. Actual physical union.

c. Satisfaction.

Included in sexual misconduct are improper sexual acts.

4. Lying

Lying occurs when four elements are present.

a. The speaker must not be mistaken about what he or she wants to say.

b. The speaker must have the intention to deceive.

c. The lie must be consciously pronounced.

d. The hearer must be deceived.

Associated with lying are all attempts to twist the truth by deceptive means and the concealment of the facts in order to cheat people.

5. Divisive speech

Here, three factors are necessary.

a. The people affected must be living in harmony or at least in a relationship of neutrality.

b. The agent speaks in order to divide the parties.

c. Discord arises between them, or at least the meaning of the speaker's words comes home to them.

Allied to divisive speech is the repetition of criticism or abuse spoken by others in order to nurture resentment.

---

* For example, underage persons, a pregnant woman, or a person falling within the forbidden degrees of consanguinity.

6. *Worthless chatter*

This comprises three elements.

    a. The conversation is motivated by the defilements.
    b. The mind strays to what is unwholesome.
    c. Futile chatter occurs, in other words, conversation productive of attachment or aversion. This covers, for instance, discussions about the sacrifices described in the Vedas, poetry, historical discourses about the rise and fall of empires, singing, recounting of legends, erotic literature, and tales of adventure and crime.

Related to worthless chatter are all unnecessary conversations about wars, crime, and so forth, even if this does not provoke attachment or hatred.

7. *Harsh words*

This depends on three factors.

    a. A specific person must be addressed.
    b. The person is spoken to harshly and hidden faults are exposed.
    c. The words pierce the person's heart, causing trauma and sorrow.

Allied to verbal abuse are all kinds of talk that, though superficially sweet, bring about the unhappiness of others.

8. *Covetousness*

Covetousness has two factors.

    a. The object in mind must be the wealth or reputation of another.
    b. One must be obsessed with the other person's qualities and belongings and want to take them for oneself.

Related to covetousness are all reflections on the wealth and advantages of others, with the wish to have them for oneself.

9. Evil Intent

Two factors are required for evil intent.

    a. The object must be a living being.
    b. The agent hates and deeply wishes harm to the other, desiring his or her misery, whether physical or mental. Wishing harm on others may be connected with any one of nine objects: those who cause trouble to oneself, those who attack one's friends, and those who aid one's enemies. These three categories, multiplied by three according to the past, present, and future, come to nine objects all together. In addition, there are five factors that accompany evil intent. These are: hatred, rancor, injured pride, vengefulness, and ignorance.

Related to evil intent is discomfort at the advantages of others, such as riches and long life, and the wish that they did not have them but rather their opposites.

10. Wrong Views

There are two kinds of false views.

    a. Disbelief in the ineluctable principle of karma.
    b. Belief in a permanent self and phenomena, or the opposite, namely, nihilism, the belief that nothing survives death.

Related to wrong views are claims, born of animosity, that a sublime being has faults when this is not the case, and conversely the denial of the qualities that such a being possesses—thus creating doubts in the minds of others.

The results of the ten negative actions

All these actions have four kinds of karmic consequence: the fully ripened effect, the effect similar to the cause, the conditioning or environmental effect, and the proliferating effect.

The fully ripened effect

Five factors are associated with actions. These are (1) motivation (virtuous or otherwise); (2) perpetration; (3) consciousness of the act; (4) result of the act; and (5) satisfaction at the finished action. However, whether or not a given act possesses all these five factors, the fully ripened effect derives principally from the first, the motivation, and this may be of three kinds. The least of these is ignorance (for example, the killer's not understanding that it is wrong to take life), on account of which, the agent creates the cause for birth in the animal realm. Worse than this is when killing is done out of desire for meat, leather, horn, ivory, pearls, and so forth. Here, the action will propel the agent into the realm of the pretas. Worst of all is when killing is motivated by hatred or anger, as when someone murders an enemy. In that case, the action is of extreme gravity and will produce a birth in the hell realms.

The effect similar to the cause

Effects similar to the cause may be experienced either actively or passively. In the first case, the result of acquiring a nonvirtuous habit in previous existences is to have a temperament inclined to the same kind of negativity, together with a conducive life situation, so that the behavioral pattern naturally repeats itself.* In the second case, even though positive karma may have resulted in birth in a higher realm, situations will be experienced that reflect the evil actions previously performed. Two specific kinds of suffering are associated with each nonvirtuous action. The consequence of killing is a shortened life dogged by illness. Stealing gives rise to poverty and the obligation to share the little one has with enemies. The result of sexual misconduct is to have an unattractive, argumentative, and slovenly spouse who will take up with one's enemies and in turn become hostile. Lying results in being abused and criticized irrespective of deserts, as well as the liability to be betrayed by those in whom one has placed one's trust. Divisive speech is the cause of having a family, servants, and attendants who are ineffective

---

* Hunters may be reborn as beasts of prey, thieves as mice, and so on.

and troublesome, quarrel among themselves, and are difficult to reconcile. The result of worthless chatter is that nothing one says wins acceptance; one's words are dismissed as nonsense and as coming from an untrustworthy source. The result of having subjected others to verbal abuse is to be constantly attacked and scolded. Everything one does to help goes wrong and becomes the cause of further friction and suffering. Covetousness begets a situation of dissatisfaction with possessions and a desire for more, coupled with the anxiety that this will prove impossible. The result of harmful intention is that all sorts of difficulties seem to arise for no apparent reason—sickness, misfortune, enemies, and so forth—while at the same time, relatives and possessions—all one's happy circumstances—simply vanish. Wrong views give rise to a lack of confidence in the Dharma and a tendency to stray to evil and untrue opinions. At the same time, one will have a crooked and deceitful temperament.*

The conditioning or environmental effect

This has a bearing on habitat and environment, making it a source of suffering. It is said in the *Saddharmasmrityupasthana-sutra*:

> Appearances of body,
> Possessions, joys, and sorrows,
> All are nothing but the mind's imagining:
> The stuff of dreams, created by the mind.

And again, in the *Bodhicharyavatara* we find:

> Who has forged this burning iron ground;
> Whence have all these demon women sprung?
>
> All are but the offspring of the sinful mind,
> Thus the Mighty One has said.
> (V, 7–8)

---

* It is said also that as a result of wrong views, people are gullible and prone to being led astray.

The karmic residue of the cruel act of killing powerfully influences the environment in which one is born. This will be unpleasant and cramped, devoid of favorable circumstances. Medicinal trees and plants will be scarce. Crops will give poor harvests. Food and drink will lack their nutritive and thirst-quenching qualities and will repeatedly prove indigestible and the cause of sickness. The environment will be dangerous, with perilous rivers and canyons, enemies, and wild beasts. The situation of having to live in harsh and frightening places is the result of killing.

The consequence of stealing is to be born in places where crops are scarce. What little there is is fragile and easily destroyed. If edible fruits and so forth are available, they are of inferior quality, without goodness or savor. The cows, female yaks, and so on, have no milk, and if crops manage to grow, they will be vulnerable to damage by frost or hail. Cattle will stray and get lost. Famine will threaten, and there is always the great anxiety that there will not be enough to eat and drink.

The result of sexual misconduct is a living environment that is squalid and suffocatingly filthy, fouled with excrement and urine, such as cattle sheds and slums. The power of previous behavior inescapably plants the vine of human birth in fetid places where there is little ease and in which one is trapped and obliged to live.

The telling of lies produces a great instability in personal influence and material fortune. Wherever one goes, one is at odds with the place and one is liable to be tricked by everyone, enemies, friends, and even people one does not know. Through a host of such adverse circumstances, the result is paranoia and a life full of nervousness and anxiety.

As for divisive speech, this will provoke birth in stark and inhospitable places full of ravines and precipitous crags where travel is difficult and full of inconvenience.

Harsh speech results in the experience of landscapes that are dry and stony, where even the fruit bushes are covered with thorns, where there are no gardens but only barren tree stumps, where the crops are poor and powerless to nourish. In such places, deadly diseases abound and good health is impossible. The water is not fresh and clear but turbid and brackish; the ground is dusty and covered with filth. People are constantly tormented in such places.

When nothing is gained in spite of all one's toil, this is the consequence of idle chatter. Fields may be plowed, cattle raised, business pursued—but nothing comes of it. The spring seems to portend a plenteous harvest, but the autumn brings no fruit. The environment is unstable, and evil threatens.

Covetousness produces the experience of places where the proportion of husk to grain is the inverse of what it should be. Even if the country has previously enjoyed prosperity, now the seasons are all topsy-turvy. Evil times are on their way, and suffering is in store.

Because of evil intent, people are born to hardship in lands subjected to wicked overlords who oppress the people with violence and wars. They are vulnerable to attack from robbers, thieves, venomous snakes, savages, and wild beasts like leopards and tigers. The crops and fruits in such places are bitter and hot-tasting. The physical constitution is weak and the environment is constantly liable to natural calamities.

On account of wrong views, the place where one is born is poor and completely without comfort and luxury such as silks and jewels. Edible and medicinal plants and trees are few or none at all. Any fruits and flowers that may be eaten have almost no power of nourishment and bring no strength to the body. One falls victim to enemies and evil forces, and one is isolated without help or protection.

The proliferating effect

In addition to the fact that actions, like killing, are connected with what happens in future lives, it is also true that their results increase with every instant. Even trivial acts may result in immense sufferings.

Conclusion

The ultimate nature of phenomena has, from beginningless time, been overlaid and concealed by the thick gloom of ignorance. But we are afflicted by an even worse darkness, namely, our deluded perceptions.*

---

* Based on the apprehension of the self of the person and the self of phenomena.

These proliferate constantly and completely blind us. In this bitter, terrible prison of samsara, which is so hard to escape from, our five aggregates must undergo long and unbearable torment, as though torn and slashed by knives. These are the consequences of the ten nonvirtues. Of all evil deeds, the worst are the five sins of immediate effect,[26] as well as the five sins similar to them, such as destroying stupas, killing Bodhisattvas and Arhats,[27] and other heinous deeds.[28]

VIRTUOUS ACTIONS

Because deluded perception is taken to be concrete reality, the appearances of high and low existences occur. While beings are under the influence of such illusions, the ten virtuous actions propel them into the higher realms. Consequently, Jigme Lingpa urges us to turn away consciously from the ten negative actions and embrace the ten virtues.[29]

It is said in the *Ratnavali* that virtuous action delivers beings from birth in the hells and the realms of pretas and animals; it brings them to the bliss of the divine and human realms and gives them the opportunity to experience the pure joys of the samadhis and limitless formless absorptions.

A RECAPITULATION OF THE PATH OF BEINGS OF LESSER SCOPE

Given the distinction between virtue and nonvirtue as laid down in the teachings, it is important to rely on virtue. The ten virtues tending to happiness will produce happy destinies, while negative action will precipitate a fall into the states of loss. To understand this distinction correctly, according to the karmic law of cause and effect, and to adopt positive rather than negative behavior is the so-called path of beings of lesser scope. It is written in the sutra:

> Those who have this perfect view,
> This perfect attitude according to the world,
> For thousands of their lives to come,
> Will not sink down to evil destinies.

How beings of medium scope practice virtue

In contrast with this, virtue tending to liberation (the preserve of beings of medium capacity) brings about a state of nirvana free from all trace of obscuring karma and defilements. "Virtue tending to liberation" means the ten virtues practiced in conjunction with the wisdom of realizing the nonexistence of the personal self. It refers also to the practice of the four samadhis of the form realm, the four absorptions of the formless realm, together with the six virtues of generosity, discipline, patience, diligence, concentration, and wisdom,[30] which are to be implemented at the same time as abandoning all that goes against them. All this is encompassed in the five paths. On the path of accumulation, the practice of virtue consists primarily in the reception and study of the teachings. On the path of joining, the main practice is that of meditation, though this is still on the mundane level. On the path of seeing, the no-self of the person is directly realized, while on the path of meditation, the principal training is in egolessness and discipline. When all these virtues have been fully practiced and accomplished, the path of no more learning is attained. In other words, "virtue tending to liberation" refers to the stainless merit accumulated on the five paths.

How beings of great scope practice virtue

In the practice of beings of great scope, namely, the Bodhisattvas, there is no conceptual view (as there is with the Shravakas and Pratyekabuddhas) to the effect that there exist ten virtues to be embraced and ten nonvirtues to be rejected. By the application of great wisdom, Bodhisattvas perfectly realize that all outer and inner phenomena are by nature empty—without self-identity, either personal or phenomenal. All aspects of the skillful means of compassion, that is, generosity and the rest, are sealed with the seal of emptiness. In this context, positive action, in which skillful means are conjoined with wisdom, is like the elixir of the alchemists. It transmutes into gold the base metal of ignorance. Here, ignorance is understood as the failure to recognize that samsara and nirvana are equal, with the result that one conceives them in terms of opposites, with nirvana as something to be chosen and samsara as something to be rejected. The ultimate buddha nature, the wisdom that abides in neither extreme (of samsara and nirvana), is thus accomplished, and the form bodies of Buddhas, together with their activities, arise effortlessly—brought forth by supramundane virtue.

As the *Bodhicharyavatara* proclaims:

> All these branches of the Doctrine
> The Powerful Lord expounded for the sake of wisdom. (IX, 1)

Those training in the four paths of the Mahayana accumulate merit through the dualistic practice* of generosity and so forth (that is to say, in post-meditation). But the fact that the practice itself is considered to be illusory—in other words, that it is associated with the nondualistic wisdom that realizes that subject, object, and action are without real existence—means that the accumulation of wisdom is accomplished at the same time. As one grows increasingly habituated to the practice of these two accumulations of merit and wisdom inseparably united, the two kinds of obscurations, emotional and cognitive, are purified, and the two kayas, the Dharmakaya and Rupakaya, are actualized.

It is said in the *Ratnavali*:

> The Buddhas' forms arise
> From stores of merit, while (if briefly told)
> Their form of truth is born
> From kingly treasuries of wisdom.

From the absolute point of view, beyond all conceptual construction, the karmic principle of cause and effect is a mere imputation. The fact that the process of cause and effect, as this is asserted in the common vehicle, has no true existence, points to the profound principle of dependent arising, which ordinary people find difficult to understand.

---

* *dmigs bcas*, normally translated as "referential" or "conceptual."

As it is written in the *Sandhinirmochana-sutra*:

> Deep truth is not for the naive.
> The Conqueror set forth the nondual and ineffable,
> But children, straying in confusion,
> Amuse themselves with doctrines, staying in duality.

THE PATH OF BEINGS OF MEDIUM SCOPE

Correct Conduct in Relation to the Four Truths

The Sufferings of Samsara

THE FOUR TRUTHS

Beings born in the higher realms of gods and humans possess for the time being a wonderful opportunity: the chance afforded them by their fortunate existence. This is like a ship in which they can sail to freedom over the ocean of samsara and which has, for the moment, eluded the ferocious jaws of the sea monster waiting to drag them down to the lower depths. Nevertheless, they have not yet reached the dry land of liberation, which is free from suffering and safe from the flood of defiled emotions. Indeed, they have not even attained the stages of the path of joining as referred to in the saying:

> The "Peak" is won—the roots of virtue unimpaired;
> "Acceptance" gained—no fall to lower realms.[31]

People in this situation should rely on the teaching of the four noble truths,* metaphorically referred to in the root verses as a captain. The Buddha taught these truths at Varanasi, explaining them in three ways. First of all, he simply pointed them out, saying: "This, O monks, is Suffering. This is the Source of Suffering. This is Cessation. This is the Path." Later, he referred to their causal aspect when he said: "Suffering is to be understood. The source of suffering is to be discarded. Cessation is to be realized. The path thereto should be followed." Still later, he indicated their resultant aspect with these words: "O monks, when you have understood suffering, there is nothing more to understand. When you have discarded the source of suffering, there is nothing more to discard. When you have realized cessation, there is nothing more to

---

* See appendix 3, p. 283.

realize. When you have followed the path, there is nothing more to follow."

The truth of suffering

The all-pervasive nature of suffering

We should understand that the six states of samsara (the three evil destinies below and the three happy destinies above) are utterly permeated by suffering: the "suffering of suffering," the "suffering of change," and "all-pervading suffering in the making." The suffering of suffering is simply pain as such, as in the case of a leper who, in addition to his disease, is afflicted by blisters. The suffering of change refers to pleasure or happiness, for this is always liable to transform into pain, as when someone is bitten by a poisonous snake while walking in the garden, or gets intestinal worms after eating delicious food. All-pervading suffering in the making refers to the fact that, due to the defiled emotional consciousness that underlies our every action, external and internal suffering is latent in everything we do. It is in fact the product of ignorance. Nowhere in the whole of samsara are beings free from the toils of these three kinds of pain. In the three lower realms, manifest suffering (of suffering) predominates, the fruit of negative action. In the states of humans and the gods of the desire realm, happiness manifests as the fruit of virtuous action, and therefore the suffering in this case is mainly of the second kind, the suffering of change. Finally, in the two higher dimensions of form and formlessness, beings experience the neutral state devoid of bliss and pain, which is the result of "unwavering actions."

> In this condition, many negative karmas previously accumulated continue to lie dormant in the mind, so that even though the painful result is not manifest, it is always there, ready to emerge. Also, the results of the previous positive actions of beings in the form and formless realms can ripen in the realm of desire, where they will bring forth the suffering of change. Thus the

sorrow of the form and formless realms is principally that of all-pervading suffering in the making.[32]

The conditions that perpetuate suffering

The roots of our present and future suffering are the harmful mental patterns of desire and aversion, which, prompted by our clinging to illusory phenomena, set in motion destructive karmic sequences of cause and effect. This "demon of desire" is like a venomous serpent rearing up to strike. External objects, shapes, sounds, and so forth, are a kind of poison. They seem pleasant when they are experienced but later reveal themselves as the source of pain. The mind is adulterated by these outer objects, for it merges with them inextricably in the same way as iron is suffused with heat when it is glowing in the fire. Because they lack the insight to appreciate the defects implicit in the attitude of craving, beings have languished in the prison of samsara and have never discovered how to escape from it. This indeed is our terrible predicament, and sadness wells up as we reflect upon it.[33]

Beings in samsara long for happiness and try their best to achieve it. But despite their tremendous efforts and the difficulties they endure, they are actually unaware of the causes of happiness and are dragged down by their own ignorance. Through sexual misconduct, for example, they create the causes of all kinds of suffering and eventually have to endure the result, transfixed on the sharp and pointed blade of pain. They wholeheartedly embrace what will bring them immediate and long-term sorrow. As Shantideva says in the *Bodhicharyavatara*:

> For beings long to free themselves from misery,
> But misery itself they race to catch.
> They long for joy, but in their ignorance,
> Destroy it, as they would a hated enemy.
> (I, 28)

Desire is the source of suffering both in this life and the next. Like moths drawn to the lovely candlelight that destroys them, people are attracted to the pleasing sound of flattery, enticed by the aroma of tobacco, the taste of meat, a lover's soft touch, and the caress of silken robes. Thus people are deceived and destroy the path to their own freedom. Lured by the sweet sound of a lute, the deer is shot with poisoned arrows; the bee is drawn by the perfume of the flower and is ensnared in its petals; the fish is caught on the hook, unable to resist the taste of the bait; and the elephant, craving contact with its mate, perishes in the quicksand. Beings are enticed by the objects of the senses and are constantly bound up with them. It is as Vasubandhu says:

> Living beings, each and every one,
> Are lured by these five senses all the time
> And overwhelmed thereby both night and day,
> What happiness can they attain?

Indeed, the intense suffering of the wheel of existence is a blazing fire destroying all it touches. Worse than wounds inflicted by lions, tigers, and ravening beasts; worse than the harm caused by savages or the punishments inflicted by kings upon lonely, friendless individuals—the sorrows of samsara are stronger, swifter to strike, and longer lasting. Beings are tormented constantly by the three kinds of misery and the eight associated sufferings that follow each other in an uninterrupted spate: birth, sickness, old age, death, separation from dear ones, meeting with enemies, the loss of what one needs and desires, and the presence of unwanted circumstances.

It is impossible to conceive how many beings, from beginningless time in samsara, have been related to us—as parents, as enemies, or as people indifferent to us. In fact, *all* beings have been linked to us in these three ways innumerable times. When they were our enemies, they injured us; when they were our parents or our friends, they cherished and aided us; when they were neither, they ignored us. It would be impossible to calculate the number of relationships that we have experienced. Once when the noble Katyayana went begging for alms, he came across a group of people and, perceiving the karmic links that bound them together, commented:

He strikes his mother, eats his father's flesh;
His hated foe he dandles on his lap.
Here is a wife that sucks her husband's bones—
At this samsara how can I not laugh?[34]

And Nagarjuna says in his *Suhrllekha:*

Were I to make a pill of mud just berry-sized,
For every mother who has given me birth,
The earth itself indeed would not suffice.

Finally, it is worth reflecting about all the times a single being (no need to mention all) has taken birth in samsara, and the number of times he or she has lost head and limbs in the quest for fulfillment. All such heads and members, small though they be, when piled up together, would make a heap more lofty than Mount Meru itself—eighty thousand leagues high! And wandering in samsara high and low, when repeatedly we had to drink the molten copper in the hot hells, or consume filth, blood, pus, and the like when born among the pretas, the tears we shed would more than fill all the rivers flowing down to the great ocean at the rim of the world. This is mentioned specifically in the *Saddharmasmrityupasthana-sutra.*

The sufferings of the lower realms

THE EIGHT HOT HELLS

There is nowhere in samsara beyond the reach of pain. But the suffering in the lower realms, and especially the hells, exceeds all limits. The first hot hell is the so-called Reviving Hell. Here, beings perceive each other as mortal enemies and fight each other to the death. But then there comes a voice saying, "Revive!" The slain come back to life and the fighting and killing start all over again—and so on endlessly. It is said in the *Saddharmasmrityupasthana-sutra* that all who have killed a human or nonhuman being will without fail be born in the Reviving Hell.

The second hot hell is the Black Line Hell. There, beings are tormented by being cut in pieces with saws following black lines (from eight to an unlimited number) that have been drawn on their bodies. As soon as the body is dismembered, it is joined together by the power of karma and becomes whole, only to be torn apart once again. As specified in the *Saddharmasmrityupasthana-sutra*, the cause of this is harming parents, relatives, and friends, lying to them, and sowing dissension. The third hot hell is the Crushing Hell. Here beings are crushed between mountains shaped like the heads of the animals they have previously killed, or else they are pulverized by hammers and clubs. The *Saddharmasmrityupasthana-sutra* says that the killing of animals—goats, sheep, foxes, pigs, rabbits, mice, deer, and so forth—is the cause of being born there. The fourth hot hell is the Hell of Screaming. There, because of their evil karma, many beings are boiled in molten metal, or crushed and pierced by white-hot hammers, swords, and the like. They scream and cry in dreadful torment. They are born there because they have tortured others, physically, verbally, and mentally and because they have led others astray and corrupted them. The fifth hell is the Hell of Great Screaming. Here the suffering is even greater than in the previous hell. Beings are driven into metal containers with double walls that are incandescent with heat. There they are roasted amid dreadful lamentation. The cause of such a destiny is stealing religious property, the sustenance of hermits, or the possessions of spiritual masters, and causing them to suffer. The sixth hell is the Hell of Heat. Here people must lie on their backs on a ground of burning metal where they are flogged and roasted, and their bodies are impaled through and through on white-hot metal spikes. The seventh hell is the Hell of Great Heat. Here, even more than before, beings are tormented by fire and blazing weapons. Their bodies are impaled on tridents and they are enveloped in sheets of incandescent metal. Alternatively, they are immersed in molten bronze in blazing iron cauldrons, so that they resemble white and black skeletons convulsed with horror. The eighth hell is the Hell of Torment Unsurpassed. Here there is the worst pain of all, constant and unwavering. Beings are trapped in a building of blazing hot metal with walls of double or fourfold thickness in which there is no breach. They are indistinguishable from the fire that suffuses and burns them. It is specified in the *Description of the Hells* that beings who do great harm to persons who have sublime qualities[35] or who kill their parents or their spiritual teachers will surely burn for an entire kalpa in the Hell of Torment Unsurpassed.

THE SIXTEEN NEIGHBORING HELLS

When the suffering of the eight hot hells becomes a little less, the beings therein have the impression that they might escape to freedom, and the doors of hell seem to open. But around the hot hells in each of the four directions are arranged four Neighboring Hells, sixteen in all. The former prisoners rush out toward what they take to be a river. But this turns out to be a trench of burning embers, and they are driven into it by iron dogs with shaggy manes. Again they see what in the distance looks like a cool and pleasant place. They hurry toward it only to fall into a swamp of rotting corpses and excrement where their bodies are gnawed by worms with jaws of adamant. On escaping from this, they see a delightful plain, but as they run toward it, their bodies are slashed and cut to pieces by the razor-leaves of the trees that grow there. Again they escape only to sink into an unfordable river of burning ashes; their suffering is greater than if they had fallen into the jaws of Yama himself.

The experience of the swamp of rotten corpses is the result of sexual misconduct. Wounding and tormenting beings with weapons gives rise to the forest of swords. Pedophilia, coveting the possessions of the Sangha, and killing fish and other animals results in the unfordable river of burning ash.

In the four directions are the hills of shalmali trees. Here, beings have visions of people after whom they had once lusted. They remember their promises of love and hurry toward them, pursued by dogs and jackals. As the former lovers climb the hill, sharp iron thorns on the trees turn downward and pierce their bodies, inflicting horrible wounds. When they reach the top, the "beloved" changes into a monstrous figure of red-hot iron and, taking them into its burning embrace, crushes their brains and reduces them to a mass of bleeding flesh. After that, vultures and carrion crows with beaks of adamant gouge out their eyes and tear out their stomachs and intestines. As the *Saddharmasmrityupasthana-sutra* says, "The adulterers will climb the hill of shalmali and will be devastated by fearful iron monsters."

With regard to the duration of life in the hot hells, it should be remembered that, as specified in the *Abhidharmakosha*, one day in the hells is equal to one day among the gods of the desire realm, and so forth.[36]

THE EIGHT COLD HELLS

In dreadful ravines, lashed by freezing blizzards and snowstorms that grip the body "with the rope of shivering" so tightly that it cannot move, beings are completely paralyzed with cold. They are utterly transfixed with pain, and yet they cannot leave their lives and die. An indescribable gale thrusts its knives into their vitals, into the very marrow of their bones again and again, and the sensation of glacial cold permeates them outside and within. They are tormented by the icy contact as though they were a grain of sesame crushed between a man's teeth. In the Hell of Blisters, the terrible cold causes great swellings to appear on the body. In the Hell of Burst Blisters, these swellings burst open and turn into wounds. Then the cold is so unbearable that beings cry constantly, and this is the Hell of Lamentation. After this, in the Hell of Groaning, lamentation is no longer possible and only protracted moans can escape from the mouths of the beings caught there. In the Hell of Chattering Teeth, even moaning is impossible, the hair stands up in bristles, and the body and mind are feeble and listless. In the Hell of Utpala Wounds, the skin turns blue and splits open, forming patterns like the six petals of an *utpala* flower. Then, in the Lotus-Wound Hell, the flesh breaks open into eight pieces like lotuses. Then, in the Great Lotus-Wound Hell, the flesh opens in patterns of sixteen pieces and more until the fragments are innumerable, and from the fractured skin drip blood and pus. Worms with iron jaws appear in the wounds and burrow into the flesh, devouring it. The suffering experienced in such states is inconceivable. In order to have an idea of the life span of beings caught there, imagine a basket filled with sesame seeds to a quantity of twenty large *koshala* measures.* The length of life in the Hell of Blisters is equivalent to the time it would take to empty the container by removing one seed every hundred years. The life span in the cold hells increases exponentially to the power of twenty for each successive hell.

* Koshala (*bre*): an ancient Indian measure of volume corresponding to two pints.

THE EPHEMERAL HELLS

Beings in the ephemeral hells, which exist in addition to the main hells, suffer because they identify logs of wood and so forth as their bodies, and these are chopped and split. In a similar way, they may be imprisoned in small stones or large boulders in which there are no openings. Again they may be caught in doors, pillars, fireplaces, ropes, glaciers, or twigs, or else they are blown hither and thither in the sky. All these hallucinatory experiences, in which they identify these objects as their bodies, and which give rise to suffering, whether constant or intermittent (being perhaps restricted to the daytime or the nighttime, or just for an instant)[37]—all are due to different negative actions such as appropriating and exploiting the property of the Sangha.

Maudgalyayana has said:

> Within this world no bliss is to be found.
> For just as if they were in transitory hells,
> Beings are tormented by their private woes,
> Caught as though in blazing furnaces.

Just like tremendous floodwaters forced through a narrow gully, the lives of beings are buffeted by the stormy waves of suffering. If the tumult is not immediately calmed by the wisdom arising from hearing, reflecting, and meditating upon the teachings, then this human condition, which is far superior to that of a god, being a basis for Dharma practice, will be ruined like a collapsing breakwater. After death and in the lives that follow, one will wander and circle again and again in the fearful wasteland of samsara, where all is pain and desolation.

The sufferings of the higher realms

THE SUFFERING OF THE GODS

Now, even if an existence in the higher states is obtained, this is of no real benefit. In the four lofty realms of formlessness, beings are suspended in an indeterminate absorption of blank neutrality, which is devoid of both bliss and suffering. When the positive propelling karma that establishes such an existence is exhausted and the absorption comes to an end, earlier karmas are revived by Craving and Grasping,* and this produces the next existence, in which many kinds of suffering will have to be experienced. The gods of the form realm, from the heaven of the Pure up to the heaven of Great Fruit, enjoy the bliss of the four samadhis. But when the karma that caused them to be born there and the resulting bliss (contaminated as it is with defiled emotion) are exhausted, these gods experience intense suffering. For they must then fall into the realms of hell or the other states of loss.

Brahma enjoys passionless bliss. Devindra Kaushika is the most perfect and glorious of all the gods of the desire realm dwelling upon the surface of Mount Meru. A Chakravartin wields power over the four cosmic continents. All such beings are what they are, lapped in pleasure, through the ripening effect of their previous positive actions. But their bliss is like the sun emerging momentarily from behind the clouds. When the effect of past virtue is exhausted, every pleasure and excellence fades away like dwindling lamplight as the oil is gradually consumed. As Nagarjuna says in his *Suhrllekha*:

> One who has become high Indra worthy of respect
> Must fall to earth again through karma's power.
> And one who has become a universal king
> Will later be a slave of servants in the wheel of life.

The pavements of the celestial city *Fair-to-See*, high on the level summit of Mount Meru, are soft and yielding to the tread, rising back in place at the lifting of the foot. This is where Indra reigns supreme, clothed in divine raiment of silken *panjalika*, soft to touch. As Vishnu and the gods of the realm of the Four Great Kings, as the naga and *kinnara* lords bend low before him, the lotuses beneath his feet blush in the radiance of their ruby diadems. Yet, when the propelling force of his karma is spent, even Indra himself will fall and be born in hell, there to be tormented and impaled on burning iron spikes. Such are the defects of the desire realm. Here the gods recline in bliss, cradled on the superb, youthful bosoms of divine maidens skilled in the sixty-

---

* See the section on the twelve links of dependent arising later in the chapter.

four arts of dance. They enjoy delightful groves of wish-fulfilling trees, garments, and gems, beautiful pavilions contrived of jewels and adorned with canopies of pearls, bells, and chimes and every other elegance. But at the last, they lose it all and fall headlong into the pit of fiery embers and the forest of swords. As a sign of their approaching death, their robes grow foul and rank; they find no comfort on their couches; their garlands wilt; and they are abandoned by the goddesses who had previously attended them. And drops of sweat, which until then they had never known, now break out upon their brows and limbs. Gone are the divine maidens who used to bathe them. They are beside themselves with dread; perceiving with the eyes of divine foresight the places of their next birth, they faint with terror. Unable to approach, their friends and family can only call to them from afar, sending them wishes that they might be born again among the gods or in the human realm. And as they gaze upon their friends, they weep in terrible grief. For seven days, according to the reckoning of the heavenly realm, they experience the agony of death and transmigration—a depth of suffering utterly unknown in the human state.

The gods of the sun and moon dwell in mansions of light that illuminate the four cosmic continents of our universe. These palaces are shaped like parasols and are of such immensity as to block out the sky above the Yugandhara mountains rising up to half the altitude of Mount Meru.* And yet at some future time, these divine beings will find themselves in the darkest of regions, in places of such impenetrable gloom that they will be unable to see even their hands in front of their faces.

THE SUFFERING OF THE ASURAS

Although the lord of the asuras, Vemacitra, lives in *Well-Guided*, his palace on the ground of gold, and although *Golden City*, his capital, and *Perfect Jewel*, his council chamber, are filled with riches, the asuras themselves are consumed with jealousy at the greater wealth and glory of *Triumphant*, the palace of the gods of the heaven of the Thirty-three, and at their city *Fair-to-See*, and *Perfect Law*, their council chamber. Over-

---

* For a more detailed discussion, see Jamgon Kongtrul Lodro Tayé, *Myriad Worlds*, p. 109.

powered by the sheer force of their envy, they go to war against the gods. But the army of the gods has at its disposal a fearful arsenal, and the gods themselves cannot be vanquished unless their heads are severed from their bodies. By contrast, the asuras are like humans and are killed when wounded in their vital organs. With their dreadful weapons, the gods can cut off the heads and limbs of the asuras, who suffer intensely. The text *Description of the Asuras* gives the reasons for birth in such a state: "Those whose conduct is false and crafty, who commit many wrongs and who take delight in conflict, but who are nevertheless generous, will become powerful asuras."

THE SUFFERING OF HUMAN BEINGS
Suffering of suffering
This life is but a fleeting moment, a bubble on the water. Human existence is indeed brief and uncertain: one moment it is there, the next it is gone. People are frustrated in their desires and find no satisfaction. They clash with others and come to grief. Sufferings follow one after the other. First one's father dies, and then one's mother; one is attacked by enemies and overwhelmed by disease and wickedness. We are like lepers who must suffer other hurts and injuries in addition to our leprosy.

Suffering of change
The higher realms are like a pleasure garden where delight seems all prepared and where the five objects of sense pleasure are eagerly sought. They are sweet indeed at the moment of their enjoyment, and yet to indulge in them is like eating contaminated food. At first it delights the tongue and produces a pleasant sensation in the stomach, but little by little the poison makes its presence felt, and the pain begins. A complete physical change takes place. The body weakens and is filled with agony; the complexion darkens and the mind is filled with anguish. In just the same way, all joys and pleasures gained through past action and present conditions are like a mirage. They turn to suffering.

All-pervading suffering in the making

All-pervading suffering in the making is suffering that is not manifest in the present moment but which is latent, stored in the *alaya*, the fundamental level of the mind. It also refers to the fact that most of what we do for the sake of happiness is in fact the cause of future pain.[38]

Once upon a time in a land called Shining, there was a king by the name of Radiant. King Radiant could not bear to go anywhere on foot and therefore ordered that an elephant be domesticated for his use. The elephant was duly broken in with goads of steel, and in the end it was so tame that it would do anything the king wanted. "I am tired of having to walk," the king said to himself and, climbing on the elephant's neck, went about without a care in the world. However, the elephant's thoughts were unsubdued by the vows of Dharma taught by the Buddha for the taming of the afflictions, and so when it caught the scent of a female elephant, its mind became wild with excitement. It raced along with such speed that the earth itself seemed to be turning somersaults. Finally, the great beast leapt into a crevasse so that the king barely escaped with his life. His terrible experience is an illustration of all-pervading suffering in the making.

The eight complementary sufferings

Thus, in accordance with their karma, beings are afflicted through and through by these three principal kinds of suffering. Their lot is really terrible. It is as if they had gone astray in a desolate wilderness where the ills of birth, old age, sickness, and death lie constantly in wait and are a source of great affliction. Beings are pained. They suddenly encounter what they do not want, such as enemies hostile to them. They lose the company of their loved ones who abandon them and go away. They are deprived of what they wish for: wealth and possessions, sympathetic company, influence, and pleasures. Humiliated, they want only to hide themselves. And they must submit to unwanted hardships, immersed in sorrow. These, then, constitute the eight unrelenting types of suffering that are intrinsic to the human condition. This is what we have to contend with all the time.

Birth

The mother's womb is like a doorless iron trap, a foul and fetid place, slimy like a muddy swamp. It is tight and cramped and utterly lightless, sunk in deep obscurity. Consciousness pervaded by ignorance enters the womb and finds its support in the intermingled sperm and ovum. During the first week of pregnancy, the embryo is round and trembling like a drop of quicksilver. During the second week it becomes elongated and resembles a string of nasal mucus. In the third week it is oblong and shaped like a finger, in the fourth it takes the form of an egg, and in the fifth it is round and flat. In the sixth week it has the form of a fish, while in the seventh week it resembles a tortoise, with head and limbs protruding slightly. Thereafter, and for the space of twenty-six weeks, the baby passes through many transformations. In what is at first an ugly, wormlike thing, there form the bases of the five sense faculties (the eyes and so forth)[39] and the baby's limbs with their lesser appendages such as fingers. The five vital organs also take shape—heart, lungs, liver, pancreas, and kidneys—and likewise the six vessel-like organs—stomach, great and small intestines, gallbladder, urinary bladder, and ovaries or testicles. The veins and arteries, wind energies, and essences will manifest, together with the blood, lymph, and body hair, developing until they are fully formed. By the thirty-seventh week, the fetus strengthens, nourished by the essential ingredients of what the mother eats and drinks, which it receives via the umbilical cord. When the baby has grown sufficiently, it will quicken in the womb and cause some discomfort to its mother. It is then too that the baby also begins to feel uncomfortable, caught in a narrow place that is dark and rank, and it suffers on account of its mother's behavior. When she is hungry, it feels as though it is falling into an abyss; when she is thirsty, it feels as though its body is all dried up. When the mother is warm, for example, when she is out in the hot sun, the baby feels as though it is being burnt. When the mother is cold, it feels as if it is being frozen in ice. If she eats a big meal, the baby feels crushed as by a mountain; when she makes any movement, the baby feels as if it is being thrown from a precipice. Whatever the mother does, whether she eats or drinks, the baby undergoes countless pains. After eight months and twenty-six days, the time for delivery arrives. The baby is turned upside down by the action of the karmic wind energy and, squeezed through the mother's pelvis, feels as if it were being pulverized between the colliding mountains in the Crushing Hell. At that moment either the mother or the infant, or both, lose their lives or at least come near to doing so. Such are the agonies of childbirth.

When the baby emerges from the womb, it is enveloped in a slimy, evil-smelling substance. If it slips onto a cushion, it is terrified, feeling as if it had fallen into a pit of thorns. When the substance is being cleaned from its skin, the baby feels as if it is being flayed alive; when washed and anointed with butter on the soft part of its scalp, it feels as though wounds were breaking out on its tender flesh, and it experiences great pain. All this suffering obliterates the memory of life in the womb, and the infant virtually loses consciousness. The child suffers because all contact is frightening and painful; it suffers because of its own filth, or through illness, heat, cold, hunger, or thirst. And throughout all this, the baby is unable to tell anyone what is happening to it.

Old age
The rosy color of youth and the grace and beauty of fresh young bodies are blighted and withered by the dreadful scourge of age. The time will eventually come when you will be afflicted with the misery of being dependent on others, an object of contempt and ridicule, without even the strength to attend to the needs of nature. You will not be able to shift for yourself and must stumble along leaning on a stick. Whenever you move, just to get up or sit down or walk from one place to another, your joints will be wrenched and you will fall. Your faculties will be impaired; your sight and hearing will fail, and your tongue will become thick and inarticulate. Delight in beauty, the enjoyments of the senses, and the company of members of the opposite sex will no longer seem pleasant. And even if you feel drawn to them, your mind will be numb and muffled like the heat and light of the sun behind the clouds. All joy will evaporate. Your body will begin to lose its heat and strength; you will have difficulty digesting your food and drink, and extremes of heat and cold will be intolerable. Though confined to bed, your mind will ramble here, there, and everywhere, and you will be confused to the point that you will hardly be able to tell day from night. You will fail to recognize other people and even yourself. This is why respect and

care for the old is so important and meritorious. The great master of Orgyen* has said: "Do not be the heartbreak of the aged; treat them with courtesy."

Illness

For beings possessed of bodies composed of the four elements (earth, air, fire, and water), perfect health is compared in the root text to a limpid pool in which the humors of wind, bile, and phlegm are in perfect balance. When the pool is disturbed and muddied, the torments of disease occur. And pained and exhausted by their illnesses, people, who in fact are no more than the combination of the five aggregates,[40] are troubled in mind and terrified lest they die from their affliction.

Death

Life is such a precious thing that all the riches of the world could not be exchanged for it. Yet no one can escape the pains of death. When the moment comes and you are lying on your deathbed, you must take leave of relatives and friends, wealth, and possessions, just like a hair pulled from a lump of butter. Alone you must go forth into the unknown. As it is written in the *Maharajakanishka-lekha*:

> When the King of Death arrives to take you hence,
> Only virtue and misdeeds will keep you company.
> All others will draw back, with none to follow you.
> Understand this well and mend your ways!

Meeting unwanted circumstances

When unwanted situations arise, such as meetings with enemies, evil forces, or other obstacles, people are distressed, tormented by the prospect of suffering. It is like when exhausted porters find a place to lodge their heavy burdens and rest themselves, only to have the resting place collapse and their bodies wrenched and even injured. This illustrates how impossible it is to find such a thing as permanent relief. We are under constant threat of intense and lasting travail.

* Guru Padmasambhava.

Separation from what is loved

When people who have been living together in a warm and loving relationship are separated, they undergo intense emotional pain merely at the thought of their partner's appearance and character. If such a suffering had form and could be seen, how immense it would be! All this is illustrated in the tale of Prince Norzang, son of Norchen, who for love of a beautiful elf maiden journeyed into peril, through lands of terror filled with savage beasts and evil wraiths. Such karmic links are long-lived and must be experienced without end.

Not having what one wants

Some people make the greatest of efforts in trying to get the things they want. But all to no purpose: they finish destitute. Deprived of wealth, they are reduced to poverty and to an unrelenting hunger and thirst. They try everything and yet fail to escape their desperate situation.

Having what one does not want

Hopes and fears make people the slaves of business and various other negative actions.* People wear themselves out and suffer continually, exhausting both their body and speech, those excellent bases for the practice of Dharma. People who are rich never feel that they have enough and are tormented by the craving to possess more. They think only of their bodily sustenance. Constantly occupied, without free time and leisure, they are no different from hungry ghosts running here and there.

The truth of origin

The Form aggregate is devoid of true existence, yet it is apprehended as a body and clung to as real. This is the basis for the experience, or Feeling, of pain, whereby the body is known in its true nature. Perception cognizes the unwantedness of suffering. There arises the desire to be rid of it, and one is thus caught up in action. Conditioning Factors multiply the seeds or causes of later suffering. Finally, Consciousness

---

* In many cases, business is seen to involve dishonesty and exploitation.

appropriates the pain as the pain of a self, and the thought arises, "I am suffering." These five aggregates concomitant with ignorance are the source and basis of all pain.* They are the vessel in which suffering occurs, for they contain its seed and ripened fruit. They are the cause of future aggregrates, the effect of past aggregates, and the present experiencer of suffering. It is important to understand that this is what they are and thus grow weary of our situation, giving up negative actions and defiled emotions, the sources of samsaric misery.†

The truth of path and truth of cessation

The Shravakas and Pratyekabuddhas, those who "ride in the chariot of the four truths," are beings of medium scope. They have rejected the ignorance of clinging to "I" and "Mine," which is the root and origin of suffering.[41] Yet they do not strive for the welfare of others. They train themselves on the path of Freedom and achieve cessation, the exhaustion of "all that is overcome through seeing and meditation."‡ They reach primordial wisdom wherein they know that all afflictions have been overcome and will never arise again. They pass beyond suffering into nirvana, whether with or without remainder,[42] thus attaining supreme liberation untouched by defilement.

> According to their tradition, Shravakas and Pratyekabuddhas believe that they will attain arhatship simply through following their own path alone and that, entering the expanse of cessation, they will remain there forever. The Mahayana teachings, however, say that after abiding in cessation for a period commensurate with their accumulations of merit and wisdom, the Shravakas and Pratyekabuddhas will arise in the buddhafields (Sukhavati, for example) in the heart of lotus flowers. Because of their ingrained propensity to nescience and their subtle cog-

* See appendix 4. "As long as the five aggregates persist, the continuity of suffering is not broken." [YG I, 354]
† "This is to be done through the eradication of all ego-clinging." [YG I, 354]
‡ I.e., the wisdom of the paths of seeing and meditation. See chapter 6.

nitive obscurations,[43] they remain enclosed in the lotus flower for a period of seven years. Then, due to the compassion of the Buddha presiding over the buddhafield, the lotus will open and they will arise from their concentration. Joyfully they will embrace the Mahayana and through meditation will attain buddhahood in that very life.[44]

It is said in the *Saddharmapundarika-sutra:*

> The Arhat Shravakas, till the Buddhas call them,
> Rest in wisdom bodies drunk on concentration.
> Roused, they take on various forms
> And work with joy for beings' sake.
> Merit and wisdom gathered in,
> They reach the awakening of buddhahood.

The *Lankavatara-sutra* speaks of this in a similar vein.

THE TWELVE LINKS OF DEPENDENT ARISING[45]

The doctrine of dependent arising is explained under five headings: the necessity of this teaching, the definition of each link, four ways of presentation, the number of lifetimes required for an entire cycle, and the method of meditating on this doctrine.

The need for this teaching

A person who understands this teaching—namely, that all phenomena of both samsara and nirvana are nothing but illusory appearances that manifest interdependently—will be free of false views and ultimately will attain the state beyond suffering.

It is said in the sutra:

> When this is, that is;
> This arising, that arises.

For thus it is: because of ignorance,
Conditioning factors and the rest arise.

The phrase "When this is, that is" indicates that all phenomena arise from existing causes. This contradicts the view of the Charvakas, who believe that phenomena are uncaused. The words "This arising, that arises" are the assertion that causes themselves arise through other causal conditions and is thus a denial of the view of a permanently existent cause. Finally, the sentence "It is thus: because of ignorance, conditioning factors and the rest arise" is a denial of the theory that the world manifests as from the premeditated design of a divine Creator.[46]

Definitions of the twelve links

1. *Ignorance:* This means ignorance of the nature of the four noble truths, the karmic law, and so forth, and, due to this, the mistaken assumption of a self.

2. *Conditioning Factors:* Through believing in and clinging to the notion of "I," beings accumulate three types of actions: positive acts "tending to happiness," negative acts, and unwavering acts, the latter being the cause of birth in the realms of the higher gods.

3. *Consciousness:* Propelled by karma into a new life, consciousness has two aspects. First, there is the "cause moment" consciousness, in other words, the consciousness at the moment of the performance of an action. Second, there is the "result moment" consciousness, which is the consciousness experiencing the karmic result of an action.

4. *Name and Form:* This refers to the gradual formation of the aggregates after the consciousness has entered the womb. The four aggregates of feeling, perception, conditioning factors, and consciousness are grouped together as "Name," and to them is added the aggregate of Form.

5. *The Sense Powers:* These are the five faculties of sight, hearing, smell, taste, and touch, and to these is added the mental faculty.

6. *Contact:* This is the coming together of external objects and the inner consciousness via the operation of the sense faculties, whereby phenomena are detected.

7. *Feeling:* The feelings of pleasure, displeasure, or neutrality, arising when objects are encountered.

8. *Craving:* Following from the above, this is the desire to experience what is pleasant and to avoid what is unpleasant.

9. *Grasping:* This is the impulse to seize the desired object once craving arises.

10. *Becoming:* Due to craving and grasping, subsequent existence arises, the infallible result of actions accomplished.

11. *Birth:* Due to karma, birth follows in one of the states of existence.

12. *Aging-and-Death:* The period of aging corresponds to the entire span of life, from the moment of birth onward. When this is over, death occurs. Old age and death are grouped together here as a single link, although it is true that some beings die before they grow old, so there is no certainty that these two stages will manifest in all cases. Suffering is many-faceted. It covers mental sorrow and lamentation due to unwanted events, and also physical ills, frustration, and agitation arising through quarreling and strife. Not everything happens to everyone. For this reason, suffering is not posited as a separate link. But in order that we might experience sadness with regard to the miseries that are part and parcel of samsaric birth, suffering is discussed under the heading of Aging-and-Death.

Four ways of presenting the principle of dependent arising

Presented as a cycle of twelve links, the principle of dependent arising throws light on our past, present, and future. The links of Ignorance and Conditioning Factors are related with previous existences, while those of Birth and Aging-and-Death refer to subsequent existences. The eight intervening links relate to the present existence. Thus this doctrine reveals the interdependence of past, present, and future lives.

The twelve links are also presented in terms of the three "paths" of defilement, karma, and suffering. The first, eighth, and ninth links (Ignorance, Craving, and Grasping) are related to the defilements; the second and tenth links (Conditioning Factors and Becoming) are related to karma; the remaining links—in other words, the third, fourth, fifth, sixth, seventh, eleventh, and twelfth (Consciousness, Name and Form,

Sense Powers, Contact, Feeling, Birth, and Aging-and-Death)—are related to suffering. Thus three links form the path of defilements, two links form the path of karma, and seven links account for the path of suffering.

Again, the twelve links of dependent arising are presented with regard to the karmic principle of cause and effect, that is, of actions leading to birth. On the causal side, there are two links associated with karma (the second and tenth: Conditioning Factors and Becoming) and three links associated with the emotions (the first, eighth, and ninth: Ignorance, Craving, and Grasping). To these five links may be added the cause-moment aspect of Consciousness, thus making up six links that are cause-related. On the result side are the six links associated with suffering: Name and Form, Sense Powers, Contact, Feeling, Birth, and Aging-and-Death. To these may be added the result-moment aspect of Consciousness, thus bringing the total to seven links that are result-related. It is possible to consider Consciousness as a single link, in which case it is placed with the causes, with the result that the two groups of cause-related and result-related links each contain six items. Of course, since each link makes possible the one following it, each link possesses both causal and resultant aspects. But in the present instance, they are grouped as cause and effect with regard to the production of lives.

Finally, the twelve interdependent links may be thought of in terms of two groups: "propeller–propelled" and "accomplisher–accomplished." Motivated by Ignorance concomitant with ego-clinging, Conditioning Factors give rise to karma that creates the impulse for a subsequent life. These two links are therefore "propellers," to which is added the cause-moment Consciousness. By contrast, the result-moment Consciousness and the following four links of Name and Form, Sense Powers, Contact, and Feeling constitute the "propelled." They are what is engendered by action. In addition, the three links of Craving, Grasping, and Becoming are said to be "accomplishers" of the subsequent life, while the two links of Birth and Aging-and-Death are the "accomplished." Thus, there are two propelling links, five propelled links, three accomplisher links, and two accomplished links.

The number of lifetimes required for an entire cycle

At the longest, a cycle of twelve links set in motion by one propelling action is completed in three lifetimes. According to this perspective, the two propellers (Ignorance and Conditioning Factors) occur in one life; the three accomplishers (Craving, Grasping, and Becoming) manifest in the second existence; and the five propelled links (Consciousness, Name and Form, Sense Powers, Contact, and Feeling) together with the two accomplished links (Birth and Aging-and-Death) occur in the third life.*

In the course of every lifetime, actions are accumulated due to ignorance—and these give rise to subsequent existences. It is thus that Ignorance marks the beginning of every cycle of twelve links. In other words, Ignorance and Conditioning Factors, occurring in some previous life, have propelled the five links of Consciousness, Name and Form, Sense Powers, Contact, and Feeling now being experienced in the present existence, and which therefore form the middle part of the cycle. In the same way, the three accomplishers of a preceding life (Craving, Grasping, and Becoming), themselves propelled by the actions of still earlier lives, have brought about what is accomplished in the present life, namely, Birth and Aging-and-Death. These last bring to an end a complete cycle of twelve links. This is how the wheel of life has rolled on from beginningless time.

At the shortest, two lives are required for an entire cycle of twelve links to unfold. The propellers (Ignorance and Conditioning Factors) accumulate actions, aided and abetted by (the accomplishers) Craving and Grasping. These will infallibly bring about a subsequent life, a process corresponding to the link of Becoming. These links, together with Consciousness in its causal aspect, make up six links that are played out in a single life. Because of them, Birth into a subsequent existence takes place, and gradually the four links of Name and Form, Sense Powers, Contact, and Feeling are perfected and are concluded by Death. These are the six resultant links that are completed in another life.

* These three lives need not be consecutive.

Now, even if a propelling karma has been accumulated, if at the moment of death it is not nourished by Craving and Grasping, no subsequent birth can occur. For there must be both propeller and accomplisher links occurring in the same life for a new existence to be produced. And, since "accomplished" links manifest only within the environment of Birth and Death, it is clear that the propelled and accomplished links must also go together. However, the propeller links and the accomplisher links (of the same twelve-link cycle) may in fact be separated by many lives, but it is impossible for this to happen in the case of the accomplisher links and the accomplished links. It might be thought that this contradicts the idea of a twelve-link cycle taking three lives. But this is not true, because the lives interposed between the propellers and accomplishers of one cycle belong to other twelve-link cycles. This, then, is the doctrine of dependent arising expounded according to the theory that one propelling action engenders one existence. A single cycle must be complete in either two or three existences, there being no other alternative.[47] A successful examination of this doctrine will impart a deep understanding of the fact that the root of samsara is Craving and Grasping, and that with them (for they are true origins) suffering is always experienced. Indeed, if they are destroyed, no further birth can ensue, even though karma may still remain. This may be observed in the case of certain Arhats.[48]

How to meditate on the principle of dependent arising

There are two ways of meditating on the twelve interdependent links, each involving a forward and a reverse direction.

According to the first way, the forward order considers the process leading to birth in samsara, while the reverse order shows how this process is arrested. According to the second way, the forward direction describes both the production and the cessation of samsaric existence starting from Ignorance and working forward. The reverse order depicts the production and cessation of samsara also, but this time beginning with Aging-and-Death and working backward.

With regard to the first way, in the forward order one considers that Ignorance gives rise to Conditioning Factors; Conditioning Factors give rise to Consciousness, and so forth. Or, and this amounts to the same thing, one can consider that Birth gives rise to Aging-and-Death; Becoming gives rise to Birth, and so on. On the other hand, the reverse order entails the reflection that by halting Ignorance, Conditioning Factors are halted; by halting Conditioning Factors, Consciousness is halted. Similarly, one can reflect that by halting Birth, Aging-and-Death are halted; by halting Becoming, Birth is halted, and so forth.

By contrast, according to the second way, the forward order consists of meditating that due to Ignorance, Conditioning Factors arise, and therefore by halting Ignorance, Conditioning Factors are also halted; due to Conditioning Factors, Consciousness arises, and thus by arresting the Conditioning Factors, Consciousness is also arrested. The reverse order, according to the second way, consists of thinking that Aging-and-Death arise from Birth, and thus by halting Birth, Aging-and-Death are also halted; Birth arises from Becoming, and therefore by arresting Becoming, Birth is also arrested.

The forward and reverse orders according to the second method may be used as a means to understanding the four truths as expounded in Asanga's *Abhidharmasamuccaya*. If one applies the forward order leading to birth, one will arrive at an understanding of the truth of origin, while by applying the reverse order leading to birth, one will establish the truth of suffering. In like manner, both the forward and reverse orders leading to the halting of birth demonstrate the truths of path and cessation.

For example, the truth of origin is defiled emotion, the root of which is Ignorance. Due to Ignorance, Conditioning Factors accumulate karma. Thus, the first links referring to origin start with the two factors of karma and defiled emotion. Establishing with the help of wisdom that Ignorance gives rise to Conditioning Factors, and Conditioning Factors to Consciousness, and so on, the truth of origin (defiled emotions) is grasped. On the other hand, the greatest of all sufferings in samsara is Aging-and-Death, and this arises from Birth. Applying thus the reverse order, the result of the afflictions, the truth of suffering is understood.

Through the wisdom of realizing no-self (which is the essence of the truth of path), Ignorance, the root of the truth of origin, is eradicated.

By stopping Ignorance, Conditioning Factors are stopped, and so on up to Aging-and-Death. Thus, the forward order leading gradually to the halting of birth reveals the truth of path, and this is the source of liberation. Finally, the greatest sorrows of samsara from which we want to free ourselves are Birth and Death, and the halting of these is the truth of cessation. Thus, by stopping Birth, Aging-and-Death are stopped, and so on down to the halting of Conditioning Factors whereby Ignorance is halted. By reflecting in this way, the perfect result, namely, the truth of cessation, is demonstrated.

A careful consideration of all this will reveal that the root of the overwhelming burden of samsaric suffering is Ignorance, the belief in the true existence of the self. Conversely, one will understand that the wisdom realizing the truth of no-self is the root of all true paths. One must endeavor to gain conviction in this. This conviction, however, can only be the result of profound reflection, extending far beyond a casual or even a close perusal of the teachings. Of the entire treasure house of the profound and truthful utterances of the Conqueror, the doctrine of dependent arising is the most crucial.[49]

The doctrine of dependent arising shows that Ignorance is the root of samsara, while the wisdom of no-self is the root of nirvana. From Ignorance come Conditioning Factors, namely, the three kinds of action—positive, negative, and unwavering—that propel beings into the samsaric state. From these comes Consciousness. Because of Consciousness, there is Name and Form, from which develop the six Sense Powers. These in turn bring about Contact, the coincidence of object, sense organ, and consciousness, as when the eye perceives an object and so on. Because of Contact, any of the three kinds of Feeling—pleasant, unpleasant, and neutral—are experienced. From these comes Craving: the desire to experience pleasure and to be free from what is disagreeable. Craving produces Grasping,* and this gives rise to its result, Becoming (i.e., the five aggregates). And because of Becoming, the Birth of the next life occurs. Once born, beings fail to get what they want and are tormented. Because of elemental imbalances, they fall ill, and all

---

* "Craving (sred pa) is the indirect cause, while Grasping (len pa) is the direct cause. Craving means desire in the most general sense. Grasping is the obsessive desire for a particular object." [YG I, 372]

the time they get older and older, only to lose their lives in Death. Thus an immense mass of suffering is produced.

By arresting the continuous process of taking birth, experienced as a concrete reality in samsara, all suffering will be removed. The profound principle of cause and effect as manifested in the chain of dependent arising is extremely difficult to fathom for those who are outside the Buddhadharma. It is the most precious of the teachings of the Buddha, the Speaker of the Truth. It is something to be profoundly cherished.

The unoriginated nature of dependent arising

In their understanding of dependent origination, the Shravakas and Pratyekabuddhas do indeed resemble the practitioners of the Mahayana in their grasp of no-self. But for the former, this is restricted to an understanding of the no-self of persons. The Shravakas and Pratyekabuddhas know that the cause of existence is action performed in the belief that the collection of perishable aggregates constitutes a self. Such actions give rise to the higher or lower states of samsara together with their joys and sufferings. Wholesome actions tending to liberation, regarded from the point of view of cause and effect, refer to the truths of path and cessation. In the same way, from the point of view of cause and effect, negative actions arising due to afflictive emotion refer to the truths of origin and suffering.[50]

Ultimate truth is beyond all discrimination, beyond all adoption and rejection with regard to the phenomena encompassed by the four truths.* It is beyond mind and mental factors, beyond the dichotomy of compounded and uncompounded; it is beyond the extremes of samsaric existence and the serene cessation of nirvana. The absolute truth is the Unborn, the ultimate nature of phenomena, forever free from all elaborations of the mind. It is to be realized only by all-discerning, mind-transcending wisdom.

---

* See appendix 3.

THE EXTRAORDINARY PATH
OF BEINGS OF GREAT SCOPE

Meditation on the Twofold Bodhichitta

CHAPTER 5

The Preparation: The Four Wheels

PREREQUISITES FOR THE PRACTICE

People who embark upon the path of the Mahayana, the supreme path of beings of great scope leading to omniscience, should try to acquire four circumstances. They should (1) live in solitude, in a place that has all the necessary conditions and is in harmony with the Dharma. They should (2) frequent a teacher who is learned in the Tripitaka and steeped in the practice of the three trainings. By doing this, they will avoid the inferior attitudes of ordinary folk as well as the wrong behavior that leads to suffering, and they will acquire all the good qualities deriving from the Dharma of transmission and realization. They should in addition (3) nourish an intense wish to practice in accordance with the teaching expounded by their master and should (4) zealously adopt the supreme protection afforded by the merit accumulated in their past and present existences. The venerable Nagarjuna refers to these four conditions as the "four wheels," the idea being that, just as someone riding in a (horse-drawn) chariot can cover in a short time a distance that would take many days for a cow or ox, a Bodhisattva taking advantage of these four conditions will progress speedily toward omniscience. Nagarjuna refers to them in his *Suhrllekha* when he says:

> Your dwelling place befits the task,
> You keep the company of holy beings.
> With highest aspirations and a store of merit,
> You have indeed the "four wheels" all complete.

SOLITUDE

Living in the midst of many people, in a town, for instance, or even living in solitude if you continue to behave negatively and neglect your studies, is the source of many defects. Such a habitat is like poisonous food because, although you may be happy in the immediate term, your happiness will turn sour. You will get caught up in the likes and dislikes of people; you will get involved in disputes and things like agriculture and trade, entertainments, wealth and reputation, crowds, and distractions. You will accumulate possessions which you will then want to look after and increase. You will receive gifts from people who look up to you, and offerings for ceremonies to be done for the dead.* You must shun such a ruinous environment and in solitude yearn for the path of serenity that leads beyond suffering. You should be rather like the wind, without a care for wealth and reputation, like a bird that lays no claim to land and livelihood, and like the animals that live wild upon the lonely hills. To be able to live in such perfect solitude, untroubled by reckless distractions and irreligious behavior, is fortunate indeed, and you have every reason to rejoice in it sincerely. If on the other hand you base yourself in one place, a village, for example, or even a monastery, and stay there all the time, you will inevitably fall in with people and build up commitments to family and friends. If you are well known and influential, you will become the object of jealousy, and though you may be able to put up with it for a time, it will eventually wear away your patience and resolve.

Consider the nature of a cat. A cat's mind is intractable and cruel, and it gives itself to acts of wickedness such as killing. Yet outwardly it appears to be the most peaceful and good-natured of creatures. Whether it moves or sits still, you hardly notice it. Its voice is so soft, and you would never think that it had claws. But let it see a bird or mouse, and the cat will leap on it with all its might. Therefore, have a care for the company you keep. Bad friends at first seem pleasant companions—so considerate and generous. But in the long run they bring ruin to beginners in the practice who naively consort with them and whose compassion is fragile. The pleasant, amusing society of such friends will quickly draw you away from the sacred Dharma.

Dharma practitioners should nevertheless be on friendly, easygoing terms with everyone—just like the sun and moon, which, thanks to

* These remarks, though generally relevant, are here specifically addressed to monks and yogis.

their steady and continuous motion, are appreciated by everyone the world over. Quarrels over wealth and so forth come from staying constantly in one place. On the other hand, if you move on as soon as you get to know people and are on familiar terms with them, you will find that wherever you go, there will be no reason for disputes and everyone will consider you a friend.

It may appear that spiritual masters sometimes speak angrily or with words of attachment, and sometimes they seem to enjoy gossiping like ordinary folk who are driven here and there by their uncontrolled thoughts. But for such masters, who have perfect control of their minds, good and bad circumstances have but a single taste. And regardless of what they say, sharp or sweet, they remain free from craving and resentment. Their minds are not entangled in their words, which resound simply like an echo; they are beyond all sense of indulgence and rejection. They strive impartially for the welfare of all beings. To such masters as these, what was said about the proper place to live does not apply; they can live anywhere. By contrast, if *you* wish to embrace the utterly pure discipline that leads to the perfection of nirvana and to set yourself single-mindedly in authentic samadhi, and if *your* practice of the three trainings is not yet stable, you should take great care. If you are able to remain in solitude and with good companions, your practice of the three trainings will bear rich fruit. It will not amount to much if you stay in a crowd and keep bad company.

Livelihood

To humble his disciples' pride in social rank, physical appearance, and wealth, our Teacher, Lord Buddha, authorized the begging for alms. If the giving of alms is performed with the three purities of preparation, main part, and conclusion,[51] it generates merit for the benefactor. In addition, it reduces the worldly involvements of the Dharma practitioners, for they have all that is necessary to feed and clothe themselves without having to curry favor or engage in commerce or agriculture. As a result, their practice of the three trainings will not decline. Begging in such a way as this (in circumstances where there is merit for both practitioner and benefactor) is in harmony with the Dharma and is like a wish-granting jewel.

Of the many impure ways of finding sustenance, mentioned in the teachings there are five that are extremely improper. First, there is a kind of indirect stealing which consists of pretending that you are poor while in fact concealing your possessions. Second, there is trying to get someone to give you something by pointedly praising the past generosity of others or else by giving small tokens in the hope of some large recompense. Third is to cajole people into giving you things either by flattery or by suggesting in a roundabout way that you are a good person. Fourth is to pretend to be a great Dharma practitioner when in reality you are a woeful disgrace. Finally, there is the attempt to secure ample provisions by parading your rank and pedigree. These are five incorrect ways of securing a livelihood. For anyone wishing to progress toward liberation, they are highly discreditable.

With regard to diet, the *Lankavatara-sutra* says:

> Killing animals for profit's sake,
> And giving money for the meat thereof
> Are evil acts that lead to being boiled
> In Lamentation or the other hells.

And also:

> There is no meat that's pure in these three ways
> And so I will refrain from eating flesh.[52]

For this reason it is said that one should refrain from eating meat. If you do eat it, you should feel responsible for the dead animal and with compassion recite dharanis, mantras, and prayers of dedication for it.

Thus you should keep to a solitary place and an excellent seat of grass,[53] relying on alms, the best of livelihoods. You should associate with virtuous friends whose conduct is wholesome. If you endeavor in this way with faith and respect, and diligently train yourself in the techniques of shamatha and vipashyana, your wisdom will gradually become sharper and your determination to persevere in the practice will be roused.

RELIANCE ON A SPIRITUAL MASTER

To cultivate the qualities of the three trainings not yet possessed, and to perfect the qualities already gained, it is essential to rely on a fully qualified spiritual master, expert in the key points of the three trainings. It is said that when an ordinary tree happens to grow in the forests of Malaya, that great garden of medicinal plants, it will be impregnated with the moisture dripping from the leaves of the sandalwood trees and will gradually imbibe the sweet perfume of sandal. In just the same way, if you are able to frequent a spiritual master, you will quickly acquire the latter's qualities.

Fully qualified masters

In times gone by, in the period of the Teachings' immediate result,[54] disciples with pure minds had no trouble in meeting great spiritual masters and siddhas who exhibited all the signs of authenticity as described in the sutras and the tantras. But in the present age of decadence, it is extremely difficult to come upon such masters. Nevertheless, it is essential to rely on spiritual friends whose minds are like excellent earth, well tilled both by the knowledge of the precepts of the three vows, as explained in the texts, and by faultless conduct, unstained by negative emotion.* The earth of their minds should be moist with the knowledge of both the words and meanings of the sacred texts and their commentaries, themselves the source of their own freedom; and it should be saturated with great compassion and a loving concern for all that lives. It should yield, too, a harvest that is rich in a proficiency in the vast array of ceremonies and rituals of the Tripitaka and the four classes of tantra; in a practice that is not merely verbal but penetrates to the essence; and in the overflowing stock of stainless wisdom resulting from the elimination of the twofold veil and the realization of all

---

* This is a free interpretation of the Tibetan term *dgag dgos tshang ba*. For a full explanation of this, see chapter 9, p. 207.

the qualities of liberation. It is thus that brilliant flowers will blossom: the four ways in which masters attract disciples who are fortunate in treading the path of liberation. The latter are like bees that come and savor the quintessential nectar of instruction. These four ways are: (1) a generosity that is completely free from attachment; (2) a way of teaching that is attuned to the disciples' minds; (3) the ability to introduce them to the practice that leads to freedom; and (4) the fact that the teacher practices what he or she preaches.

The Buddha said in the *Mahabheri-sutra*:

> Ananda, do not sorrow!
> Ananda, do not weep!
> In future I will come again
> Appearing as your spiritual friend,
> To act for your and others' sake.

We should therefore understand that a true teacher is the Buddha come again.

Vimalamitra has said that authentic teachers, who expound the special pith instructions of the diamond vehicle of the Secret Mantra, and who thus set forth the absolute truth, must possess the following eight characteristics. (1) They themselves must have received the empowerments related to all the mandalas of the outer and inner tantras, and their minds must be filled with wisdom. (2) Their body, speech, and mind must be serene and disciplined through their observance of the vows and samayas. (3) They must have perfectly understood and assimilated the meaning of the general and specific tantra texts. In other words, they must have integrated the ground tantra, which is the nature of the *sugatagarbha*; the path tantra, namely, the stages of generation and perfection that nurture the qualities of elimination and realization; and finally the fruit tantra, the naturally present kayas and wisdoms of buddhahood. (4) They must have a complete experience of all the signs of proficiency in the phases of approach, accomplishment, and activation.[55] (5) They must have an unconfined view, having realized the equality of samsara and nirvana, and, (6) having direct experience of this, their minds must be liberated. (7) With boundless compassion, they must be guiding beings to liberation, and (8) their activities must be exclusively for the sake of others.

In addition to these, the omniscient master Jigme Lingpa has added two other characteristics. (1) True spiritual masters have few activities. They are exclusively preoccupied with the Dharma, fully committed to it in thought, word, and deed. They have a great weariness of samsara and a powerful determination to depart from it. Their presence has a transforming effect on the perceptions of all who meet them, so that the latter are inspired to seek for liberation. (2) A spiritual master knows many skillful ways of leading others out of samsara and possesses the blessings of an unadulterated lineage that is untainted by breaches of samaya. By following such a master, it is possible to attain the supreme and ordinary accomplishments swiftly and in this very life.

False teachers

Some teachers, however, are like "wooden millstones." They practice the Dharma dishonestly and out of pride, merely in order to preserve a line of incarnate lamas or a family lineage, no different from what a Brahmin priest might do. They practice merely out of concern for the reputation of their monastery, fearing that their ecclesiastical residence or tradition might otherwise decline. Trying to secure wealth or religious patrimony with such an evil motivation is like bathing in a filthy pond; such people are made even dirtier by the experience. Thus to receive, study, and explain the teachings, and to build stupas, make statues, and so forth, with such motives as these is not true Dharma. Indeed, it will be the person's ruin. This is why the root text speaks of bathing in a filthy pond. Empty and noisy boasting about qualities contributes nothing to the mind's discipline, just as a wooden millstone is incapable of grinding barley and cannot produce flour. Such teachers bring their disciples to ruin.

Again, there are some people who, though their minds are filled with defilements, no different from ordinary beings, have, as the karmic result of some trivial generosity in the past, obtained the position of a teacher in this life. They put on airs and persuade themselves that they are somebody after all, preening themselves and becoming puffed up with pride because they receive offerings, honors, and service from their devotees who go bowing and scraping in front of them—fools who know nothing about the true characteristics of a genuine spiritual master! Such spiritual friends are like "well frogs," as described in the famous story.[56]

Then there are other imposters—those who have only a smattering of the teachings. They have taken the vows and embraced the tantric commitments. But they are ignorant of the precepts, and their discipline is quite distorted. They have no idea of the three trainings, and their minds, awash with defects, are base and degenerate. They pretend to teach and give instructions, but it is sheer guesswork, and they behave as though they were soaring in the skies of realization. Moreover, they do not actually care for their disciples, and the drawstrings of love and compassion have broken. Attendance on such "insane guides" inevitably leads to the precipice of negativity, to the abyss of the lower realms, and to ever-increasing evil.

The teacher's knowledge should be greater than that of the disciple. If this is not the case, and if people who are supposed to be teachers are lacking in bodhichitta, it is a great mistake to follow them, attracted perhaps by their fame and personal charisma. It is evident that the blind cannot be led by those who are themselves "blind guides." Therefore, to place one's trust in someone whose eye of wisdom is closed is a serious error in both the immediate and the ultimate term. Teachers like this are unconcerned that their disciples are acting contrary to the Dharma. They make a pretence of caring for them because they enjoy being served and respected. And their disciples help them, believing that they are serving their teachers, despite the fact that such "masters" are immersed in the eight worldly concerns and their actions quite destitute of any underlying wisdom or valid purpose. Associating with such people and in such a way deprives disciples of any chance of understanding what behavior is to be adopted and what is to be rejected. They will consequently wander in the darkness of the lower realms.

For the above reasons, aspirants may well be devoted and sincerely interested in practicing the Dharma, but if they fail to check whether their teachers are truly qualified and commit themselves regardless, they will be throwing away their present qualities as well as those to come in relation to the path. Their very human existence, endowed with eight freedoms,* which they have only just obtained after waiting so long, will be rendered meaningless. Their situation is like someone going toward a dark mass of poisonous snakes thinking that it is the cool shadow of a tree. Expecting shade and coolness, they hope to refresh themselves but will be punished for their mistake with a poisonous bite. As it is said in the *Vidyadhara-pitaka:*

> They, disciples, fail to judge him truly;
> He is ignorant and has no answers to their questions:
> This teacher is a demon for his students.

Evoking the sublime qualities of an authentic teacher

But masters who are steeped in the sacred scriptures and their commentaries, whose eyes of wisdom are open wide, and who, through their extraordinary realization of the three trainings, are skilled in liberating their disciples' minds—teachers such as these are supreme, their minds replete with every quality of doctrine and realization.† They manifest from the self-arising, ever-present expanse of vast nonconceptual compassion within the state of primordial wisdom beyond thought, the Dharmakaya of all the Buddhas of the ten directions. In the world of living beings, they appear in countless forms, and for human beings who are now born in the residual period of Buddha's teachings, they manifest as spiritual friends. They are the peerless source of all qualities on the path and of all supreme and ordinary accomplishments. As the tantra *spyi mdo dgongs pa 'dus pa* says:

> Buddhahood can never be attained
> Without reliance on a teacher.
> Such a thing indeed I never saw.
> And if it does occur, the scripture is disproved.

---

* See chapter 1, p. 27.
† This refers to the Dharma of transmission and realization.

Authentic spiritual masters act with the intention of leading beings of every kind along the path of Freedom. This is the only reason they engage in apparently worldly behavior. In truth, however, they are untouched by anger even when they appear to be subjugating opponents, and likewise they are without attachment even though they appear to be taking care of their families. While in the midst of entertainments, their minds are undistracted. Though they may accumulate wealth, they are free of grasping, and they have no pride, though they may have property and influence. Seeing all appearances as dreams and illusions, their minds are like space. Even if their actions and words seem at variance with mundane conventions, it is a mistake to judge them wrongly, for there are many purposes behind such actions, as they train beings according to their wisdom.

True spiritual masters are greater than anyone in the world. They are expert in cutting through the doubts of their disciples related to the words and meaning of the teachings or to the practice and the dispelling of obstacles. Spiritual masters are not downcast when others abuse and criticize them. However exhausted they may become, physically, verbally, and mentally, in the service of others, they bear everything with patience. And it is through the practice of their essential instructions that beings cross over the sorrowful ocean of existence and reach the land of Freedom. Spiritual masters are thus like great ships. They are true guides, able to teach the common path without mistake and can explain the sense of the sublime sutras of ultimate meaning* as well as the tantras. They are like a rain of nectar, for with the three kinds of wisdom, they extinguish the flames of defiled emotion and karma accumulated from beginningless time. They are like the sun and moon, scattering with the radiance of their wisdom the darkness of not knowing what is to be adopted and what is to be rejected. They are like the earth, strong and forbearing, unaffected by circumstances whether good or bad. Since they reveal the path to the higher realms and ultimate excellence, they are like wish-granting trees, a source of the ultimate excellence of buddhahood and of temporary happiness—the joys and

---

* These scriptures describe the ultimate truth in direct language, divested of any circumlocution or parable. See chapter 9, p. 246.

prosperity of the higher realms. They are like the vase of miracles, for they contain the treasure of all the words and meanings of the sutras and tantras. As the source of all realization, they are even greater than a wish-fulfilling gem. Making no distinction between those who are close and those who are unfamiliar, they behave like parents to all beings, caring lovingly for them without partiality, wishing to establish them all in happiness and the level of omniscience. Their compassion is like a river, immense and swift, aiming to free all beings from suffering and its causes. Spiritual masters are like Mount Meru. Unswayed by jealousy, they delight in the perfection of beings. Like a rain cloud, they impartially soothe the negative emotions of all with an equanimity untroubled by hatred or attachment. Such teachers are the peer of all the Buddhas, even if they do not display the major and minor marks of attainment. Merely to see them, hear them, or remember their actions is highly significant. Even if one does them harm, if one has remorse and confesses one's fault, one will find the path to happiness, whether in this or future lives, and become their disciple. Those who rely properly on such teachers with faith and unfeigned devotion will automatically acquire all the advantages of favorable samsaric birth (health, longevity, beauty, good fortune, family, wealth, and intelligence), together with all the qualities of enlightenment (loving-kindness, compassion, and so forth). Such qualities will shower upon them like falling rain.

Relying on the teacher with a twentyfold attitude

The way in which the disciples should rely on the teacher is set forth in the *Gandavyuha-sutra*. Here it is said that disciples should cultivate four attitudes. They should consider themselves as invalids, afflicted from beginningless time by the disease of defilements; they should look upon the Dharma teachings as medicine; and the teacher should be regarded as a skillful physician, while the practice diligently pursued should be considered as the healing process. With four attitudes analogous to these, disciples should think of the teacher as travelers might consider an escort protecting them from enemies. They should depend upon their teachers as on courageous friends guarding them from danger. Again, they should rely on them like merchants who are dependent on their captain or voyagers dependent on their navigator. If disciples seriously entertain these twenty attitudes (five sets of four) and do not leave them as mere lip service, they will be protected from the dangerous enemies of birth, death, and negative emotions. This, then, is the correct way to rely upon a spiritual master.

The characteristics of bad disciples

The compassion and blessings of a perfect spiritual master are impartial, untainted by favoritism and dislike. It is, however, a fact that, just as the quintessential milk of the lioness cannot be contained in a vessel made of base metal, a disciple who listens to the master's teaching but who lacks the qualities of faith, intelligence, diligence, and determination to be free of samsara will not be benefited by the elixir of the master's instructions. These are general points. More specifically, some people who lack confidence in the profound Dharma may have a superficial devotion because they are pleased by circumstantial trifles: gifts, smiles, and other marks of favor. Such shallow, artificial devotion serves no purpose. It is as changing as the weather—there in the morning, gone by the afternoon. Abandon it, for it is fragile and easily altered.

Even with the help of many different methods, some people are very difficult to coax into the Dharma. At first, they are like wild yaks—difficult to herd into the cattle pen. Then they are fractious and unruly when they are instructed and made to study, and anyone who is diligent in the Dharma they detest. The present life is their only interest. In the end, they neglect their vows and samayas and take up with unsuitable friends. They go from bad to worse and stray from the teacher and their Dharma friends, eventually becoming like the wild men of the forests and the outlands, who shun the company of human kind.

Then there are people who, even when they are in the teacher's presence, are constantly preoccupied with all manner of plans. They think that, better than staying with the lama, they ought to be away, practicing in solitude. They rush away, but no matter where they go, they take up with bad friends; their practice and actions degenerate, and they get caught in evil ways. On the other hand, if they are actually told to go into solitary retreat and apply themselves steadily to spiritual practice, they may well stay there, but they disregard their teacher's instructions and their practice falls apart. They give themselves up to idleness and distractions, failing to do even one session a day. They are no different from the tips of kusha grass, bending here and there as the wind blows.

Then there is a bad sort of person, skilled in trickery and unsatisfied by mere wealth and reputation. People like this covet the prestige of receiving empowerments, transmissions, and instructions as if these were items of merchandise, and they approach the spiritual master with deceitful intentions, laying a trap as though for a musk deer. Without any thought of the master's kindness, their one intention is to get the musk, in other words, the sacred Dharma, and when they have it, the samayas and vows are tossed away. Just like hunters who, having killed the deer, are excited at the prospect of selling the musk, these disciples are thrilled at their new standing, proud of having received such a teaching. People like this, who throw away the samaya with their teachers, will be wretched in this and future lives.

Then there are the disciples whose plans far exceed their capacity. They receive all the essential and direct instructions on the key points peculiar to the phases of generation and perfection, but they do not practice them, thinking that, in order to do so, they need an explanation of the entire Dharma. And so, forgetting about their practice, they search here and there for different texts, making copies of them and busying themselves with notes and annotations and tiring themselves out. Even before they catch sight of something new, they will have already forgotten the little that they had previously understood.

There are, in general, many individual types of disciple, but they can all be classified in the following three categories, which it is important to understand. To begin with, there are those who have genuine faith, who sincerely receive, reflect, and meditate upon the perfect teachings. They have great interest and devotion and are determined to free themselves from samsara. Then there are those who have the appearance of practitioners, but they are lacking in genuine determination and settle only for success and honor in their present life. Finally, there are those who belong neither to the first nor second category. They are lukewarm, neither hot nor cold. They are foolish and false in their Dharma practice, embracing it simply because other people do so. Without prior consideration, they engage in it rashly and without faith or sincere intention. Their practice of the Dharma is like the meditation of a monkey or the recitations of a parrot. They end up like stray dogs wandering the streets; they are neither practitioners of Dharma nor straightforward worldly people.[57]

The characteristics of good disciples

By contrast, good disciples don the armor of devotion like Nagabodhi, who realized the Truth.* They have steadfast minds and like Pelgyi Yeshe serve the teacher and the Doctrine without a care for life and limb. Like Jetsun Mila, they do whatever their teacher tells them, without regard for their own comfort. Disciples like this are liberated merely by their devotion.

Disciples should have faith, the source of all spiritual qualities, and a clear, lucid intelligence unafflicted by doubt. They should have acquired the knowledge that enables them to distinguish virtue from non-virtue. They should have the great compassion of the Mahayana and a deep respect for vows and samayas. They should be serene and disciplined in thought, word, and deed. They should be broad-minded and on friendly terms with their neighborhood as well as with their Dharma kindred. They should act with generosity toward the pure fields† and should have pure perception with a sense of propriety toward others.

Good disciples should be (1) like well-behaved children, knowing how to please their teacher and how to avoid displeasing him or her. (2) Even if their teacher scolds them severely and often, as need arises, the students should behave like intelligent horses and restrain their anger. (3) In order to accomplish their teacher's purpose, disciples should be like boats, sailing back and forth without weariness. (4) Like a bridge, they should be able to withstand any circumstance—good or bad, happiness or suffering, praise or blame. (5) Disciples should be like an anvil, unmoved by the summer's heat and the winter's cold. (6) Like servants, they should be obedient and meticulous in carrying out their

* I.e., he realized the no-self of persons and phenomena.
† This refers to the field of exalted qualities and fields of benefit and compassion. See chapter 3, p. 49.

teachers' instructions. (7) They should be respectful toward their teachers and the spiritual community, with the humility of a street sweeper. (8) They should reflect upon their own shortcomings and avoid all arrogance, like the old bull whose horns are broken and who takes the last place in the herd. In the *Bodhisattva pitaka* it is said that if disciples act in this way, they will be relying on their teacher correctly.

How to serve and follow the teacher

Spiritual teachers are embodiments of the Three Jewels; indeed, the Guru is the Fourth Jewel. As the *Sarvabuddhasamayayoga-tantra* says: "Buddha, Dharma, and Sangha: added to these, the teacher is the Fourth Jewel." And Guru Rinpoche says, "The teacher is Buddha, the teacher is Dharma, the teacher is likewise Sangha. The peerless all-accomplisher, the teacher is the glorious *heruka*." In view of this, there are said to be three ways of pleasing the teacher.

First, if one possesses material wealth, it is extremely important to make offerings.[58] Second, in order to serve the teacher and to show respect, one should perform any necessary physical action, from household chores and practical tasks of stitching and preparing a seat, to making gestures of reverence with your hands joined. One should speak up for whatever the teacher requires and, in relation with his or her teaching of the Dharma, one should do whatever is necessary, by way of explanation and so forth. The merit of all such actions is never wasted. These two kinds of action pleasing to the teacher—material offerings and physical and verbal service—are considered of lowest and medium importance respectively. The third and best way of serving the teacher is to put the teachings into practice.[59]

Spiritual masters have already accomplished their own aim. It is now their task to labor for the sake of others. It is important to understand that their various activities are displayed as appropriate to the inclinations and feelings of different beings and are the inconceivable operation of enlightened activities. Bearing this in mind, one should refrain from misinterpreting them. The siddhas of India like Saraha appeared for the most part as social outcasts. They adopted a way of life that was conventionally disreputable and lived without a concern for purity or impurity, getting their livelihood as menials of the lowest caste or as "sinful" hunters and fishermen—living in the humblest way possible. But since their minds were undeluded, their actions were never wrong. We, by contrast, are as deluded as if we were under the power of hallucinogenic drugs. If we who have not gained freedom through the three doors of perfect liberation, and have not realized the infinite purity of all phenomena,[60] ascribe defects to our teacher, we commit an immeasurable fault. Bhikshu Sunakshatra committed to memory the entire twelve collections of the teachings, but, overpowered by his wrong views, he regarded as perfidious and underhand the actions of Buddha Shakyamuni himself, who was utterly without fault and possessed of every excellence. We should take all this to mind and confess and repair the slightest fluctuation in our faith. As it is said in the text *'khor lo chub pa rol pa*:

> If in the visions of your dreams,
> The teacher seems to have a fault,
> As soon as you awake, confess!
> For if you fail, the fault will grow
> And lead to Hell of Torment Unsurpassed.

If spiritual masters become apparently angry and scold their disciples, chiding them and behaving fiercely, the latter should understand that some fault has been perceived in them, a wrong thought perhaps, or negative behavior, and that the moment to practice discipline has come. They themselves vow never to commit the mistake again. They should never consider that the teacher is at fault. Intelligent disciples, who thus understand the underlying wisdom and purpose behind the master's behavior, will not fall under the power of demonic forces.

How to behave in the presence of the teacher

There is a certain etiquette to be followed in the presence of spiritual masters. When they stand up, you should not remain seated but rise immediately. When they take their seat, you should inquire about their health and offer them refreshments and anything that might please them. When they walk from place to place, you should sweep the ground before them and sprinkle it with scented water, put down carpets, and offer them a horse or some other conveyance. When accompanying them as an attendant, do not walk directly in front of them, because it is disrespectful to show your back. Do not walk directly behind either, since that would mean treading on their footsteps. Neither should you walk on the right side, since that is a place of honor. You should keep rather to the left. If you verbally disparage the teacher's seat or horse, if you step or sit on them, or if you complain about the sound of the teacher's voice, walk on the teacher's shadow, and so on, your merit will decline. In addition, when the teacher is present, avoid slamming doors, wearing extravagant ornaments, and the like, and never lose your temper. Never lie, and always be moderate and sensible in your actions. Loud laughter and impertinent, overfamiliar banter should be avoided. Never be indifferent to the teacher's presence, behaving as though you were with an ordinary person, without respect and awe. Follow your teacher with humility and keep your thoughts, words, and deeds on a tight rein.

You should not form ties of friendship with people who revile and criticize the teacher with animosity and dislike—even if they are generous benefactors and are kind to you. Try to restrain their evil behavior either with suitable words or even with force if necessary. But if the situation is beyond your control, avoid relating to such people on easy terms; if you do otherwise, the great strength of their evil actions, as well as demonic influences, will rot your samaya. For this involves a "breach of samaya through relations with others."* The defect of this kind of association is described in the tantra *bdud rtsi 'byung ba*:

> If the vajra master is reviled,
> Prevent this, using mild or wrathful means.
> But if you are unable,
> You should stop your ears.
> Do not associate or speak

* *zlas nyams.*

With those who pay the teacher insults,
Or else you too will boil in lower realms.

Do not make distinctions among the teacher's attendants and disciples, liking some and disliking others. And do not make a nuisance of yourself. Try rather to be like a belt, fitting easily with any company, and like salt, easily adaptable to anyone, high or low, influential or obscure. Be a pillar of strength against weariness, irritation, and any kind of assault. This is how to serve the teacher and to respect the teacher's attendants and benefactors as well as the vajra kindred.

You should aspire to dwell constantly in the company of spiritual masters, custodians of the treasury of Dharma—like swans living in beautiful creeks and flower-filled pools that gently taste the weeds and plants, and like bees that sip the nectar of the blossoms without damaging their color or perfume. It is marvelous indeed to be able to observe the proper conduct as just described, leaving aside all incorrect behavior and cultivating every wholesome attitude. Attend the spiritual master steadfastly without weariness, trying not to be a cause of displeasure. Taste, by the power of faith alone, the qualities of the master's realization!

All activities of the teachers of the Mahayana are geared to one thing only: enlightenment. Not one of their activities diverges from the six paramitas. Having embraced the uncommon path of means and wisdom, such masters practice the accumulation of merit associated with extraordinary skillful means, for instance, by making offerings, distributing charity, building temples, and explaining and listening to the Dharma. They also practice the accumulation of wisdom. They seal their activities with the understanding that the subject, object, and action itself are lacking in inherent existence; and they rest in the sphere of ultimate reality. If you associate yourself with the activities of such masters, participating in a material way or helping them physically and verbally, or meditating with them and so forth, all your actions will be in harmony with their activity. It is thus that the accumulations of merit and wisdom of both master and disciple are perfected at one and the same time.

Reasons for serving the teacher

All the energy put into serving the spiritual master—carrying messages, even sweeping the house—is never a meaningless waste of effort. It is the supreme path whereby the accumulations are perfected and the fruit of liberation is attained. There is a reason for this. Whichever visualized field of merit you use (whether peaceful or wrathful) when taking refuge or generating bodhichitta, if you consider that the field is the display of the teacher's mind, this is the outer level of guru yoga. If in order to purify the mind you meditate upon the teacher seated at the crown of your head as the embodiment of all the Buddhas, this is the second and inner level of guru yoga. If as a means to receive the direct transmission of his blessings you meditate on the spiritual master in your heart center, this is the secret level of guru yoga. Finally, to train in the generation stage, considering that the uncontrived state of your body, speech, and mind and the three secrets of the teacher* arise inseparably as the yidam deity, is the most secret level of guru yoga. To train in the perfection stage is the conclusion of all these practices. You mingle your mind with the teacher's wisdom mind and rest therein, never diverging from primordial wisdom, the inconceivable radiant clarity of the ultimate nature. Becoming acquainted with this natural state of the wisdom mind of the teacher, totally free from mental activity—all this is the ultimate level of guru yoga. This shows how the essence of all practices is present in the practice of guru yoga. For this reason, the sutras of the Mahayana teach that one must acquire the habit of seeing the teacher as the Buddha, fully awakened. This is the teaching of the tantras also. It is written in the tantra *phyag rdor dbang bskur ba'i rgyud*: " 'Lord of Secrets, how must the disciple look upon his teacher?' 'He must consider him in the same way as he considers the Buddha, the Blessed Lord.' " In the same vein, the tantra *nam mkha'i klong yangs kyi rgyud* says:

> Meditation on the teacher
> Is meditation on the Dharmakaya.
> Compared with this, all meditation

---

* The enlightened Body, Speech, and Mind.

On a hundred thousand deities
Is seen as nothing.
Therefore every act
Of wholesome Dharma—
Hearing, teaching,
Meditating, and upholding,
Torma offerings and all the rest—
Are but preparations for the guru yoga.
For the teacher is the glorious Buddha
Of the past, the present, and all future time.

The majority of people, ignorant and foolish, meditate on pictures of their teachers (made by themselves or others), but they do not actually serve their teachers devotedly and in practical ways while they are still alive and present in the world. When their teachers die, in order to create a good impression of themselves, they have reliquaries made of gold and silver. Thus, their deeds and their intentions do not correspond. They say that they are meditating on the profound ultimate reality, but they have not the slightest clue of the innermost profundity of the teacher's mind—a state utterly beyond distraction and meditation. On the contrary, they put their confidence in the meditation of idiots, clinging to true existence. Their worldly, discursive minds try to accomplish a wisdom that lies beyond the intellect itself. What a foolish waste of time! The discursive mind is completely incapable of producing such a result! Such people have no pure perception; they are destitute of yearning and devotion, and yet they expect to meet the teacher in the bardo! Did you ever hear such nonsense?

Conclusion

So at the outset, you should keep your distance and make inquiries about the life of the teacher you wish to follow. Later you should examine him or her more closely—from a position that is not too far but not too close either. Then you should participate in the teacher's activities skillfully, examining them carefully and in detail.

If the teacher turns out to be someone who should not be followed, take your leave and go. But if the teacher proves to be the person you are seeking, stay, and become a disciple. Subsequently, regardless of how the teacher's behavior later appears to you, whether good or bad, you should be skillful in examining yourself, and you should persevere in your relationship.

Finally, when you have received instruction, and studied and meditated upon the view and action thus explained, you should be skillful in imitating your teacher's manner of thinking, speaking, and acting. Disciples who act accordingly will make progress on the authentic path to enlightenment, unhindered by obstacles and without losing the way.

Even so, when people give themselves to the practice of the true path, evil forces, demons, spirits, and the like, who hate everything related to peace beyond suffering, will appear in various human forms: family, friends, and even Dharma friends, behaving evilly and deceitfully. Insofar as you associate with those who pursue the side of nonvirtue, hating all that is virtuous and despising and repudiating true spiritual masters, to that extent the storm of negativity will lay waste the harvest of learning and virtue that you had before. How unwise it is to keep evil company! It will prevent you from acquiring good qualities in the future, and you will be overwhelmed and ruined by demonic powers. Your ultimate goal will be lost.

On the other hand, people who rely on a true, authentic spiritual master and keep the company of virtuous friends will enjoy physical and mental well-being, and in this very life they will acquire all the marvelous qualities that derive from the Dharma of transmission and realization. The Buddhas and the Bodhisattvas will always think of them. In the immediate term, they will be richly endowed with the advantages of the higher realms and will finally achieve the ultimate excellence. They will complete the two accumulations, purify the two obscurations, and thereby attain the supreme and common accomplishments. They will gradually progress to the highest of the grounds and paths.

If you practice guru yoga with faith and devotion, making offerings and singing praises; if you recite the mantra that invokes the teacher's mind and take empowerments, you will perfect the accumulation of merit. And if at the conclusion of this practice, while still a beginner, you mingle your mind with the teacher's mind in a single stream and rest evenly in this, or if you constantly preserve the understanding that all phenomena are primordially of the same taste in the sphere of the ultimate nature, you will perfect the accumulation of wisdom. Guru yoga is the quintessential method of completing the two accumulations by taking as the path the two kayas of the result. For this reason, the Victorious One has said that to be mindful of the teacher for an instant is better than worshiping the Buddhas and Bodhisattvas for many kalpas, and better than meditating on hundreds of generation-stage practices. It is also said in the *Dashachakra-sutra*: "If you serve the teacher with respect, you will acquire inconceivable merit. You should understand that all the excellent qualities and activities of buddhahood derive from following the teacher." And the tantra *yid bzhin mchog gi rgyud* specifies: "To meditate on the teacher as the yidam above the crown of your head is a hundred or a thousand times greater than traversing the three-thousandfold universe with thousands of mandalas in your hands and dissolving them a thousand times into your heart."

PERFECT ASPIRATION

The essence of perfect aspiration is an earnest wish to practice the teachings. It involves the application of four excellent principles. The first of these is the *excellent aim*, namely, the wish to assimilate by means of the three kinds of wisdom the supreme Dharma of transmission and realization, that unfathomable oceanic treasury of immortal ambrosia. This in turn depends on the *excellent teacher*, learned in the sutras and tantras and unmistaken in the exposition of them. Third, the disciple must employ the *excellent method*, the whole array of conceptual practices, generosity, and so on, whereby the desired goal is attained and the wisdom of the profound stages of generation and perfection (referred to in the root verse as pith instructions) is kept from distortion and decline. Fourth, the *excellent determination to be free from samsara* is a powerful enchantment cast over the demon of complacency, by means of which each and every practice will propel one further along the path to liberation.

The contrary of these four principles is a grudging practice of the Dharma, engaging in it through a sense of obligation imposed by a spiritual friend or someone else. Some people, for example, may adopt the external tokens of the saffron robes and so forth, but they are bored by the teachings and studies, however light and undemanding they may be. And even if this is not the case, no matter how much they learn, reflect, and meditate, if their motivation is contaminated by a poisonous concern for this life—material gain, reputation, and so on—the result will only ever be a continuation of samsara. This is a situation totally opposed to the path of Freedom. Alternatively perhaps, although the Dharma is the last thing they think about, there are some people who are too inhibited to contravene the instructions of the spiritual master or their Dharma friends, and so they carry the precepts and vows around with them as a burdensome duty. This shows that they are motivated by the eight worldly concerns. Even though to all appearances they act for the sake of others and the Teachings, their Mahayana practice is overthrown. It is as though a powerful sorcerer were to provoke a disaster, calling down curses to stop the rain and induce a drought. The eight worldly concerns are indeed like the face of Rahu, which eclipses the bright autumn moon, a symbol of the determination to persevere in one's excellent aspiration.

Mindful of the three scopes or categories to which spiritual practitioners belong, the Buddha our Teacher set forth three kinds of path. To practice any of them is compared in the root text to riding the chariot of skillful means. Each of them is a direct and powerful antidote to the poison of the entire range of defiled emotions. Indeed, a path that does not counteract the afflictions is not a Buddhist path. Beings of the first scope know that actions motivated by the three poisons will thrust them into the lower realms and therefore they reject them, if only for the time being. Beings of the middle scope know that the root cause of the sufferings of existence is clinging to the self, and consequently they overcome affliction by eradicating this clinging. Beings of the great scope purify the afflictions by realizing that they lack true existence, or else they make positive use of these same emotions by applying to them the profound stages of generation and perfection, or again they employ the method whereby the emotions "self-liberate," that is, dissolve by themselves.* Do not remain enmeshed in the thoughts of the past, nor

---

* This applies to the practices of the Vajrayana.

go to meet those of the future, and do not allow your present mental state to be pulled this way and that by different circumstances. Instead, practice constantly and without tiring, confidently allowing all that should be eliminated—and even the antidotes themselves—to fall away into the fourth and ultimate time of equality.[61] In this way, by virtue of your reflection on the Dharma, and through the instructions of the teacher, everything you perceive by means of the six consciousnesses will impress upon you the truth of impermanence and will inculcate a determined wish for freedom from samsara, together with a sense of compassion and devotion. All these factors will bring forth the wisdom of omniscience, the full accomplishment of your excellent aspiration.

THE SUPREME PROTECTION OF MERIT

There are five things that, on coming together in a single living situation, are indisputable signs that in previous lives one has accumulated, consistently and with devotion, a great deal of merit. The first of these is to enjoy the seven qualities of the higher realms. Vasubandhu enumerates them as follows:

> Longevity and perfect health,
> Beauty, fortune, family,
> Wealth, and clear intelligence
> Are seven qualities.

The second factor is the perfect attainment of high samsaric status, exempt from the eight conditions in which there is no freedom to practice Dharma. The third is the absence of ill health. The fourth is the ability to concentrate and thus to create a flexible and positive state of mind. The fifth is the intelligence to understand the meaning of the teachings.

It may be that, with the help of a little study and learning, you might realize that virtue is to be adopted and nonvirtue avoided. But if you do not train yourself, this knowledge will be lost. If you take pride in your social status, erudition, appearance, and so forth, the wealth of the teachings you have received and studied, as well as the three trainings, will not remain with you, and all your virtue will be brought to nothing. Most especially, merit is completely annihilated by anger. As Shantideva says in the *Bodhicharyavatara*:

> Good works gathered in a thousand ages,
> Such as deeds of generosity,
> Or offerings to the Blissful Ones,
> A single flash of anger shatters them.
> (VI, 1)

And it is further said in the scriptures that desire is the ruin of discipline and destroys even the attainment of divine and human status in the higher realms.

Your present situation, in which you are able to use your body, speech, and mind in a wholesome way, is evidence that you have accumulated merit in the past. You have attained a human form, which is a basis for the practice of the Buddhadharma; you have attained a wholesome mind, undisturbed by karma, defilements, and the wrong behavior of thought, word, and deed; you have the ability to discern what has to be avoided; and you possess the methods for doing so. Finally, you enjoy the fortune of receiving the sacred teachings.

As the *Sutralankara* says:

> Joy and birth endowed with freedom,
> Absence of disease, ability to concentrate,
> Intelligent discernment, all these qualities
> Are signs of merit gained in previous lives.

Yet it is not enough merely to see the importance of the accumulation of merit. Your mind should be powerfully focused and determined to practice the teachings of the Great Vehicle. This should be like a suit of armor, so strong that you will not forsake it even at the cost of your life. After hearing and reflecting on the teachings, the vast and profound ocean of Dharma, you should arrive at an incontrovertible certitude and draw the teachings into yourself through meditative experience. A giant of tremendous strength will be able to bend the bow of Indra if he has courage and does not hesitate. In the same way, you should be confident that if you are persistently determined and brave, you *can* assimilate and practice the Buddha's teachings in their entirety; you *can*, with the help of antidotes and countermeasures, overcome all adverse conditions. Then it will be just like throwing wood on the fire: the more difficulties arise, the firmer will your resolution be; whatever defilements occur, the more powerful will the antidotes become. Your following of the path will never be overpowered by mere circumstances; neither will your practice be complacent and slack; and your every action of thought, word, and deed will contribute to the practice of the six paramitas, becoming thus the cause of final omniscience.

To follow the path, fortified with the armor of determination, also includes the accumulation of merit through the seven-branch prayer (a formula expressing such things as refuge and so forth) and ranging from the slightest meritorious acts such as offering water tormas and the burnt offerings of *sur*, to major ones like the gift of your very body. Conversely, it includes the purification, through the use of antidotes, of every fault down to the most trifling actions committed in dreams. If with mindfulness and meticulous vigilance and care you assess your actions correctly, adopting what is to be adopted and repudiating what is to be repudiated, down to the slightest gesture of your hands, the mouthing of a single syllable, or the conception of a single thought, you will not be brought low by any adversity threatening your practice. Everything you do will be transformed into the perfectly pure practice of the path, the all-important accumulation of merit.

In conclusion, the correct application of these four wheels of training is the fundamental basis of the path of great beings, the Bodhisattvas.

CHAPTER 6

The Foundation of the Path: Refuge

THE REASONS FOR TAKING REFUGE

Sentient beings, driven by the power of their karma to wander through the realms of existence, live in dread of a multitude of dangers. They fear samsaric suffering, which is opposed by the path of the Shravakas and Pratyekabuddhas. Less generally, Bodhisattvas dread the attitude of self-concern, which is so much at variance with the path of the paramitas. Most particularly, the practitioners of the Secret Mantra feel the menace of a deluded clinging to phenomena experienced as ordinary, again the antithesis of their path. Taken together, beings are constantly tormented by these three perils, as though buffeted and engulfed by the waves of the deep, the lair of dreadful monsters. And though the gods like Indra may be thought of as protectors, such deities are deceptive refuges, for they are also bound within the world and are thus not immune to such dangers themselves.

By contrast, the only true objects of refuge—true in being genuinely able to give both immediate and ultimate protection—are the Rare and Precious Ones, known more poetically as the Three Jewels, the infallible guardians for those who perfectly trust in them. They are renowned throughout the three worlds of existence and are like a white parasol that gives shade from the heat of karma and defilement. At the very outset, upon embracing the Buddhist teachings, it is essential to take refuge in them. For it is proclaimed in the *Seventy Stanzas on Refuge*, "The Buddha, Dharma, and Sangha are the protection for those who yearn for liberation."

Faith as the cause of taking refuge

True and unfailing refuge in the Three Jewels consists in a commitment:[62] the commitment to be a basis in which the path to liberation can unfold, in other words, to undertake the practice of the three trainings, thereby becoming a vessel for all the qualities of elimination and realization. An attitude of faith is the necessary preliminary for such refuge, and in order to cultivate this, it is vital to understand the qualities of the Buddha, the qualities of the sacred Dharma, his teaching, and the qualities of the Sangha by whom this teaching is upheld. It is in fact a general principle that faith is the sole root of everything positive.[63] The *Dashadharmaka-sutra* and the *Ratnakuta* are alike in saying:

> Green shoots cannot come
> From roasted seeds,
> And perfect qualities will not arise
> In faithless hearts.

People who are of the noble lineage,[64] with fortunate karma, experience powerful faith from the very outset. By contrast, there is no telling when faith will awaken in the minds of ordinary people, whose karmic potential has not been stirred. On encountering a Buddha in person, in whom all is harmonious—or simply seeing a representation of one—it is possible for one to be completely inspired with faith. The same can occur on meeting a spiritual master. And it sometimes happens that on reading the sacred texts of scripture, people are moved to tears and their skin stands up in gooseflesh, as in the case of Shura-charya.[65] This first experience is known as *vivid faith*. It is a sense of joy felt in response to the qualities of sacred objects or the scriptural teachings. Subsequently, there arises a desire to emulate such qualities within oneself, with the same urgency and eagerness with which bees are drawn to flowers. This is called *yearning faith*. Later, one experiences a sense of complete trust in the doctrine of the four noble truths and a confidence in the spiritual master who sets forth the teachings on what is to be abandoned and what is to be adopted. This is *confident faith*. Finally, there arises an *irreversible faith*, by virtue of which it becomes impossible to turn away from the Three Jewels, though one's very life be at stake. Generally speaking, when receiving and reflecting on the teachings, and especially when taking refuge, one should have irreversible faith: the commitment not to forsake the object of refuge even at the cost of one's life.[66]

The causes of faith

There are many factors able to instill faith in the mind or to intensify it where it already exists. All, however, may be summarized in four crucial circumstances. First is attendance on an authentic spiritual master; second is association with wholesome friends; third is mindfulness of the qualities of the Three Jewels; and fourth is reflection on the miseries of the round of existence, so bereft of meaning and sense, and the ruin of this and future lives. Thoughts like these give rise to a determination to leave samsara, and a natural and authentic faith comes into being.

The qualities of the Buddha

The qualities of the Body, Speech, and Mind of the Buddhas are like an inexhaustible array of ornaments. It is said in the *Samadhiraja-sutra* that if one were to live for as many kalpas as there are grains of sand in the Ganges, one would still not have sufficient time to praise the wisdom qualities of a single hair of a Buddha's body.

THE QUALITIES OF ELIMINATION
The ultimate qualities of elimination are attained when the emotional and cognitive obscurations are overcome by the two kinds of wisdom generated on the paths of seeing and meditation.

The one hundred and twelve obscurations eliminated on the path of seeing

The different categories of obscurations to be thus eliminated may be outlined as follows. As it is said in the *Abhidharmasamuccaya*:

> One hundred and twelve things are driven out by seeing.
> Desire and wrath, pride, ignorance and doubt,
> The transitory composite, the extreme and the false,
> To hold one's view as best, to hold one's discipline as best—

Of these root obscurations driven out by seeing,
Five are views, the other five are not.
These ten run counter to the noble truths,
Five directly so:
The view of "transitory composite,"
The "extreme" and "false" views,
And with them, ignorance and doubt.
The conditioning power of anger undermines the noble truths
And four things indirectly counter them.
Though all these ten are found in regions of desire,
There is no anger in the form and formless realms.
One hundred and twelve things we therefore count.

This may be explained as follows. One hundred and twelve obscurations are eliminated by seeing. Ten of these are root obscurations, and of these, five are views and five are not views. Those that are not views are the emotions of attachment, anger, pride, confusion, and doubt. Those that are views, or opinions, are the view of the transitory composite (the belief in an "I"), the view of extremes, wrong views, the view of doctrinal superiority, and the view of ethical superiority.* In the realm of desire, these ten factors are detrimental to each of the four truths, thus making forty factors to be eliminated. In the form and formless realms, anger does not occur, with the result that here only nine factors run counter to the four truths. This makes twice thirty-six, or seventy-two items. Add to this the previous forty elements and the total comes to one hundred and twelve obscurations eliminated through seeing.

How the obscurations militate against the understanding of the four truths

The three views and the two nonviews that run directly counter to an understanding of the four truths act in the following way. The *view of the transitory composite* asserts the four truths in terms of "I" and "mine."[67] The *view of extremes* is the belief that this self is either permanently existent or completely annihilated at death. *Wrong view* will simply deny the law of karma (among other things). The "nonview" of *ignorance* will

---

* See appendix 4, p. 291

simply not know what the four truths signify, while *doubt* will hesitate over them and question their veracity. All these factors jeopardize a proper understanding of the four truths, and because they do so, unless prevented by other extraneous factors, they are regarded as directly running counter to them.

Two nonviews and two views are indirectly injurious. Of the former, *attachment* clings to the mistaken views mentioned in the previous paragraph, and through *pride* the mind arrogantly persists in its erroneous opinion. The *view of doctrinal superiority* regards false teachings as superior, while the *view of ethical superiority* will consider these erroneous ideas, together with all connected disciplines, as effective means to liberation. Running counter to an understanding of the four truths, these four factors are based on *wrong view,* and the latter is therefore seen as interposing itself between the truths and the factors themselves. It is for this reason that these factors are said to run counter to the four truths indirectly.

Anger, as the verse says, is generally detrimental on account of its conditioning power. For in addition to holding erroneous views, people may well be irritated when others disagree with them. When this happens, their anger is not, of course, directed at the four truths or their own view. Consequently, anger is regarded as inimical to the four truths only by its conditioning power.*

There are a few subtle differences in the way these factors run counter to the truths of cessation and path.[68] One should, moreover, be familiar with the systems† that teach that cessation involves the complete destruction of the mindstream and that the path is the process that brings this about.

The four hundred and fourteen obscurations eliminated on the path of meditation
It is said:

> Craving, anger, pride, stupidity,
> The transitory composite,

---

* In other words, by the negative effect it has on the general situation and the process of understanding.
† I.e., the Hinayana.

And extreme views: these six
Are driven out by meditation.
Within Desire all six are found,
While Form and Formless realms have only five.
Arranged by level and intensity,
Four hundred and fourteen obscurations thus are numbered.

As this quotation shows, there are six root obscurations eliminated by meditation. These are attachment, anger, pride, ignorance, the view of the transitory composite, and the view of extremes. If these are calculated according to the three realms of existence, they come to a total of sixteen—in the desire realm, there are six obscurations, while in the form and formless realms, where anger does not occur, there are five apiece. Alternatively, if these obscurations are categorized according to the levels of mundane existence, there are six for the desire realm, five in each of the four levels of samadhi in the form realm (i.e., twenty all together), and five in each of the four levels of the formless realm (again twenty). By adding them together, this comes to forty-six obscurations. According to intensity, each of these forty-six can be further broken down into nine subdivisions. This comes to a grand total of four hundred and fourteen obscurations. Moreover, the five obscurations, discounting anger, can be categorized according to a system of nine mundane levels and nine degrees of intensity. This comes to four hundred and five, and, with the nine degrees of anger in the desire realm, we again have a total of four hundred and fourteen.

Within the three realms of desire, form, and formlessness, there are nine mundane levels. The first of these levels corresponds to the whole of the desire realm, while the remaining eight comprise the four samadhis of the form realm and the four levels of the formless realms (Infinite Space, Infinite Consciousness, Utter Nothingness, and Neither Existence nor Nonexistence). There are also nine levels of intensity. For example, attachment in the desire realm may be broken down into nine degrees: great, middle, and small of the great; great, middle, and small of the middle; and great, middle, and small of the small. All told, this comes to nine levels of intensity for each obscuration.

The difference between the Hinayana and the Mahayana approaches to the removal of obscurations

The obscurations eliminated on the path of seeing are the mind's incorrect imputations.[69] These are eliminated by the simple "seeing" or realization of the four truths. By contrast, the obscurations eliminated on the path of meditation are coemergent or innate.[70] These cannot be annihilated by the mere realization of the four truths. They can only be removed gradually by dint of an increasing immersion in this realization.

The practitioners of the Hinayana claim that the obscurations eliminated by seeing are only to be removed on the transmundane path.* On the other hand, they say that the obscurations eliminated by meditation can be removed even on the mundane path. In their opinion, it is thus possible to rid oneself of the obscurations eliminated by meditation while still in the desire realm, in other words, prior to the elimination of obscurations by seeing. They call this the path of "leap over" and assert that there are two kinds of Shravakas abiding on this path: candidates for the stages of Once Returner and of Nonreturner.[71]

It was, however, only for the sake of encouraging his disciples, and in order to inspire them with interest for the path, that the Buddha skillfully taught this doctrine. In point of fact, nothing on the mundane path can counteract obscurations to be eliminated by meditation. These obscurations can only be *removed* on the superior, or supramundane, level. According to the Mahayana, this kind of obscuration is not eradicated but only suppressed on the mundane path. And by "mundane path" is meant the concentrations of the form and formless realms. These are concentrations that lack the wisdom of *vipashyana*. By contrast, the transmundane path is the union of *shamatha* and vipashyana, linked with the wisdom of realizing the nonexistence of the personal and phenomenal self.

The Hinayana and Mahayana ways of removing the obscurations by seeing

Taken all together, the path of seeing comprises sixteen instants, four for each of the four truths. They are called acceptance, understanding,

---

* I.e., the Hinayana path of seeing.

subsequent acceptance, and subsequent understanding.* The realization of the truth of suffering thus comprises four instants. At the first instant, when there occurs a fearless *acceptance* of the nature of suffering,† ten obscurations eliminated by seeing (related to the truth of suffering of the desire realm) are discarded.[72] At the second instant, there occurs an *understanding* of the nature of suffering, and here wisdom arises as the antidote.[73] At the third moment, that of *subsequent acceptance*, eighteen obscurations eliminated by seeing (related to the truth of suffering of the form and formless realms) are discarded. At the fourth moment, that of *subsequent understanding*, the wisdom again arises as the antidote. If these same four moments are applied to the other three truths, we have all together four groups of twenty-eight obscurations. Thus, we arrive once again at a total of one hundred and twelve eliminated obscurations.

The Mahayana teaches, on the other hand, that the obscurations eliminated by seeing that are related to the three realms (desire, form, and formless) are abandoned totally all at the same time. It is believed that they are abandoned at the very moment when the nature of each of the four truths is understood.[74]

The eighteen shravaka schools[75] of Hinayana Buddhism are said to have explained the sixteen instants of the path of seeing in many different ways. And in the Mahayana also, the master Haribhadra says that there are two distinct ways of setting them forth. First, it is said that with regard to the moment of discernment, these sixteen instants arise successively, while from the point of view of the moment of absolute reality, these sixteen are but one single instant. Second, there is the opinion of those who believe that an instant of discernment and an instant of absolute reality are in fact a single instant.[76] Haribhadra himself adopts the first alternative, that the sixteen instants arise successively. It is impossible for one so-called instant of discernment to destroy all misconceptions concerning the four truths. Therefore, taking each of the truths into consideration, the gradual eradication of misconceptions passes through sixteen instants. Nevertheless, the so-called instant of absolute reality is regarded as the single instant in which the

---

* The Tibetan terms are, respectively, *chos shes kyi bzod pa, chos shes, rjes bzod, rjes shes.*
† This means the acceptance of the four aspects of the truth of suffering. See appendix 3.

absence of self is seen directly. It is a single instant because the ultimate nature cannot be divided (into a succession of categories).[77]

In one of his writings, the noble Asanga explains the sixteen instants of the four truths as follows. First, at the time of acceptance of the knowledge of the nature of suffering, everything eliminated by seeing falls away. At the moment of understanding the nature of suffering, the wisdom antidote arises. Through subsequent acceptance, an understanding dawns that the wisdom of accepting and the wisdom of understanding the nature of suffering constitute the ground of the noble path of meditation. Through subsequent understanding, there is the realization that subsequent acceptance is the ground of the noble path. Acceptance and understanding of the nature of the four truths pertain more to the object apprehended, namely, the truths themselves. By contrast, subsequent acceptance and subsequent understanding refer to the wisdom, namely, the apprehending agent in the inquiry. In Asanga's tradition, the system of sixteen instants[78] is drawn up to describe how incontrovertible knowledge is achieved in the post-meditation period. This is regarded as a scholastic classification for the sake of those inclined to an intellectual approach. On the other hand, from the point of view of the state beyond all conceptual constructions, as experienced in meditation, these sixteen instants occur at once.

The master Nagarjuna likewise says in his writings that the system of sixteen instants is merely an analytical procedure describing the destruction of misconceptions of the four truths. Acceptance consists in a confidence in the four truths that bestows a fearless assent, and through understanding their nature, one realizes them directly. Through subsequent acceptance, fearlessness regarding the nature of the four truths is obtained even during post-meditation. Finally, through subsequent understanding, a perfect knowledge of the four truths arises even in the post-meditation state. It is in this context that the division into sixteen instants is made. In point of fact, however, the instant in which one sees all phenomena as unborn and beyond all conceptual constructs is indivisible (into sixteen). As it is said in the *Lankavatara-sutra*:

> The unborn nature is the only truth,
> While "four truths" is the talk of mere children.

For those abiding in the essence of enlightenment
Not one is found; why speak of four?

In conclusion, therefore, these sixteen instants are merely a schematic description of a single meditative instant.*

How the obscurations are eliminated on the path of meditation

Turning now to the obscurations eliminated by meditation, it is said that through familiarity with the practice, the antidotes to these obscurations, which in fact constitute the path of meditation itself, will gradually develop, beginning from the most general and progressing to the most penetrating. As a result, the obscurations will disappear in the same order, starting from the most gross and proceeding to the most subtle.

As we have said, the obscurations eliminated by seeing are imputed misconceptions, whereas the obscurations eliminated by meditation are innate thought patterns. Imputation refers to the view of the transitory composite (the belief in "I"), the extreme views of eternalism, nihilism, and so forth. They are the conceptions imputed newly (in each existence) under the influence of mistaken theories. People who take up a philosophical position maintain these false doctrines openly; on the other hand, even those who are "innocent" of philosophy are nevertheless always liable to entertain such mistaken views.[79] The expression "innate thought patterns" refers, by contrast, to the fact that the mind is already "configured" in a self-oriented way. This configuration, which thinks "I am," is accompanied by desire and other afflictive thought patterns, which turn outward toward objects. The mind has been oriented in this way from beginningless time.

Thus, the obscurations eliminated by seeing[80] run counter to the nature of the four truths. The obscurations eliminated by meditation run counter to the sense objects such as form and so on.[81]

Even though the obscuration of strong anger is completely eliminated only on the path of meditation, it is already attenuated by the powerful sun of wisdom arising on the path of seeing, which withers it

* *mnyam bzhag skad cig.* See the definition of "instant" given in note 76.

like a rotting shoot. This is why it is said that the Aryas are free from such afflictions once they have attained the noble path, even though these same afflictions are said to be fully eliminated only on the path of meditation.

The obscurations eliminated by seeing are the misconceptions newly imputed in every lifetime under the influence of false tenet systems. This is why non-Buddhist tenets are unable to influence someone in whom the path of seeing has arisen. And this will remain true throughout all subsequent lives.

THE QUALITIES OF A BUDDHA'S REALIZATION
In addition to the qualities of elimination, Buddhas possess qualities arising from their realization.* These are: the five kinds of eye (powers of vision), which are the fully ripened effect of positive action; the six kinds of preternatural knowledge accomplished through concentration, such as the knowledge and ability to perform wonders; and the ten powers owing to which no intended action is impeded (as in the case of the power of Buddhas over their own lifespan). Buddhas also possess the four dharanis, all of which are grounded in extraordinary memory and supreme intelligence. The first dharani is the power of understanding that all phenomena are unborn. The second is the mantric dharani accomplished through concentration and wisdom. The third is the word dharani, which is the ability to hold in unforgetting memory every word of the Doctrine. The fourth is the meaning dharani, which is the power to remember infallibly the sense of all the teachings. Buddhas have the ten strengths, defined as an unobstructed cognition of all objects of knowledge, such as the strength of knowing the different aspirations of beings. They have the four fearlessnesses in the face of all opposition to the assertions they make about themselves and others, and the four perfect knowledges of all the ways of helping beings.

Buddhas possess eighteen distinctive qualities that are not shared by the Shravakas and Arhats. Six of these refer to the way Buddhas behave. (1) Their physical conduct is without delusion. (2) Their voices are not strident or inconsiderate. (3) Their mindfulness is unimpaired and seamless. (4) Their minds are always in meditative equipoise. (5) They

---

* See appendix 5, p. 297.

do not impose discriminations on their perceptions. (6) Their equanimity nevertheless involves full discernment. In the same sequence, there now follow six distinctive qualities of a Buddha's realization. (7) Buddhas have a constant, joyful keenness to act for the sake of beings. (8) They possess a mindfulness that never turns from the welfare of others. (9) They are tireless in endeavor. (10) They have a supreme knowledge of all phenomena, (11) one-pointed concentration, (12) and complete freedom from the two kinds of obscurations and habitual tendencies, together with a realization of omniscient wisdom. Then there are three qualities comprising the three distinctive aspects of primordial wisdom whereby Buddhas embrace all objects of knowledge—without impediment (due to the fact that the cognitive veils have been removed) and without attachment (because the emotional veils are also eliminated)— (13) in the past, (14) in the present, and (15) in the future. Finally, the three distinctive qualities of a Buddha's activities of (16) Body, (17) Speech, and (18) Mind proceed from, and are accompanied by, wisdom. This means that wisdom is the driving force of the entire range of a Buddha's activity. Taken all together, these are the eighteen qualities peculiar to a Buddha. They are not shared by Shravakas, Pratyekabuddhas, or Arhats.

It is said in the *Seventy Stanzas on Refuge*:

> Awaking from the sleep of ignorance,
> His mind made vast through primal wisdom,
> The Buddha is a lotus fully opened.

The Buddha is Dharmakaya, primordial wisdom expressed in twenty-one perfect qualities,* supreme over all, the expanse of purity and equality† in a single taste. For the retinue of Bodhisattvas on the tenth ground, a Buddha manifests as the Sambhogakaya, the appearance aspect of the ground nature, an empty form endowed with five certainties. In the perception of ordinary beings, however, a Buddha manifests as the Nirmanakaya, the Teacher.

---

* See appendix 9, p. 341.
† See glossary entry *Purity and equality*.

The qualities of the Dharma

DHARMA POSITED AS THE TWO TRUTHS OF PATH AND
CESSATION

The term "dharma"[82] covers three areas. First, it signifies virtuous action
or skillful means such as generosity. Second, it signifies the path, which
in turn refers to the wisdom of realizing the absence of self. Third, it
signifies nirvana, the freedom from obscurations that results from following the path. All these are the subject matter of the Dharma of
transmission. For the nature of Dharma is twofold. On the one hand,
it is the supreme resultant state free from all stains; on the other, it is the
very activity that eliminates these stains. These two aspects of Dharma
correspond to "the two truths of perfect purity," namely, the truth of
cessation and the truth of path,[83] while meritorious action is ancillary
to the path.

DHARMA DEFINED AS THE DHARMA OF TRANSMISSION
AND REALIZATION

The Dharma of transmission and realization may be discussed in terms
of the three collections of the teachings, or Tripitaka, and the three
trainings set forth therein.

The Dharma of transmission

The Dharma of transmission may be subdivided in various ways. Arising from the "dominant condition,"* namely the Tathagata himself, it
is perceived by beings as the twelve branches of the sacred scripture, the
sutras, poetic epitome, and so forth.[84] And when these twelve branches
are systematized in terms of antidotes to the three poisons, one arrives
at the Tripitaka, namely, the Vinaya, the Sutra, and the Abhidharma.
Finally, even more profound than the Tripitaka and endowed with even
more skillful means is the *pitaka* of the Vidyadharas.

　　It is said in the tantra *kun byed rgyal po*:

> As remedy for craving,
> Twenty-one thousand sections

---

* See note 114.

Of Vinaya were set forth.
As remedy for anger
Twenty-one thousand sections
Of the Sutra were set forth.
As remedy for ignorance,
Twenty-one thousand sections
Of the Abhidharma were set forth.

For Vidyadharas over all the rest,
And as the all-subduing remedy,
The twenty-one thousand sections
Of the Fourth Collection
Were set forth.[85]

The basis for the composition of the scriptures is the letters or sylla-bles which combine to make words and so on to form phrases and sentences. Sentences are grouped together in stanzas (*shlokas*); these form chapters, sections, and volumes. The scriptures therefore consist of col-lections of letters, which thus form the basis of the refuge commit-ment.[86]

The Dharma of realization

The Dharma of realization[87] refers to all the qualities to be gained on the five paths, from the path of accumulation onward. For example, in the lesser path of accumulation, the Dharma of realization refers to the four close mindfulnesses; in the middle path of accumulation, it refers to the four genuine restraints; and in the great path of accumulation, it refers to the four bases for miraculous powers, and so forth.*

In addition, the Dharma of realization refers to the wisdom resulting from elimination and realization, which suffuses the minds of supreme beings. Now all the qualities of the path and of wisdom are nothing but the actualization of what is already the essential nature of the mind—the tathagatagarbha. These qualities are not causally produced as something new and extraneous, for the ultimate nature is actualized

---

* See appendix 6, p. 301 for a presentation of the five paths.

in no other way than by the elimination or removal of obscurations. In the Mantrayana, these obscurations are removed by following the profound pith instructions which lead straight to the true reality of body, speech, and mind. In the generation-stage practice, which is conceptual, the practitioner meditates on the three seats of the deities,[88] thus causing the coemergent primordial wisdom to arise. Through the perfection-stage practice, which is nonconceptual, the primordial wisdom is cultivated, together with the dharanis of unforgetfulness, the ten limitless *ayatanas*,[89] and nine successive absorptions[90] and so forth. Therefore the Dharma of realization comprises all the qualities possessed by beings abiding by the main practices of the path of learning (i.e., the paths of accumulation, joining, seeing, and meditation) and also the path of no more learning (or buddhahood).

The grounds or stages of realization

In the expository vehicle of causality, the basis of such qualities is the ten grounds. These are as follows:[91]

1. *Perfect Joy* (*rab tu dga' ba*): This is the basis of the qualities of the extraordinary primordial wisdom of the Mahayana path of seeing. In Asanga's *Sutralankara* it is described thus: "Seeing that one is approaching enlightenment and that beings can be benefited, the Bodhisattva feels intense joy, and this is the reason why this ground is so called."

2. *Immaculate* (*dri ma med pa*): This is the foundation for the qualities associated with the extraordinary primordial wisdom of the lesser level of the lesser Mahayana path of meditation. It is described in the *Sutralankara* thus: "Since at this level, there is no need of effort to preserve a spotless discipline, it is called Immaculate."

3. *Luminous* (*'od byed pa*): This forms the basis of the qualities of the extraordinary primordial wisdom of the middle level of the lesser Mahayana path of meditation. It is described in the *Sutralankara* thus: "Since the bright light of the understanding of reality is shining forth, this ground is called Luminous."

4. *Radiant* (*'od 'phro ba can*): This is the basis of the qualities of the extraordinary primordial wisdom associated with the superior level of the lesser Mahayana path of meditation. In the *Sutralankara* it is described thus: "Since the Bodhisattva possesses qualities conducive to enlightenment that burn away the two-fold veil, this ground is called the Radiant."

5. *Hard to Uphold* (*sbyangs dka'*): This is the basis of the qualities of the extraordinary primordial wisdom of the lesser level of the middle Mahayana path of meditation. In the *Sutralankara* it is described thus: "Since bringing beings to complete maturity and taking care of one's own mind is difficult to achieve, even for a wise Bodhisattva, this ground is called Hard to Uphold."

6. *Clearly Manifest* (*mngon du gyur pa*): This is the basis of the qualities of the extraordinary primordial wisdom of the middle level of the middle Mahayana path of meditation. In the *Sutralankara* it is described thus: "Since on this level, for the Bodhisattva who relies on the paramita of wisdom, the nature of samsara and nirvana is openly evident, this ground is called Clearly Manifest."

7. *Far Progressed* (*ring du song ba*): This is the basis of the qualities of the extraordinary primordial wisdom of the superior level of the middle Mahayana path of meditation. In the *Sutralankara* it is described thus: "Since this ground feeds into the one great way (the eighth ground or first pure level), it is called Far Progressed."

8. *Immovable* (*mi g yo ba*): This is the basis of the qualities of the extraordinary primordial wisdom of the lesser level of the superior Mahayana path of meditation. In the *Sutralankara* it is described thus: "Since the Bodhisattva cannot be shaken by the two types of perception,[92] this ground is called Immovable."

9. *Perfect Intellect* (*legs pa'i blo gros*): This is the basis of the qualities of the extraordinary primordial wisdom of the middle level of the superior Mahayana path of meditation. In the *Sutra-*

lankara it is described thus: "The ground where the Bodhisattva gains the four perfect knowledges* is called Perfect Intellect."

10. *Cloud of Dharma* (*chos kyi sprin*): This is the basis of the qualities of the extraordinary primordial wisdom of the superior level of the superior Mahayana path of meditation. In the *Sutralankara* it is described thus: "Since the expanse of the Bodhisattva's mind is filled with every kind of concentration and dharani as though with two clouds, this ground is called Cloud of Dharma."

According to the resultant vehicle of the Secret Mantra, there are thirteen grounds.† In other words, above the ten sutra grounds, we find the eleventh ground of Universal Light, which is the Nirmanakaya level, the twelfth ground of Lotus Free of All Desire, which is the Sambhogakaya level, and the thirteenth ground of Vajra Holder,‡ otherwise known as Great Wheel of Collections of Letters,§ which is the Dharmakaya level. There are, however, different methods of classification. Indeed, the different systems of Vajrayana grounds, as set forth in the various tantras, are innumerable.[93] For example, in the *mdo dgongs pa 'dus pa*, an anuyoga tantra, the names given are the Keen, the Distinguished, the Encouraged, the Confident, and the Greatly Powerful.

The Sacred Dharma, then, is the extraordinary wisdom of elimination and realization that suffuses the minds of those abiding on the grounds and paths.[94]

The qualities of the Sangha

Generally speaking, the Jewel of the Sangha is the spiritual community of those who are endowed with realization, that is, those who possess a measure of wisdom together with freedom from some of the stains of the two kinds of obscuration.[95]

---

* These are the same as those described in appendix 5, p. 299.
† This enumeration is according to the Mahayoga tantra.
‡ *rdo rje 'dzin pa.*
§ *yi ge 'khor lo tshogs chen.*

If we group the Shravakas and Pratyekabuddhas together and if we take into account the two stages of "candidate for" and "abiding by the result" associated with any given level, we can distinguish four pairs of Shravakas and Pratyekabuddhas. We thus arrive at a total of eight kinds of beings.

The four kinds of Shravakas and Pratyekabuddhas are therefore as follows:[96]

1. *Stream Enterer* (*rgyun du zhugs*). The Shravakas who abide in the understanding of the fifteen instants of the path of seeing, as described in the Hinayana Abhidharma, and the Shravakas who abide by the path of joining and the fifteen instants of the path of seeing, as described in the Mahayana Abhidharma, are all candidates for the degree of Stream Enterer. When they reach the sixteenth instant of the path of seeing, they become Stream Enterers who abide by the result. They are called Stream Enterers because they enter the "stream" of the path whereby they will attain the result.*

2. *Once Returner* (*lan gcig phyir 'ong ba*). The Stream Enterers who have rid themselves of the five degrees of obscurations in the desire realm eliminated by meditation are candidates for the state of Once Returner. On relinquishing the sixth degree, they become Once Returners abiding by the result. They are so called because they return only once more to the desire realm.

3. *Nonreturner* (*phyir mi 'ong ba*). The Once Returners who have rid themselves of obscurations in the desire realm eliminated by meditation, to the seventh and eighth degree, but who have not yet eliminated those of the ninth, are candidates for the state of Nonreturner. When they discard all such obscurations, they become Nonreturners abiding by the result. They are so called because they will not be reborn in the desire realm.

---

* They will be reborn no more than seven times in the desire realm.

4. *Arhat* (*dgra bcom pa*). The Nonreturners who are free of all the obscurations of the higher realms (i.e., form and formless) eliminated by meditation, right up to the eighth degree in the Peak of Existence, are candidates for arhatship. When they discard all the remaining obscurations of the three worlds, they become Arhats abiding by the result. Arhat means "Foe Destroyer." They are so called because they have destroyed their enemy, afflictive emotion.

The Hinayana path has its own system of eight grounds.[97]

Those belonging to the Sangha of the Mahayana are called the children of the Conqueror.[98] They dwell on the *bhumis*, or grounds, of realization produced by the practices of the expository vehicle of causality; their qualities are inexpressible.

WHAT IS REFUGE?

The Sacred Dharma is the path leading beyond suffering; it is the protection from the two extremes: samsara on the one hand, and the peace of nirvana on the other. The Dharma has come to us from the Buddha our Teacher, and those who have embraced the three trainings and who assist us in our own efforts to accomplish them are the Sangha. These three are the Three Jewels, the refuge of those who strive for liberation. It is said in the *Seventy Stanzas on Refuge*: "The Buddha, the Dharma, and Sangha are the protection for those who yearn for liberation."

Causal and resultant refuge

According to Jigme Lingpa's root text, within the Mahayana, the Sutrayana refuge is the "causal refuge," while the Vajrayana refuge is the "resultant refuge." The vows of both of them should be taken with utter sincerity and not as mere lip service. The refuge of the expository vehicle of causality is the vow to practice with a view to accomplishing the Three Jewels in the future (after three measureless kalpas or more). The ultimate focus of interest is the state of buddhahood,[99] for it is here alone that all the qualities of the Three Jewels are complete. The resultant refuge which is the special refuge of the Vajrayana, deriving from the view peculiar to that vehicle, is the vow to actualize the nature of one's own mind—understood to be the Three Jewels themselves—now in this very moment and not as something to be accomplished at some point in the future. The result, buddhahood, is sought for in one's own mind and nowhere else.

Generally speaking, however, according to the Mahayana expository vehicle of causality, the object of refuge is the Three Jewels: the Buddha endowed with the four kayas and five wisdoms, the Sacred Dharma of transmission and realization, and the Noble Sangha dwelling on the grounds of accomplishment. To take refuge in them as Teacher, Path, and Companions is the causal refuge, whereas the resultant refuge is the aspiration to "actualize" the Three Jewels in one's mind in the future. According to the vehicle of the Secret Mantra, however, the nature of the Three Jewels[100] is embodied in the lama, the spiritual master. One's root teacher is the embodiment of all the Buddhas. The teacher's Body, Speech, and Mind are the Sangha, Dharma, and Buddha, respectively. With this understanding, to take refuge in him in a nondual manner (that is, without seeing a difference between the one who is seeking protection and the one who is giving protection) is the causal refuge. Finally, to understand that one's own mind is, in that very instant, the Three Jewels, is to take resultant refuge. This involves the recognition of one's mind as the wisdom of luminosity. It involves the recognition that the mind is without defect from the very beginning and that it is endowed from the first with every perfect quality. There is nothing to purify and there is nothing new to gain. The mind itself is Buddha. This resultant refuge involves, too, the recognition of the mind's stainless ultimate nature, primordially unchanging, as Dharma, and of its inalienable qualities as Sangha.

The different motives for taking refuge

There are three possible attitudes of mind in those who take refuge. First, there are those who wish to accomplish a temporary, ephemeral happiness. Then there are those who wish to accomplish permanent happiness. Finally, there are those who have the unsurpassable attitude of wishing to accomplish the happiness of others.

As to the first type, we may refer to them as beings of lesser scope. Such people are afraid of the lower realms and take refuge in the Three Jewels in order to gain the happiness of the higher realms of gods and humans; and they take such refuge until they do so. The beings of middle scope, the Shravakas and Pratyekabuddhas, fear the suffering of existence as such and take refuge in the Three Jewels with a view to their own liberation. In the immediate term, they take refuge for the rest of their lives while, ultimately speaking, they take refuge until they attain the fruit of the Hinayana path, which is arhatship. Finally, beings of great scope, the practitioners of the Mahayana, repudiate the attitude of wishing for their own happiness alone and neglecting the plight of others. They take refuge until they attain great enlightenment in order to liberate every being in samsara and place them in the condition of Great Freedom, or buddhahood. In fact, those who have internalized the profound sense of the sutras of ultimate meaning, together with the tantras, realize that there are no truly existent samsaric defects or qualities of nirvana to be eliminated or attained. From the very outset, the fundamental state of the mind is free from compounded phenomena, deceptive and relative, which nevertheless arise in the sequential order of cause and effect due to the mechanism of acceptance and rejection. To "see the face of the sugatagarbha," the ultimate reality, and to rest in it is to take unsurpassable refuge in its resultant aspect.

How to take refuge

Beings constantly wander upon the five pathways,[101] the path of dreams, the path of habitual tendencies, the path of karma, the path of uncertain feelings, and the path of the uncertain effects of causes. For them, the Buddha's compassion is always timely and is beyond attachment or impediment.

In the *Karmashataka-sutra* it is said:

> The tides of serpent-crowded seas
> May fluctuate and change.

Yet for his children, those whom he might train,
The Buddha's acts are always timely.

So immense are the qualities of the Tathagata that even the powerful
Bodhisattvas dwelling on the tenth ground, whose vast treasury of wisdom has been opened wide, are unable to describe the tiniest pore of
his body. Were they to attempt such a feat, they would be like birds
trying to fly to the edges of the sky—at length, they fall to earth.

Samsara is like the wheel of a water mill. From the Peak of Existence
down to the Hell of Torment Unsurpassed, beings revolve constantly
through the sequences of the twelve interdependent links. All who have
committed evil actions through wrong views and strong emotions, be
they universal sovereigns or gods like Brahma and Indra, or the rich and
powerful of this world—all must wander in samsara. Failing to realize
the ultimate truth, they rush headlong into the fearful abyss. It is true
that on a temporary basis, such beings may help or harm us. But people
who possess the threefold motivation (fear of samsara, faith in the
Three Jewels, and compassion for those who are ignorant of where to
turn) know perfectly well that they are deceptive protectors both now
and in the long run. Such disciples should, like the great Bodhisattvas,
cast behind them all self-centeredness. They should cultivate the enlightened mind for others' sake and be mindful of the qualities of the
Three Jewels. Wishing from the depths of their hearts to accomplish such qualities in themselves, they should take refuge, reciting the
seven-branch prayer in the presence of the field of merit.

THE BENEFITS OF TAKING REFUGE

The benefits of causal refuge

Just as it is impossible to encompass the immensity of space in any of
the ten directions, it is likewise impossible to fathom the benefits and
defects resulting from positive and negative actions performed in connection with the Three Jewels. Such is their tremendous importance.
The merit resulting from taking refuge is limitless. Indeed, if it were
able to assume physical form, space itself could not contain it. The

Vimala-sutra says: "If the merit of taking refuge possessed shape and mass, it would fill the whole of space and still there would be more."

In brief, it is by taking refuge that one becomes a Buddhist. Refuge, therefore, is the criterion distinguishing those who are within the Dharma from those who are not. Refuge is the basis of all the vows of Pratimoksha, Bodhisattvayana, and Mantrayana. Through taking refuge, all actions that are negative by their nature, all transgressions of the vows, and all obscurations will be purified.[102] It is impossible for anyone who has taken refuge to be harmed by any evildoer, human or divine. Even a person in whose mindstream is the cause for falling into the lower realms will be safeguarded from such a destiny. Those who take refuge, regardless of where they are born and throughout the sequence of their lives, will be blessed by the presence of the Three Jewels. In this very life, they will enjoy the excellence of samsara and nirvana. And having completed, on the conceptual level, the accumulation of merit, they will at length accomplish the two form bodies, the Sambhogakaya and Nirmanakaya.

The benefits of resultant refuge

Resultant refuge, absolute and infallible, is the recognition of the true and uncontrived nature of the mind, the realization of the equal taste of samsara and nirvana as referred to in the expression "the three doors of liberation." The first of these is that all phenomena encompassed by the mind and mental perception are without inherent existence; they are empty. The second is that even though the creative display of the mind is unfettered, it eludes all description and definition, for it is beyond all characteristics (and description), pure or impure. The third is that this manifestation is beyond all discriminative acceptance and rejection, all action and refraining from action; it transcends all expectancy. No result is aspired to; no result is hoped for; no reliance is placed in some extraneous refuge separate from the nature of one's mind. This is because one settles evenly in the naturally pure expanse, the deepest fundamental nature of the mind, unshaken by dualistic thoughts of subject and object—the state of wisdom of uncompounded vajra luminosity. Being free from clinging to conceptions of the three spheres, one fulfills the accumulation of wisdom, attaining the Dharmakaya endowed with twofold purity: the natural primordial purity and the purity resulting from the removal of all adventitious stains.

THE PRECEPTS OF THE REFUGE VOW

The precepts of causal refuge

The precepts regarding things to be avoided

It is possible to speak of common and uncommon precepts. The former state that the Three Jewels must not be forsaken even at the cost of one's life. No need to mention, then, that they must not be denied for the sake of social and ecclesiastical preferment or gifts of gold and silver. In particular, since spiritual masters are the embodiments of the Three Jewels, once one has taken refuge, one must refrain from addressing them in disrespectful and unpleasant ways. The same applies to all beings worthy of respect. Likewise, one should abandon all deceitful and false behavior toward one's teacher—all improper talk, all blaming, and all kinds of grumbling.

As for the uncommon precepts, once one has taken refuge in the Three Jewels there are three things to avoid. Taking refuge in the Buddha, one should stop paying homage to the gods, Brahma, Vishnu, and so forth, who are not only incapable of truly helping beings but, due to their karma, are themselves caught within the cycles of existence. Even less should one pay homage to the pretas or spirits that inhabit the upper air and who possess miraculous powers.[103] Taking refuge in the Dharma, one should not harm other beings. One must not kill or beat them, and, in the case of animals, one should not ride on them or weigh them down with burdens. Taking refuge in the Sangha, one should shun fellowship with those who are hostile to the Buddhist teachings or who have no faith in the Three Jewels.

The precepts regarding things to be accomplished

One should have a respectful attitude toward all representations of the Three Jewels, regarding them as their embodiments. One should never trade or pawn any image or likeness of them, whether new or old, whether skillfully or poorly executed. The same applies to even a single syllable, the support of Buddha's Speech. One should never step over anything that has been written upon. One should never disrespectfully turn one's back on the scriptures or soil them with one's spittle. One should avoid criticizing and scolding the Sangha, even those whose observance of the vows is poor.[104] With devotion, one should touch the crown of one's head with even a patch of their red and yellow robes. One should call to mind the qualities of the Three Jewels as many as three or six times every twenty-four hours, or at least once during the day and once during the night. One should take refuge in them and encourage others to do the same.[105]

The precepts of resultant refuge

Turning now to the precepts of the resultant refuge, the Dharmakaya of the Buddha is the ultimate nature of the mind. Thus, one becomes fully enlightened when all the manifestations of the mind's creative power (the mind and mental factors operating together as the sun and its rays) dissolve into the expanse where there is nothing to rid oneself of and nothing to gain, and where all concepts subside. For this reason, in the case of the resultant refuge, one does not apprehend the Three Jewels as the protector and oneself as the protected. This resultant refuge utterly transcends the conventional refuge taken with the help of a ritual. It is therefore impossible to speak of its precepts and disciplines.

When the refuge vow is broken

The causal refuge is abandoned when one gives way to doubt and wrong view[106] with regard to the Three Jewels, the true object of refuge. It is abandoned also when, unable to keep the precept, one gives it back. If any of the precepts concerning what has to be abandoned and what has to be adopted is impaired (even when the vow is not completely broken), one will fall to nether regions of the lower realms. For this reason, just as one takes care of a physical injury, one should be vigilant in observing even the slightest precept.

Attitudes incompatible with refuge

Due to "effects similar to the cause," certain people, like foxes unable to resist their instincts, are trapped in their wrong attitudes and thoughts. They recite the refuge prayer loudly, but in reality their behavior contradicts their commitment. They have no faith in the Three Jewels and their minds are impervious to their blessings; they are cynical "unworthy vessels." They have recourse to what worldly folk regard as gods, spirits, and ground-lords* but which in reality are pretas that move in the air and possess magic powers and clairvoyance, the fruit of their past karma. Such behavior shows that these people do not believe the Three Jewels to be definitive and infallible refuges. In this very life their fortunes will decline and their deaths will be untimely.

The benefits of observing the precepts of the refuge vow

When this universe, the earth, the sky, Mount Meru, the four cosmic continents, all that now exists is destroyed and dissolves into the void, the sun and moon will lose the energy[107] propelling them in their heavenly courses and could fall upon us. But even if such a thing were to happen, it would be impossible for the Three Jewels to deceive us. It is extremely important to be completely convinced of this truth.

If in a dream one has the impression of falling into a river, or of being pursued by enemies and wild beasts, as soon as one sees or remembers the Three Jewels and prays one-pointedly to them, all such dangers will fade away. One will acquire carefulness, mindfulness, and all the qualities of the three trainings. If in past lives one had faith in the Three Jewels, in subsequent lives wholesome qualities will be developed easily and with pleasure. To see the Buddhas and Bodhisattvas even in the bardo state will not be difficult, and one will easily progress toward liberation. Finally, by becoming an embodiment of the Three Jewels oneself, one will be able to protect other beings, soothing their anguish and leading them not only to the higher realms but even to the ultimate perfection of buddhahood itself.

* *sa bdag*, spirits occupying certain localities.

CHAPTER 7

Cleansing the Mind by Training in the Four Boundless Attitudes

THE MAHAYANA PATH

Since its characteristic attitude and practice are limited, aimed solely at the pacification of one's own defilement and suffering, the Hinayana is likened in the root verses to a pool of muddy water. As yet, the seed of the Mahayana,[108] the potential for bodhichitta, lies unstirred in the minds of the Shravakas and Pratyekabuddhas, and they enter the peace of cessation. But they are at length roused from this by the Buddhas, who are guides to the wisdom of emptiness and universal compassion. With bodhichitta thus awakened, the Shravakas and Pratyekabuddhas embrace the Dharma of the Great Vehicle, as deep and vast as the sea itself, and set out for the land of jewels, the omniscience of buddhahood.

As long as generosity and the other four virtuous actions are not combined with wisdom, they do not constitute transcendent perfections—the *paramita*s that bring forth great enlightenment. Nevertheless, as when alchemy transmutes base metal into gold, the union of wisdom and skillful means can transform these lesser virtues into the invaluable causes of great enlightenment.

Bodhichitta is the indispensable prerequisite for achieving nonabiding nirvana and is the fusion of the skillful means of compassion and the wisdom of emptiness.[109] It arises in the mind through repeated training in the four boundless attitudes,[110] whereby a person's thoughts and actions are transformed into the path of the Mahayana. The four boundless attitudes are therefore to be seen as guides. Once the mind is purified by them, the cultivation of bodhichitta in aspiration and action and the training in the precepts become possible. On the paths of accumulation and joining, this bodhichitta, the union of skillful means and wisdom, is, however, no more than a foretaste of the fully authentic bodhichitta that arises on the path of seeing.

THE FOUR BOUNDLESS ATTITUDES

Love is essentially the wish that beings who suffer—for instance, in being deprived of the bliss of the upper realms—should have happiness, both immediately and ultimately. The love that a Bodhisattva feels toward other beings resembles the love that a mother feels for her own dear child. Therefore, our person, our possessions, and our merits gained in the past, present, and future should all be devoted to the benefit of beings in the immediate and ultimate term. In addition, we should train ourselves to endure with love even the harm that others do to us, returning them good in exchange.

The essence of *compassion* is a valiant resolve to free absolutely all beings from their miseries—beings who are by nature entangled in the three or eight types of suffering. It is a sensation felt in the very roots of the heart, an inability to tolerate the fact that beings suffer. It is as when a man unhesitatingly jumps into a filthy pit to retrieve his child. Such compassion is incapable of leaving matters simply as they stand; it is a resolute determination to free beings from their pain. People with such compassion see that the beings of the six realms are like cornered deer, unable to escape from the pain arising from their ego-clinging. And with tears of compassion in their eyes, they strive by every means to liberate those who would never otherwise be able to free themselves.

Sympathetic joy is a sincere pleasure, untainted by jealousy or a sense of competition, at the happiness and prosperity that others have. It also involves the cultivation of the excellent thought "How wonderful it would be if all beings had perfect prosperity and well-being!" It is a sense of delight that, due to their past karma, beings have attained happiness, and gives rise to the wish that they will never lose their contentment and bliss.

Impartiality,[111] or lack of bias, is freedom from the fixed, conventional attitudes of exclusive attachment to the objects of one's love (parents, relatives, husband or wife, etc.), hatred toward enemies and those inimical to one's interests, and indifference toward those who fit into neither of these categories. Impartiality is the ability to see that all beings, regardless of their associations and alignment, are equal, and to consider them all—friend, enemy, or neither—with the same benevolence.

The four boundless attitudes are thus the wish that others be happy, the wish that they not suffer, the joyful desire that they never lose their happiness, and the aspiration to view them all with an open heart free of partiality. It is important to understand that the object of the practice, namely, other beings, and the form of the practice, that is to say, these four attitudes, are devoid of true existence. They are like dream visions or reflections in a mirror. In other words, this training should be performed in a state that is free of clinging to a truly existent subject, object, and action.

By contrast, the loving attitude of wishing happiness for one's friends and relatives out of attachment; the kind of compassion that, for instance, spares animals from toil only out of miserliness; the conceited exhilaration that comes from being more prosperous than others; and the formless, mindless indifference of wishing neither to help nor to harm—these have nothing to do with the authentic path of liberation. They are more akin to the four so-called Brahmaviharas,[112] the four attitudes that provoke rebirth in the form and formless realms. Since they approach their objects with partiality and bias, and since their character is one of clinging, they are a distortion of the four boundless attitudes of the Mahayana and should be utterly discarded.

In the context of the Mahayana path leading to the nonabiding nirvana beyond the two extremes, the focus of the four boundless attitudes is the entire aggregate of beings and is completely without bias. Moreover, although such beings, and for that matter the four attitudes themselves, are manifest phenomena, they are without inherent existence, being primordially beyond all conceptual construction.[113] Through repeated training, the four boundless attitudes, in which both skillful means and wisdom are combined, will strengthen and eventually give rise to relative and absolute bodhichitta. This is why they are referred to as extraordinary. They are endowed with a skill and wisdom that are not to be found among the Shravakas, Pratyekabuddhas, and those who follow worldly paths.

How to meditate on the four boundless attitudes

The four boundless attitudes[114] may be meditated upon either in the direct order described here or in any sequence, as when the meditation on impartiality is taken first. To begin with, one should get used to the practice by focusing on objects toward whom these attitudes may be entertained easily. However, in order to counteract attachment, should it arise while meditating in a fixed order, the sequence of meditations should be changed. It may happen, for instance, that, in the course of sustained meditation on love and cherishing, the practice itself provokes attachment. If this happens, the meditation on impartiality, which is free from bias toward those who are close as opposed to those who are distant, will remove such attachment. On the other hand, if during the meditation on impartiality the mind becomes simply addled and neutral and loses its benevolent impulse, then by shifting to the meditation on compassion and reflecting on how beings sow and reap the crop of suffering, this worthless kind of impartiality will be averted. Again, if, while meditating on compassion and reflecting on the immense sufferings that beings experience, the mind becomes excessively downcast and depressed, by turning to the meditation on sympathetic joy and focusing on the happiness and prosperity of beings, it is possible to avoid discouragement. Finally, if meditation on joy leads to overexcitement and distraction of the mind, one should begin to meditate on love, and so on.

The benefits of this meditation

Training in the four boundless attitudes gives rise to four results. (1) The fully ripened karmic result will be birth in the higher levels of samsara with the perfect form of a human being or a god of the desire realm. With the support of such a body, it will be possible to complete the two accumulations and achieve ultimate excellence, the grounds of the twin paths of learning and no more learning. (2) With regard to the two effects similar to the cause, *actively* (action similar to the cause) one will continue to meditate on the four boundless attitudes in all one's subsequent lives, and *experientially* (experience similar to the cause) one will attain perfect happiness free from the four unfavorable factors of malevolence, cruelty, jealousy, and craving taken together with anger. (3) As for the conditioning environmental effect, the practice of love will result in the experience of congenial places with pleasant company and amenities. Through compassion one will find fortunate conditions of both body and mind; because of sympathetic joy, the environment will be adorned with medicinal trees and plants and will be a pleasure to live in; through impartiality, one will find oneself in a country where the people are friendly and live in harmony. (4) Due to the proliferating effect, one's practice of the four boundless attitudes will gain in strength, and every excellent quality related to the twofold aim (one's own and others' benefit) will be gained.

As one becomes proficient in the practice of boundless love, one will come to cherish all beings as a mother would love her only child. Through the power of such love, in which anger and hostility have no place, one will receive the affection and appreciation of others. By meditating on the fact that love is by nature empty, that it is devoid of inherent existence, one will achieve the unobstructed knowledge of mirrorlike wisdom and gain the Sambhogakaya endowed with the oceanlike infinity of the major and minor marks of buddhahood. As it is said in the *pad ma rtse mo* tantra, "By love is anger driven out and the mirrorlike wisdom and Sambhogakaya are perfected."

Likewise, in becoming proficient in great compassion, one will be able to bear the burden of all the sorrows of others as though they were one's own. Unable to tolerate the fact that others suffer, one will think only of ways to free them from their sorrow. One will never entertain thoughts of aggression even for an instant and will approach other people as friends, with an attitude free from any trace of passionate desire. Compassion is nothing but the glow and display of emptiness, from which it is inseparable. It embodies a clear understanding of the principle of cause and effect that dominates all samsaric phenomena, including living beings. It leads finally to the realization of all-discerning wisdom, which perceives clearly and distinctly all objects of knowledge, and thence to the attainment of the Dharmakaya, naturally endowed with every quality. As the *pad ma rtse mo* tantra says, "Through compassion is desire cleansed. This is wisdom all-discerning, the Dharmakaya."

As one becomes proficient in the practice of sympathetic joy, all jealousy and resentment at the happiness and prosperity of others will evaporate. On account of the unusual pleasure one feels at the happiness of others, one's own wholesome qualities will be stable, and one will enjoy an uninterrupted satisfaction free from the torment of jealousy. As a result, one's meditative concentration will be undisturbed. Sympathetic joy is essentially a sense of happiness at the perfect endowments of others, free from the strain that arises from the dualistic apprehension of subject and object. Accordingly, on the ultimate level, all-accomplishing wisdom, which effortlessly achieves the benefit of others, will come into play. One will attain the supreme Nirmanakaya and strive for the welfare of others. As it is said in the *pad ma rtse mo* tantra, "Jealousy is purified by sympathetic joy. This is wisdom all-accomplishing, the supreme Nirmanakaya and the supreme, spontaneous activity of buddhahood."

As one becomes proficient in the practice of impartiality, one will benefit oneself and others equally, whether friends, enemies, or neither. As a result, all self-cherishing or conceited (artificial) altruism and pride will subside. For the mind is empty; it is empty even though it now strays from the evenness of the middle position, its true and ultimate nature, and so clings to the conceptual extremes of existence and nonexistence. It is within this emptiness, in the expanse of peace wherein all conceptual activity subsides, that the extraordinary realization of impartiality is born. Essentially, impartiality is simply the absence of ignorance, the confused apprehension of distinctions (between friend and enemy); it is the pacification of extreme notions. Ultimately, the wisdom of the dharmadhatu that knows that all phenomena are equal, beyond acceptance and rejection, will be realized and the Svabhavikakaya will be attained—the expanse that is utterly pure and free from all obscurations. As the *pad ma rtse mo* tantra says, "Impartiality—the great impartiality—purifies stupidity and pride. It is the wisdom of equality together with the wisdom of the dharmadhatu: the body of manifest enlightenment and the vajra body, respectively."

It is thus possible to train in the four boundless attitudes according to the extraordinary Mahayana, bringing into play an understanding of the ground, path, and fruit. The path of the two accumulations, which bring to birth the two kayas (as understood on the level of the sutra teachings), and the path of skillful means and wisdom, which purify the two veils (as understood in the context of tantra) are, as far as the ground nature is concerned, one and the same. Because these two paths, by means of which ultimate reality is actualized, are not by nature different, the same is also true of their respective results, namely, the two kayas.[115] This practice is extremely profound and gives rise to limitless qualities, which infallibly lead to the attainment of the ultimate level.

Finally, the *Shrimaladevi-sutra* says: "All who meditate upon the four boundless attitudes will attract the notice of the Buddhas. They will acquire limitless qualities surpassing the very vastness of the sky." False paths and non-Buddhist traditions do not possess the teaching and practice of the four boundless attitudes. Their tenets result in samsaric existence. The commentary on the *Praise of the Grounds* says: "The four boundless attitudes are the path to liberation. Neglect them and you will go astray."

We should not diverge from the true path of compassion combined with the wisdom of understanding the primordial emptiness of phenomena. Jigme Lingpa requests us to train ourselves on the supreme path of the Bodhisattvas, leading to liberation free from the two obscurations and stilling the turmoil of our minds, our self-centeredness, and our belief in the true existence of phenomena. And we should actually do it and train ourselves, and not be satisfied with a merely intellectual understanding!

The Vow of Bodhichitta

WHAT IS BODHICHITTA?

Bodhichitta, the mind of enlightenment, is the greatest, most precious thing in the whole of samsara and nirvana. It is the supreme and essential element that brings about perfect enlightenment, the fruit of the path. This sublime disposition of mind is obtained through repeated training in the four boundless attitudes. And when disciples have engendered it, in aspiration and in action, they must go on to school themselves correctly in its attendant precepts. Indeed, it is by their keen enthusiasm, as firm as the earth, and their sublime nobility of heart, as excellent as gold, that their bodhichitta will strengthen and grow. And as the "miraculous chariot" progresses higher and higher on the path, the improper desire for individual peace and bliss will wither away, and the two goals will be perfectly achieved.

If the supreme thought of bodhichitta arises in the minds of even the most abject of creatures, bound in samsara by their defilements and suffering (the dreadful consequences of evil deeds), as though in the dungeons of a terrible king—such people undergo a complete transformation of identity. They are ennobled with the title of "children of the Conqueror" and raised to an entirely new status. The powers of light rejoice and place their confidence in such people, praising them and making them offerings. Gods and humankind, the lords among the beings of the six classes, will pay them homage and shower them with gifts and eulogy.

The nature of the mind is primordially immaculate, and yet it is veiled by ignorance and defilement whereby samsaric action is engendered. Thus the virtue of ordinary beings is feeble and inconstant; it is like lightning that flashes briefly between the clouds in a dark black sky lit by neither sun nor moon. Such virtue, practiced fitfully, produces mere merit and nothing more. After yielding its result, happiness in the divine or human realms, it is exhausted like the plantain, the castor-oil plant, or the bamboo cane, which bear their fruit and wither. By contrast, the miraculous tree of virtue combined with bodhichitta is like a seed planted in fertile, well-farmed land. It brings forth a copious and proliferating harvest: the abundant happiness of the upper realms of samsara, which constantly increases until the peace of great enlightenment is attained.

Samsara is an ocean fed by the rivers of all-pervading suffering in the making. It is surrounded by the fiery abysses of karma and defilement and is turbulent with the surging waves of wrong thinking. It is fraught with danger for the fragile boat sailing to the haven of liberation. But beings fail to recognize samsara for what it is. They take delight in it and cling to it as if it were their home. Thus they deny themselves the chance of liberation. To don the armor of a powerful and courageous determination to bring such beings out of samsara: this is the sole meaning of supreme bodhichitta. As Shantideva says in his *Bodhicharyavatara*:

> Those who wish to overcome the sorrows of their lives,
> And put to flight the pain and sufferings of beings,
> Those who wish to win such great beatitude,
> Should never turn their backs on bodhichitta.
> (I, 8)

Beings of great scope do not consult their own interest in the way that those of small or middle scope do. They long to free limitless beings from their sorrows in just the same way that a hungry and thirsty man craves food and drink. This is the measure of their great compassion. Through compassion they focus on the benefit of others, and through wisdom they focus on complete enlightenment, aiming to bring all beings to omniscience. This is the meaning of bodhichitta, encapsulated in the definition given in the *Abhisamayalankara*: "Bodhichitta is the wish for perfect enlightenment for the sake of others."

CLASSIFICATIONS OF BODHICHITTA

Bodhichitta in aspiration and action

The pledge to accomplish perfect enlightenment is known as aspirational bodhichitta, and for this the training is threefold: the recognition of the equality of self and other, the exchange of self and other, and the cherishing of others more than oneself. These constitute the key precepts of bodhichitta in aspiration and are essentially none other than the four boundless attitudes of love, compassion, sympathetic joy, and impartiality.

Bodhichitta in action consists of the pledge to practice the six transcendent perfections that lead to enlightenment, and the undertaking of such a pledge. Its precepts comprise the training in the same perfections and all the methods whereby neutral activities such as walking and sitting are rendered virtuous and pure through aspirations made for the benefit of others.

Other classifications of bodhichitta

According to classifications associated with the different stages of the path, it is possible to distinguish from two to six types of bodhichitta. In connection with the two accumulations, there are two kinds of bodhichitta. Likewise from the point of view of the two truths, there are also two: the relative bodhichitta of ordinary beings and the absolute bodhichitta of superior beings.* Again, there are three types of bodhichitta associated with the three trainings of discipline, concentration, and wisdom, while there is another tripartite classification related to the three aspects of discipline: the abstention from negativities, the practice of virtue, and the benefiting of others.

A fourfold division of bodhichitta is also possible, based on the different paths. While training on the paths of accumulation and joining, taken together, it is impossible to have a direct vision of ultimate reality

---

* In the first case, the focus of attention is the plight of sentient beings; in the second case, the focus is on the nature of the mind.

because the obscurations concealing the buddha nature have not yet been purified. They have not even been partially removed. The consequence of this is that, for the time being, ultimate reality can only be understood conceptually, by way of a mental image. The bodhichitta generated at this stage therefore must be *practiced through aspiration*. By contrast, from the first to the seventh ground (that is, on the paths of seeing and meditation), there is an understanding of the equality of self and others, and the veils obscuring the buddha nature are partially dissipated. Primordial wisdom is experienced directly, and bodhichitta of *the utterly pure attitude* occurs. As the three pure grounds (eighth, ninth, and tenth) are traversed, the remaining veils that obscure the ultimate nature are gradually removed. On the eighth ground, the defiled emotional consciousness is arrested, with the result that the wisdom free of concepts is realized. On the ninth ground, the mental consciousness and the five sense faculties are arrested. At the same time, the primordial wisdom of the four perfect knowledges is realized, together with the infinite purity of all phenomena. On the tenth ground, the functioning of the mental consciousness is purified and buddha activities are perfected.[116] When these four realizations are possessed, the *fully ripened* bodhichitta occurs. By the end of the tenth ground, the veils covering the buddha nature, which are the instinctual patterns of the mind and mental factors, together with the alaya, are entirely purified. On this level, the level of buddhahood, bodhichitta *totally free from all obscurations* occurs.

In connection with the five paths, bodhichitta may again be divided into five. On the path of accumulation, there is the bodhichitta "of the beginner." On the path of joining, there is "completely trained" bodhichitta. On the path of seeing, there is the bodhichitta that "sees the nature of phenomena." On the path of meditation, there is "totally free" bodhichitta, and on the path of no more learning, there is "inconceivable" bodhichitta. Finally, in relation to the six paramitas, bodhichitta is classified sixfold.

Bodhichitta classified according to twenty-two similes

There is a further division of bodhichitta into twenty-two aspects made from the point of view of the grounds and paths. These are expressed metaphorically in the *Abhisamayalankara* as follows:

Earth and gold and moon and fire,
Treasure, mine of jewels and sea,
Diamond, mountain, healing draught,
Virtuous teacher, wishing gem,
Sun, melodious song and king,
Treasure house and broad highway,
Perfect steed and flowing spring,
Strain of music, river, cloud:
Two and twenty aspects thus are shown.[117]

The first three similes, of earth, gold, and moon, refer to the three stages of the path of accumulation, while firelike engagement refers to the path of joining. The following ten similes indicate the ten grounds (covering the range of the path of seeing and the path of meditation), which correspond to the ten paramitas. Kinglike clairvoyance and the four that follow (from treasure to spring) point generally to the three pure grounds (on the path of meditation). The music of the Dharma feast and the last two similes of river and cloud refer to the tenth ground alone. Other classifications exist, but all may be subsumed under bodhichitta in aspiration, the wish to realize the wisdom mind and enlightened activities of the Buddhas, and the actual implementation of that wish, or bodhichitta in action.

Bodhichitta classified according to its benefits

People who strive to attain the excellence of the higher realms for their own sake alone are careful to keep an ever-open door. They take from their possessions and give liberally to beggars, providing them with sustenance and saving them from distress. Such people are referred to as open-handed benefactors. They are certainly worthy of praise, and their actions will bring them birth as kings and queens in the desire realm. If this is the case, what need is there to speak of those who aspire constantly to attain the level of buddhahood for the benefit of others? Indeed, if aspiration bodhichitta is generated even for an instant, the doors of the lower realms are closed and birth is assured in the high state of gods and humans, where life will be long and free from illness and where excellent qualities, the karmic fruit similar to the cause, will burgeon.

The qualities of bodhichitta in action are even greater than those of aspiration. As it is written in the *Bodhicharyavatara*:

> Bodhichitta in intention bears rich fruit
> For those still wandering in samsara.
> And yet a ceaseless stream of merit does not flow from it;
> For this will rise alone from active bodhichitta.
> (I, 17)

When, with the wish to attain enlightenment for the sake of others, practitioners take the vow of bodhichitta in action and pledge themselves to the practice of the six paramitas, they take the irreversible decision to bring beings to freedom in the state of buddhahood. From that moment onward, the strength of their determination is such that their minds are constantly equipped with an abundant source of merit, even in moments of distraction and sleep and even in the making of neutral, routine gestures. This is mentioned in the *Bodhicharyavatara*:

> For when, with irreversible intent,
> The mind embraces bodhichitta,
> Willing to set free the endless multitudes of beings,
> In that instant, from that moment on,
>
> A great and unremitting stream,
> A strength of wholesome merit,
> Even during sleep and inattention,
> Rises equal to the vastness of the sky.
>
> This the Tathagata
> In the sutra Subahu requested,
> Said with reasoned demonstration,
> Teaching those inclined to lesser paths.
> (I, 18–20)

Bodhichitta classified according to the speed of progression

For those who have excellent means and wisdom, a training in each of the bodhisattva activities will produce, within a short time, an immense accumulation of merit. For someone who lacks this advantage, however, the same accomplishment would require a training in virtue extending over many kalpas. Bodhichitta can therefore be classified according to the speed with which Bodhisattvas progress toward the supreme goal. In the *Niyataniyatagatimudravatara-sutra*, this is illustrated with five similes: the ox chariot, the elephant chariot, the chariot of the sun and moon, the miraculous powers of the Shravakas, and the miraculous powers of the Buddhas.*

Parallel with the difference in speed with which progress is made upon the grounds and paths, bodhichitta may be distinguished according to the strength of the determination (basic, medium, or supreme) with which individuals generate it. This will be explained in due course.† Bodhisattvas who have great determination, perfect skill, diligence, and a wisdom that is profound and sharp will overcome the two obscurations in which they are enmeshed and will attain buddhahood after only three measureless kalpas.

How to cultivate bodhichitta

To have a fully ripened fruit, it is first necessary to have a seed. In addition to this, however, the main condition for maturation is not simply that the seed should be planted in the earth, but rather the coincidence of other, secondary factors.‡ In like manner, it is first necessary to stimulate, indeed fabricate, the mind of enlightenment. This contrived bodhichitta is naturally much less important than a totally authentic and spontaneous bodhichitta.

---

* The first two similes refer to ordinary beings who are unstable (i.e., they wish to go beyond the realms of samsara but finally fall back and fail to accomplish their goal). The third refers to beings who are ordinary but nevertheless stable. The fourth is an allusion to beings who dwell on the seven impure grounds, while the fifth is a reference to those who dwell on the three pure grounds. The last three kinds of beings will certainly attain enlightenment; they will never regress. [YG II, 69]
† See chapter 9, p. 190; and see YG II, 194.
‡ I.e., water, warmth, fertilizer, etc.

The causes of bodhichitta

Bodhichitta comes to birth in a perfectly pure mind through the operation of three strengths. The first of these is the meditative development of compassion, the root of bodhichitta. The second is the correct accumulation of merit, brought about, for example, by the seven-branch practice.* Finally, by taking refuge in the Three Jewels, negative tendencies are surmounted and a powerful support for bodhichitta is created. These three strengths are thus the strength of attitude (compassion), the strength of practice (the accumulation of merit), and the strength of cause (the taking of refuge).

Who can generate bodhichitta?

There are two traditions, associated with the Chittamatra and Madhyamika schools of Mahayana Buddhism, concerning people who are able to generate bodhichitta. According to the Chittamatra school, while there is no restriction with regard to bodhichitta in aspiration, the vow of bodhichitta in action may be taken only by people who have taken one of the seven pratimoksha ordinations. (Naturally, this does not include the one-day *upavasa* discipline, which is only a temporary commitment.) On the other hand, the Madhyamika tradition considers the main factor for the generation of bodhichitta to be aspiration. As it is written in the *Ratnolka-sutra*:

> Through faith in Buddha, faith in Buddha's doctrine,
> Through faith in unsurpassed enlightenment,
> Through faith in all the works of Buddha's children:
> The truly wise give birth to bodhichitta.

Moreover, scriptures like the *Gandavyuha*, *Bhadrakalpita*, and *Akashagarbha* sutras specify the different physical supports appropriate for the generation of bodhichitta.† This is taken up by the Prasangika Madhyamika

---

* See also chapter 8, p. 171. It is said that if the mind lacks merit, it is an unsuitable vessel. Bodhichitta will not arise there—just as a king would refuse to live in a beggar's hovel.

† In the *Ratnakuta-sutra* it is said that innumerable beings, gods, nagas, asuras, garudas, and other nonhumans have turned their minds to unsurpassable enlightenment.

school, which is more inclusive than the Chittamatra and affirms that, provided the wish for bodhichitta is perfect, any physical support will serve.[118] Both traditions agree, however, that a prerequisite for the perfect arising of bodhichitta is the accumulation of merit.[119]

The ritual for taking the vow of bodhichitta

Inculcating the correct attitude

The "extraordinary causal condition"* for the birth of bodhichitta is the luminous nature of the mind. This is present in all sentient beings and contains within itself all the immense qualities of the Sugata, which are by nature apt to ripen. It is like a seed that holds the potential shoot within it. As the *Chandrapradipa-sutra* says:

> All beings have within themselves the buddha-seed.
> Provided that they generate the bodhichitta perfectly,
> They all, without exception, will be Buddhas.

The "dominant condition" for the coming to birth of bodhichitta is perfect attendance upon an authentic spiritual friend. As a holder of the vows and an expert in the Great Vehicle, the guru must be in sovereign possession of all supreme qualities and, like a wish-fulfilling jewel, must be able to fulfill the hopes of his or her disciples. Such a guru, whose heart is filled with bodhichitta, is the person from whom the vow should be taken. It is written in the *Samvaravimshaka*:

> Gurus who are faithful to their vows
> Possessing wisdom and ability—
> From gurus such as these should vows be taken.

Teachings received from such a source are excellent in the beginning, for they stimulate a feeling of weariness and revulsion toward samsara. They are excellent in the middle, for they prevent attachment to nirvana,

* See note 114.

which is the other extreme. Finally, they are excellent in the end, for they inspire the heart with enthusiasm for bodhichitta, the mind of enlightenment, emptiness endowed with the core of compassion that abides in neither samsara nor nirvana. Such teachers are able to expound the infinite qualities of bodhichitta as described in scriptures like the *Sutralankara* and the *Gandavyuha, Ajatashatru-parivarta, Kashyapa-parivarta,* and *Ratnarashi* sutras.

Accumulating merit

PREPARING THE PLACE
The place where the vow of bodhichitta is to be taken should be beautifully adorned and cleansed with various kinds of perfume and fragrant substances. It should be well swept and sprinkled with saffron water and *bajung*,[120] and scented with incense, and so forth. Then, as a gesture of respect rather than vanity, one should bathe and put on clean clothes. In a spirit of intense devotion and faith and without any pretentiousness or self-advertisement, with a mind preoccupied only with the Three Jewels, one should prepare every kind of offering—hanging tassels, parasols, banners of victory, canopies, and so forth, and every kind of substance pleasing to the senses: the seven attributes of royalty,[121] the eight auspicious symbols,[122] the eight substances,[123] and so forth. Everything should be laid out tastefully and with sincere rejoicing.

INVITING THE FIELD OF MERIT
Proclaiming the truth—in other words, the power and compassion—of the Three Jewels, one should visualize that one's house (or the room in which the ceremony is to take place) is a vast palace. This is located in the center of an immense pure land and is greater than the three-thousandfold universe. It is made entirely of precious substances and is exquisitely adorned. In the center of this palace, numerous beautiful thrones have been set up. They are encrusted with gems and spread with silks, and upon each of them is a lotus, sun, and moon. One should then invoke the Three Jewels, requesting them to enter the consecrated representations of the enlightened Body, Speech, and Mind, such as images of the Buddhas and Bodhisattvas, and the volumes of the Mahayana scriptures. As a formula, one may use the text taken from the

Chandrapradipa-sutra: "Arise! Arise! Buddhas who possess the ten powers . . . etc."; or again one may recite the prayer in the tantra *rig pa mchog gi rgyud* beginning, "Protectors of all beings. . . ." Thus, with speech and melody, one invokes the wisdom beings from the expanse of ultimate reality, requesting them to come and remain inseparably in the consecrated supports. According to the images given in the root text, the Buddhas will forsake all the other buddhafields of the ten directions and will come as soon as they are summoned—quicker than a mother will rush toward her only child who has been lost and found, and quicker than a lover runs when he remembers a tryst promised with his beloved. As the *Ratnakuta* says:

> In front of those who think of them with faith
> The Buddhas stand
> Radiating blessings
> And dispelling faults.

In the root text there now follow some verses of entreaty.

First, an invocation is made to the supreme protectors, the guardians of all who dwell in samsara, the sublime friends who shield beings from suffering. Summoning them to act as the field for the accumulation of merit and as objects of refuge, the disciple calls upon all the Buddhas and Bodhisattvas of the ten directions, the enlightened destroyers of the hosts of evil, who are free from the two veils of emotional and cognitive obscuration and who thus know and perceive without attachment or impediment all phenomena in their multiplicity as well as in their ultimate nature.

OFFERING CLEANSING WATERS AND CLOTHES

Then, as a gesture of reverence, there follows the offering of cleansing waters. The Buddhas are visualized as coming to a bathing chamber built not of ordinary materials produced by the common karma of the world's inhabitants, but of precious substances perfumed with sweet fragrances that fill the air. The ground is made of crystal and jewels. It is smooth and even, decorated with checkered inlay like a chessboard. The roof is supported by magnificent pillars, gleaming and bright, and the hall is embellished with every kind of ornament, dazzling canopies of turquoise, coral, and pearls. The Buddhas and the multitude of their supreme offspring, the Bodhisattvas, appear and take their place. In order to perform the ceremony, the disciples imagine that offering goddesses emanate from themselves and bathe these supreme beings with thirty-two kinds of perfumed water poured out from jars and amphoras of lapis lazuli. The goddesses vie with each other, accompanying the bathing ceremony with countless songs of praise, with ravishing dances and the strains of sweet melody. They are skilled in gentle massage, in softly drying, dressing, and adorning. They array the Buddhas in embroidered silks and fragrant substances, and with various unguents they massage their bodies respectfully and with perfect concentration. They offer clothes and every kind of adornment. The material of the robes, moreover, is not of one single hue; it shimmers with different colors. Neither is it woven in the ordinary manner; it is the raiment of the gods, as though "purchased (or rather self-manifested) through the strength of merit." It is, in other words, the five-hued *panjali cloth*, effortlessly supplied by the wish-fulfilling tree. As to their form, these materials are worked into five kinds of raiment, and for those who have the pure monastic vows, the three Dharma robes. Far from being heavy and cumbersome, they are fine and diaphanous, so that the physical form is discernible beneath them. Moreover, they are soft and very light to the touch. Clothing in the northern continent of Uttarakuru weighs only one *pala*-measure,* those of the heaven of the Four Kings only half of one such measure, gradually getting lighter according to the elevation of the divine realm. Robes in the heaven Enjoying Magical Creations weigh only a sixty-fourth part of a measure, while those of the realm of the Pure are so fine as to be impossible to weigh. This is the sort of garment with which the Buddhas are arrayed. They are perfumed with many fragrances and are of many different kinds, appropriate for the manifestations of both the Sambhogakaya and Nirmanakaya. The goddesses also offer eight kinds of ornament, all of immense value, "so expensive indeed that one would be embarrassed to mention their

---

* *srang,* Skt. *pala.* This was an ancient Indian unit of weight corresponding to approximately forty grams.

price." These include bracelets, armlets, earrings, crowns, and so forth, an immeasurable quantity. All these things are offered to the Buddhas, the mightiest among the Sages, for they have abandoned even the subtlest habitual clinging to sense objects and have acquired every perfect quality resulting from realization and elimination.

The disciples should then pray in such words as these:

"For many lifetimes, I have gained no merit, and I need and thirst for it. Although I have no wealth, and although you are far beyond the need of gifts, please accept these imagined offerings of mine so that I might accumulate some merit." Thus the disciples should imagine that the whole sky is filled with offerings and should wish that a perfect accumulation of merit is achieved both for themselves and others. They should pray that all might clothe themselves with a sense of shame and decency and thus be protected from the torments that are the fruit of wrong behavior. They should pray too that they and others might acquire the perfect ornaments of unfailing memory, intelligence, concentration, and the major and minor marks of buddhahood.

In the same way, offerings should be made to Avalokiteshvara and the other seven Close Sons of the Buddha, as well as to the sixteen Bodhisattvas of this Fortunate Kalpa: to the Guide of Those in the Lower Realms, to the Loving One, to Meaningful to Behold, and to Destroyer of Sorrow's Gloom, to Musk Deer, Intrepid, Sky Treasure, Wisdom Ornament, Boundless Light, Moonlight, Sustainer of Good, Radiant Net, Diamond Essence, Endless Intelligence, Manifold Courage, and Entirely Good and also to the lay Bodhisattvas: Dharmodgata, Saraprarudita, Licchavi Vimalakirti, and so forth.

A thousand universes, each with its Mount Meru, four continents, and celestial realms, are referred to as a thousandfold universe. This multiplied by a thousand constitutes a two-thousandfold universe, and this multiplied by a thousand yet again is a great three-thousandfold universe. One imagines that this great concourse of universes, a billion strong, is pervaded with the scent of sandalwood and perfumes wafted on the wind. With that same perfume one should anoint the bodies of the enlightened ones, the brilliance of whose forms outshines to insignificance the lustrous glow of refined gold, who are adorned with the major and minor marks, and whose bodies are the source of boundless, ever-multiplying merit.

REQUESTING TO BE SEATED

The array of a buddhafield spontaneously manifests solely through a Buddha's prayerful aspiration joined with the merits of the Bodhisattvas. Accordingly, for a person who has completed the accumulations through training in the four boundless attitudes, and in accordance with what a Buddha in perfect possession of these same attitudes perceives through wisdom, there manifests an immense ground of crystal, the expression of the Buddha's vast impartiality for beings (which knows no discrimination between close and distant ones). Upon this ground there is a thousand-petaled lotus in full blossom. Its pistils are expressive of love bedewed with benefit. Upon this, there is a beautiful seat composed of the gleaming sun and moon. The cool light of the moon symbolizes the compassion that soothes the torment of beings, while the brilliance of the sun scatters the darkness of ignorance. The disciples then request the Buddhas and their entourage of Bodhisattvas, whose nature is joy transcending all impure attachment, to take their seats and to remain there for countless ages, and to accept them as disciples.

EXPRESSIONS OF RESPECT

The posture of the body naturally expresses the inner disposition of the mind. Therefore, putting aside all negligence, the disciples should join their hands at their hearts—a gesture that indicates faith and devotion, awe, attention, modesty, and a consideration for the feelings of others. The hands when joined should have the shape of an opening lotus or a small locket holding a flower bud.

The Buddhas' wisdom is like an eye that sees the ultimate reality of all phenomena. Their compassion is like feet on which they go forth in aid of beings. They progress in bliss upon the blissful path, the vehicle of the Bodhisattvas, and reach the fruit, the bliss of buddhahood. All the qualities of the Buddha, and indeed all the qualities of the holy Dharma and of the noble Sangha, are not manifest to ordinary perception until one has attained one of the sublime grounds. Thus the Three Jewels seem far away. And yet, as soon as the Buddhas come as invited guests to the garden of one's devoted mind, one is overwhelmed by the qualities of the Three Jewels, and the skin of one's body rises in gooseflesh—not in fear or grief but in faith and a sense of fervent yearning.

THE PRAYER OF SEVEN BRANCHES

Once the Buddhas and Bodhisattvas have been reverently invoked, the offering of the seven-branch prayer is made.

1. Prostration. Rigdzin Jigme Lingpa paints a picture of a crystal-clear pool. Its immaculate surface reflects the unclouded autumn moon so perfectly that it looks as if it is actually bathing in the water. There on the shore beside the pool, a ravishing peacock is dancing. And the water throws back its image so clearly that it is hard to tell which is the bird and which is the reflection. With the same clarity, one emanates literally thousands of youthful bodies, as many as the grains of dust in the entire world—all so clear that one would lose one's mind trying to distinguish them from one's own form. And thus one makes prostrations with all of them, in a perfect union of thought, word, and deed.

2. Offering. Bodhisattvas give in charity all the material wealth that they possess. And through ridding themselves of the seven kinds of attachment[124] and by embracing four special qualities,[125] they perfectly accomplish the six paramitas, from generosity onward. In the present context, that of a beginner, it is important to practice generosity by making material offerings, and this should be done in a manner accompanied by four special qualities and three pure elements.[126] The practitioner also imagines immense, boundless clouds of offerings, unfathomable and quite beyond anything that could exist on the material plane. As the verses of the *Ratnolka-sutra* say:

> Flowers everywhere and canopies of flowers,
> Flowers radiating myriads of beams
> Of every kind and color I spread out
> And offer to the Buddhas and their bodhisattva children.
>
> The single blossom held here in my hand
> And all the myriads that I now imagine,
> These I offer to a single Buddha,
> And just as all to him, now all to all the Buddhas,
> To match the concentration of the holy sage.

And as the root text figuratively says, in making offering to all the Buddhas, the practitioner competes with the inconceivable offerings emanated by the sublime Bodhisattva Samantabhadra.

3. Confession. The nonvirtuous actions performed due to the outrageous "impudence" of the faculty of speech*—indeed, all seven negativities of word and deed, together with all sins and evil propensities committed in the past and which have not yet come to fruition—are for the moment held in check by the results of virtue, manifesting in this present human existence. It is as if they have been "alarmed and chased away"—which is a way of saying that in the immediate term, the inescapable result of these evils, namely, the torments of the lower realms, has been temporarily suspended. This, however, does not mean that the effect of these evils has been annihilated. On the contrary, their karmic traces are concealed in the alaya, the thick envelope of ignorance that enshrouds ultimate reality and is the root of samsaric existence.† Even so, everything that is lurking there may be exposed and purified through confession fortified with the brilliant sunlight of the four strengths: remorse for past evil, firm resolution to abstain from evil in the future, the antidote (to exert oneself in virtue), and the support, which is the taking of refuge in the Three Jewels and the generation of bodhichitta in their presence.[127]

4. Rejoicing. Rejoicing is the only method whereby one can instantaneously appropriate all the good qualities and wholesome actions of the Buddhas, Bodhisattvas, Shravakas, Pratyekabuddhas, and ordinary beings—"stealing it like a robber!" It is accomplished by a single perfect thought without having to exhaust oneself in the accumulation of merit.[128]

5. The request for teachings. In samsara—rhetorically described as endless—beings abandon themselves to wrongful actions, and their wickedness is not restrained by antidotes. They are not by nature inclined to harmony but are corrupt and deceitful. When it comes to the practice of generosity for the Dharma's sake, they are hard like walls of steel. Through habit, they are apt to evil, and their inclination to vice is as

---

* "The mouth is the door and source of all evil deeds." [YG II, 105, 4]

† Ready, in other words, to fructify when the appropriate circumstances present themselves.

strong as adamant. Destitute of the wish to free themselves from samsara, their minds are as though parched and desiccated. They are barren land incapable of bringing forth a harvest of virtue. Apart from the sacred Dharma, nothing has power enough to tame them. With this in mind, the disciples supplicate the Buddhas and Bodhisattvas to turn the wheel of the Teachings in ways attuned to the different aptitudes of beings. Indeed, the wheel of Dharma has three levels.[129] These are the three trainings set forth in the Tripitaka with its expedient and ultimate teachings, which are remedies for the three poisons. Moreover, the sharp spokes of the Dharma wheel sever the conception of "I" and "mine" (the two kinds of obscurations and their accompanying tendencies) and fix practitioners "to the rim" of high rebirth and the ultimate excellence of enlightenment—so that they cannot fall off!

6. *The supplication that the enlightened beings should not pass into nirvana.* If it were to happen that the Buddhas and their bodhisattva children dwelling in the infinite universes of the ten directions withdrew into nirvana, we would be cut off from the means to liberation. We would be unable to distinguish virtue from non-virtue and to identify the authentic path. We would be sunk in misery, the result of our evil actions, and we would never be able to free ourselves from it. With this understanding, a plea is made that the Buddhas might live, that their lotus feet might remain upon the diamond throne for an ocean of kalpas, and that they might not pass into nirvana. To support this supplication, the request is made accompanied by an offering of everything one possesses, including all one's merit and even one's body.

7. *Dedication of merit.* Conditioned as they are by the agent's belief in the real existence of the person and phenomena, actions aiming at samsaric happiness are productive of merit alone. But since they are not endowed with extraordinary means and wisdom, the fruit of these good actions is unstable and may be wasted through the effects of anger and so forth. And even if it is not destroyed in this way, it will give no more than a single samsaric birth in the higher realms of gods and human beings. Here it will be exhausted by the fact of being experienced, so that in the following existence one will inevitably fall into unavoidable suffering and grief. Bearing this in mind, we should consider all phenomena as illusory. And we should dedicate, in a way free from duality,

all our positive actions, the roots of merit, accumulated in the past, present, and future, for the sake of the enlightenment of all beings. This kind of dedication acts like an alchemical process, transmuting base metal into gold. With such an aspiration, our merit will convey us to enlightenment. This is an extraordinary teaching, expressive of the skillful means of the enlightened ones, and is unknown outside the Buddhadharma.[130]

In the *Sagaramati-paripriccha-sutra* it is said:

> As when a drop of water falls into the sea,
> And will not dry until the sea itself runs dry,
> So merit pledged to gain enlightenment
> Is not consumed till buddhahood is gained.

OFFERING ONESELF IN SERVICE

To be content with what you have is like drinking an elixir that annihilates the thirst of covetousness. If you have contentment, then even if you are not wealthy enough to make extensive offerings, you can still use the little offering you have as a support and offer all those things that are unowned by anyone.* You can also imagine things and offer those. In this way you will accumulate merit as if you were offering your very own wealth. On the other hand, if you are not content with bare necessities and are constantly striving to increase your possessions; and if you are tight-fisted and unable to make offerings from what you own, then no matter how elaborate your words of imagined oblation may be ("everything unclaimed in the realms of gods, nagas, and humans, etc."), it will be nothing but empty talk. Your offering will be without substance and will amount to lying. Apprehensive of the fact that you could easily find yourself doing this, you should offer even your own body as the "seat" or servant for those to whom the offerings are made. It is very important to be constant and diligent in the offering of your body to the Buddhas and Bodhisattvas. The reason for this is that people who really do pledge themselves to the service of the Three Jewels will be sheltered in the cool shade of their compassion, as though sheltered from the hot sun beneath a leafy tree covered with flowers.

* See *The Way of the Bodhisattva*, II, 2–7.

People who are committed to the Three Jewels will be shielded from suffering and will live prosperously. At death they will be led to pure lands by Buddhas and Bodhisattvas. And if, because of bad karma and loose discipline, they must confront the cruel messengers of Yama, the memory of the Three Jewels will free them from fear and the terrible visions will melt away. This shows how meaningful such a commitment is.

CONCLUSION

Ignorance of the ultimate truth and of the workings of karma, the principle of cause and effect, results in a powerful inclination to negativity and the obscuring of the mind. Nevertheless, the mind may be purified and the welfare of others achieved. Merit may be accumulated and mental obscurations removed. When a crystal is cleaned, its surface becomes bright and able to reflect objects. In the same way, the mind, though thick and murky now through its lack of merit, can be purified. Clear and limpid, it is able to hold within it the image of the peerless vow of bodhichitta—which is taken externally through the symbolic gesture of the ritual.

In addition to being in the grip of our own negativities, we are also exposed to the evil demon of desire and his lotus-garlanded consort, whose heads are adorned with a crown of five flowers. When they throw these flowers at those who labor on the path of liberation, they are like soft but penetrating darts and are the source of every obstacle. The first arrow is the bringer of arrogance: pride in spiritual and temporal affairs. The second sows confusion about what actions are to be adopted and forsaken. The third leads one astray with wrong views. The fourth induces forgetfulness and saps the strength of awareness. And the fifth brings distraction through the eight worldly concerns. These demons shoot their arrows at spiritual practitioners, aiming at whichever emotion is the most developed, aggravating it so that it grows exceedingly strong. Would-be practitioners are thus overwhelmed and fall into the abyss of countless faults from which it is difficult to escape. There they remain, cut off from liberation and the higher realms. Such people are like chronic invalids, tormented by every kind of sickness, the result of the six root emotions and their twenty subsidiaries.[131] However efficient ordinary drugs may be in healing merely physical ills, they are powerless to cure such plagues as these. Physical medicine is the remedy only for the four hundred and four corporeal ailments* arising from the imbalance of the elements. They are, however, unable to eradicate the cause of the imbalance itself. This can be remedied only by the supreme physician himself, the Buddha, the Blessed One. Refuge in him leads to liberation in the state beyond suffering. When he is requested by prayers of strong devotion, the Buddha comes to the place where the bodhichitta vow is taken. Indeed, the Buddha, the Supreme Teacher, holds the infinity of beings constantly in his unobscured sight, and he considers them with the wisdom of knowledge and compassion that is free from attachment and impediment, in other words, the emotional and cognitive veils. He reigns supreme, surrounded by the assembly of Bodhisattvas, beings who have attained the Mahayana level of Nonreturner.[132] He is like the moon amid a host of stars, or like Mount Meru encircled by ranges of lesser peaks. Bright and resplendent, his Body, Speech, and Mind are utterly majestic, and in him there is nothing that jars or is discordant. With fervent devotion, the aspirants for the vow should pray to him and take him as a witness.

The ritual of the bodhisattva vow

Generally speaking, according to the tradition of Vast Activities of Asanga, vows of bodhichitta in aspiration and action are taken separately in two different ceremonies. In the tradition of the Profound View of Nagarjuna, as explained by the great master Krishnapa in his commentary on the difficult points of the *Bodhicharyavatara*, it is also possible (though not necessary) to distinguish two rituals for the taking of the vow, according to the capacity of the individual concerned. If one takes only the vow of aspiration bodhichitta, one should recite thrice the first two lines of stanzas 23 and 24 of the third chapter of the *Bodhicharyavatara*. For the vow of bodhichitta in action, the third and fourth lines of the same stanzas should be recited.

In either case, as pointed out in the *Seventy Stanzas on Refuge*, no vow

---

* A way of categorizing diseases according to the four medicine tantras.

can ever be taken without first going for refuge. All vows, from those of Pratimoksha onward, must of necessity be preceded by refuge, which itself acts as their foundation. Indeed, before taking the vow of bodhichitta, one must first take refuge three times according to the extraordinary way of the Mahayana and thus create the proper basis for the commitment.

According to the *Treasury of Precious Qualities*, the vows of bodhichitta in aspiration and action are taken together. If the vow is taken in the presence of a teacher, the latter will normally prepare the mind of the disciple in the way previously explained. Those who do not take the vow from a teacher must be sure to prepare themselves properly. The aspirants should make prostrations and offer a mandala. Then, kneeling and with hands joined, they call three times upon all the Buddhas dwelling in the ten directions, all the great beings, the Bodhisattvas on the tenth ground, and all the great vajra-holding masters to be their witnesses. The power of this prayer arouses their great compassion. Directed at all beings, perceived to be illusory, their compassion is beyond all conceptuality, for it arises from their sustained state of meditative evenness in the expanse of dharmadhatu. The aspirants then recite the formula saying that just as the Buddhas and Bodhisattvas cultivated bodhichitta for the sake of others and undertook the practice by training successively in the six paramitas (all of which are implied in the three trainings and the four ways of attracting disciples), in the same way they too will enter and embrace the practice. This is by way of a general commitment; the promise is made more specifically as follows.

Shravakas, Pratyekabuddhas, and Arhats have, through the realization of the absence of personal self, put an end to the torment caused by the emotional obscurations that obstruct liberation. But the cognitive obscurations that veil omniscience remain for them, for their realization is incomplete and has not penetrated to the no-self of phenomena. This is why they are said to "cling to the taste of sense objects." In other words, they discriminate between samsara and nirvana, avoiding the one and preferring the other, and are unable to counteract and eradicate such clinging. Would-be Bodhisattvas therefore reflect that they will also liberate the Arhats, Shravakas, and Pratyekabuddhas from the cognitive obscurations that still confine them. They consider too that they will liberate all beings, beginning with those on the most ordinary level, completely enmeshed in the two kinds of obscurations and so on, up to the beings dwelling on the ten sublime grounds of the path of learning and who are thus still not free from all obscurations. This includes all those who are outside the Dharma (even the god Brahma himself), who adhere to false views or who do not subscribe to any tenets at all. Finally, they reflect that they will liberate all the beings in the lower realms, tormented by ceaseless and unbearable suffering. They will relieve them utterly—temporarily speaking in the higher realms of samsara, and ultimately on the level of supreme liberation. In short, aspiring Bodhisattvas promise from the core of their being to bring all beings to the great citadel of nirvana, the primordial wisdom that transcends the two extremes of existence and peace. And in this context, "all beings" means everything that possesses animate life. This includes ordinary beings who, trapped by their karma in the ever-grinding mill wheel of the twelve interdependent links, have a direct experience of suffering. And it embraces even the Bodhisattvas on the tenth ground, who, although they no longer wander in samsara through the effect of karma, have not yet dissolved in the ultimate expanse their perception of mere appearance,* the result of habitual tendencies with regard to phenomena arising through interdependence.

As for the text of the ritual that combines the vows of bodhichitta in aspiration and action, Jigme Lingpa says that it should be drawn from the tradition of the master Nagarjuna and his spiritual heir Aryadeva. In this way, he says that the text should be based on any vow-giving formula, whether detailed or abridged, as recorded in the scriptures of the Mahayana Madhyamika tradition. It is also possible to use the text given in *Treasury of Precious Qualities*, reciting it three times.

From the moment of taking the vows of bodhichitta in aspiration and action, and for as long as one keeps them, the commitment should be consistently renewed (using the formula taken from the *Bodhicharyavatara*)[133] three times during the day and three times during the night. This, however, should not be done out of a sense of duty, like paying a

---

* *gnyis snang*, a perception that implies not a clinging to external phenomena and the perceiving mind as really existent, but a continued tendency to experience these two poles as separate, the one observing the other.

tax. It should involve the genuine cultivation of the bodhichitta attitude and a sincere training in it.

As the sutra says:

> All depends upon conditions,
> Specifically upon the keenness of your will.

Everything arises from causes and conditions, and above all it is one's inner aspiration that renders acts of thought, word, and deed virtuous or otherwise. In this particular circumstance, when the vows of the two bodhichittas are pronounced together thrice, at the first recitation, the vow of aspiration is firmly taken; at the second recitation, the vow of bodhichitta in action is taken; and with the third recitation, the vows of the two bodhichittas are taken in unison. This explanation reflects the unsurpassable teaching of the master Sagaramegha.

The conclusion of the ritual: the uplifting of one's own and others' minds

In the course of our previous lives, when we occupied the position of fathers or mothers, when we were exalted sages or even Brahma, we failed to consider our own true benefit, still less that of other beings.* Not even in our dreams did we conceive of such a positive and sublime thought, more precious and valuable than the most exquisite jewel. It is a thought that bestows a peculiar significance on our human existence, rendering it inconceivably precious. This is the meaning of the parable of the prince who, losing his royal position, wanders among the meanest and most despised classes of society and adopts their ways. Later, when he is recognized as a prince, he immediately assumes the royal status of his father's house. In just the same way, having recognized the nature of one's mind as being of the dharmakaya lineage—in other words, that it is the seed of the Tathagatas†—and having embarked upon the practices that lead to the activities of buddhahood, one becomes instantaneously

---

* See *The Way of the Bodhisattva*, I, 23–24.
† *de bzhin gshegs pa'i rigs*, the luminous nature of the mind, the tathagatagarbha, as expounded in the sutras of the third turning of the Dharma wheel.

the child of the Buddhas. One is crowned and receives the title of Bodhisattva and is fit to reign in the kingdom of the Mahayana.

Those who enjoy lordship in the three levels of existence (above, below, or upon the earth)—the kings of the celestial realm called Mastery over Magical Creations of Others, Brahma and the other gods, and all the other heavenly lords, the nagas, and the powerful rulers of the human world—all of them fondly think of themselves as supreme in the universe. And even princelings and ministers looked up to as rich and influential regard themselves, in their conceited ignorance, as great. But in samsara, there is nothing and no one inherently high or low. Greatness in samsara is but a fitful, transient dream of pleasure. And yet it is enough to make men highly regarded and arrogant. No matter how often such status has been experienced, it is utterly without substance. But on the day that the bodhisattva vow is taken, one assumes the name and receives dominion of the realm of the Mahayana. One becomes the protector of beings. Thus one can invite every being to a banquet of happiness and fulfill them totally. Such is one's altruism that it never forgets or fails to bring them benefit. It is in this spirit that one can uplift the minds of others, calling upon them, even the gods and other nonhuman beings, to come and share in this "flower garland" of happiness.*

True Bodhisattvas possess such tremendous merit that, on the temporary level, they are free from the scourge of untimely death. When they attain the sublime grounds, they are beyond birth and death altogether in the ordinary sense and ultimately accomplish nonabiding nirvana utterly transcending the two extremes of existence and peace. They possess the nectar of immortality that renders powerless the demon Lord of Death. By virtue of their treasure of the two accumulations of wisdom and merit, they dispose of an inexhaustible fund of material wealth. Thus they are wishing-jewels to dispel the hunger and poverty of all. They are the supreme remedy that soothes away the afflictive emotions and the ills that are their fruit. They are the locus of happiness and benefit for beings, the place of repose for those who wander wearily the pathways of existence, worn out by sorrow and longing for happiness. In this spirit, the disciple makes the resolve: "From now and until samsara is emptied, I will be the ground and basis for the sustenance of beings."

* See The Way of the Bodhisattva, III, 34.

CHAPTER 9

The Precepts of Bodhichitta in Aspiration and Action

THE BODHISATTVA COMMITMENT

When people have an enthusiasm for some worldly assignment, they often commit themselves to it rashly without considering the difficulties involved or even whether the activities in question are good or bad. But when it turns out that the goal is hard to accomplish, the worst that can happen is that they give up their resolve and are a source of disappointment to others. The situation is much more serious when it comes to our commitment to the teachings of the Mahayana. For when we abandon our pledge to act according to the profound and utterly reliable precepts that in their wisdom the Buddhas and Bodhisattvas have studied, pondered, and meditated upon for innumerable measureless kalpas, we are in effect turning our backs on all living beings and betraying them. And because of this, we will pass our future lives wandering endlessly in the realms of sorrow. It is written in the *Bodhicharyavatara*:

> How can I expect a happy destiny
> If from my heart I summon
> Wandering beings to the highest bliss
> But then deceive and fail them?
> (IV, 6)

It is hardly necessary to discuss so great a fault. In sum, if the undoing of a single being's happiness, whether through killing or the theft of property, leads to a fall from the states of happiness into the lower realms, it stands to reason that we must not injure even a single being in the slightest way.

Of course, it could be argued that unlike the vows of Pratimoksha, the vows of bodhichitta can always be repaired. Even so, a person who oscillates between a determined attitude of bodhichitta and serious downfalls will for a long time be barred from the higher levels of the aspirational practice,* to say nothing of the level of the Perfect Joy† and the other bodhisattva grounds.‡ The precepts of conduct must be kept as instinctively as one protects one's eyes. A person who knowingly abandons them is like a madman destroying himself.

The causes of falling from bodhichitta are many.[134] Of these, the root cause is defiled emotion, which should therefore become for us an object of intense resentment.

In this connection, consider the following. Ordinary people react with a strong sense of pride and indignation at even the slightest injury, as when someone does something to reduce their influence or property. And in a real conflict, such people will staunchly resist the attacks of their enemies, refusing to back down until they have got what they want. It is the same when we are training on the path. In the struggle against the great horde of our defilements, foes from beginningless time, our enemies that have never done us any good nor even been neutral toward us, we too must retaliate with antidotes. In terms of the three trainings, we may say that discipline inculcates a sense of disgust for defilements, concentration will in turn suppress them, while wisdom will eradicate them totally. We should bear a bitter grudge against our defilements and never overlook any means to destroy them. Who indeed would ever think of abandoning the observance of the precepts before the sublime level has been attained?[135] The *Bodhicharyavatara* says:

> Those who wish to keep a rule of life
> Must guard their minds in perfect self-possession.
> Without this guard upon the mind,
> No discipline can ever be maintained.
> (V, 1)

---

* *mos spyod kyi sa*, the paths of accumulation and joining.
† *rab dga'*, the first bodhisattva ground, corresponding to the path of seeing.
‡ See *The Way of the Bodhisattva*, IV, 11.

In our present situation, habitual deluded perception is extremely tenacious. We are tightly bound by our clinging to self and are thus locked in the prison of defiled emotion. We have scarcely any idea what the enormous task of abandoning our own defilement involves. How could we have promised so rashly to free beings from *their* defilements and evil habits and establish them in the state of buddhahood? This powerfully underlines the fact that in order to free others from their defilements, we must first possess the means to remove our own. The first of these prerequisites is *careful attention:** the earnest and meticulous implementation of the rules of conduct concerning what behavior is to be adopted or repudiated. Then there is *mindfulness,*† whereby the crucial points of the training are never forgotten. Finally, there is *vigilant introspection,*‡ which keeps a close watch over our every action, whether of thought, word, or deed. If the mind has these three qualities, it is like well-tilled soil. Not only can the seed of bodhichitta be planted there, but the shoots of the extraordinary attitude of universal responsibility can be cultivated easily. It is therefore important to realize the immense significance of these three factors.

Nevertheless, simply maintaining bodhichitta and its connected trainings, so that they do not decline, is not in itself sufficient. Jigme Lingpa requests us to follow a spiritual friend with great earnestness and to hear and reflect upon his or her teachings. He exhorts us to implement all the trainings of the Mahayana, accumulating wisdom and merit, purifying downfalls and obstructions, and enhancing our bodhichitta, its attendant trainings, and all favorable conditions.

THE PRECEPTS CONCERNING WHAT IS TO BE AVOIDED

In the scriptures generally, it will be found that a total of twenty bodhichitta downfalls is mentioned. The *Akashagarbha-sutra* gives eighteen, and to these a further one is added in the *Mahaguhyaupayakaushalya-sutra* and another in the *Ratnakuta.*[136]

* *bag yod.*
† *dran pa.*
‡ *shes bzhin.*

Five actions, beginning with the confiscation of religious property dedicated to the Three Jewels, are the downfalls of a king.[137] Five actions, beginning with the destruction of towns and regions, are the downfalls of a minister.[138] In addition to these ten are eight downfalls associated with ordinary people,[139] such as giving teachings on the doctrine of emptiness to those whose minds are unprepared.

As we have just said, to these eighteen,[140] two further downfalls are to be added. These are the abandoning of aspiration bodhichitta by embracing the attitude of the Shravakas and Pratyekabuddhas (this is mentioned in the *Mahaguhyaupayakaushalya-sutra*) and the relinquishing of bodhichitta in action by allowing one's vows of generosity and so forth to decline (see the *Ratnakuta*). This comes to a total of twenty downfalls, all of which are to be utterly repudiated.[141]

Repairing faults[142]

Generally speaking, any negative action, including those committed in dreams (being the result of the propensities generated in the waking state), should be confessed without delay by practicing the *Triskandha-nama-mahayana-sutra*, consisting of prostration, confession, and dedication. It is hardly necessary to add that faults and downfalls perpetrated while awake should also be confessed in the same way.

Faults against bodhichitta may be divided into three categories. The first is to turn away from even a single being. This results in the complete loss of the bodhichitta of aspiration—the very basis of all bodhisattva trainings and qualities. The second involves the commission of any of the specific root downfalls that go contrary to the training. The third is the complete loss of bodhichitta, by consciously giving back the vows.[143]

Downfalls should be confessed as follows. The day and night are each divided into three time periods. If, for instance, a fault is committed in the first morning period, it must be confessed at the latest in the second period, and so forth. If the fault is left unconfessed beyond the given time limit, it is regarded as "having exceeded the limit" and cannot be repaired at a later stage merely by confession. In this case, the fault must be confessed with a strong spirit of repentance and firm purpose of amendment. Then the vow must be taken again according to the prescribed ritual.

People of basic faculties should make their confession in the presence of ten upholders (or at least one) of the Mahayana vows. For individuals of moderate faculties, the prescribed procedure is as follows. Rising before dawn, they should wash and make themselves meticulously clean. They should then kneel down facing the east and invoke in front of them the presence of the Bodhisattva Akashagarbha or their yidam deity and, reciting the extraordinary seven-branch prayer, they should make their confession. In this way, they repair their downfall. Persons of superior capacity[144] should confess their faults in the way described in the *Mahamoksha-sutra*:

> Those, repenting, who would purify themselves
> Should sit up straight and watch the "perfect purity."
> This perfect purity they watch with perfect purity,
> And seeing it, are utterly set free—
> Thus supreme repentance and the highest cleansing.[145]

THE PRECEPTS TO BE IMPLEMENTED

The four precepts of aspiration bodhichitta

The first precept: taking suffering and giving happiness

It is important to be grounded in the sublime and courageous practice of giving and taking.* Using the rhythm of your breath, as you exhale, imagine that all your happiness, knowledge, and good qualities are given away to others so that they come to perfect development and fulfillment in them. Then, summoning all your strength, generate the thought that you yourself, alone, will patiently take their sorrows upon yourself. Imagine that others are set free from their pain and defects, and imagine that these same sufferings and faults are loaded into yourself, borne on the stream of your inhalation. Pray without ceasing that beings might

---

* *gtong len.*

be forever free from pain and that they might never lose their happiness until they attain enlightenment.

The second precept: the seven-point causal sequence giving birth to the attitude of bodhichitta

Train your mind in the perfect attitude of the four boundless qualities, and in the equalization and exchange of self and other.[146] This means remembering the goodness that all beings have shown you, who from beginningless time have repeatedly been your parents and done the very best for you. The ensuing wish to repay their kindness gives rise to love. From love springs compassion, and this in turn gives birth to bodhichitta. This is the teaching of the authentic scriptures of the Mahayana pitakas and was expounded in a causal sequence by Lord Atisha, the master from Bengal, in his seven-point instruction. This sequence is: first, the acknowledgment that all beings have been one's mother; second, the remembrance of their kindness; third, a sense of gratitude toward them and a desire to repay their kindness; fourth, the experience of loving warmth toward them; fifth, the feeling of tender compassion toward them; sixth, the extraordinary attitude of universal responsibility; and seventh, the unsurpassable result, which is the attitude of bodhichitta.

1. *To recognize that all beings have been one's mother.* There is not a single living being who has not, at one time or another, been joined to us in the relationship of mother and child. As the master Nagarjuna has said:

> Were I to make a pill of mud just berry-sized,
> For every mother who has given me birth,
> The earth itself indeed would not suffice.

2. *To reflect on the kindness of all mother sentient beings.* As soon as a baby is born, its mother unhesitatingly takes it on her knees—this unclean worm, this evil-looking, implike creature—and making a basin, so to speak, of her own lap, she gently wipes away the baby's dirt with her own hands, afraid that a cloth would be too coarse. The infant is unable to take solid food and so she feeds it with her own milk, giving it her

body's warmth and doing all that she can to make the child comfortable and happy. Her greatest terror is the death of her child, a fear closely followed by that of sickness. And she is constantly anxious that the child might be hungry, thirsty, or cold. She does everything to protect her baby from harm, preferring to die herself than that her child might fall ill. For her child's sake, she will become angrily protective and will bear all difficulties, putting up with heat and cold and every kind of insult. To disregard the kindness of one's mother is thus the worst, the most shocking, and the most degenerate behavior imaginable. It is therefore said that to carry on one's back the whole universe, weighed down with Mount Meru and the peaks of iron that surround the great ocean, is nothing compared with the load of suffering that will result from the failure to repay the kindness of one's mother. Such suffering is counted as endless and inexhaustible as if one's whole body were engulfed in virulent poison. It is said in the *Vinayavibhanga*:

> The earth and seas and mountains,
> Their weight for me is light.
> That I did not repay her good,
> Is now my heavy load.

Thus we should reflect that all sentient beings without exception have been our mothers many times. They have helped us and shown us intense kindness in ways that no other person would. Reflecting on this again and again, we should acknowledge the fact that every single being we meet has been kind to us.

3. *To have a sense of gratitude.* We should therefore endeavor to help others in every way we can, thinking constantly how we might be of service to them in order to repay the great goodness they have shown to us.

4. *To generate feelings of warmth.* By accustoming ourselves to this way of thinking, we will stop reacting angrily when we come across unpleasant and hostile people. On the contrary, we will feel sincere love for them, wishing them to be happy and feeling the affection for them that a mother has for her child.

5. *To have tender compassion.* From such a feeling of love a boundless

sense of compassion will naturally arise. And on seeing the objects of our love acting in negative ways that will lead them into suffering, we will have an unbearable longing to free them. At the same time, when we see that others are prosperous and happy, we ourselves will have a joy greater than if the good fortune were happening to ourselves. We will perceive the essential equality of beings and approach them with an impartiality that annihilates the distinctions between those that are close and those that are distant, uprooting favoritism and dislike accordingly. It is thus that the four boundless attitudes develop and intensify.

6. *To gain the extraordinary attitude.* In this way, as our minds become imbued with these four boundless attitudes, we will find that others have become dear to us and the focus of our compassion; and we will experience a deep sense that we ourselves are responsible for establishing them in a state of permanent happiness and freedom.

7. *The unsurpassable fruit.* People who have this attitude and act accordingly, who reflect that all beings have been their mothers and feel great gratitude to them, will naturally be endowed with the seven sublime riches of faith and so forth. They will gain the unparalleled fruit, which is to aspire to enlightenment for the sake of others.

The third precept: the four black and four white factors

The mind that aspires to enlightenment is characterized by the excellent attitude of not rejecting anyone. It shines its light impartially on all, like the bright moon of autumn. Four black factors militate against this attitude, however, and are able to obscure it worse than the face of Rahu.[147] Antidotes must be used to drive them far away. These four factors are as follows:

1. To mislead and deceive those who are worthy objects of homage—teachers, spiritual masters, abbots and monks, and all who possess true spiritual qualities.

2. To place doubt and anxiety in the minds of people accumulating "merit tending to happiness" or who have entered any of the three vehicles of the Dharma and are accumulating "merit tending to liberation." One does this when, for example, one tells them that they have

not received the vows authentically or that the teachings they are practicing are bogus and inauthentic.

3. To criticize superior beings openly and to denigrate those who have truly generated the attitude of bodhichitta, spreading rumors behind their backs.

4. To deceive others by hiding one's faults and laying claim to qualities one does not possess, and also to cheat others through any kind of sharp practice.

The presence of any of these four factors will lead to the loss of aspiration bodhichitta. If one fails to confess the fault with a powerful sense of remorse, if the antidotes are not applied, whether at the beginning, the middle, or the end of the period in which the fault occurs, and if the time limit for confession is exceeded, bodhichitta is lost.

The best antidotes to the four black factors are the four white factors. These are:

1. Never to lie or intentionally deceive anyone, even at the cost of one's life.
2. To respect and praise all Bodhisattvas as if they were Buddhas.
3. With utter sincerity, to strive in thought and deed for the benefit of beings.
4. To inculcate an attitude of aspiration bodhichitta in those one is able to influence and to lead them wholeheartedly on the stages of the path to perfect enlightenment.

The fourth precept: the four attitudes that strengthen bodhichitta

There are four attitudes of mind that strengthen bodhichitta and protect it from decline. They are set out in the *Samadhiraja-sutra* as follows:

1. To consider as a real Buddha the master of the Mahayana from whom one is receiving the unmistaken teachings on the path.
2. To consider as the path the profound and vast teachings.
3. To consider as one's friends all other Bodhisattvas, who are practicing the Mahayana path and whose views and actions are in harmony with one's own.

4. To approach the infinite multitude of living beings as though each one were one's only child.

All these trainings, beginning with the practice of *tong-len*—giving and taking—and concluding with these four attitudes, constitute the authentic precepts of aspiration bodhichitta, as distilled from the teachings of the Mahayana texts.

The precepts of bodhichitta in action

A brief explanation of the paramitas

The precepts to be observed by those who have taken the vow of bodhichitta in action[148] comprise the six paramitas, or transcendent perfections.[149] The first five—generosity, discipline, patience, diligence, and concentration—are related to the sublime accumulation of merit, while the sixth paramita corresponds to the great accumulation of wisdom.[150] Aside from these two accumulations of wisdom and method united, there is no other means of attaining buddhahood. In addition to the usual six paramitas, a further four may be added.[151] These are: (7) skillful means, which is the dedication of generosity and so forth to the great enlightenment of all beings (on account of which the merit generated becomes inexhaustible); (8) strength, which by overcoming all adverse conditions transforms merit into enlightenment; (9) aspiration, whereby the practitioner is always eager to engage in virtue and on account of which the qualities of generosity and the other paramitas will always arise in subsequent lives; and (10) primordial wisdom, wherewith all the paramitas are practiced, bringing others to spiritual maturity. These therefore are the ten transcendent perfections possessed by all true Bodhisattvas.

A CATEGORIZATION OF BODHISATTVAS ACCORDING
TO THEIR STRENGTH OF MIND
According to the criterion of courageous determination, there are said to be three kinds of practitioners on the bodhisattva path. First, there are those of basic faculties, who perfect the two accumulations in order

to attain buddhahood for themselves first, so that they might afterward be able to liberate others. Theirs is called "bodhichitta of great aspiration in the manner of a king." It was the way in which the noble Maitreya first generated bodhichitta. Second, there is the bodhichitta generated by those of medium faculties, who wish to free themselves and all beings together simultaneously. This is known as the "bodhichitta of sacred wisdom, in the manner of a ferryman." Finally, there is the bodhichitta generated by those with superior faculties, who wish to establish others in buddhahood before themselves, while they remain on the tenth ground. It is only after all others are saved that they wish to enter the peace of nirvana. This is the unsurpassable way of generating "bodhichitta in the manner of a shepherd." This is the bodhichitta of the Bodhisattvas Manjushri and Avalokiteshvara. The *Ratnakuta* says that Bodhisattvas of basic faculties will reach the goal of the path and attain enlightenment after thirty-three measureless kalpas. They require three measureless kalpas for the paths of accumulation and joining and three for each of the ten grounds. Bodhisattvas of medium capacity need four measureless kalpas for the paths of accumulation and joining, one kalpa for the path of seeing, one for the seven impure grounds, and one for the three pure grounds. They will therefore attain buddhahood after seven measureless kalpas. Bodhisattvas of supreme faculties need one kalpa for the paths of accumulation and joining, one for the seven impure grounds, and one for the three pure grounds. Consequently, they attain nirvana after three measureless kalpas.

The Paramita of Generosity

The nature of generosity is to have no attachment to material wealth and to have a giving, open-handed attitude toward others.[152]

There are three kinds of generosity: the giving of material possessions, the giving of protection from fear, and the giving of the sacred Dharma.

THE GIFT OF MATERIAL THINGS
There are three degrees of material generosity. The first is "ordinary generosity" at a stage when the mind has little strength. "Great generos-

ity" occurs next, when the habit of giving has been acquired. Finally there occurs "peerless generosity," when the training has been perfected. The first kind of giving, ordinary generosity, will involve, according to the strength of one's resolve, the donation of food, clothing, chariot, oxen, and land. Great generosity involves the giving up of things that are extremely dear and precious to oneself, for example, one's beloved son, daughter, wife, or husband.[153] Peerless generosity is the most difficult of all. It involves the giving up of one's limbs and organs, even one's head, in a way that is completely free of attachment, as the king Chandraprabha did.[154]

Those who are only beginning to train in the general activities of the Bodhisattvas—and this is particularly true for the practice of giving—will find themselves much hampered by feelings of niggardliness and will experience difficulty even in making gifts of food. They must train themselves gradually like the man in the story who started out by transferring small objects from one hand to another, with the thought that he was simply *giving*. In the end, he was able to perform feats of great generosity. Likewise, we should start by training ourselves in giving away small things, cooked vegetables, and so forth. Gradually, our possessiveness will be overcome and generosity will increase in strength. And our training should continue until we are able to practice peerless generosity.

THE GIFT OF PROTECTION FROM FEAR

This means to protect the lives of those who are imprisoned or are being punished and tortured. It means to protect wild animals that are being chased by hunters, or cattle and sheep destined for the slaughterhouse, and to help people who are endangered by disease and evil forces. It also means to train one's mind in the aspiration actually to liberate all beings from the endless sufferings of samsara—the source of constant fear—and to bring them to the perfect ease of nirvana.

Beginners should practice generosity according to their true capacity. For the danger is that, if they do not have the ability to give what is difficult to give, and overreach themselves imprudently, they will fall into discouragement and regret, and there will be a great danger that the attitude of the Shravakas and Pratyekabuddhas might gain a foothold in their minds. Therefore, such injudicious acts of giving are to be shunned. Shantideva says in his *Shiksasamuccaya*:

A tree of paradise so lovely to behold—
Its seeds and roots will bear a rich delight.
So do not take them from the ground before their time:
The healing tree of buddhahood is just the same.

Thus, the giving up of one's body and life with a "compassion" that is soiled by attitudes of malevolence or jealousy and so forth is forbidden in the *Shiksasamuccaya*, as we have just seen. Moreover, to practice generosity in a spirit of hostility, jealousy, or boasting, or in a way that injures others—to give away harmful things such as poison or weapons (a knife to a butcher, for example, or alcohol to an alcoholic), or again to distribute wealth to people to whom one is passionately attached—all such generosity is sullied by impure intentions and will only increase negativities. Far from being the practice of the Bodhisattvas, this is something that they would utterly despise. By contrast, the sign of perfect generosity is to abandon all miserliness in one's heart. It means to give up all clinging to possessions: one's house, one's body, one's enjoyments, and one's merits.

THE GIFT OF DHARMA

The supreme gift of Dharma is likewise subdivided into three degrees. The *Arya-Lokadhara-paripriccha-sutra* contains the following admonition: "What is meant by the gift of Dharma? The giving of pen, ink, and books is the small gift of Dharma. To teach the Dharma of the Shravakas and Pratyekabuddhas and to teach the unsurpassable Dharma, according to the capacity of the hearer, is the great gift of Dharma. To bring people to the cultivation of bodhichitta and to teach a Dharma inconceivable like space is the peerless gift of Dharma."

The true gift of Dharma is to impart instruction to others according to their mental capacity. However, it is difficult for people who are on the level of aspirational practice to give teachings in this way, since they are unable to expound the Dharma clearly either in word or meaning. At this stage, one should consider the altruistic attitude as the main practice and endeavor earnestly, with mindfulness and vigilance, in the task of clearing away defiled emotions according to the instructions of the teacher. With love and compassion, one should read aloud the general teachings of the Buddha and in particular the sutras of the Mahayana. Others who hear them will purify the negative actions and obscurations of many past lives. A spirit of altruism will naturally appear in them, and innumerable qualities will arise.[155] Gods and nagas who are drawn to virtue will indeed come and listen to the sound of Dharma and, freed from karma and defiled emotions, will strive to protect the Buddha's teachings. In sum, it is important to pray that all beings become vessels of the Mahayana teachings and strive to attain the unsurpassable goal.

When one's mind is free, untouched by the eight worldly concerns and uncluttered by distraction and busyness, the main thing is to bring benefit to others. One should teach the Dharma to others according to their type, capacity, aspiration, and character, from the principles of karma and continuing through to the Great Perfection.

The Paramita of Discipline

The essence of discipline is the firm decision to refrain from harming others and even from having the idea of doing so. It is a repudiation of all that is contrary to the precepts. The teachings on discipline are expounded under three headings: (1) the avoidance of negative actions of thought, word, and deed; (2) the undertaking of positive actions, such as the six transcendent perfections; and (3) the benefiting of others, either directly through the four ways of attracting disciples or indirectly through the purification of one's own mind in order to be of help to others.

THE DISCIPLINE OF AVOIDING NEGATIVE ACTIONS

The difference between the vows of the Hinayana and Mahayana

Generally speaking, those who enter the lower or higher vehicles are the same in striving to avoid negativities and embrace virtue. The discipline of the Bodhisattvas, however, is distinguished by four special features, which place it on a level superior to that of the pratimoksha discipline of the Hinayana. In the Pratimoksha, one avoids injury to others by avoiding all evil actions and the evil thoughts that produce them. The Bodhisattvas add to this the practice of actively helping beings. As we have said, their discipline comprises the three facets of avoiding evil, embracing virtue, and bringing benefit to others. Moreover, in all seven pratimoksha disciplines, there are seven things to be abandoned: the three negativities of the body and the four of speech. On this level, therefore, stress is laid on physical and verbal actions. By contrast, Bodhisattvas strive to abandon all ten negative actions.

In the context of actions to be abandoned, there is a further distinction separating the pratimoksha from the bodhisattva vows. Having in mind self-interested persons who have taken the vows and who apprehend phenomena as truly existent, the Buddha did not allow (in a pratimoksha context) the seven aforesaid negative actions of body and speech to be perpetrated, even in situations in which others might benefit. The precepts as formulated are not to be transgressed. Bodhisattvas, however, are permitted to disregard them if this would be of benefit to others. In this situation, an examination must be made to see whether three conditions are present. First, the Bodhisattva must know that a given negative action (i.e., one of the seven, physical or verbal) is of direct benefit to others, and, second, that it will be so in future. Finally, the Bodhisattva must be sure that such an action will not obstruct the accumulation of merit but will rather augment it. These three conditions being present, the Bodhisattva is allowed to act in an apparently negative way. This is illustrated in the story of Captain Goodheart, who killed Black Spearman in order to protect him from the full ripening of his actions and thereby perfected the accumulation of merits of eighty thousand kalpas.* Then there was Tararamana, the son of the Brahmin, who practiced chastity in the forest for forty-two thousand years. One day, he went to a village to beg for alms and was seen by the daughter of a merchant, who fell violently in love with him. She became so infatuated that she was ready to kill herself. In order to prevent this, the ascetic relinquished his vow of chastity and in this way accumulated the merit of eighty thousand kalpas. Other stories can be found that

* See *The Words of My Perfect Teacher*, pp. 125 ff.

give similar examples of stealing and so forth. In the case of the four negative actions of speech, if those actions are truly meaningful, the Bodhisattva is allowed to perform them. They may have the appearance of faults, but they are in fact virtues. However, given that it is the intention that creates the powerful effect of an action, it stands to reason that the three negative actions of mind are not permitted to anyone under any circumstances.[156]

Therefore, within the context of the Mahayana, the seven negative actions of body and speech are (under certain circumstances) permitted. It is said in the teachings, however, that in the case of someone new to the bodhisattva commitment, who is still involved in his or her own concerns and desire for happiness, and who gives up the precepts because they are difficult to keep and not through any intention to bring direct or indirect benefit to others, the perpetration of all such actions is simply a downfall.

Avoiding negativity according to the Mahayana

Thus, for the beginner on the bodhisattva path, the first task is to discipline the mind. The most important thing is to train oneself in such a way that qualities like renunciation and faith constantly increase. Beginners must train to bring their minds under control, progressing steadily day by day and month by month. Indeed, if at the outset, when the mind has not yet been purified by the discipline of avoiding negative behavior, too much emphasis is placed on the other two aspects of the bodhisattva discipline (namely, undertaking positive actions and bringing benefit to others), many hindrances will occur that impede progress in the three trainings, the path to buddhahood.

A Bodhisattva who has embraced the monastic life is superior to a Bodhisattva who is a householder.[157] The *Sutralankara* says:

> Bodhisattvas who embrace monastic life
> Are boundless in the qualities they have.
> Compared with layfolk who uphold the vow of bodhichitta,
> The ordained are declared to be supreme.

The Mahayana sutras do not say, however, that *all* Bodhisattvas must follow a discipline based exclusively on the pratimoksha ritual. For it is said that an extraordinary bodhisattva discipline is also open to gods, nagas, and other nonhuman beings.

In the case of people who have previously trained in the two accumulations and have a powerfully determined mind able to assimilate the profound and vast teachings, it does not matter whether they are ordained or layfolk. The most important factor is intention. This is illustrated by the story of Indrabodhi, the king of Oddiyana, who took all three vows in a single instant simply by receiving an empowerment.[158]

Lay practitioners who uphold any of the *upasaka* vows (as will be explained in due course) or the twenty-four-hour discipline of upavasa, whether on a temporary or lifetime basis, and who in addition constantly maintain the twofold bodhichitta of aspiration and action, are known as bodhisattva upasakas. Ordained people, who keep the vows of bhikshu or *bhikshuni, shramanera* or *shramanerika,* or *shiksamana* (female novice in training for full ordination),* and who in addition have bodhichitta in aspiration and action, are considered to uphold the bodhisattva discipline of avoiding negativities.

The levels of ordination
The precepts of laypeople
There are two kinds of lay upasaka: the so-called complete upasaka and the upasaka of pure conduct. If one renounces a single negative action out of the four (killing, for example), one is said to be "keeping a single precept." If then one vows not to steal, one is said to be "keeping a few precepts" or having "a part" (of the ordination). If in addition one vows not to lie, one is said to be "keeping a major part of the precepts." If again one formally renounces sexual misconduct, one is said to be keeping "three and a half" vows. The expression "three and a half" is explained by the fact that if sexual misconduct alone is renounced, the vow is said to be only half fulfilled, as distinct from its full observance, which implies complete abstinence. Finally, if, in addition to the three and a half vows just mentioned, one renounces alcohol, one is said to be a "complete upasaka,"† given that without refraining from alcohol it

---

* In Tibetan these ordinations are *dge slong* (*bhikshu*), *dge slong ma* (*bhikshuni*), *dge tshul* (*shramanera*), *dge tshul ma* (*shramanerika*), and *dge slob ma* (*shiksamana*).
† *yongs rdzogs dge bsnyen.*

is impossible to observe the other commitments perfectly. The upasaka of pure conduct* is one who has renounced all four root downfalls, namely, killing, stealing, lying, and all sexual activity, together with the consumption of alcohol.

Laypeople who are practicing the twenty-four-hour upavasa discipline are obliged to observe nine of the ten precepts of the shramanera ordination. They renounce all but the use of gold and silver, which they are allowed to accept as a means of sustaining their families. Their discipline is, however, commonly referred to as the eight-branch discipline, for all kinds of dancing and the wearing of ornaments are counted as a single, minor fault for them. All this is explained in the *Yogacharabhumi-shastra* of Asanga. Those who maintain this discipline every day without a time limit, in other words, for the rest of their lives,† are described as upasakas "after the manner of Chandragomin."

The monastic precepts[159]

The precepts of shramaneras[160] · Those who have received the shramanera ordination are bound to abstain from four root faults. They vow not to perpetrate the act of killing a human being or human embryo. They vow not to steal the property of another. They vow not to indulge in sexual intercourse through any of the three openings. Finally, they vow not to lie to someone who understands speech, who knows what is being talked about, who is in a normal state of consciousness, and who is not a hermaphrodite or without sexual differentiation.[161] If any of these four root faults is committed in such a way that the four fundamental elements of basis, intention, act, and result‡ are all present, the ordained state of shramanera is torn asunder. Whether the ordination can be repaired depends on whether there is any intention to conceal the act. The same applies here as in the case of fully ordained monks.

There are, moreover, six additional faults which, if committed, must be confessed. These are: (1) the taking of alcohol or any other intoxicat-

---

* The category of upasaka of pure conduct (*tshangs spyod dge bsnyen*) includes all who are observing the twenty-four-hour precept of upavasa, a vow which was given for the sake of layfolk who find it too difficult to renounce sexual activity completely. They can thus observe pure conduct for a day at a time, on which occasions they observe the precepts of the shramanera ordination. [YG II, 241]

† I.e., renewing the vows each morning.

‡ See chapter 3, p. 53.

ing substance, because they impair vigilance; (2) the indulgence in all that is a cause of pretension and attachment for the things of samsara, such as art, dancing, singing, and the playing of music; (3) the wearing of ornaments, garlands, perfumes, and cosmetics; (4) the use of valuable furniture, seats, and beds adorned with precious substances (all such accoutrements should be of plain wood and in any case no more than a cubit in height); (5) the consumption of food at improper times, such as after midday (all meals should be confined to the period between the hours of dawn and noon); and (6) the acceptance of precious gifts, such as gold and silver, and the use of these as though they were personal possessions.

Shramaneras are considered superior to the upasakas. To save them, however, from being overwhelmed by a multitude of regulations, their vows have been condensed into ten general precepts, as mentioned before. This was established after the incident of the sons of Bridzi as recorded in the Vinaya. Nevertheless, in considering the matter in more detail, the vows of the shramanera ordination specifically prohibit thirty-three transgressions. These comprise, first of all, the four root transgressions of homicide, lying, theft, and sexual intercourse. Linked with these are three kinds of killing: the slaughter of animals, the flooding of vegetation that is the habitat of insects, and the drinking of water in which there are insects. Then there are twelve kinds of mendacity: (1) to tell lies without due reason; (2) falsely to accuse another of broken vows; (3) to provoke disturbance in the religious community by the spreading of false rumors or (4) to be in agreement with someone who does this; (5) to scandalize the laity by criticism of the monks, accusing them, for instance, of drinking alcohol; (6) to utter a falsehood deliberately; (7) to decry the teacher; (8) to denigrate the administrators of the monastery; (9) to accuse another of teaching in order to get sustenance; (10) to accuse someone of committing residual faults (see below); (11) to express contempt for the precepts; and finally (12) to conceal one's share of food with the intention of getting more. All this comes to a total of nineteen transgressions. In addition, there is the fault of drunkenness, the three kinds of dancing, wearing the three kinds of ornaments, sleeping in high beds, sleeping in costly beds, taking food after midday, and accepting gold and silver. Finally, there is the failure to renounce the manners of the laity,* the failure to assume the specific demeanor of a monk,† and the failure to show deference to one's abbot. All together, this comes to thirty-three transgressions.

The precepts of a woman novice in training for full ordination · In addition to the ten major transgressions listed above, women novices in training for full ordination must renounce twelve things. They must avoid the six root faults of touching a man and so on.[162] They must also avoid the six related faults such as the possession of precious metals and stones.[163] The teachings say, moreover, that, given the strength of their emotions, such novices should be tested for two years to see whether they are capable of observing the vow. It is only then that they should receive full ordination.

The precepts of full monastic ordination[164] · *The precepts concerning what is to be avoided* · The fully ordained monk or bhikshu must observe two hundred and fifty-three precepts. He must abjure:

1. The four radical defeats,[165] namely, killing a human being, stealing, sexual intercourse, and lying.
2. Thirteen residual faults,[166] such as masturbation.
3. Thirty downfalls requiring rejection,[167] such as the faults of "keeping and separation" with regard to the robes (see below). Added to these are ninety "mere downfalls,"[168] such as speaking in a consciously equivocal way, gossiping about the faults of people who are fully ordained, slandering a bhikshu, reviving old disputes, and so forth.
4. Four faults to be specifically confessed.[169]
5. One hundred and twelve wrong actions.[170]

Taken together, these five classes of precepts represent a total of two hundred and fifty-three actions to be avoided.

The fully ordained nun or bhikshuni must observe three hundred and sixty-four precepts of renunciation. In addition to the four radical defeats common to both monks and nuns, the bhikshuni must avoid four specific defeats. She must not touch a man; she must not lie on her

---

* For example, not to shave one's head.
† In the sense of wearing the robes and not carrying weapons.

back in the presence of a man; she must not conceal the fault of another nun; and she must not try, either physically or verbally, to prevent another nun from being reinstated into the Sangha after a proper confession has been made. Buddhist nuns must therefore guard against eight root defeats. Following this, there are twenty residual faults, thirty-three downfalls requiring rejection, one hundred and eighty mere downfalls, eleven faults requiring specific confessions, and one hundred and twelve wrong actions. All these come to three hundred and sixty-four things to be rejected. In addition to all this, there are many different kinds of related faults and infractions[171] common to fully ordained monks and nuns in which all the karmic conditions are not operative when they are committed.

The four or eight radical defeats entail the complete loss of the ordination. Whether this can be subsequently restored depends on whether there was the intention to conceal the fault. This is laid down in the Vinaya. It is consequently disconcerting to come across shramaneras or even fully ordained monks and nuns who claim to be upholding the precepts correctly but yet are ignorant even of the names of the five classes of downfall. Such people are a disgrace! To say that they are ordained is like pointing to some dry earth and calling it a well! It might be objected that, given that they do not abide by the precepts, there is hardly any point in their knowing what they are. True enough, but ignorance can never be justified! To be aware of what the downfalls are and to understand how reparation might be made is what makes purification possible. And Asanga himself has said that of the four doors to transgression, ignorance is the most serious.[172]

The precepts concerning what is to be done · According to the teachings, there are three basic rituals[173] to be performed: the confession ritual,[174] the ritual of the summer retreat,[175] and the ritual for ending the summer retreat.[176] All in all, there are seventeen precepts that form the basis of the three trainings. These have been set out in the *Vinayavastu* in the form of a mnemonic:

> Taking ordination,
> Ritual of confession,
> Retreat in summer months,

The lifting of the same,
Wearing fur and leather,
Medicine and clothing,
Leaving robes in monasteries,
Kaushambi or the smoothing of divisions,
All activities, the red and yellow disciplines,
The faults of individuals and demotion,
Refusal to confess, and rules for living space,
The settling of disputes, the healing of divisions.[177]

Training in these precepts constitutes the discipline of what has to be implemented.

If it happens, in the course of observing the precepts, that one is called upon to do something that is not normally allowed (this does not include actions evil by their nature, such as the killing of animals, or the seventeen major transgressions of the rule, namely, the four radical defeats and the thirteen residual faults), the action must be "blessed." For example, if one is obliged to eat at an improper time of the day, one considers that one is an inhabitant of the northern continent of Uttarakuru, where people are naturally endowed with discipline.[178] If the monk does this, he is permitted to eat. For it is said that once, when the Buddha was in Koshala, a large group of merchants offered him and the monastic community a meal. The meal was prepared and the monks were summoned, but just as they were about to eat, a fire broke out in the merchants' shops. Everyone ran to put out the blaze and so it happened that the time for the midday meal passed by. The monks turned to the Lord and asked what they should do. "O monks," the Buddha replied, "don't hesitate, just eat your meal. But as you eat, bless this moment as if you were in the northern continent of Uttarakuru."

In similar fashion, if one is obliged to bathe more often than twice a month, one should regard oneself as ill and the bath as a medicinal cure for the disease. Likewise, if one needs to use extra clothes, or garments that are of an inappropriate color, such as white, or of an improper material, such as leather or fur, one should be mindful that since there are no other possibilities, one would be completely deprived if one did not use them. It is then permissible to use such clothing in order to protect one's life and maintain the practice of virtue. Again, if it happens that one is constrained to touch or possess precious substances, one should consider that this is permissible as a means of making offerings to the Three Jewels and giving sustenance to others.

As for other things that do not clearly fall into the categories of what is specifically advocated or banned, the question of whether they are permitted is judged according to the degree to which they approximate or diverge from the spirit of the precepts.

After the Buddha's parinirvana, eighteen shravaka lineages came into existence. Seven of these belong to the Sarvastivada school of the royal lineage of Rahula. Five belong to the Mahasanghika school, which is of the priestly lineage of Mahakashyapa. Then there are three lineages of the Sthavira school in the lineage of Katyayana the arrow-maker, and three lineages of the Sammitiya school in the lineage of the barber Upali. Of these four main groupings,[179] it was the Sarvastivada school of precepts that spread mainly in Tibet.[180] There are slight differences in the precepts of these four traditions, but, as King Krikin[181] saw in his dream, each of them belongs to the Buddha's teaching and covers the five kinds of ordination, with the result that each of these traditions embodies his teachings on correct conduct. Therefore, one who lives by the precepts of one school is naturally an upholder of all. It is therefore important to maintain all one's precepts correctly.

How the three kinds of vow may be observed simultaneously[182]

The Tibetan translation of the term *nirvana* literally means "to pass beyond suffering." Here, "suffering" refers to the miseries of samsara, the cause of which is karma and defiled emotion. To "pass beyond" such causes severs the continuum of suffering and is the supreme level of peace or nirvana. This state of enlightenment is the goal of all true Pratimoksha, a discipline which is thus superior to any ethical observance, the object of which is simply the happiness of the higher realms. If, in addition to upholding the Pratimoksha, one wishes to attain perfect enlightenment for the sake of benefiting others on a vast scale, and if one duly takes the vows of bodhichitta in aspiration and action according to either of the two traditions of Vast Activities and Profound View, one becomes a holder of the vow of bodhichitta. Furthermore, one may, with the high motivation of benefiting others, receive empowerment according to the mantrayana rituals, which express the perfect view of the great classes of tantra. Thus one receives the authentic mantrayana vow of the Vidyadharas. This in turn is the foundation of the profound practice of the generation and perfection stages. A person who takes all three kinds of vow and who observes their many precepts concerning actions to be adopted or forsaken, as they are explained according to each level, will achieve all the qualities of the path and fruit.

Since the three kinds of vow transmute into each other, they partake of a single essential nature and are not considered as separate entities. However, they are distinct with regard to their respective aspects,* so that they remain, unmingled in the mind of the individual, until such time as they are broken. This principle of distinction according to aspect is a key point, on account of which each of the three vows must be kept at its own level, without being confused. This being so, it may be objected that the different vows contradict each other. For example, the act of killing, which is forbidden by the pratimoksha vow, is said to be permitted in the case of a Bodhisattva, while in the context of the unsurpassable Mantrayana, it is advocated as an act that one should willingly perform, being the samaya of the vajra family. What is one to make of this?

In the tradition of the learned and accomplished masters of the past (who were thinking of practitioners who were well versed in the extraordinary attitude of altruism and had confidence and expertise in the stages of generation and perfection), it is said that the greatest emphasis must be placed on the practice of bodhichitta and mantra. The essential meaning of this is explained as follows. To kill apparently violates the basic precept of Pratimoksha, which is not to harm others and therefore to abstain from killing. But a Bodhisattva who kills, for example, an evil and dangerous man, interrupts the stream of the man's actions and thereby reduces his suffering. The purpose of this deed is manifestly in

---

* *ldog pa.* For the sake of convenience, this is here simply rendered as "aspect." In fact, it is a highly technical term used in logic. See D. E. Perdue, *Debate in Tibetan Buddhism,* pp. 441ff.

agreement with the goal of the pratimoksha vow not to harm but to establish in happiness and to plant the seed of liberation.[183]

If, however, an action truly contradicts the three vows, which the Buddha, skilled in means, set forth in accordance with the various capacities and aspirations of beings, then it is in no way admissible. Conversely, if certain apparently unvirtuous actions *are* permitted, the reason is that they do not ultimately violate the precepts. For all the teachings of the omniscient Buddha, whether expedient or absolute, are all united in one essential intention. This is especially so in the context of the extraordinary view and meditation of the Mantrayana. Alcohol, the taking of which is a downfall according to the shravaka Pratimoksha and constitutes a fault in the bodhisattva discipline, is regarded in the Mantrayana as a substance of samaya that must always be present. The *Guhyagarbha-tantra* states:

> Meat and alcohol must not be lacking
> For they are substance of accomplishment,
> Food and drink, essences and fruits
> And all that is a pleasure to the senses.

and also:

> In particular, it is improper for meat and alcohol to be lacking.

It is taught that such substances are to be enjoyed by yogis who, by means of the practice of the stages of generation and perfection, are able to overcome the power of their thoughts—which at first seem so solid and real but which at length appear as the very deity. In general, this refers to the *aspirational deity*, for those who are on the path of accumulation; to the *deity of energy-mind*, for those who are on the path of joining; to the *deity of luminosity*, for those who are on the path of seeing; to the *deity of the united level of learning*,[184] for those who are on the path of meditation; and to the *deity of the united level of the Dharmakaya and Rupakaya*, for those who are on the path of no more learning.[185]

Practitioners of the inner tantras of the Mantrayana act without dualistic clinging, in such a way as to support their view of the purity and equality of phenomena. Through the skillful means of the generation stage, their own aggregates and elements, the universe itself, and all the beings that inhabit it arise as the display of the deity, mantra, and mudra. Such practitioners bless the substances of the sacred feast, or *tsok* offering, transforming them into *amrita*. And when they enjoy them, the alcohol is no longer ordinary; neither is their attitude one of ordinary indulgence. Within this state of great purity and equality, their perceptions are transmuted and they experience themselves as the deity and the alcohol as amrita. In such circumstances, yogis and yoginis are allowed to consume alcohol. They do not cling, out of self-interest, to ethical precepts concerning what is to be adopted or abandoned, regarding them as truly existent and immutable values, and they are not attached to their self-image as bhikshus and bhikshunis. Neither do they cling to the notion of altruistic generosity in the relative, materialistic sense, clinging to the idea of being Bodhisattvas. Yogis and yoginis who are thus allowed to partake of alcohol are not like Shravakas, who must repudiate desire because they have no means whereby defilements and sensual pleasures may be harnessed on the spiritual path. Neither are such practitioners like ordinary people, who, in the grip of negativity, accumulate actions that propel them into samsaric existence. Through the profound yogas of generation and perfection, all perceptions are transmuted. All appearances become the infinite mandala of deities. The samaya substances, alcohol and so forth, are enjoyed as amrita, and for that reason they may be consumed. Not only is no fault committed but merit increases, for yogis and yoginis who enjoy such samaya substances are in fact making offerings to the Three Jewels and the Yidam deity. It is thus that their accumulation of merit and their development of spiritual qualities are enhanced far more intensely than if they were to make offerings to the Sangha—the Sangha, that is, composed of monks and nuns confined to the pratimoksha discipline, or of ordained Bodhisattvas who strive for the sake of others but who as yet lack the view of purity and equality.

The observance of the three vows as taught in the Nyingma tradition
When harnessing negative emotion and desire for sense objects, with a view to progress on the spiritual path, the yogi must know how to apply

the same reasoning to all other aspects of the precepts, both major and minor. Beginners in the practice of the three vows must, however, strive to keep as well as possible all the precepts of all three vows. To this end, it is essential to understand the teaching of our tradition on this question, summarized as it is under six headings.

1. **The aspects remain distinct.*** · The respective aspects of the three vows are not confused. The authorities from whom one receives the three vows, the attitude with which one takes the vows, and the rituals wherewith one takes them—all these aspects have their own particular character. They are distinct. Even the duration of the vows is clearly different. The characteristics of the vows are peculiar to each level and do not overlap. Because the vows are differentiated in this way, they must be observed according to their respective character. And if an infraction occurs, it must be repaired according to the provisions established for each vow.

2. **The three vows are the same both in purpose and as antidote.†** · Each of the three vows fulfills two functions. Each is an antidote to negativities, and each fulfills the purpose of freeing the mind. As an illustration of this, consider a garden in which a poisonous plant is growing. An ignorant gardener without experience will dig up the plant and throw it away. By contrast, a physician may be able to prepare a medicine from the plant, which will be beneficial in treating diseases. Finally, a person skilled in mantra is able, through the application of mantric power, to give the poison an even greater beneficial potency. Each of these approaches is a way of neutralizing the poison, and, arranged hierarchically, each method outstrips the one preceding it in terms of ease and efficiency. In parallel with this image, the Shravakas, who regard negative emotions as existing entities, not merely on the relative but even on the absolute level, "tether" their minds with the vows of Pratimoksha. By binding the doors of the senses, they curb their behavior, principally that of word and deed. This is the shravaka method for dealing with defilement. As the *Pratimoksha-sutra* says:

---

* *rang ldog ma 'dres.*
† *dgag dgos tshang ba.*

The ever striving, ever restless mind—
A stallion wild and difficult to tame!
The harness of the pratimoksha vow
Is bit and bridle for the curbing of the mind!

The Bodhisattvas, for their part, consider that emotional defilement, though without ultimate existence, nevertheless imprisons them on the relative level. They therefore strive to disperse it in the expanse of ultimate reality.* In the *Bodhisattva pratimoksha-sutra*, the Buddha speaks about this at some length: "When a Bodhisattva, O Shariputra, perfectly observes his own desire, he examines the ground (the phenomenon) from which desire has sprung. Searching perfectly, he finds nothing. Whence does desire originate? Who gives birth to it and how? Indeed the Bodhisattva finds no arising, nor any subject to experience it, nor any way in which arising might occur. No desire is found. For the Bodhisattva, therefore, desire does not result in wrong actions. On the contrary, it is productive of positive qualities. Thus the Bodhisattva does not impugn desire but praises it."

In the general context of the Vajrayana, negative emotions, even on the relative level, are not regarded as defects. Like hard ice melting into liquid water, they are brought onto the path, being of the nature of deities (the five Buddha families) and wisdoms. And in this way, the fruit is swiftly gained. As it is said in the tantra *rgya mtso'i rgyud*:

Defilement is a pure and skillful path,
And objects of desire the supreme ornament.
By tasting of them, each and every one,
You speedily become the glorious heruka.

Indeed, for those who have truly realized the ultimate reality, defiled emotions are the sublime ornament of wisdom. It is said in the tantra *kun byed rgyal po*:

Craving, anger, ignorance
Arising on the path of great enlightenment,

* I.e., by the realization of its emptiness.

The five sense objects that are all enjoyed:
These wondrously adorn the great expanse.

It is like the peacock that feeds indiscriminately on poisonous flowers, thereby becoming ever more youthful and beautiful in its plumage.

A monk who chastely refrains from sexual intercourse, though he has the capacity for it, remains unstained by lust. The yogi practicing on the path of the third initiation indulges in sexual intercourse, and he too is unstained by lust. Both monk and yogi fulfill the vital point of antidote and purpose and thereby perfectly observe their vows concerning defilement. The ground in which a poisonous plant grows has no intention either to help or harm. By analogy, yogis and yoginis remaining in the view of the Natural Great Perfection are untouched by defilement. They do not reject it; they do not transmute it. Neither do they take it as the path. They are totally free from any such exertion. As it is said in the *kun byed rgyal po*:

> All appearances are one in suchness:
> Therefore let no alteration be imposed.
> This kingly state of uncontrived equality
> Is thought-free Dharmakaya, simple presence.

3. **The transmutation of the vows*** · Gyalwa Longchenpa's autocommentary on his *Absorption's Easeful Rest* gives a quotation from the tantra *gsang ba cod pan*:

> For thus we may observe that copper
> Is derived from stone; from copper, gold.
> When copper has been smelted out, the stone is gone.
> Transmuted into gold, the copper is no more.
> The Buddhas have not taught
> That pratimoksha and the bodhichitta vow
> Remain within the minds
> Of "inner monks," the Vidyadharas.

---

* *ngo bo gnas 'gyur.*

Commenting on the meaning of this, Gyalwa Longchenpa says that the pratimoksha vow and the bodhichitta vow do not persist in the mind as separate entities when the state of tantric Vidyadhara is attained. They are rather transmuted into the substance of the mantrayana vow. He says: "On the level of Secret Mantra, the two lower vows are transmuted into a single entity. Nevertheless, the specific aspects of the three vows do not merge and mingle into one. From the moment the vows are taken, and until they deteriorate, these aspects remain separate and distinct."

With regard to the notion of the transformation of the vows, some authorities interpret the expression "inner monks, the Vidyadharas," and a statement occurring later in the present text* that "transformation is produced by wisdom," as implying that unless the extraordinary "example" or "absolute" wisdoms manifest, no transformation (of the vow) can be said to take place. The teacher of our lineage has said that there was good reason for this assertion. Others, however, think that transformation occurs merely on the reception of an empowerment. My own view is that it is possible to speak of transformation happening even when the extraordinary wisdom,[186] which is uncompounded in all its aspects, has not yet occurred. However, I do not believe that transformation occurs just through sitting in an assembly and receiving an empowerment, touching one's three centers† with the blessed substances, and tasting them. The essence of the pratimoksha vow is the determination to free oneself from samsara. The essence of the bodhisattva vow is the promise to benefit others. The essence of the mantrayana vow is pure perception. However, the vows or ordinations will not be true and authentic simply through a vague desire for freedom, a vague wish that others be well, or a vague notion of pure perception. The vows must be held with a clear and definite attitude. It is when this occurs that one can speak of a transformation taking place.

The definition of the pratimoksha vow is the discipline of refraining from wrong action, combined with the determination to free oneself from samsara, and this within the environment of the desire realm. In

---

* I.e., Jigme Lingpa's root verses.
† The centers of body, speech, and mind.

his *Vinayamula-sutra*,* Gunaprabha sets forth "the discipline related to the determination to free oneself from samsara." The Abhidharma goes on to define the types of people eligible to take the vow in this way: "With the exception of neutered persons ('male' and 'female'), hermaphrodites, and the inhabitants of the northern continent of Uttarakuru, all human beings are capable of 'positive vows' and 'negative vows.' "† And this is taken up by Sakya Pandita in his book *The Three Vows Distinguished*, which states, "Besides the human inhabitants of the three cosmic continents, ordination is forbidden to other beings."[187]

The vow of bodhichitta is defined as the extraordinary practice of the six transcendent perfections combined with the wish to accomplish unsurpassable enlightenment for the sake of others. The vow is the state of consciousness‡ concomitant with the mental factor of intention: the firm resolve to abstain from all faults of thought, word, and deed that run counter to the six transcendent perfections. It is said in the *Abhisamayalankara*:

> Bodhichitta is the wish to gain
> Perfect, pure enlightenment for others' sake.

And in the *Bodhicharyavatara* it is said:

> Deciding to refrain from harming them
> Is said to be perfection of morality.
> (V, 11)

The mantrayana vow is defined as the state of consciousness concomitant with the mental factor of intending to arrest (by means of the primordial wisdom wherein knowledge and method are united) the mental processes which apprehend and cling to phenomena as really existent—together with the negative thoughts, words, and deeds that derive from this. As it is said in the *Garland of Light*:§

---

* *mdo rtsa.* The basic text from which the Vinaya commentaries derive.
† *sdom, sdom min,* lit. vow and nonvow. See appendix 4, p. 287.
‡ I.e., the main mind (*gtso sems*); see appendix 4, p. 294.
§ The text on the three vows by Bhutichandra studied in the Kagyu tradition.

Showing coemergent wisdom through the use of signs,
Restraining all defiling thought:[188]
All this defines, as long as space remains,
The tantric vow of Vidyadharas.

And it is said in the tantra *rgyud phyi ma* that a vow is the promise to observe the samaya without breaking it, even in dreams.

The three vows must be received according to their own respective rituals. However, even if the vows of the lay or monastic state are taken in accordance with the pure rituals of the Pratimoksha, if the underlying intention is to practice discipline only as a protection from suffering and as a means to gain temporary benefits, the vows themselves remain of only nominal value. But as the story of Nanda shows,* it is when the determination to leave samsara really takes birth within the mind that the mere vow is transformed into the authentic commitment of Pratimoksha. Nevertheless, even though the intention becomes more vast and there is a change of attitude, the original commitment to avoid negativities is not canceled. Thus it is that, as one receives the three successive types of pratimoksha precept, the lower aspects of the Pratikmoksha are not at all superseded. On the contrary, the commitment to reject negative behavior is fortified and developed. This is shown by the vinaya teaching that if at some later stage the higher precepts are given back, the person in question reverts to the lower ordination, for example, that of shramanera, taken before. However, when the highest ordination is taken, the lower two do not remain as separate sets of vows. If this were the case (i.e., if it were possible for two sets of vows to remain as distinct entities), it would follow that a man who has the vow of upasaka and who later takes full ordination is simultaneously monk and layman, since the upasaka ordination belongs to the lay state.

The same applies if, in addition to the pratimoksha vow, one goes on to take the vow of bodhichitta that aims at the welfare of others. While the specifically pratimoksha aspect is associated with the bodhisattva commitment, the determination "to free only oneself" from samsara is transmuted. It becomes indistinguishable from the attitude of

* See *The Words of My Perfect Teacher*, p. 95.

bodhichitta endowed with the twofold aim. When copper ore is smelted, the extracted copper is not substantially different from the original mineral. Yet if the *quality* of its preceding state persisted in the copper, the end result would have to be both ore and extracted copper at the same time, which is impossible. Likewise, when the determination to free oneself from samsara is improved (by bodhichitta), the resulting attitude of mind is not *substantially* different (from the previous one).*
Yet if it did not lose its earlier inferior *quality*,† the resulting mind-set would be both selfish and unselfish at the same time, and this is impossible.

In exactly the same way, when in addition to the bodhisattva vow one receives the vow of the Mantrayana, the altruistic attitude is itself raised to a higher power. This happens thanks to a confidence that arises through just a slight understanding of the state of purity and equality, to say nothing of when the absolute wisdom of empowerment actually occurs—which is said to happen during the bestowal or practice of the four empowerments that are the basis of the generation and perfection stages. The altruistic attitude is thus enhanced and transmuted into the mantrayana vow, so that, although the mantrayana attitude is not substantially distinct from the bodhisattva attitude, the difference now is that no discrimination is made, even on the relative level, between samsara and nirvana, accepting the one and rejecting the other. When beginners like ourselves reflect about the way in which we hold the three vows simultaneously, all we can say is that, when and as pure perception—the essence of the Mantrayana—and the view that results from hearing and reflecting on the teaching increase and strengthen, we do undergo a transformation of attitude, although this is not the same as the birth of the wisdom that comes through the power of meditation. When, through meditation, the "example wisdom" or "extraordinary absolute wisdom" is realized, this implies that the ordinary mind has been transmuted into primordial wisdom, and the mastery of the expanse of ultimate reality has been gained. The direct realization of ultimate reality gives control of all sense objects

---

* One still retains the determination to free oneself from samsara, though now it is in order to be able to liberate others.
† I.e., to free oneself *alone*.

and afflictions, so that, whatever yogis or yoginis do, they cannot be defiled by downfalls in the ordinary sense of the word. And although it may seem to an outside observer that such practitioners are acting in accordance with the precepts, from their side there is no clinging to the precepts of the lower vows as external independent entities, and they are thus beyond any intentional acceptance and rejection.[189] Here, the three vows undergo a complete transformation; it goes without saying that they are not separate entities. At that stage, the yogi and yoginis are bhikshus and bhikshunis in the truest, most spontaneous sense. It is said in the *Guhyagarbha-tantra*:

> The discipline arising from the Vinaya
> And the inconceivable array of all the vows
> Are all contained, are pure without exception,
> In supreme and unsurpassable samaya.

And Saraha, who was later the ordaining abbot of Nagarjuna himself, said:

> Till yesterday I was still a Brahmin,
> Till yesterday I was not a monk.
> But taking to myself an arrow-maker's daughter
> I am indeed a monk henceforth,
> A supreme monk and glorious heruka.

In relation to the three vows, therefore, there are, in brief, two kinds of transformation. The first is a change of attitude (experienced in the mind of the individual). The second is the complete transformation of the ordinary mind into wisdom,[190] of imperfection into perfection. If, when the mantrayana or bodhisattva vows are ritually received (by someone who already has the pratimoksha vow), no transformation of attitude occurs, it might be objected that the new vows have not in fact been received. For we have already seen that the vows themselves are not distinct entities.* However, within the tathagatagarbha, which is the

---

* In other words, the change of attitude is the only way of distinguishing them.

utterly pure nature of the mind, all the qualities of the paths and fruit are already present, waiting to be activated. It is when they are awakened and empowered by circumstances* that the qualities of each of the paths become manifest. This is through the inconceivable power of dependent arising, and the wonderful way in which it works is not to be explained away by any kind of rationalization. Things posited as dependent arisings cannot be categorized as identical or distinct.† Moreover, the range and workings of virtuous and nonvirtuous habitual tendencies are generally inconceivable, and in particular the minds of those practicing on the path may harbor merit that is both stained and unstained. If it is said that the nature of these different propensities is identical, this would mean that virtue and nonvirtue are identical. On the other hand, if their nature is asserted to be different, this would be the same as saying that the mind is likewise multiple—or else that virtue and nonvirtue must exist separately from the mind, which is equally unacceptable. As it is said:

> To trust in academic theorizing will bring no certainty.
> It's inconclusive, pitiful, and it obscures the issue.
> To trust in this is to rely on children!

It is important for the followers of our tradition to reflect about these matters carefully and to gain a deep conviction for themselves.

4. The gradual qualitative enhancement of the three vows‡ · On the level of the pratimoksha path, where wisdom and method are incomplete, the commitment to avoid negative action aims only at the liberation of oneself from samsara. The resulting qualities are therefore limited. If, however, this commitment becomes part of the bodhichitta vow, the Pratimoksha is kept within the framework of unbounded means and wisdom and becomes the cause of unsurpassable enlightenment. The ensuing benefit is far greater than when the vow is maintained outside the bodhichitta commitment. Furthermore, if the pratimoksha and bodhichitta vows are observed as part of the mantray-

---

* Blessings or initiations, etc.
† And likewise the vows cannot be designated as either the same or different.
‡ *yon tan yar ldan.*

ana commitment, unsurpassable enlightenment will be attained quickly and easily, because the Mantrayana is the profound, vast, and swift path of skillful means and wisdom. The qualities arising from such an observance are vastly increased.

5. **The absence of contradiction in the practice of the three vows*** · Beginners are unable really to benefit others on a vast scale, and they are unable to display powerful yogic activities. If on the level of word and deed their practice consists mainly of the observance of the pratimoksha vow, but at the same time they adopt, as far as they can, the attitude, view, and meditation of the bodhisattva and mantrika vows, it might seem that they are being inconsistent if they do not actually train in the extraordinary activities of Bodhisattvas or Mantrikas. But they are not at fault. It is only at a later stage, when self-interest has completely vanished or has been greatly reduced, that practitioners can focus mainly on the altruistic attitude. And when their view and meditation of the Mantrayana matures and their ordinary clinging is purified, they are able to undertake the activities of "union" and "liberation," in order to perfect the two accomplishments for the sake of beings. At this point, it may seem that they are acting contrary to the lower, more fundamental precepts to which they had earlier committed themselves. Yet none of the elements[191] of a downfall can occur, in the sense understood at the pratimoksha level, for the latter involves a clinging to the real existence of phenomena. Such practitioners are like peacocks able to consume poison. Not only is no fault incurred, but wisdom is served and enhanced, and therefore in the most important sense the lower vows are not contradicted. As Aryadeva has said, "Those who want to rid themselves completely of defilement must go to the most essential meaning."

6. **Observance should be appropriate to the moment†** · Generally speaking, from the level of beginner up to that of accomplished yogi, the behavior of practitioners should be appropriate to their capacity and also to the situation in which they find themselves. In the midst of a gathering of people, they should act impeccably and with care and concern for others. Their deportment should be in accordance with the

---

* *gnad kyi mi 'gal ba.*
† *dus skabs gang gtsor spyad pa.*

five customs of Samantabhadra. The first of these is to live in a solitary, wholesome place or hermitage. The second is to have a pure livelihood that is in harmony with the Dharma and unspoiled by wrong means of subsistence.* The third is to observe the vows purely. Beginners should concentrate mainly on the Pratimoksha. Then, as their capacity for great compassion and skillful means for the benefit of others increases, and as they grow in understanding of the ultimate, unoriginated nature of phenomena and the absence of real existence, they should gradually observe the higher vows. In this way, the three vows will be practiced faultlessly. The fourth custom of Samantabhadra is to keep good company, frequenting those who maintain a pure observance. Finally, the fifth is to practice the perfect Dharma of compassion and emptiness. As the *Guhyasamaja-tantra* says:

> Be, outwardly, like Shravakas
> And inwardly enjoy the quintessential meaning.

The perfect Buddha, the Lotus-Born Guru, has said the same.

When a yogi is engaged in secret practice, actions that are considered downfalls on all levels of vow should be rejected totally. However, in the case of those actions that may be assessed differently at different levels, or in the case of one who is training in "fearless and unconventional" yogic activities, preference should be given to the mantra point of view, although in no case should the lower vows be disparaged. Since the practitioners here are acting with the means and wisdom of the higher vows, no fault is committed. Nevertheless, if their behavior is liable to give scandal to ordinary people and cause them to lose faith, they should adhere to the precepts of the lower vows. For as it is said in the *Bodhicharyavatara*:

> All that you have seen, or have been told,
> To be offensive—this you should avoid.
> (V, 93)

---

* See chapter 5, p. 99.

Again, in *The Three Vows Distinguished*, it is said:

> Behave like Shravakas and guard yourself
> From sins and all unvirtuous ways.
> And when you are beyond all selfishness
> Behave like Bodhisattvas, avoiding every wrong.
> Behave like both and strenuously guard yourself
> From any deed that scandalizes simple folk.

The great commentary on the *Kalachakra-tantra* states that one should behave correctly according to the level of one's practice, either by acting or refraining from action according to circumstances. It is important not to confuse the conduct proper to different stages of the practice: that of a beginner with that of a yogi on the path, that of a siddha with that of an omniscient Buddha.

The three vows as presented in other traditions

All the practices of the oceanlike teachings of the Tathagata are expressed in the observance of the three vows. Taken together, the different teaching traditions give six ways of describing how it is that the three vows may be combined and practiced by a single individual. These six ways fall into two opposing camps: those asserting that the vows have an identical essence and those that deny this.

1. It is said in the tantra: "When the wisdom of the unsurpassable vehicle is possessed, all actions that appear defiled to others are performed but not stored.* They will result in the accumulation of merit. This is the supreme vow of discipline." A practitioner who reaches this level of realization is like the majority of the great beings of India and Tibet who had no clinging to the concepts of vow and absence of vow; they had overcome all belief in the true existence of phenomena. For them, all discursive thought was transmuted into wisdom, and as far as the vows were concerned, they were quite beyond all talk of essence or aspect. Nevertheless, in Tibet in times past, it was said by Atsara Marpo[192] that if one receives empowerment, it is sufficient to observe the mantrayana vow alone. Some people who followed him believed

---

* See chapter 3 on karma, p. 57.

that both the aspects and the essence of the vows transform, with the result that when the higher vow is received, there is no further necessity to observe the lower vow, since this is entirely contained within the essence of the superior vow of the Mantrayana. This may appear to agree with what we have just been saying, but it is only admissible in the case of a yogi whose mind is completely liberated through the realization of the equality of phenomena. However, if beginners act in this way and ignore the lower vows, they merely accomplish their own downfall.

2. It is taught in our tradition that when the pratimoksha and bodhichitta vows are transformed into the mantra vow, the different aspects of the former remain distinct (i.e., operative) within the mantra vow itself. This is the teaching of all the great masters of India and Tibet as clearly set forth in the Ancient Translation tantras such as the *sgyu 'phrul dra ba*. Furthermore, the *Garland of Light* clearly states, "Some believe that the three vows relate to each other in the same way as the earth, water, and boat.[193] This is wrong. The great masters Ashvaghosha and Lilavajra have said that the three vows are differentiated only according to their aspects." This in turn is the unmistaken view of the learned and accomplished masters of Tibet. These include Rongdzom Chökyi Zangpo, the majority of the teachers of the Zur lineage and especially the second Buddha, Longchen Drimé Özer, as well as the great tertön Gyurme Dorje (Terdag Lingpa), of the Ancient Translation school, and also the great translator Rinchen Zangpo, Sakya Pandita (who was Manjushri in person) and his followers, all of whom belong to the New Translation schools. The manner in which the transformation takes place has already been explained. Those who maintain the contrary view argue that if the three vows have the same essence, it follows that, like the pratimoksha, the bodhichitta and mantrayana vows must be relinquished at death, or conversely that the pratimoksha vow continues until the state of nirvana (like the bodhichitta and mantrayana vows).[194]

3. According to another view,[195] the three vows are presented in terms of the following example. If a sapphire is placed in a vessel of transparent crystal filled with clear water, the liquid and the vessel will take on the color of the sapphire while nevertheless remaining separate entities. It is the same with the pratimoksha, bodhichitta, and mantra

vows. They coexist in one mind as separate entities and as such are mutually exclusive. Nevertheless, as the respective qualities of the three vows are gradually enhanced, pratimoksha and bodhichitta are considered as the subsidiaries of the mantra vow. This means that the vows relate to each other in the manner of a support and something that is supported.[196] This view is admissible in the case of a person whose mind is unable to go beyond the lower vows in terms of superior wisdom and means. For such a person, the vows do indeed have different and separate aspects, and this involves no contradiction. Nevertheless, if one asserts that the three vows are all equally related in the manner of support and supported, it would follow that when the pratimoksha vow is relinquished, the bodhichitta and mantra vows, which are based on it, are also relinquished. And this is not acceptable.

4. The vows may be distinguished in terms of the time and circumstances in which the vows are taken and relinquished. It may be said, perhaps, that this is the general view of the Kagyupas. For they affirm that the vows themselves each possess a distinct nature because the rituals in which they are taken differ from each other and because they are relinquished in a variety of circumstances of time and cause. Other authorities, however, interpret this as meaning that when the higher vows are received, the lower ones are relinquished. Nevertheless, this kind of distinction, they say, is not to be taken at its face value; it was made with the specific intention of keeping people of limited capacity on the path of liberation. In the early stages, one is obliged to speak like this in order to cater to persons such as the sage Suryaratha who through sheer narrow-mindedness rejected the profound meaning. It is like suggesting that it would be better for such people to engage in the Mantrayana at some later stage.[197]

There is another good reason for presenting the vows in this way. Having in mind people whose monastic observance is fragile, who are lacking in extraordinary means and wisdom,[198] and who are therefore liable to give up their monastic commitment, Atisha said in his *Lamp for the Path*, "One who practices the path of purity* should not receive the secret empowerment and the wisdom empowerment." In such a context,

* I.e., the monastic life.

the present (fourth) view is acceptable. But if it is asserted as a general principle binding in all circumstances, the false conclusion would follow that there can be no such thing as a Vajradhara, a holder of the three vows. It would also run counter to the facts. For it is impossible to attain buddhahood without receiving the four empowerments.

5. According to the fifth view, as expounded by Abhayakara in his *Munimatalankara*, golden ornaments are all made of the same substance and yet they have different forms according to the purpose they are intended for, whether as ornaments for the head or feet, bracelets, and so on. Abhayakara explains that although the nature of the three vows is identical—namely, the firm resolve to refrain from evil actions—the vows themselves are of different form. This is the same as saying that the three vows exists separately and unmixed within a single mind. They are like three coins, one on top of the other, and do not intermingle. It is correct to say this from the standpoint of the respective aspects of the vows, for on this level the vows are indeed distinct. But it is wrong to understand this on the level of the vows' essence, because this would be the same as saying that three types of mental factors (for example, the three kinds of firm resolve to refrain from killing) could coexist simultaneously in a single mindstream.

6. The sixth point of view is the tradition of Bhutichandra, a disciple of Shakya Shri, and is explained in the *Garland of Light*.

The light of the sun, moon, and stars may be classified according to a scale of intensity. When the moon rises, it outshines the stars. But though the starlight is hidden, it is itself unweakened. It is not annihilated and remains a distinct light. The same thing is thought to occur when the higher vows are received: the lower ones are outshone and, as it were, eclipsed due to their difference of strength.

This way of speaking is admissible only in the case of people who are free from the duality of known object and knowing mind and in whom the ability to observe the two higher vows is greatly enhanced by skillful means and wisdom. For them, the lower vows are not relinquished but remain latent, subsisting in the natural quality of discipline that has been instilled in them. They are present, though their aspects are hidden. As the great master Vimalamitra said, "It should be understood that whoever grasps that the mind, the instigator of action, is devoid of intrinsic identity, or whoever meditates on the fact that phenomena are without inherent existence, possesses perfectly pure discipline." Any other interpretation of this view of the distinct but latent characteristics of the three vows is unacceptable. For if one still needs to guard oneself from transgressions,* the lower vows are not eclipsed. And if one has no such need, it follows that the vows do not retain a distinct existence.

Concluding summary

It is the nature of the ordinary mind to fabricate thoughts; and words and expressions proliferate accordingly. Therefore, any examination of the way in which an individual can observe the three vows together naturally gives rise to endless assertions. They can all, however, be condensed into the following principle according to the teaching of the four reliances. People not bound by vows may not be liable to commit downfalls, but they are also incapable of extraordinary merit. Their positive actions will generate what is called intermediary merit and will not lead out of samsara. Those who strive for liberation must first receive the vows, and, like farmers apprehensive of droughts and hailstorms, they must observe the vows correctly and be careful not to break them. Earlier, in the section describing the rituals for receiving the vows, it was explained that, on the level of their imputed existence,† they all possess their distinct aspects and should be observed accordingly. And when emphasis is placed on one or other of the three systems of vows, there is no contradiction between them, provided one proceeds in such a way that what is to be discarded is duly repudiated and the specific purpose (of liberation) is respected. For virtue and nonvirtue have no real existence in themselves—they are but reflections of thought; and vows, which are compounded phenomena, fall within the field of thought. Their transformation into uncompounded discipline[199] occurs through the power of extraordinary wisdom free from every concept of vow or the absence of vow, and which arises when the discursive activity of the eight consciousnesses blends with ultimate reality and the

---

* I.e., at all levels of the vows.
† *btags yod.*

absence of intrinsic existence is realized. All this is explained in the sutras.

The six points pertaining to our tradition (regarding the distinct aspects of the three vows and so on) are general considerations. More specifically, it should be said that unless a particular attitude arises, such as the determination to free oneself from samsara, the vows lack true authenticity. For authenticity does not automatically come from merely receiving the vows. Therefore, practitioners must strive skillfully to enhance their inner attitude, beginning with their determination to leave samsara. And even when their attitude has been transformed, the specific aspects of the various vows must still be observed. When, however, the extraordinary wisdom, absolute luminosity, is fully generated, distinctions between the separate aspects cease, and whatever is done will be faultless. It is important to be able to distinguish these two cases. As it is said in the commentary on the *Ratnavali*, "In the shastras, it is well known that there are exceptions to the general teachings."

When rivers flow into the ocean, they are all united in the one salt sea, but while flowing in their different courses, they are not mixed. In the same way, the three vows are different ways to embrace happiness and banish suffering, the fruits, respectively, of the virtuous and nonvirtuous mind, the origin of all action. Thus the basis of discussion concerning what is to be done and what is not to be done, within the context of each of the vows, is necessarily the question of their aspects. A tradition that asserts that the aspects of the lower vows are immediately transformed when one receives the higher vows possesses no means of mending the damage when the lower vows are broken. For example, it would be impossible to use the blessing ritual in accordance with the pratimoksha view in order to repair the fault of failing to keep the patched dharma robe always with one. For the specific aspect of Pratimoksha would have already been transformed, leaving nothing behind. There would in fact be no downfall to repair. It would be impossible to remedy the fault from the point of view of the bodhichitta or mantrayana vows since, at this level, no downfall would have occurred. Any idea of reparation would be out of place, and in any case no provisions have been made for it.

To recapitulate, the Vaibhashikas assert that the vows are imperceptible substantial forms, the product of perceptible actions of body and speech. The Sautrantikas claim that the vows represent stages of mental transformation. The Chittamatrins hold that the vows consist of the constant resolve and the associated habitual tendencies to refrain from wrong behavior. These three tenet systems regard the vows as possessing true existence.[200]

The fact of entering the Mahayana, receiving empowerment, and practicing the corresponding paths does not automatically mean that one gains a perfect knowledge of emptiness and compassion and thus the ability to render defilements helpful for the practice. It does not mean that one is in possession of the extraordinary methods of the Mantrayana whereby affliction is utilized on the path. It does not mean, in other words, that one has instantaneously attained the level of Vajradhara, holder of the three vows, for whom the extraordinary transformation of compounded mind into uncompounded wisdom has occurred. One still remains vulnerable to afflictive emotion, just as one is liable to be harmed by poison until it has been neutralized by the blessing power of a mantra.

It is one's attitude that renders the vow pure and authentic. When the determination to free oneself from samsara occurs, the pratimoksha vow becomes authentic. When true aspiration to accomplish perfect enlightenment for the sake of others occurs, the vow of bodhichitta likewise becomes authentic. But even a person who has these two attitudes will still consider phenomena, the aggregates, and so on, as impure, adopting and rejecting accordingly. To overcome this kind of discrimination, it is necessary to consider that the three seats[201] are mandalas of deities and to master the yoga of the generation stage. Any clinging to the deity that may arise in the course of the generation stage, through considering it supreme and wonderful, will be dissolved in the perfection stage, the essence of which is the cultivation of thought-free wisdom. When the realization of this wisdom is fully perfected, the yogi becomes like space, impervious to defilement. For the yogi, there are no more breaches of the precepts, downfalls of the kind that earlier had been caused by the afflictions experienced in the ordinary way, and which are phenomena on the level of relative truth, subject to origin and cessation. The reason for this is that for such an individual, ordinarily experienced defilements and actions no longer occur. Virtuous thoughts cannot benefit such people by bringing them a further increase in spiritual qualities. Evil thoughts cannot harm them, nor cause them to degenerate through failure to apply the antidotes.

Out of concern for people who successively pursue the stages of the path, the Buddha stipulated specific periods for the observance of the three vows. First, he taught that beginners should practice the precepts of pratimoksha discipline in order to banish emotional defilements and the negative actions of thought, word, and deed, which are a hindrance to liberation. Then, as a means to restrain selfish attitudes and the consequent actions of body, speech, and mind that obstruct the welfare of others, he set forth the precepts of the bodhisattva discipline. For those who have gained proficiency in this, and whose attitudes and behavior have become truly other-centered, he then expounded the tantric discipline of the Vidyadharas, as a method for halting the ordinary perception of the three doors of body, speech, and mind, and halting the deluded clinging to samsara that impedes the swift and effortless accomplishment of the welfare of others. The three vows are like medicines administered to a sick person at the beginning, middle, and end of an illness. They do not in any way contradict each other. They are essentially relative and interdependent phenomena, having the status of the mental factor of intention. In the immediate term, their observance effects a transformation of attitude, which becomes increasingly refined, while on the ultimate level, it brings about a transmutation of the perceptions of the compounded mind into uncompounded wisdom.

Most people nowadays lack all proficiency in learning, reflection, and meditation. For them, therefore, nothing[202] is ever transmuted into deity or amrita. Their thoughts of craving and desire remain on the ordinary level, and they regard prohibitions and permissions as real. They receive the three vows and undertake an aspirational practice of the training in united means and wisdom, abiding in each of the three vows separately until such time as a breach or degeneration occurs. While such people abide by the three vows, the specific aspects of the latter remain separate within them. From the point of view of observance, they must therefore combine all the various points of the vows with regard to adoption and rejection. If they keep the vows in this way, their observance will be flawless. Instead of observing the lower vows merely on their own level, they will maintain them in a manner that is enhanced by, and in accordance with, the higher vows. But if the need arises to repair a vow, this should be done separately according to the level of the vow infringed. In this way, the vows are perfectly restored.

If, driven by craving, one consumes alcohol, or if one teaches Dharma out of jealousy, one is acting wrongly, and such behavior is proscribed[203] even if the actions appear good in themselves. On the other hand, if one acts wholesomely and with good results, whatever is done for the benefit of others is permissible, whether it be an act of generosity or something that has the appearance of a wrong deed, such as giving someone a beating. In sum, all that is said to be permissible or forbidden in accordance with the nature and aspiration of beings is not to be understood in a narrow, literal sense. It must always be seen in relation to the varying attitudes of the people concerned; it is only then that the principle is properly applied.

THE DISCIPLINE OF GATHERING VIRTUE
The complete and infallible means to attain enlightenment are the six transcendent perfections—which is the same as saying the two accumulations. The practice of the perfections using a specific object of focus and attitude results in the accumulation of merit, while the practice of the perfections in a state of nonconceptuality, in which the three spheres (of subject, object, and action) are seen to be without true existence, gives rise to the accumulation of wisdom. Taking advantage of every favorable opportunity and skillful means, it is vital to develop the superior qualities, not shared by the Shravakas and Pratyekabuddhas, which have not yet been generated in the mindstream. This should be done gradually, following the commitment of the bodhichitta vow that one will train oneself step by step. All this, together with the continued cultivation of the qualities already possessed, constitutes the "discipline of gathering virtue." Of the three trainings, this practice belongs to the higher training of the mind, in other words, concentration, since the one-pointed virtuous mind is in fact the essence of the six transcendent perfections of generosity and so forth.

The six perfections are said to be implicit in every positive action qualified by love and compassion (such as giving or the study and contemplation of the teachings). If accomplished for the sake of others, the act is one of generosity since there is no desire to take the results for oneself. Being free from self-interest, it is discipline. If performed without weariness or irritation, it is patience. If, in view of the resulting qualities, it is performed with joy, it is diligence. If done intently and unwaveringly for the sake of others, not straying to other things, it is concentration. And if the act is performed in a manner such that the three spheres are not apprehended as truly existent, it is wisdom, for this will mean that, while interdependently produced phenomena are not overlooked, they are not clung to in terms of acceptance and rejection. Therefore, as the six paramitas are all present in a single good deed, through the constant application of skillful means and wisdom, all positive actions, physical, verbal, and mental, will partake of the six transcendent perfections and there will be no obstacles to the attainment of buddhahood.

Moreover, even while performing the four (morally neutral) everyday activities of eating, sleeping, moving, and sitting, Bodhisattvas are always in a state of mindfulness and vigilance. And being able constantly to accumulate totally pure merit by making prayers of aspiration in accordance with every deed they do,[204] they advance effortlessly on the path of the six paramitas. This is true of any action they perform, even walking—merely lifting up and putting down their feet. Endowed with such skillful means, they swiftly complete the accumulations.

It is said that the bodhisattva vow has four aspects. These are mentioned in Shantideva's *Shiksasamuccaya* as follows:

> My body and my worldly wealth,
> My virtues present, past, and those to come,*
> I will *give* them all to every being
> And *protect* and *purify* and *increase* them.[205]

* In other words, the bases of every kind of clinging.

As regards the aspects emphasized in the course of training in the discipline of gathering virtue, it is said that beginners should concentrate mainly on *protecting*. On the level of aspirational practice, disciples apply themselves to *purification*. On the impure bodhisattva grounds (i.e., the first to the seventh), they should emphasize *generosity*, while on the pure grounds (the eighth to the tenth), they should concentrate on *increasing*.

THE DISCIPLINE OF BENEFITING OTHERS

Bodhisattvas pursue to their ultimate limit the three aspects of skillful means: they perfect the two accumulations, they bring others to spiritual maturity, and they have the ability to perceive and manifest pure fields.* It is thus that they labor earnestly for the immediate and ultimate welfare of others. Directly, they give in charity to the needy, while indirectly, they give the gift of Dharma, encouraging beings to engage in positive action. They are rich, too, in the four methods of attracting disciples. These four methods are: material generosity; skill in teaching the Dharma in ways that are delightful and appropriate to the individual hearer; the ability to inspire people to undertake the practice; and practicing perfectly what one preaches. Bodhisattvas are in themselves expert in the discipline of gathering virtue, and this in turn nourishes the four abilities just mentioned. It is thus that they throw open wide the door of generous giving, and their capacity to work for others is immense.

It is said that working for others involves six considerations: oneself, others, material poverty and wealth, and spiritual poverty and wealth. The categories of self and other encompass those of poverty and wealth (both spiritual and material) because they naturally form the context in which the latter occur. And self-concern and altruism themselves depend on the strength or weakness of one's Dharma practice. Those who truly possess the Dharma qualities of transmission and realization, and who never diverge from the teachings because of distraction and the pressures of daily life, must devote themselves mainly to working for others. If, however, altruistic action is a matter of external appearance only, others are not genuinely helped thereby, and one's own qualities

---

* *rdzogs smin sbyangs gsum.*

deriving from the three trainings will degenerate. Discipline will become distorted, concentration dissipated, and wisdom obscured. It is consequently important for beginners in the practice, who are prone to such eventualities, to examine themselves mindfully and with vigilance. They must identify their deluded thoughts and defilements and apply themselves to training in skillful means, reinforcing the antidotes that will eliminate their faults. By doing this, they will be genuinely working for others. It is only when one is in a position to bring really great benefit to the Doctrine and beings that one is permitted to lay aside the lesser rules, such as the precepts of the lower vows that are themselves geared toward one's ultimate benefit and the immediate welfare of others. To save a city, one may sacrifice a village; to save one's life, it is reasonable to give up one's house. And for the sake of spreading the Dharma of transmission and realization on a vast scale, one may sacrifice oneself.

The Paramita of Patience

When practitioners are engaged in the training of discipline, fearless patience is their great resource and mainstay. Patience is essentially the tenacious ability to bear with suffering. It is the fertile soil in which the flowers of Dharma (in other words, the three disciplines) can grow and spread their perfume of good qualities. Encircling these flowers like a protective fence are the three kinds of patience. The first is the patience to bear the sufferings and difficulties that occur while one is striving for the twofold goal: buddhahood for one's own sake and the accomplishment of the welfare of others. The second kind of patience is the ability to put up with the injuries that others might inflict, while the third kind is the ability to confront, without fear or apprehension, the doctrine of emptiness and other profound teachings.

Indulgence in anger and all its dreadful manifestations is like a darkness that throws a pall over every joy and happiness, hardening the mind and making it pitiless and cruel. The creeping tendrils of every kind of evil spread out from it: killing, striking, wounding—acts that propel the agent into one of the hell realms whence there is no escape. Those who fear the prospect of falling into hell are careful never to give the slightest rein to thoughts of anger. As it is said in the *Bodhicharyavatara*:

No evil is there similar to anger,
No austerity to be compared with patience.
Steep yourself, therefore, in patience—
In all ways, urgently, with zeal.
        (VI, 2)

The mischiefs that flow from anger are boundless. Just as it is impossible to remove the briers from a forest of thorns (so that the only way to escape harm is not to go there), it is impossible to halt the onslaught of adversity. It befalls us constantly and without reprieve. Irritated and dismayed by what we do not want, we experience impulses of anger and resentment that are hard to control. Everyone's mind is infected in this way. The first thing to occur is the perception that a given object is in some way unwanted, and then feelings of displeasure arise. If, however, we are able to bring the impulse under control before it hardens and becomes established, the arduous practice of patience will prove a good friend. As the proverb says, "Hit the pig on the nose; clean the lamp while it is still warm."[206]

When we are criticized by someone, our hearing faculty and consciousness all interact so that the statement provokes a strong feeling of displeasure. A sharp sensation of pain is experienced as if an arrow had pierced our heart and torn it open. Nevertheless, if the situation is examined properly, we can see that the *words themselves* have an echolike quality.* Even if they appear to hit their mark, they are (in themselves) unable to inflict real damage. But what normally happens in this kind of situation? Our habitual way of thinking, which identifies the word with the thing,† takes the words as genuinely harmful, and the interplay of assailant and assailed is set in motion. Thus we are disturbed and suffer.

In our present situation, all the causes of physical and mental suffering—beating, fighting, robbing, slander, and the like—seem to come from other people. But the cause of them all is in ourselves. They are like booming echoes returning to their source. Indeed, if we had no

---

* They are mere sound. And, as mere sound, they come from no one and are directed at no one.
† *sgra don 'dres 'dzin gyi rtog pa.*

ego-clinging, there would be no one for the enemy to attack, so we should reflect how situations of conflict are called forth by our own past actions. Moreover, if we think about it, we can see that patience can only ever arise in adversity, which is consequently not negative but extremely beneficial! Thanks to the hostility of enemies, we can embark on the ship of patience and sail upon the ocean of the Mahayana, gaining for ourselves the precious jewel of bodhichitta, the source of immediate and ultimate benefit for self and others. Enemies should therefore be looked upon as the object and source of patience. They are as worthy of offerings as the sacred Dharma itself!

As regards patience in connection with ultimate reality, it is important to reflect on the following point. If one investigates closely to see where the injury lies—in the aggressor, in the action itself, or in the victim of aggression—one will discover that it cannot be found anywhere. As we have explained, when different circumstances coincide, it is the mind, with its tendency to construct existential situations,* that fabricates the problem there and then. And if one examines the mind, it will be found not to possess any constant and immutable characteristics. When one tries to trace a design on water, the pattern dissolves in the very instant of its drawing. In the same way, as soon as the violence of hostile thought is allowed to subside (for it is incapable of remaining on its own, unsupported by other factors), a totally pure and spacious state of mind appears—the primordial great emptiness free from concepts. To preserve this state of openness, this simple presence, which is not something to be lost or gained, accepted or rejected—to preserve this without being distracted by other things is called, on the profound path of the Madhyamika, the "purification of defilement in ultimate reality."†

In conclusion, the arduous practice of patience has three phases: the earnest embracing of hardships, the patient toleration of the wrongs done by others, and the patience that is a fearless conviction with regard to ultimate reality. If the last kind of patience is lacking, the other two can never rise above the worldly path. On the other hand, if these two

---

* *nyer len.*

† This is also called *chos la nges sems kyi bzod pa*, patience that is a certainty with regard to the ultimate reality of things. [YG II, 362]

are absent or weak, then however much one may wish to acquire the qualities of the path and fruit, through the practice of generosity and the other five paramitas, it will be difficult to achieve the object of one's aspirations. It is comparable to the difficulties encountered in trying to go somewhere, all alone and without an escort, following a path that is haunted by enemies, robbers, and wild beasts. Therefore, we should summon up our courage and train in patience, cultivating strength of heart.

*The Paramita of Diligence**

It is extremely important never to lay aside our efforts to hear and reflect upon the teachings and never to give up the practice of the three trainings. With a fully perfected sense of diligence, we should apply ourselves to virtue without delay, not leaving it abandoned and forgotten in the ravine of the three kinds of laziness. Rather we should be like swans who hatch their eggs in a thicket but take to the water as soon as their chicks are strong enough.

THE THREE KINDS OF LAZINESS†
(1) People are inextricably entangled in the affairs of this world. They are engrossed in them, overwhelmed by the bustle of mundane activities and society. They cling to their dear ones; they repudiate their adversaries; they immerse themselves in the accumulation, preservation, and increase of wealth. And from all these cares, they cannot free themselves; they are like silkworms imprisoned in the cocoons of their own making. (2) Moreover, they are overpowered by the laziness of discouragement and tell themselves that they are unable to accomplish even those achievements of Dharma that are only slightly difficult. Destitute of energy in the practice of virtue, they constantly postpone it. (3) And they put themselves down with thoughts like, "Oh, but how could I ever do such things?" To wallow in this kind of depression is to cut

---

* Essentially, the one-pointed state of mind of taking delight in the practice of virtue.
† The three kinds of laziness, as explained in the following paragraph, are (1) an inclination to unwholesome ways; (2) discouragement; and (3) self-contempt. See Shantideva, *The Way of the Bodhisattva*, VII, 2.

oneself off from the Dharma. People like this have no chance of gaining freedom, foundering as they do in the ocean of the three kinds of laziness. It is as though they are on a leaking ship; they have no prospect of gaining the other shore.

THE THREE KINDS OF DILIGENCE

The armies of the four demons,[207] which obstruct the path of the Mahayana are overcome by three things. The first is a *courageous, armorlike diligence*, impervious to any adverse circumstance.

The second antidote to the four demons is *diligence in action*. This is the gradual implementation of the threefold discipline of the four paths of learning,[208] whereby—never losing the defenses of one's courageous pledge—one brings to completion the five paths and perfects the ten grounds. The third and final protection against the four demons is never to transgress one's pledge to benefit others, nor to allow one's diligence to weaken, either in intention or action. This indeed should be irreversible under all circumstances, regardless of the qualities of the path that might arise. This is referred to as *insatiable diligence*. Those who are endowed with this threefold diligence will without any doubt accomplish their aspirations both immediately and ultimately.

Our life is like a bright, sunny day. At the moment, we may have everything: dear friends, wealth, every kind of enjoyment. But moment by moment, life gradually wears away like the sun journeying toward the mountains in the west. The deep darkness of death is creeping ever closer like the shadows of the hills. And when death arrives, we will fitfully perceive relatives and friends sharing out all our belongings, telling each other what they are going to do with them.[209] This is the final conclusion of our worldly works. Though they be more numerous than the stars at night, they all come to this. And if we have failed to practice virtue before death comes, there will be no reprieve from the terrors and dangers of the bardo state, the offerings and the positive actions of the living notwithstanding. As the *Bodhicharyavatara* says:

> And when the vanguard of the Deadly King has gripped me,
> What help to me will be my friends or kin?
> (II, 41)

Diligence is a friend that purifies the cloudy, muddy waters of laziness. Thanks to it, progress on the path becomes steady and continuous like the four rivers[210] flowing to the great ocean, which never stagnate or run dry like lesser streams. In the same way, until reaching the ocean of omniscient wisdom, the powerful diligence of unremitting and respectful practice, devoid of the extremes of excessive tension and slackness, will carry us forward irresistibly to the level of perfect fruition.

The Paramita of Concentration

THE PREREQUISITES FOR CONCENTRATION

In praise of forest dwellings

In the forest, marvelously arrayed and colored like the iridescence of the peacock's throat, the ground is carpeted with green grass and every sort of flower. The branches of the trees are decked with leaves and blossoms of various kinds. It is a delightful place filled with wholesome plants, caressed by the fresh, scented breeze. Cool streams babble gently amid lakes and pools encircled by green and grassy swards, populated by a host of swans, wild ducks, and other waterfowl sweet-voiced and harmless. On the mountain slopes are natural caves set amid wonderful cliffs that are smooth and gleam like oil. Above and below are rocky walls of various colors. Near their summits, the mountains are adorned with ledges, the nesting place of birds. On the lower slopes live little deer, charming and playful, a delight to see. The forest is a natural source of joy and heart's ease; it is lovely like a goddess, her waist encircled with woven girdles of fresh moss. Cuckoos, fearless of harm, call with their sweet voices and sing of the weariness that draws one out of the world. People who wish to cultivate concentration should go to such delightful solitudes, so replete with pleasures that are in harmony with the Dharma.

Giving up attachment to wealth

Why is it necessary to seek solitude? The fleeting pleasures of this world are like the canopies of clouds that appear one moment in the sky and are gone the next. People immerse themselves in these enjoyments, claiming that they are necessary for their livelihood and indispensable for their survival. And yet the life of humankind is no more than a flash of lightning—a swiftly passing interlude, which can in no way be extended beyond its term and is all the while attended by three sufferings, rampant like a gang of thieves: the suffering of change, the suffering of suffering, and all-pervading suffering in the making. In particular, wealth and enjoyments are the occasion of ruin in this life and those to come. Beings are in a situation that is like a turbulent river rushing irresistibly toward the sea. They are constantly tormented and exhausted by the tasks of accumulating, preserving, and augmenting their possessions. Their minds are pulled this way and that by desires, and they are never satisfied. When they possess a few riches, they become puffed up and look down on others. Fearful of losing what they have, they grow mean and stingy. They are so tight-fisted that they do not even eat their own food or wear their finery. As a result, they wander after death in the limitless ocean of the lower realms.

Wealth and precious possessions gained by evil means, and sinful thoughts and actions issuing from false and deceitful attitudes, are black like summer clouds heavy with rain. They are the source of unbounded suffering both in the present and in future lives. By contrast, those who own little are safe from enemies and robbers. Those who know contentment have reached the summit of riches.

Giving up attachment to bad company

On the whole, ordinary people are foolish and behave like spoiled children. Their mindstreams are clogged with wrong thoughts and their actions are unvirtuous. They praise themselves and say unpleasant things about others; they are filled with the venom of the defilements. Their attitudes and conduct are as poisonous as a snake's tongue, and they are surrounded by the harsh atmosphere of conflict. For such people, negative states are constantly on the increase. They think the fleeting, vacuous splendors of the world will last forever, and they are not grateful when spiritual friends do things to help them. They are irritated at the sight of people endeavoring virtuously and in harmony with the Dharma. Instead of being pleased, they are frowning and sullen. Whenever they feel the slightest resentment, which nevertheless burns into them like a fierce fire, they provoke quarrels and stir up the whirlwind of slander. They are as unstable and unpredictable as monkeys; their actions are contrary to the Dharma, and they are great troublemakers. Their minds are centers of mischief—like the vast belly of a sea monster, gulping down all sorts of fish. Like venomous snakes with their deadly breath, they bring to ruin everyone they meet, and with the fires of their hatred, they scorch and destroy in an instant the wholesome fruit trees of their own and others' minds. One must keep as far away as possible from such childish and destructive company.

Giving up attachment to objects of the senses

The six senses stray constantly to the objects of desire, form and so forth. And these, when carelessly enjoyed, are more dangerous than powerful and swift-acting poison. Ordinary toxins, however, when not neutralized by medicine or the power of mantra, result only in the destruction of this present life. By contrast, the fully ripened effect of the wrong enjoyment of sense objects is extremely damaging, resulting in the lower realms for many lives to come. To repeat, if people swallow poison, sweet as it may taste, they will suffer. They can, however, be cured by medicine and mantra. But through wrongly enjoying the objects of desire, beings will have to face the suffering of many lives, not just of one. Medical remedies are powerless against such a predicament, for their purpose is to treat only the four hundred and four kinds of physical disease.[211]

Until one is able, through the practice of vipashyana, to tame the elephant of one's mind, which is intoxicated and driven wild by the deceptive poisons of desire objects, one will never truly perceive the latter's defects, for they always appear as positive qualities. There is nothing more specious and liable to deceive people than the objects of the senses. Therefore, until the time comes for the compounded aggregate of this physical form to fall apart—in other words, when death occurs and the body is placed on a bier and carried away by four men or loaded on an ox and transported to the cemetery—Jigme Lingpa encourages us to dwell in peaceful woodland glades or other places of solitude, away from the distractions of business and society.

In praise of solitude

"Secluded place" and "solitude in the wilds" are actually technical terms. The first refers to a location a mile distant from a village, at the limit of what is considered to be the village territory. By contrast, "solitude in the wilds" is more than two miles distant from a village. Such places, where there are no irritating and harmful circumstances, are a delight to the spirit. It is there that a weariness with samsara will develop. There one will avoid the society of people whose attitudes are false, who are engaged in the worldly occupations of trade, agriculture, and so on. Likewise, one will not be harassed by the obligation of paying taxes, or commissioned for compulsory service and the payment of duties. One will no longer be fretting about whether one has enough to live on; one will be free from the troubles of wage earning and the need to depend on helpers or attendants or indeed on anyone else. Out in the wilds, there are only the carefree birds and wild animals, the sound of whose voices does not grate upon the ear. In places such as these, noble beings find a joyful abundance of all that they need: pure water and all kinds of fruit and edible plants. Natural caves are found in the rocks and shelters of grass and leaves, spacious enough to accommodate the four kinds of activity.* How wonderful if we could find such pleasant dwellings, rejoicing in the cool shade of the trees!

One who lives in such a place is like a traveler constantly arriving in a different place. For outwardly the forest transforms itself to reveal the passage of the seasons, changing its raiment as summer turns to autumn. And yet in all this there is nothing to provoke the arising of defilement. It is thus that Jigme Lingpa praises solitude and instructs us to attend to the Buddha's utterly reliable words when, for example, he declares metaphorically that to take seven steps toward such a place brings unlimited merit! The *Samadhiraja-sutra* says: "Greater than making offerings of flowers, incense, food, and every pleasing thing to the Buddhas for an entire kalpa is to take seven steps in the direction of a solitary place with a mind that is weary of samsara. The merits of such an act are unbounded.

---

* I.e., eating, sleeping, walking, and sitting.

"Leaving on one side all cares for life and limb,
Meditate in solitude in perfect peace,
Work upon your mind with diligence,
And dwell in loneliness like hart and hind."

CONCENTRATION ITSELF

The essence of concentration

Practitioners should stay in solitude and rest in concentration without allowing themselves to be carried away by distraction even for a moment. This constitutes the higher training of the mind. Because body and mind are interrelated, if one adopts a correct physical posture, the subtle channels with their energies will be straight, and this will facilitate the birth of realization in the mind. It is therefore important to sit on a comfortable seat and adopt the seven-point posture of Vairochana. (1) The legs should be crossed in the full or half vajra position.[212] (2) The eyelids should be lowered and the eyes should be gazing along the line of the nose. (3) The body should be kept straight, not leaning to one side or another. (4) The shoulders should be level. (5) The chin should be slightly tucked in so that the nose is in line with the navel. (6) The tip of the tongue should rest on the palate behind the teeth. (7) The breath should be allowed to rise and fall slowly and naturally. This posture is referred to as the life-tree or vital axis* of the mind, for it helps to prevent it from getting lost in distraction, like tying a feeble sapling to a firm support. One must then strive in concentration, keeping the mind balanced in equipoise and focusing it exclusively on the specific object of concentration, without letting it stray elsewhere, even to virtuous objects (let alone negative ones), and without letting it lapse into a sort of shapeless blankness. The object on which the mind should focus one-pointedly may be with or without form,[213] and from time to time, by consciously examining the object of concentration, the mind should fasten itself to its positive target. It is thus that one engages alternately in the practices of analytic and "resting" meditation. A beginner might concentrate on an image (of the Buddha), for example.[214]

The time of meditation should be gradually extended. At length, all that appears to the mind, contrived and fixed upon by thought, will

* *srog shing.*

vanish into emptiness, the ultimate reality. This is not a state of nothingness in which nothing can be perceived. All phenomena, forms and so forth, appear unobstructedly, but they have no true existence; they lack all concrete attributes, with the result that there is in fact nothing real to observe. This is because dualistic perception,* which apprehends things as truly existent, completely vanishes. For the mind has merged with the fundamental nature of things.[215] When the mind remains in such a state, without torpor or excitement, dwelling one-pointedly on its object, undisturbed by thoughts, this is "meditation," namely, *shamatha*. The perfect recognition of the mind's nature of primal wisdom or the absence of clinging to the object of concentration is "post-meditation," namely, *vipashyana*. Shamatha and vipashyana partake of the same nature.†
The *Ratnamegha* gives the following definition: "Shamatha is the one-pointed concentration of the mind; vipashyana is perfect discernment."

The categories of concentration

There are three kinds of concentration. First, there is the "childish" concentration of ordinary beings. This is the concentration enjoyed by beings who have not entered one or other of the three vehicles.‡ The second is the clearly discerning concentration of the worldly mind. This is the concentration of those who have entered one of the vehicles and is the cause of the realization of the path of seeing. Finally, there is the excellent concentration of the Tathagatas, which is the preserve of those who are on the noble path.§

Childish concentration

There are four levels of samadhi belonging to the realm of form, distinguished according to four criteria, namely the presence or absence of: (1) gross discursiveness; (2) subtle discursiveness; (3) joy; and (4) bliss. In addition, there are four absorptions associated with the formless realm (the absorption of "infinite space" and so forth). These eight absorptions together constitute the first kind of concentration, known

---

* *bcos ma'i 'du shes.*
† In other words, shamatha and vipashyana are two aspects of the one state of mind. This distinction in terms of meditation (*mnyam bzhag*) and post-meditation (*rjes thob*) is discussed at greater length later in the chapter.
‡ Those of the Shravakayana, Pratyekabuddhayana, and Bodhisattvayana.
§ I.e., on the paths of seeing and beyond.

as the *childish enjoyment concentration*,[216] so called because they pertain to ordinary beings who have yet to enter one or other of the three paths. We will now consider certain details of these concentrations.

1. *The four levels of samadhi of the form realm.* The first samadhi comprises the preparatory stage* of the samadhi and the actual samadhi itself. Various kinds of meditation may be used as preparation. However, practitioners who are only on the worldly path meditate on the harsh character of the desire realm and the peaceful serenity of the superior states. At the outset, the mind of the realm of desire is considered as something coarse, agitated, and inferior. From this perspective, the state of the first samadhi is seen as peaceful, happy, and supremely advantageous. One is thus continually preoccupied with it, learning and reflecting about it. The time will come when learning and reflection are transcended and the samadhi will be experienced in meditation. Until the six defilements of the desire realm† (in their great and moderate degrees of intensity) are discarded, the meditator is considered to be in the preparatory stage of the samadhi. Subsequently, as the emotions of the lesser degree associated with the desire realm are discarded, the samadhi itself is experienced.

The first samadhi has five aspects: gross discursiveness, subtle discursiveness, joy, bliss, and concentration. With regard to the first two aspects, the qualification as gross and subtle is made in accordance with the Abhidharma. Indeed, "gross discursiveness" refers to a rough judgment as to whether the mind is in correct concentration, while "subtle discursiveness" is a more refined investigation of the same thing. As the mind rests in concentration, the consciousness is suffused with happiness. This is what is meant by joy. A physical sensation of bliss arises from perfect flexibility.[217] Finally, "concentration" refers to the fact that the mind remains focused one-pointedly.

The second samadhi has four aspects: perfect limpidity, joy, bliss, and concentration. Perfect limpidity normally denotes mindfulness, vigilance, and mental evenness, but in this context it refers to the fact that

---

* *nyer bsdogs.*
† See chapter 6. These six defilements are: attachment, aversion, pride, ignorance, doubt, and wrong views.

one is never separate from the flow of mental joy. The three remaining aspects are the same as for the first samadhi.

The third samadhi has five aspects: bliss, evenness, mindfulness, vigilance, and concentration. The meaning of bliss is the same as above. Evenness refers to the fact that the mind rests (effortlessly) in its natural flow, free from all torpor or agitation. Mindfulness means not to forget to concentrate. Vigilance is the constant confirmation that neither torpor nor agitation is occurring. Finally, concentration is as previously described.

The fourth samadhi has four aspects: mindfulness, neutrality of feeling, evenness, and concentration. Mindfulness and concentration are as just described. Neutrality of feeling refers to a state of undifferentiated sensation, while evenness is as described in relation to the third samadhi.

The possession of the five aspects of gross and subtle discursiveness and so on belongs to the rudimentary stage* of the first samadhi. When rough discursiveness is relinquished but subtle discursiveness remains, the extraordinary first samadhi is attained. When both gross and subtle discursiveness are relinquished, the second samadhi occurs. When both gross and subtle thoughts together with mental joy are absent, the third samadhi is attained, while the absence of these three factors together with that of physical bliss is characteristic of the fourth samadhi.

Regardless of whether the meditator attains actual samadhi, the authentic and pure preparatory stage for the first samadhi constitutes the foundation of vipashyana, for which reason it is referred to as the "all-sufficing preparation."† The preparatory stage and the rudimentary and extraordinary phases of the first samadhi are sometimes counted separately, so that, taking them together with the three remaining samadhis, one comes to what is referred to as the *six levels of samadhi*.

2. *The formless realm.* The absorptions of the formless realm are not classified according to respective aspects, but are differentiated mainly according to their referent and accompanying attitude.

When the fourth samadhi is attained, three kinds of perception are arrested: the perception of shape (square, round, etc.), the perception of

---

* *bsam gtan dang po'i dngos gzhi tsam po pa.*
† *nyer bsdogs mi lcogs med.*

color (white, yellow, red, green, etc.), and finally the perception of the solidity of objects such as houses or mountains. Meditating on the spacelike nature of all phenomena, the practitioner goes beyond all form-related perceptions and rests in a state that is similar to space, in an absorption that is called *infinite space*. When even the apprehension of space is relinquished, the meditator remains simply in the state of consciousness within which the notion of space had been conceived. This absorption is called *infinite consciousness*. When the apprehension of this mere consciousness, is relinquished, a perception of nothingness appears; the absorption is therefore referred to as *utter nothingness*. When even this apprehension is discarded and the experience of apprehending nothingness is analyzed, all coarse movements of perception cease and the mind dwells in an extremely subtle state which is the absorption of *neither perception nor nonperception*. This absorption is also called *neither existence nor nonexistence*.

Clearly discerning concentration

For people who have entered one of the three vehicles and are abiding on the paths of accumulation or joining, it is through the concentration associated with vipashyana that the path of seeing (i.e., liberation) is attained. This state of mind is known as *clearly discerning concentration*, where the name of the result is given to the cause.

The excellent concentration of the Tathagatas

Perfect Joy, the first ground of the noble bodhisattva path, is where the concentration of noble beings begins. By nature, it is immaculate, perfect wisdom.* Later, on the path of no more learning, the wisdom of the Buddhas is the perfect union of shamatha and vipashyana, the ultimate stainless virtue. This excellent concentration is the transcendent perfection of concentration itself.

It is an essential feature of all concentrations that the mind is held one-pointedly within and not allowed to stray to any external distractions. This is accomplished and perfected by an uninterrupted mindfulness that never loses its referent and attitude, and is accompanied by

---

* "The term 'immaculate' (*zag med*) is used here to denote the fact that this wisdom is an antidote for the belief in the self." [YG II, 404]

enthusiastic diligence. These are the factors on which concentration depends. If one loses one's concentrated mindfulness and is distracted to extraneous objects, one should at once vigilantly retrieve it and diligently meditate, thus mending or "patching up" one's concentration. Training in the common samadhis constitutes the basis for the bliss that arises from the well-trained flexibility of the body and mind, and for various miraculous powers. The accomplishment of the samadhis results in qualities enjoyed also by Shravakas such as preternatural knowledge (the recollection, for example, of previous existences) and the "eight dominant ayatanas."[218]

In each of the six types of attention[219] occurring in the preparatory stage of the first samadhi, discursiveness, both gross and subtle, is present. However, in the first samadhi itself, although subtle discursiveness persists, gross discursiveness vanishes. The remaining three samadhis are devoid of both gross and subtle discursiveness. The samadhis proceed in order, each preparing the way for the one following; the first lays the ground for the second, and so on. In the same way, the fourth samadhi is the preparation for the (formless) absorption of infinite space. This in turn is the preparation for the second absorption, and so on. For this reason, the nine absorptions[220] are referred to as the foundation of the paths of seeing and meditation for the three kinds of noble beings (Shravaka, Pratyekabuddha, and Bodhisattva).

The qualities resulting from concentration
Shamatha and vipashyana[221] bring forth all the qualities of the paths and fruit of the three vehicles.

In particular, the concentration that produces all the qualities of the paths and fruit of the Mahayana is associated with a compassion for other beings and is linked with a supreme wisdom that is free from concepts. In proportion as practitioners gain in compassion and wisdom, they acquire the different levels of concentration[222] that share their nature.* Accordingly, meditators will accomplish all the qualities of the grounds and paths of the extraordinary Mahayana and will discard all obscurations.

---

* *rang dang ngo bo gcig pa.*

There are two ways in which meditation, or remaining in equipoise, may be distinguished from post-meditation. The first way presupposes that they both possess the same nature.* According to this perspective, as the mind rests one-pointedly in meditation, all gross movements of the mind and mental factors vanish and a state free of thoughts occurs. This is "meditation." Throughout this experience, the sense consciousnesses are not arrested but continue to function. Phenomena still appear, but there is no clinging to them. This aspect of clarity is regarded as "post-meditation." Partaking of the one substance of the mind, meditation and post-meditation gradually eliminate dualistic thoughts of subject and object.

A distinction is sometimes made between the terms "duality of subject and object" and "dualistic thought of subject and object." While the apparent object (which lacks inherent existence) is the thing perceived, the apprehension, or perception, is regarded as the perceiver. This is the "duality of subject and object." By contrast, the apprehension of an object of the eight consciousnesses (form and so forth) is the "percept-thought," while the apprehension of the "thinking aspect" of the eight consciousnesses performing the perception is the "perceiver-thought."[223] The removal of duality and the removal of dualistic thought amount to the same thing. When dualistic thoughts (i.e., those of subject and object) are discarded, duality is also discarded. Intelligent people should examine for themselves whether this is true.

The second way of distinguishing meditation from post-meditation presupposes that the two are different by nature. On the one hand, when the mind dwells one-pointedly in equipoise, this is meditation. When the meditator rises from this and engages in daily activities such as eating and sleeping, while never losing the awareness that all is like an illusion, this is post-meditation. When in the course of such activities as walking or sitting the six consciousnesses are carried away by outer objects, the practitioner is dissipated.† It is said that until they reach the seventh ground, even noble beings sometimes fall into this kind of dissipation.

---

* I.e., they occur simultaneously.
† *rgya yan pa*. In other words, no longer in the post-meditation state.

There now follows an exposition of wisdom, the third of the three trainings, covering both its nature and its various categories. Essentially, wisdom is a pure intelligence that accurately knows phenomena and their ultimate nature.

THE CATEGORIES OF WISDOM

The wisdom that is the fruit of meditation arises naturally in three ways. To begin with, it is the result of the preliminary training of samadhi. Later, it derives from the main practice of samadhi, which is limpid and free from all obscuration and opacity, occurring when the mind has become pliable and positive. This at length gives rise to the wisdom of perceiving (even in post-meditation) that phenomena are without true existence.

In all, there are three kinds of wisdom: the wisdom of hearing, the wisdom of reflection, and the wisdom of meditation. Gradual training in these will result in the perfect accomplishment of vipashyana, primordial and nonconceptual wisdom. This wisdom destroys the defilements that prevent the attainment of liberation and removes the cognitive obscurations that prevent omniscience. It is the unmistaken knowledge, first, of ultimate reality, the profound nature of things, and second, of all phenomena that arise within the sphere of deluded perception. Equipped with such knowledge, one is able to pass swiftly through the city of existence, which karma and defilements have made so difficult to cross. Thus, one goes beyond suffering and reaches nirvana with ease.

The six transcendent perfections, generosity and so forth, are causally interrelated and are arranged progressively in terms of subtlety and elevation. They are called transcendent because they are all combined with transcendent wisdom.

THE WISDOM RESULTING FROM HEARING THE TEACHINGS

Ordinary people who have entered the path and who are not well grounded in the wisdom of hearing the teachings are in danger of becoming pretentious and conceited about their qualities of reflection and meditation. Because of this, they run the risk of wandering into error. The *Samadhiraja-sutra* says:

A man who binds himself with pure discipline
But proudly fails to listen to much teaching—
The fruits of his good life will go to waste,
And dreadful suffering will be his lot.

Indeed, the wisdom arising from hearing the teachings is said to be the cause of the wisdom of reflection and meditation. As master Ashvaghosha has said:

The man of little learning is as if born blind.
How can he meditate, on what can he reflect?
Study then with diligence, reflect and meditate;
Through this, vast wisdom will arise.

The keys that open the treasure chest of Dharma

The twelve branches of scripture, which set forth the doctrine of the two truths, are evaluated by the wisdom that arises from hearing the teaching. This evaluation involves the making of two distinctions: (1) the distinction between the teachings of ultimate meaning and the teachings of expedient meaning; and (2) the distinction between the four kinds of implied teaching* and the four kinds of indirect teaching.† This assessment can only be made by applying the principle of the four reliances.[224]

The ultimate and expedient teachings

The fundamental state of all phenomena, of samsara, nirvana, and the path, is the naturally pure expanse of absolute reality, the luminous nature of the mind itself. Transcending origination, abiding, and cessation, this state is expressed as the three doors of perfect liberation: it is empty, devoid of attributes, and beyond all expectancy. This is the ultimate meaning.

Taking as his frame of reference phenomena as they appear to deluded minds—in other words, everything occurring on the level of the relative truth—and in order to lead beings on the path, the Buddha

* *dgongs pa can.*
† *ldem dgongs.*

referred to things that in truth have no existence. Thus, with regard to the ground, he spoke about the aggregates, the *dhatus* and ayatanas. With regard to the path, he gave teachings on the three vehicles. And in reference to the fruit, he expatiated upon the three kinds of nirvana. All these doctrines comprise the teachings of the expedient meaning. The scriptures that set them forth are the "pitaka of expedient meaning," and their commentaries are the "shastras of expedient meaning."[225] Those who understand the distinction between the teachings of the sutras of expedient meaning and those of the sutras of ultimate meaning will know in which they should place their trust. The previous mention of the four reliances has made this clear. All this is the first key that opens up the treasury of the teachings, enabling us to imbibe its rich and varied contents.

The implied teachings and indirect teachings
Once we have understood the difference between the ultimate and expedient teachings, we can go on to explore the latter, namely, those the real meaning of which is not explicitly stated. In order to assess both the Buddha's didactic purpose and the content of his thought,* as these underlie the sutras of expedient meaning, and in order to establish a meaning that is ultimately valid, it is helpful to distinguish four kinds of "implied" teaching and four kinds of "indirect" teaching.

We will begin with the four kinds of implied teaching. Here, the Buddha merely expressed himself in words that were, and are, open to interpretation. The case is different with the indirect teachings, in which the Buddha taught his hearers by means of expressions employed on an ad hoc basis, suited to the situation. This was to lead them to an understanding of what he actually meant. It should be noted that in the case of implied teachings, although the underlying meaning is uppermost in importance, it may in fact elude the grasp of the hearers, even though the immediate purpose of the utterance is achieved.

Implied teachings · *1. Teachings implying the equality of all phenomena.* In the most general terms, phenomena are, according to their fundamental nature, beyond the categories of good or bad. They are beyond any such

* *dgongs gzhi.*

differentiation. In this sense, the Tathagatas are all essentially equal—identical in the expanse of the Dharmakaya. Having this in mind, the Buddha said: "At that time, I was the perfect Buddha Vipashyin." He was thus teaching that phenomena appearing as separate in time, or as opposites—samsara and nirvana, good and bad, to be accepted or rejected accordingly—are all one. In addition, it was with these words that he confounded those who disparaged him for his short life span and the size of his body.

2. *Teachings implying the absence of inherent identity in phenomena.** Having another sense in mind (in other words, the absence of inherent identity with regard to the *imputed, dependent,* and *completely existent* natures),[226] the Buddha said that when phenomena are analyzed—from form right up to omniscience—nothing is found. Thus, by appealing to analysis and so on, he counteracted the tendency to grasp at phenomena as real.[227]

3. *Teachings implying fulfillment at a future time.* Having in mind the fact that, once the seed is planted, enlightenment eventually occurs at some future moment, the Buddha said that by the single recitation of certain dharanis or mantras, or by simply pronouncing the name of the Buddha Nirmala Chandraprabha, enlightenment "would be effortlessly achieved." He said things like this in order to entice people who are otherwise slow and lazy in the practice of virtue.[228]

4. *Teachings for the humbling of pride and conceit.* Seeing that people are barred from liberation by the pride they take in their practice of generosity, the Buddha belittled it, saying it was demon's work (though of course it was not) and praised discipline. And thinking that people become self-satisfied on account of their discipline, the Buddha deprecated it and extolled charity. In this way he destroyed conceit and undermined pretentiousness.

Indirect teachings · In the so-called indirect teachings, the Buddha expressed himself in terms that are not to be taken at their face value. He acted in this way because if he had set forth subjects like the indivisibility of the two truths or the extraordinary qualities of the Buddhas and Bodhisattvas in straight and unvarnished terms to people of limited capacity, their minds would have been unable to accept them, and they

* *ngo bo nyid med.*

would have fallen into doubt. To people of this kind, who could not otherwise be introduced to such doctrines, the Buddha expressed himself artfully and with tact, using words and arguments that were engaging and liable to make an impression on his hearers. In order to direct them to an understanding of his wisdom intention, he taught in words that were on a level with his hearers, even though his own true meaning was not.

The *Sutralankara* distinguishes four categories of indirect teachings: (1) indirect teachings aimed at introducing people to the path; (2) indirect teachings on the nature of phenomena; (3) indirect teachings connected with remedial methods; and (4) indirect teachings that are couched in metaphors.

1. *Indirect teachings aimed at introducing people to the path.** If from the first the Buddha had taught people of lesser capacity and aspiration the teachings of, for example, the *Prajnaparamita-sutras*, in which the no-self (or the absence of inherent existence) of phenomena is openly expounded, his hearers would have missed the point, namely, that phenomena arise in interdependence. They would have taken the teaching as a nihilistic view of nothingness. And dismayed by both the words and the meaning, they would have rejected both the path and the teachings of the Mahayana. In one of the sutras, the Buddha therefore said, "Form, O Subhuti, has attributes. Sound has attributes." He thus made an assertion implying the existence of form and the rest. The people listening to him were consequently not shocked, and in the belief that phenomena truly exist, they entered the path. This was the purpose of the Buddha's saying what he said. Yet what the Buddha himself knew was that everything that appears to the deluded mind does so in the manner of a dream.[229]

2. *Indirect teaching on the threefold nature of phenomena.*† To say that phenomena in their fundamental nature[230] have no inherent identity does not mean that they are completely lacking in existence, but rather that they are characterized by the three doors of perfect liberation—in other words, that there are three kinds of nature or reality. First, there is

* *zhugs pa ldem dgongs.*
† *mtshan nyid ldem dgongs.*

imputed reality, or reality as understood by ordinary beings. Second, there is *dependent reality*, the condition of phenomena as they arise through interdependence. Thirdly, there is *completely existent reality*, in other words, the truly Real, emptiness, beyond all conceptual constructs.

On the level of the imputed or assumed reality of things, absence of inherent identity means that phenomena have no inherent existence at all. Phenomena that are merely mistaken perceptions have no reality whatever. This is exemplified by someone seeing a rope and thinking that it is a snake.

On the level of dependent reality, absence of inherent identity means that phenomena are unborn. For, although phenomena seem to have origins, if they are analyzed it will be found that none of the four possible kinds of origination applies to them.[231] In this sense, they are like illusions.

On the level of completely existent reality, absence of inherent identity means that even the absolute truth cannot be said to exist inherently. This is so because the absolute is outside the range of concepts and predicates (of impurity, purity, or whatever). It is like the unclouded sky. With these three realities in view, the Buddha gave profound teachings, difficult to fathom. He said, for instance, "All phenomena, from form to omniscience, lack true existence. They have no origin."

The above is presented from the Madhyamika point of view, which regards the Buddha's teaching on the threefold nature of phenomena as expedient. The Chittamatrins, for their part, take the opposite view and affirm that it is rather Buddha's teaching on the absence of inherent identity that is expedient. In their view, when the Buddha said that the imputed reality lacks existence, he meant that there are no substances outside and separate from the mind. When he said that dependent reality lacks true existence, he meant that the causes of phenomena are not found in themselves. When he said that the completely existent reality does not exist, he meant that it is not something separate from the dependent reality. This is the reason why he affirmed their lack of inherent existence. But this view is specific to the Chittamatrins and is not the same as the one just given.

*3. Indirect teachings connected with remedial methods.** Certain coarse and nar-

---

* *gnyen po ldem dgongs.*

row-minded persons thought that, of the thousand Buddhas who would manifest, the Buddha Shakyamuni was inferior due to the fact that, as it was reported in the *Bhadrakalpita-sutra*, his body was slight, his light radiated only to the distance of an arm's length, his following was meager, and his life span short. In order to correct such disparagement, the Buddha taught that the life span, lineage, and physical stature of the Teachers are beyond measurement. He was thinking of the fact that the Rupakayas of all the Buddhas are equal in appearing only for the benefit of beings, that they are equal in the unborn Dharmakaya, that they are equal in having perfected the twofold accumulation, and that they are equal in their enlightened activity, which is effortlessly deployed for the sake of others.

Likewise, in order to remedy contemptuous attitudes toward his Dharma of transmission,[232] the Buddha said, "The ability to understand the Mahayana is the fruit of worshiping Buddhas equal in number to the grains of sand in the Ganges." He was thinking, so it is taught, of the mahayana Dharma of realization.

4. *Indirect teachings expressed in metaphors.** In order to prevent people from saying things like, "Gautama the ascetic teaches unsolicited," the Buddha said, "Profound and peaceful, beyond all concepts, and so on," and he remained silent. And in order to prevent people from saying, "If he attained such excellence after a mere six years of ascetic practice, his Dharma must be easy indeed!" the Buddha said, intending to introduce his hearers to profound teachings, that one should kill one's father and mother (whom one should not kill under any circumstances). He said that liberation would be attained by those who bring down the king and the two classes of pure conduct (Brahmins and virtuous ascetics) and by those who destroy both country and royal court—all of which are not to be destroyed. Actually, with these words, the Buddha was referring to Craving, Grasping,[233] and the alaya. Thus, in the *Udanavarga*, he said:

> Father, mother—slay them both,
> Your king, the two of pure life,

---

* *bsgyur ba ldem dgongs.*

The country and the royal court[234] destroy!
Liberation is for those who do so.

It would obviously be a calamitous mistake to take such words literally.

The difference between implied and indirect teachings · In whichever way the implied and indirect teachings are presented, their meaning comes essentially to the same thing; they are separated only by a difference of emphasis. When a discourse of the Buddha is being explained in which the meaning is not literally expressed in the words used, and when the commentator emphasizes this underlying meaning, saying, "The Buddha said this, but in fact he meant that," as distinct from what the commentator understands to be the specific pedagogical purpose behind the Buddha's speech (namely, to lead people on the path), we have what are called the implied teachings. By contrast, when the commentator interprets the Buddha's words in a manner that particularly highlights their pedagogical purpose, saying, "The reason the Buddha did not speak directly but in a roundabout way was to guide certain people onto the path," we have what are called indirect teachings. Of course, the interpretation of the Buddha's words, meaning, and purposes is a vast and complex subject. But in short, the wisdom that correctly identifies the implied and indirect teachings constitutes the second key that opens the scriptures of sutra and tantra.

An explanation of the treasury of Dharma
A general exposition of the two truths
As an antidote to the eighty-four thousand types of defilement, the Buddha, expert in methods and rich in great compassion, set forth eighty-four thousand sections of teaching, classified as the four pitakas, or "baskets." Each of the first three pitakas counteracts one of the three principal defilements, while the fourth pitaka is an antidote to all three together. The range of these teachings is inconceivably vast, but they are all summarized in the doctrine of the two truths.

The relative truth embraces all the phenomena of samsara or the world, in other words, the mind and the phenomena that manifest from the mind. The absolute truth refers to supramundane primordial wisdom, all-discerning awareness, which has the same nature as the dharmadhatu. It follows from this that all possible knowledge-objects are accounted for in the two truths; there is no third truth.

The relative truth is subdivided into two aspects: unmistaken and mistaken, following the distinction made between accurate and defective cognition. All phenomena that appear to the deluded mind and are efficient (in the sense of the moon shedding light, fire giving heat, water being wet, and so on)—together with the consciousnesses that cognize them—are regarded as the "unmistaken relative truth."* They arise from their respective causes, although, when examined, they are found to be empty of inherent existence. By contrast, things like a mirage of water, a rope that is mistaken for a snake, or the vision of two moons instead of one (all of which might appear in hallucinations but are incapable of producing normal effects, in the sense of moistening, giving a poisonous bite, or shedding light)—together with the consciousnesses that cognize them—are referred to as "mistaken relative truth."† Thus the difference between mistaken and unmistaken relative truth depends upon the ability to function on the conventional level.[235]

The term "absolute truth" refers to the fundamental state of all things. It is primal wisdom, wherein samsara and nirvana are seen to have the same nature.‡ From the very first, neither the phenomena of samsara nor the phenomena of nirvana possess inherent existence, and they are not two separate classes of things. Phenomena have always been beyond the range of conceptual construction. And since the absolute truth is beyond all thought and verbal expression, it cannot be said to exist for those who have realized it and not to exist for those who have not done so. Whether it is realized or not, the absolute truth is the unchanging nature of all things. The regent Maitreya has said: "It is the unchanging ultimate nature, the same in the past and in the future."

The two truths are not separate like the two horns of a buffalo. From the beginning, they are blended together inextricably: appearance and emptiness inseparably united. Therefore, phenomena arising through interdependence are not totally nonexistent like a horned rabbit. They are rather like the reflection of the moon in a clear pool.

* *yang dag pa'i kun rdzob.*
† *log pa'i kun rdzob.*
‡ I.e., as seen at the level of buddhahood when mind and object are "of the same taste."

Phenomena appear, and this aspect of appearance corresponds to the relative truth. Nevertheless, in the very moment of their arising, they are lacking in true existence. This aspect corresponds to the absolute truth. Thus, while a distinction can be made between the two truths, these same truths have no intrinsic existence separate from each other.

For the moment, while we are on the path of aspirational practice, phenomena, the objects to which the senses are attracted (forms, sounds, and so forth), all appear clearly to our five sense consciousnesses, like the brilliant colors of the rainbow. But the mere appearance of the five sense objects is not what entangles us. It is rather that, when the duality of subject and object arises, the perceiver identifies a perceived object as something to be enjoyed and so on. Endless delusory perceptions of mind and mental factors occur, resulting in the rejection of the undesirable and indulgence in the desirable. Nevertheless, all these appearances are lacking in real existence. They are beyond the eight ontological extremes. One should reflect on them and analyze them according to the eight examples of illusion. Like appearances in a dream, phenomena have no origin; like an illusion, they are not subject to destruction; like a mirage they have no permanence; like a reflection of the moon in water, they are not completely nonexistent; like an optical illusion, they come from nowhere; like an echo, they go nowhere; like a castle in the clouds, there is no distinction in them; like magical displays, they are not identical. We must generate conviction in the inseparability of appearance and emptiness and, having done so, rest one-pointedly in it.

Merely to understand the indivisibility of the two truths and the absence of inherent existence according to the eight ontological extremes (using the eight similes quoted above), and to familiarize oneself with this, does not in itself mean that one attains to the ultimate nature of things. For no object of intellectual affirmation can be the absolute truth. The intellect pertains only to the relative truth and is itself the factor that veils the state of nonduality. The absolute truth can be realized only by thought-free primordial wisdom, wherein there is no duality of subject and object. The state beyond all conceptual constructs is incompatible with concepts of one and many, existence and nonexistence. Primordial wisdom, the ultimate nature, can never be the object of the intellect. As Shantideva says, "The absolute is not within the reach of intellect." (*Bodhicharyavatara*, IX, 2)

The four tenet systems

This, then, is an exposition of the two truths in the most general terms. However, each Buddhist school of tenets interprets the Buddha's teaching on the two truths in its own particular way, and thus sets forth its own particular teaching on the ground, path, and fruit.

The Vaibhashikas · The Vaibhashika school considers that, with regard to the six ordinary sense consciousnesses, the absolute truth, or ultimate reality, is the indivisible moment of consciousness, which, so they say, intellectual analysis is unable to divide into past, present, and future. Likewise, the indivisible particle of matter, which cannot be further divided, also has the status of an ultimate reality or absolute truth. By contrast, all gross, nonmental phenomena, which are composed of these tiny particles, are considered to lack true existence, being subject to destruction by opposing forces.[236]

The Sautrantikas · The way in which the Sautrantikas[237] account for phenomena in terms of the two truths is as follows. Efficient objects, like vases able to hold water and pillars able to support beams, have no absolute existence in that they are no more than collections of material atomic particles (which, however, are ultimately real). Consequently, the position of the Sautrantikas is the same as that of the Vaibhashikas in that they accept the reality of two partless particles—of matter and consciousness. The Sautrantikas differ from the Vaibhashikas, however, in saying that time (the past, present, and future) has no substantial existence and in denying that space is a permanent and real entity. They say, moreover, that a mental image of, for example, a vase or a pillar, insofar as it is unable to perform a concrete function such as holding water, belongs to the relative truth. It effectively obscures the specific character of the object as it is in itself. For it is the mental image alone that appears to the deluded mind and has no inherent existence. The absolute and relative truths are explained as relating respectively to specifically characterized things* (absolute) and generally characterized

---

* *rang mtshan.*

things* (relative). The tradition of the Sautrantikas is a system established through reason and elaborated through the application of logic.[238]

The Chittamatrins, the Mind Only school · The Chittamatrins[239] say that through the power of habit, we assign a distinct existence both to the perceiving mind and to its perceived object, whereas in reality the two do not exist as separate entities. The object-apprehending mind and the percepts of this mind, which are falsely reified as truly and separately existing entities, are referred to here as imputed reality. This imputed reality is the relative truth, and everything other than it is absolute. The absolute truth refers, in the first place, to the ultimate essence of the dependent reality, namely, the underlying substratum of mental appearances or percepts. This substratum itself is the self-knowing mind, void of duality of subject and object. In the second place, the absolute truth also includes the completely existent reality, namely, the fact that the dependent reality is empty of the imputed reality.[240] Of these two aspects of the absolute truth, the first is called subjective absolute truth,† and the second is objective absolute truth.‡

The Svatantrika Madhyamikas · The Svatantrika Madhyamikas say that phenomena (form and the other objects of the six senses) have a natural existence of their own on the relative level, and this is established by conventional reasoning. Although phenomena have no *true* existence, yet on their own level, so to speak, they do exist. In this context, "existing from their own side," "existing on their own level," "existing according to their characteristics," and "substantially existing" are regarded as synonymous, and what these expressions refer to is not considered the proper object of refutation by reasoning that establishes the absolute truth. Thus, for the Svatantrikas, it seems that when the Madhyamika texts say that phenomena are without inherent existence, it is necessary to add that this is to be understood on the level of the absolute truth alone.[241] Phenomena appear like illusions, according to the interdependence of causes and conditions; they are "really there," existing according to characteristics. It is thus possible to discourse

---

* *spyi mtshan.*
† *chos can don dam.*
‡ *chos nyid don dam.*

about distinct phenomena, actions and their effects, and so forth. On the other hand, if the ontological status of these phenomena is examined using analysis and reasoning on the absolute level, they are found to be devoid of any kind of existence. They are utterly pure, empty like space. In this context, the expressions "true existence," "absolute existence," "completely existing," and "ultimate existence" are all synonyms and are equally the object of refutation by analysis at the absolute level. The Svatantrikas state that the objects of refutation are specifically the self of phenomena and the personal self. These are the general tenets of the Svatantrika Madhyamikas.

The Prasangika Madhyamikas · The Prasangika Madhyamikas accept that everything in phenomenal existence arises in interdependence; phenomena manifest like an illusion or dream. However, they refrain from investigating such appearances, to see whether they have some sort of existence or not, and group them all under the heading of relative truth, using this as a stepping-stone to the absolute truth. That phenomena are, ultimately speaking, without inherent existence and are void from the very beginning—this is their absolute truth. However, all such statements are mere labels, formulated from the conventional standpoint alone. In reality, the two truths, relative and absolute, are not correlated with appearance and emptiness, respectively. Phenomena are by their very nature ungrounded and rootless, beyond the four ontological extremes. All phenomena, forms and so forth, that are the objects of the six consciousnesses and appear to come into and pass out of existence—all arise and perish, come and go just like a reflection or a mirage. They have no ultimate existence. For the processes of origination and so forth are themselves mere appearances. They themselves have no real existence.

The Chittamatrins affirm that the self-knowing mind (i.e., the dependent reality) is really existent. The Svatantrikas assert that the phenomena dependent on causes and conditions, forms, and so forth, have an existence on the conventional level. By contrast, the Prasangikas, in their tenets, refrain from positing even the relative existence of things, let alone their absolute existence.

The great founder of the Prasangika tradition, the supreme Nagarjuna, whose birth was foretold in scripture, elucidated the sutras of ultimate meaning through the sheer strength of his own genius, without recourse to other commentaries. It was thus that he established the Madhyamika dialectic, which prevails to this day.[242] It is written in the *Lankavatara-sutra*:

> In the land of Bheta to the south,
> A glorious monk of wide renown,
> By name of Naga will be called.
> "Is" and "is not" both he will refute
> And propagate my teaching in the world,
> Explaining Mahayana unsurpassed.
> Accomplishing the ground of Perfect Joy,
> He will depart for Sukhavati.

And in the tantra *'jam dpal rtsa rgyud* it is said:

> Four hundred years after I
> The Tathagata shall have passed away,
> A virtuous monk called Naga will arise
> To propagate and benefit my doctrine.
> Accomplishing the ground of Perfect Joy
> And living then six hundred years,
> This great being will attain
> To *Knowledge of the Mighty Peacock*,[243]
> To understanding of the different shastras,
> The meaning of the absence of existence.
> Relinquishing his mortal frame,
> He will take birth in Sukhavati
> Thence to gain the perfect fruit
> Of final buddhahood.

Nagarjuna's six (main) treatises[244] were commented on by the masters Aryadeva, Buddhapalita, Bhavaviveka, Chandrakirti, and others. Of these especially, the glorious Chandrakirti, possessed as he was of incomparable knowledge and ability, penetrated the teaching of the master Nagarjuna and unerringly elucidated the *Karikas* in his commentaries *Madhyamakavatara* and *Prasannapada*.[245] He perfectly set forth the ultimate meaning of the Buddha's teaching, and it was through his writings that the tenets of the Prasangikas rose like the sun over the world, scattering the darkness of false views.

Conclusion

The proponents of the three lower tenet systems impute existence to phenomena. They do indeed manage to overcome certain conceptual constructions by reflecting on the absence of self, the unborn nature, emptiness, and the absence of ontological extremes, which are the very object of wisdom inquiry. But they still retain a certain clinging to the reality of things. The Svatantrikas, for their part, accept existence on the conventional level. It is only the Prasangikas who contest such assertions, uprooting all extremes of conceptuality. Being immune to counterattack, the Prasangika tenets are supreme; they are the summit of all systems and utterly free from error.

In India there were many philosophical systems, both Buddhist and non-Buddhist. Likewise in Tibet, numerous distinctions were made according to respective beliefs, and there are several ways of comprehending the teachings of the proponents of the Madhyamika and the Secret Mantra. From their own standpoint, and according to their own understanding, the proponents of each of these systems claim finality for their own tenets. But if one analyzes them all in detail and gains a proper understanding of them through the wisdom arising from hearing the teachings, it is possible to differentiate clearly the character of the four main systems of Buddhist thought and achieve certainty that the ultimate path of practice is that of the Prasangikas. While the Svatantrikas are in harmony with the Prasangika position, the Vaibhashikas, Sautrantikas, and Chittamatrins diverge from it. Conviction in this matter goes far beyond the manipulation of mere words and expressions.* It is the wisdom resulting from reflection, which itself derives from the wisdom arising from perfectly hearing the teachings. Through meditation on the meaning thus understood, the perfect wisdom that accurately ascertains phenomena will subdue all negative emotions and the thought patterns that fixate upon the (supposed) reality of things. It will banish them

---

* It has nothing to do with a merely academic understanding.

from the mind, and an immense courage will arise in the face of evil and adversity, which in turn will be rendered powerless.

As the great upholders of Prasangika doctrine have shown, the ultimate aim of practice is the fundamental condition of phenomena. This is the dharmadhatu, which is by nature beyond all conceptual constructs. It is unspeakable, unthinkable, and impossible to convey. It is a peaceful serenity, the absence of all conceptual construction: the ultimate, absolute truth. Its unobstructed creative power is displayed as the dependent arising of phenomena, and it is this that the mind and its mental factors interpret, or rather misinterpret, as something that can be verbally expressed, mentally conceived, and demonstrated. Phenomena that arise unobstructedly and according to imputation are described as the relative truth. If in meditation one settles in the spacious state of wisdom free from thoughts, and if in the post-meditation period one unremittingly accumulates merit on the understanding that all is like an illusion, one will avoid falling one-sidedly into one or other of the two truths. Even in post-meditation, when appearances arise, it will be impossible to stir from the fundamental mode of phenomena, and, conversely, even when one rests in meditation in a state free from conceptual constructs, such an emptiness will not be a state of mere nothingness. At all times, the two truths are united and inseparable. This is the nature of the dharmadhatu, beyond all duality imputed by the ordinary intellect, beyond the division of an object realized and a mind that realizes. It is impossible for anyone to experience it in the manner of a knowledge-object. The dharmadhatu is, of course, invisible to the referential, dualistic view. It is not at all as though something is newly attained that had not been present before, or perfected through the laborious following of the path. Even those who fail to accomplish the path and who remain in ordinariness do not, for that reason, lose it. For in the natural condition of the ultimate nature, attainment is not good, and nonattainment is not bad; they are perfectly equal.

Dwelling in emptiness, the ultimate nature, means that the mind is attuned to emptiness and all clinging to ontological extremes is exhausted. Subject and object blend into one taste. Like salt dissolving in water, the mind and the ultimate nature are not distinct. This is what is correctly designated as the "realization of emptiness" and "the gaining of the result."[246]

THE WISDOM RESULTING FROM REFLECTION

The meaning of the treasury of the scriptures is that all the phenomena of the ground, path, and fruit arise interdependently. If, from listening to the teachings, we gain a clear understanding of this interdependence, and if we are then able to bring together the key points and penetrate them with the wisdom that results from reflection—a wisdom that is uncontaminated by adhering to extreme views—we will have in our possession, so to speak, a key with which to open the door to the scriptures' profound meaning.

Dependent arising with regard to the ground nature

All phenomena, all false and deceptive appearances, the fluctuating compoundedness of life, samsara with its karma and defilements, and indeed the liberation from suffering that we call nirvana are names superimposed on the ultimate nature. As to their origin, they arise from nowhere; as to their cessation, they go nowhere; and in the meantime they have no place of abiding. From the outset, phenomena dwell in the same essential equality of the three times. They arise in interdependence, an interdependence that is rendered possible by their ultimate nature. As it is written in the *Pitaputrasamagama-sutra*, "Phenomena are equal in the equality of the three times."[247]

This could be expressed in another way by saying that all phenomena seem to arise from origins and end in extinction. But in the very moment of their manifestation, they are without inherent existence. These appearances, which are empty by nature, arise unobstructedly. They are untouched by the ontological extremes of existence, nonexistence, and so forth. If through wisdom one gains a profound conviction that this is so, one will realize that all that appears within the sphere of the common consensus is without inherent existence; it is a mere imputation of the mind and is based on emptiness. This is the teaching of the Madhyamika path, in which there is no place for extreme ontological assertions.

True and fundamental reality is beyond the categories of pure and impure. Nevertheless, though devoid of true existence, external and internal phenomena appear—according to the habitual patterns set up by the adventitious* cognitive activity of the mind. But in reality there is nothing. These appearances are organized dualistically and are considered to exist inherently, some apprehended as subject and some as object. They are seized upon as things to accept or to reject, to accomplish or to avoid. Thus we wander endlessly, caught in the uninterrupted sequences of false appearances and false cognitions.

Proponents of philosophical tenets, whether Buddhist or non-Buddhist, have reflected upon the nature of reality and repeatedly investigated it. But failing to comprehend the absence of ontological extremes, they take one of four possible positions which either overshoot the mark or fall short of it. Here we are referring, on the one hand, to those Buddhist schools which attribute true existence to either the outer object or the inner mind or which, by negating entities on the coarse level and refuting the duality of subject and object, express the ultimate reality as the mere emptiness of a nonaffirming negative. On the other hand, there are the proponents of non-Buddhist tenets. Some propound a theory of the eternal and unchanging *purusha* and *prakriti*; others hold the nihilistic view that phenomena existing here and now are purely random and that there is no causality and no past and future lives.

In addition to all this, if one intellectually elaborates a position that is free from extremes and calls it the Middle Way, proudly upholding it as supreme, this is a sign that one has failed to master the ultimate meaning.[248] Those caught in the toils of their own views and tenets are like silkworms imprisoned in cocoons devised from their own saliva.

But phenomena that are mere appearances and to which we impute real existence through the sheer power of our habits are by their fundamental nature unoriginate. (1) They are without origin. (2) They have no extinction. (3) They have no dwelling. (4) They arise from nowhere and go nowhere. And the reason for this is that (5) "self" and "other," consciousness and its objects, are neither the same (6) nor are they different. (7) They are not eternal unchanging entities, nor do they (8) have existence at the outset and fall to extinction at the end. The first

---

* *glo bur ba.*

six items of this list express nonaffirming negatives, while the last two are affirming negatives. Phenomena, in conclusion, are by their very nature devoid of the eight conceptual extremes.

As Master Nagarjuna has said:

> All things then dependently arise;
> They have no ending and they have no origin;
> They are not nothing, nor are everlasting;
> They do not come, they do not go;
> They are not different and they are not one.
> Thus the absence of conceptions is set forth.

The mind that truly understands this fundamental reality, the natural state of things as it is, has in its possession the unmistaken wisdom that arises from reflection.

The dependent arising of samsara

All that appears on the conventional level to the deluded mind—the four elements of earth, air, fire, and water appearing within the bosom of open space; and all particular objects such as mountains, woods, villages, pitchers, woolen cloth, yak-hair fabric, soil, bamboo, and so forth—all such compounded things arise from their respective causes. In the outer world, phenomena occur due to the interdependence of twelve factors. Consider, for example, a plant, which manifests in dependence on six main causal factors (root, stem, branches, leaves, flowers, and fruit) coupled with six circumstantial factors, namely, the five elements in conjunction with time as expressed in the changing of the seasons. When all these twelve factors are present and complete, and as long as one still retains the propensity to perceive external appearances, the phenomenon "plant" will continue to manifest. Thus the outer world is the result of twelve interdependent links.[249]

In the same way, from Ignorance derive Conditioning Factors, which in turn give rise to Consciousness, and so forth. The twelve interdependent links gradually unfold, each link based on the one preceding it. They are seamlessly connected without interruption until Aging-and-Death. This is how "life" goes on, from beginningless time, until the moment when the propensities of the mind and body are exhausted. This describes the twelve-linked dependent arising on the inner level.

The dependent arising of nirvana

The dependent arising of nirvana[250] consists in the four successive paths of learning, together with the resultant stage, the path of no more learning. The root of the twelve-linked chain, which proceeds from Ignorance to Aging-and-Death and is concomitant with the dependent arising of samsara, is Ignorance—ignorance of the ultimate meaning of the two truths. By listening to the teachings and reflecting on them, while on the path of accumulation, practitioners come to a full understanding of the antidote to ignorance—the wisdom of awareness that realizes the no-self of persons and phenomena. While on the path of joining, and by means of the five factors of faith, diligence, mindfulness, concentration, and wisdom, the practitioner meditates on emptiness by way of a mental image. The result of this is that Ignorance is attenuated. On the path of seeing, the practitioner beholds the wisdom of awareness directly and in its true nature. As a result, no further karma is ignorantly accumulated, and therefore no further existence is set in motion. While on the nine grounds of the path of meditation, the practitioner trains continually in this wisdom and intensifies its power, with the result that the habitual tendencies of ignorance are gradually brought to a halt. By virtue of this, the habitual tendencies of Conditioning Factors, together with the other links (of the twelvefold chain) are halted in reverse order. Finally, when the last stage of the tenth ground is reached, by means of the diamondlike concentration, all extremely subtle tendencies to Ignorance, the very root of samsara, together with the perception of mere appearances[251] will be discarded and their continuity severed. When this happens, the wisdom of the Dharmakaya will be actualized and unbounded compassion will manifest, able to assume any form. All this amounts to the interdependence of the fruit.

From this it follows that the ground, path, and fruit are interdependent; in themselves, they have no real, inherent existence. Those who correctly realize this know also that true sufferings (namely, the universe and its inhabitants) manifest simply by virtue of dependent arising and are without true existence. They know that by abandoning the cause of suffering (ignorance, the root of defilement—the truth of origin), the truth of cessation, or supreme nirvana, is actualized. Thus they meditate upon the supreme wisdom of no-self (the truth of path) and behold it directly.

THE WISDOM RESULTING FROM MEDITATION

As we have already explained, perfect wisdom arising from reflection creates the conviction that the three types of phenomena associated with samsara, nirvana, and the path are unoriginated (i.e., empty), and gives rise to an unmistaken knowledge of the fundamental nature of things. Settling the mind, unspoiled by dualistic cogitation,[252] in this ultimate reality calls forth the wisdom that results from meditation. This is the message of the extraordinary sutras and their commentaries as set forth by valid authorities.

WISDOM ITSELF

Just like space, ungraspable, impossible to indicate, formless, and without center or circumference—even so is the nature of the mind. When one rests in the primordially pure dharmadhatu, the object of meditation (ultimate reality) and the subject (wisdom) are of one taste. Within the fundamental nature of the mind, which cannot be characterized as "this" or "that," there is no such thing as five aggregates. And given that the mind's nature is uncompounded,* even the eight consciousnesses are absent. The Prasangika Madhyamikas teach that there is no origination of the kind described by any of the four possible theories. But one should not conclude from this that, once the extreme of existence has been refuted, there is a "nonexistence" to be meditated upon as something newly established. For "nonexistence" is not the fundamental nature of things; indeed, it is incompatible with the wisdom that knows this nature. The nature of the mind abides within the three doors of liberation. It is not a bare nonentity. It is the source of all the kayas and wisdoms of the Tathagatas and is indeed like a treasure house.

To be sure, only Superior Beings or Aryas see ultimate reality directly as it is. But even on the level of ordinary beings, the mind, when left unaltered by mental fabrications, is able to watch the perfectly pure and

---

* Uncompounded in the sense of having no origin, duration, or cessation.

ultimate nature of phenomena. Such a state of mind is the wisdom of vipashyana. It is quite different from the absorption of the insensate gods. Neither is it a kind of somnolence, nor a deprivation of the faculty of vision as in the case of somebody born blind. Of course, the expression "to watch" is just a metaphor. If one does not stir from the state of uncontrived nature (in the sense of being distracted elsewhere or of purposefully meditating), one is in fact meditating on the natural condition of things, as it is. This is why this kind of meditation is superior to any other. The primordial wisdom present in such meditation is without the split between subject and object. It is free from discursive thinking with its "main mind," "mental factors," and their objects. This wisdom is indeed the all-discerning wisdom. When the mind attains to such a wisdom and phenomena are known to be neither existent nor nonexistent, liberation will come by virtue of bodhichitta and the skillful methods of generosity and the rest. On the other hand, endeavoring in skillful means while lacking this wisdom, and continuing to apprehend phenomena as truly existent, is to be no different from non-Buddhist practitioners, who are unable to free the mind from the fetters of samsara.

PROGRESS ON THE PATHS AND THE ATTAINMENT OF THE RESULT

Those who gather the two accumulations through meditation on emptiness in formal sessions and through the practice of great compassion in post-meditation (first through conscious application and then through gradual habituation) are on the small, medium, or great path of accumulation. The path of joining is what links practitioners swiftly to the path of seeing and has four stages (warmth, peak, acceptance, and supreme mundane level). In each of these four stages, both in meditation and post-meditation, emptiness and compassion manifest naturally.

When the path of seeing is attained, the wisdom of emptiness is united with compassion. "Emptiness experienced in meditation" and "compassion felt during the post-meditation" are not different experiences. Emptiness and compassion manifest coemergently and inseparably. While resting in the meditation on emptiness, the mind is saturated with great compassion. In post-meditation, while training in the bodhisattva activities of generosity and so forth, everything is conditioned by the wisdom of the emptiness of the three spheres. On the first ground, named Perfect Joy, the practitioner gains the perfect, pure, unclouded eyes of Dharma and beholds directly the true, ultimate nature of phenomena.

Later, on the noble path of meditation, that is, on the seven impure grounds, skillful means and wisdom are combined, even though there is still a distinction between the practices of meditation and post-meditation. When, however, the pure grounds are reached, and due to a concentration on emptiness that is supreme in all aspects, the yogi gradually attains the perfectly pure expanse and all the inconceivable qualities of the Tathagatas. By this means, and following the nonconceptual path that is free from effort and activity, the yogi spontaneously accomplishes the two aims of self and other. Here meditation and post-meditation are indistinguishable.

When, at the end of the tenth ground, the path of meditation is perfected, the diamondlike concentration overwhelms even the subtlest cognitive obscurations, annihilating them without a trace, while on the path of no more learning, total and perfect enlightenment is attained. At this point, there is no moment when the mind is not resting in meditation. The twenty-one sections* of the stainless qualities of omniscient wisdom are actualized: the eighteen distinct qualities of the Conquerors, the ten strengths, the four fearlessnesses, and so forth. This is buddhahood.

A concluding summary of the six paramitas

All the Buddhas of the three times—those who have come in the past, those who appear at the present time, and those who will come in the future—when on the path of learning, listen to scriptures that set forth the six paramitas. They reflect upon their meaning and train in them on the path. As their view exceeds all conceptual extremes (in the final stages of their training), their practice of the path is unlimited and their exercise of the six paramitas is utterly pure (devoid of all self-regard).

* See appendix 9, p. 341.

In this way they bring the two accumulations to perfection and depart for the realm of Akanishta, adorned with the five certainties. There they attain perfect enlightenment and accomplish the two kayas.

This, then, concludes our discussion of the Expository Vehicle of Causality, as understood in the traditions of the Profound View and Vast Activities.

Impermanence demonstrated by the formation and destruction of the universe according to Buddhist cosmology

THE GRADUAL FORMATION OF THE UNIVERSE

The inanimate vessel of the universe is formed, as it were, in two directions. All that is founded in space takes shape starting from above, while all that is based on the earth begins its formation from below. All this begins with the production of the basic foundation, the mandala of the elements. Within the vast recesses of space, six wind energies arise: churning, all-pervading, compressing,* cohering, ripening, and separating. These gain in strength and form an unyielding foundation like a crossed vajra. Upon this there falls a rain from clouds that have a core of gold, and this gives rise to the mandala of water surrounded at its rim by an all-containing wind energy. Then, through the activation of the churning energy, the water is agitated and there solidifies within it a golden ground of great strength. Upon this the mountains are formed, the continents and oceans of the universe. Through the churning together of earth and water, and through the admixture of rain from the clouds of different elements, Mount Meru, composed of four precious substances, takes shape in the center. Around it are arranged seven encircling ranges of mountains, themselves separated from each other by seven oceans called the Seas of Enjoyment. Finally, between the last circle of golden mountains and the external rim of iron peaks, there is an ocean of brine. In each of the four main and four intermediate directions and positioned slightly above the level of the water, the four main continents and the eight ancillary continents of the universe arise.

Now, below Mount Kailash, at a distance of twenty thousand leagues, is the location of the eight hot hells. These are set in tiers, one above the other. Twenty leagues to the north are the eight cold hells.

---

* *rtsubs*, the usual meaning of which is "rough."

The ephemeral hells have no fixed position, while the neighboring hells are grouped around the hot hells. As for the pretas, their principal abode is five hundred leagues below Rajgir,* while their subsidiary habitations are in the human and divine realms. Animals are found in the oceans or live scattered throughout the countries of the humans and the gods. Among the races of the desire realm gods, two have their abode on the earth itself. First, the sphere of the Four Great Kings is to be found on the four great steps of Mount Meru, in the celestial mansions of the sun, moon, and stars, upon the crests of the golden mountains, and so forth. Second, the heaven of the Thirty-three is situated on the summit of Mount Meru. Finally, the remaining four abodes of the "sky-dwelling" gods of the desire realm are ranged in tiers, higher and higher, in the space above Mount Meru.

The asuras, or titans, have their homes in the crevices and chasms of Mount Meru, beginning from the level of the ocean's surface and descending to the stratum of the golden ground. Nevertheless, some asuras may be found in the human and other realms.

The eighteen spheres of the realm of form are located in the space above the desire-realm gods. These comprise the twelve dwelling places of beings who are still on the ordinary level, and above these, the five levels of superior beings.† According to some authorities, ordinary beings are sometimes to be found in these five levels also. This is in harmony with the theory that living beings start their formation and spread in a downward direction from the Peak of Existence. Above these five levels is Akanishta the Fair, the dwelling place of Bodhisattvas in their final existence before attaining buddhahood. The formless realm has no manifest location. . . .

THE GRADUAL FORMATION OF ANIMATE BEINGS

Due to the fall of nectar, the wind energy gradually manifests within the earth, and there develop a variety of plants of lotus form. As the four elements of the fundamental basis of the universe are formed, the

* Rajgir is a place in Bihar, India, not far from Bodhgaya, and was the location of the monastery of Nalanda.
† See note 14.

four goddesses of wind energy and the many dancing goddesses of water, the four goddesses of earth, and the four powerful naga youths appear within the hollow calyx of these blossoms. The sound of their merriment rouses into manifestation the consciousness, hitherto dormant, in the formless sphere at the Peak of Existence. This is one traditional explanation of how living beings come into existence.

Another tradition states that the adventitious, manifold, delusory forms of beings arise when movement occurs in the space of indeterminate awareness. The *Guhyagarbha-tantra* says:

> Emaho! From the Sugatagarbha,
> Beings arise through thought's activity.

Accordingly, by mistaking and straying from the primordial ground, beings in the formless realm[253] spread lower and lower into the four levels of absorption. Having nothing but a body of concentration, empty but knowing, they come to abide in the different levels of space. Beings in the form realm possess bodies of light which act as a basis for their conscious continuum; they delight to remain absorbed in protracted concentration. And they spread progressively through the dimensions of the space which are called according to the color of different jewels—from Infinite Space down to, but not including, the sphere of Mastery over Magical Creations of Others.[254] From these originate the gods of the desire realm, of which there are six kinds.[255] Four dwell in the dimensions of space and are called by the name of their predominant pleasure, while two kinds are inhabitants of the earth and are designated (the realms of the Four Great Kings and the Thirty-three) according to the beings that rule over them. The asuras take their origin from certain sinister races of the gods and dwell, as we have said earlier, in openings and crevices on the sides of Mount Meru. The humans of Jambudvipa, this world of ours, derive from the gods of Clear Light (in the form realm), whose merit dwindled so that they came upon this earth and gradually propagated. At that time, they were able to move miraculously through the air, with bodies of shining light. They were sustained on bliss, and their life span was measureless. Defiled emotions were unknown to them, and their manner of birth was miraculous. From them, and after a great lapse of time, there descended the family of humankind. As the life span and brilliance of these beings declined, and as their merit dwindled and their latent defilements were about to awaken, the inhabitants of the continents of Videha and Godaniya and their subcontinents descended from the higher gods,* while from the gods of the Thirty-three there derived the inhabitants of the continent of Uttarakuru and its satellites. While the humans of the continent of Jambudvipa were living distracted in a state of bliss, during the period when their life span was equal to ten million years, they took birth from eggs. When their life span was that of six million one hundred thousand years, they were born from warmth and moisture. Then their light diminished and through the force of ignorance, darkness came into being, whereupon, by virtue of their common karma, the sun, moon, and stars appeared together with temporal measurement and the changing of the seasons. In that period, sexual differentiation occurred. This marks the end of the period known as Perfect Endowment.[256] Afterward the four castes[257] came into being, and due to the strength of the three poisons, human beings began to accumulate strongly negative actions. Thereafter, lower states occurred, populated by beings who in the human state performed negative actions due to the three poisons. Finally, when the first being took birth in hell, the kalpa of formation was complete. All together, one intermediate kalpa is necessary for the formation of the universe, and nineteen for the formation of the beings that inhabit it.

THE DURATION OF THE UNIVERSE

From having a life span that is measureless, humans gradually lose their longevity by one year every two centuries until they have a life span of eighty thousand years. After this point, it decreases every century by one year until the length of life amounts to one decade. This marks the end of the so-called aeon of lengthy reduction,† and it is at this point that the life span starts to grow again, beginning from ten years and

---

* That is, those that were situated at a level higher than the level of the heaven of the Thirty-three.

† ya thog ring mo sgrib pa'i bskal pa.

gradually increasing every century in twelve successive stages until a life span of eighty thousand years is reached once more. Then again the span of life decreases to ten years, and the process continues as before. One period of increase and one period of decline together form an intermediary cycle.* When eighteen intermediary cycles have elapsed, the life of human beings once again increases until immeasurable longevity is attained. This period is called an aeon of lengthy increase.† The aeon of reduction together with the eighteen intermediary cycles, completed by the aeon of increase, all together constitute the twenty intermediate kalpas, corresponding to the duration phase of the universe. The thousand Buddhas of this great Fortunate Kalpa all appear while the life span is decreasing. By contrast, Chakravartins occur, and then in great number, only when longevity is decreasing from measurelessness to the point of the eighty-thousand-year life span. Finally, Pratyekabuddhas appear in any period.

THE DESTRUCTION OF BEINGS

The destruction of the inhabitants of the universe happens as follows. The period of destruction starts when, after the twenty intermediate kalpas of the duration phase, no more beings are born in the realms of hell. At this point, all beings living in the hells are reborn in higher states, or if their karma productive of an infernal existence is not yet exhausted, they remove to the hell realms of other world systems. The same process occurs in the other two lower states. Then, the inhabitants of Uttarakuru take birth in the heaven of the Thirty-three, while the dwellers in the other three continents attain the concentration of the second samadhi and are born in the level of Clear Light. The gods of the desire realm and the gods abiding on the level of the first samadhi of the form realm pass through an analogous process. When the world is destroyed by water, those who dwell in the second samadhi reach the concentration of the third samadhi. When the universe is destroyed by wind, beings abiding on the level of the third samadhi

---

* *khug pa.*
† *ma thog ring mo 'phel gyi bskal pa.*

attain the concentration of the fourth samadhi and take birth accordingly. At that time, all the other realms are completely empty of living beings.

THE DESTRUCTION OF THE UNIVERSE

Seven suns arise in succession and destroy everything from trees and forests to the mountains, continents, and the golden foundation of the universe. The fire then mounts upward and consumes the divine abodes of the first samadhi. There then comes a rain that washes away everything from the level of the second samadhi down. Everything disappears like salt dissolving in water. The ensuing wind scatters the remaining debris, from the level of the third samadhi down. The reason the first samadhi is destroyed by fire is that, as a characteristic of the first samadhi, there still remains a subtle form of analytical thought, which is "like fire." In the second samadhi there is an attachment to bliss that is "like water," and this is why this level is destroyed by water. Finally, the third samadhi has a factor that "resembles the inspiration and expiration of the breath." It is associated with wind, and for that reason this level is destroyed by wind. The fourth samadhi has no such defects, and for this reason this level cannot be destroyed by the elements. However, beings in this state are still subject to transmigration.

The destruction of beings that inhabit a universe takes place over a period of nineteen intermediate kalpas, while the universe itself is destroyed in one—thus making twenty intermediate kalpas in all.

THE PERIOD OF VOIDNESS

Destruction is followed by a period of voidness lasting for twenty intermediate kalpas, during which an empty, spacelike condition supervenes. The compounded entity of a universe and its inhabitants subsides into uncompounded space, and this, on the level of absolute meaning, affords an illustration of how the Rupakaya dissolves into the expanse of the Dharmakaya.

THE FOUR PERIODS REFLECTED IN THE EXISTENCE OF AN INDIVIDUAL BEING

This process of formation, duration, destruction, and voidness finds a parallel in the existence of an individual being. In the tantra *thal 'gyur*, it is written:

> In truth, destruction and formation,
> Abiding and the void are found
> Within the fabric of existence,
> As birth and aging, sickness, death.

The luminosity of the moment of death, occurring after physical death, is analogous with the mandala of space devoid of inherent existence. Within its radiance, which is unobstructed and protean in character, there is a movement of the life energy, which is itself endowed with four aspects, so that perceptions of places, minds, and living beings* begin to stir. These are indeterminate and without much precision and are accompanied by unstable feelings of happiness and sorrow. This may be compared with the mandala of wind. Because it is dominated by craving, the consciousness takes hold of the essences of the father and mother, which in turn form the substantial cause of the ensuing physical life; and this is parallel to the fall of rain. The five wind energies, but especially that of karma, which is similar to the churning energy, continue to transform the embryo, propelling it through five stages of development (during the first five weeks of pregnancy). This corresponds to the mandala of the earth. From the pure quintessence of the embryo are formed the three main subtle channels running down the center of the body, together with the six chakras, themselves analogous to the six realms. From the remaining substance are formed the arms and legs and their smaller appendages. Then, in each of the physical sense organs, the perfectly limpid sense powers[258] are themselves formed

---

* *gnas don lus gsum.*

and resemble the array of a celestial realm. When this happens, from the alaya of the individual concerned, the mental activity of the seven types of consciousness gradually matures. All this corresponds to the kalpa of formation. Subsequently, fortune and adversity are experienced by turns. Youth and freedom from illness give way to the discomforts of disease and poverty. After a period of stability, the elements degenerate, and one is crushed beneath the burden of old age. One is tormented by numerous sufferings, and at length the end of life is reached. This is the counterpart of the kalpa of abiding. Following this, after the gradual dissolution of the elements, which halts the grosser kind of dualistic experience implicit in mental activity, there occur the subtle stages of dissolution. The red essential element, which has the nature of fire, dissolves. This arrests all subtle light-appearance. Then the white essential element, with the nature of water, dissolves, and light-increase is halted.[259] Finally, the extremely subtle life wind energy ceases, and all phenomena, animate and inanimate, encompassed within the perceptions of the mind vanish. This is parallel to the kalpa of destruction. At that time, the compounded aggregates, elements, and sense powers are suspended in the state of Dharmakaya, the uncompounded luminosity of awareness. This corresponds to the kalpa of voidness. Until dualistic thought involving subject and object is dissolved through meditation in the expanse of primordial purity, the ground of liberation, the mechanism of existence continues to revolve unabated.

THE CEASELESS CONTINUITY OF THE PROCESS OF FORMATION AND DESTRUCTION

Again, after the period of universal voidness, another phase of formation begins. In the case of our three-thousandfold universe, the present great kalpa will be followed by sixty dark kalpas when no Buddha will manifest. Then there will be innumerable kalpas with countless Buddhas, and so on endlessly. According to the tantras, the infinitude of universes is symbolized by the immense Buddha Vairochana Gangchen Tso. Above his hands, folded in the mudra of equanimity, is a column of twenty-five lotuses one on top of the other. Upon each of these lotuses, there is a buddhafield. At the thirteenth level from the top, at the level of his heart and central to all the others, is Endurance, our own buddhafield or world system.[260] It has formed, and it will be destroyed, in the womb of space, just as inconceivable universes have done in the past. Moreover, in the infinite spaces in the ten directions, limitless universes likewise come into being and are destroyed.*

[Taken from the commentary of Khenchen Yönten Gyamtso, YG I, 199–210]

---

* See Jamgon Kongtrul Lodro Tayé, *Myriad Worlds*, for several descriptions of the Buddhist cosmology from the point of view of the Abhidharma, the *Kalachakra-tantra*, and the Great Perfection.

APPENDIX 2 ⊘⁓
The Bardo

THE FOUR BARDOS

The Tibetan word bardo *means "in between," an intermediary state. A life cycle consists of four main intermediary states. The natural bardo of the present life starts at birth and continues till death. The painful bardo of dying is the whole death process, beginning when an irreversible cause of death occurs and ending with the final exhalation. At that time, the five wind energies gradually disappear and the corresponding five elements dissolve in the ground nature, the luminosity of the moment of death. The body and mind separate and the luminous bardo of reality arises. If the consciousness of the deceased person fails to recognize the nature of the manifestations of the bardo of reality, these subside and the bardo of becoming begins to manifest. The wind energies of the five elements reemerge from the all-encompassing wind energy of ignorance and, combined with consciousness, give rise to a mental body. Habitual patterns and clinging reassert themselves as before, and the consciousness of the dead person must pass through the terrifying experiences of the bardo of becoming, which lasts until birth (that is, conception) into the next life. The bardo of becoming is characterized by six uncertainties. [Translators' note]*

THE SIX UNCERTAINTIES OF THE BARDO OF BECOMING

Uncertainty of location: The mental body in the bardo is unobstructed and completely random with regard to its movement.

Uncertainty of resting place: The being in the bardo searches everywhere for shelter—in stupas, in temples, under bridges—but is powerless to remain settled.

Uncertainty of behavior: Aside from their momentary quality, the activities of the mental body are quite unpredictable.

Uncertainty of sustenance: Although the bardo being can perceive the different kinds of food, good and bad, consumed by the beings in the

six realms, it is powerless to ingest them, unless they have been specifically dedicated for that purpose. In fact, they can absorb only the aroma
of the burnt *sur* food offering. Therefore, when performing the weekly
ceremonies for the dead,[261] it is important that the practitioner dedicate
the food offerings many times, with a pure attitude and unwavering
concentration.

Uncertain companionship: The mental body experiences only temporary
encounters; apart from these, it has no fixed entourage.

Uncertain mental condition: Sometimes happy, sometimes overwhelmed
by suffering, the mental body is constantly fluctuating. It leaves behind
no footprints and casts no shadow.

This is how the six uncertainties arise, short-lived and fleeting. The
people in the bardo are tormented by fear, hunger, thirst, and weariness
and flit here and there like feathers on the wind. Because the channel
structure is lacking, the mobile wind energy moves uncontrolled, and
the consciousness is powerless to control its movements, as though riding on a wild horse. Because there is no inner sun and moon of the
bodhichitta,[262] beings in the bardo have no perception of an outer sun
and moon and see only the radiance of the five subtle energies, like the
glimmer of the dawn. In the dimness of the bardo, which is like the
half-light of daybreak, the dead are pursued by flesh-devouring creatures: carnivorous ghosts and savage beasts which are nothing but the
embodied form of their own habitual patterns of mind. They are caught
in tempests, torrential rain, and snowstorms and feel that they are completely enveloped in them. They have the impression that close relatives
and friends are beckoning to them with sweet and loving words, but
when they approach they change into devouring spirits and deadly apparitions. Beside themselves with terror, they search for somewhere to
hide. The consciousness of beings in the bardo is extremely sharp, and
their feelings are proportionately more violent and intense. But there is
no escape, nowhere they can go. They have no friends, and for their
mental body there is no resting place. From this we may understand the
torment of those who have never practiced Dharma. Those who have
done so and who have built up a stock of merit have nothing to fear.
Wherever they go, sustenance is given to them, and they are escorted
by gentle companions: only pleasant appearances arise.

In the bardo, four dreadful sounds will be heard, the expression of the four wind energies. As the energy of the earth element reemerges, there will be heard a roar as of collapsing mountains; as the energy of the fire element reemerges, there will be the sound of blazing forests; as the energy of the water element reemerges, there will be the crashing of tumultuous seas; as the energy of the wind element reemerges, there will be the shrieking of a gale like the winds of the end of time. The beings in the bardo are overwhelmed; they are terrified and are constantly looking for a safe place in which to hide. Whatever evil they have done before, such as the taking of life, will take form in the bardo, and they will be hounded, wounded, and beaten. On the other hand, beings whom they have helped will appear in the bardo to assist and protect them. There will also appear three dreadful abysses, the embodiment of hatred, desire, and confusion, and the bardo beings will be terrified of falling over these chasmic precipices, white as ash, dark red, and black.

How to benefit the consciousness of beings in the bardo

During the first week of the bardo, the habitual patterns of the previous life are very pronounced, and so it is important to perform immediately the virtuous actions and the appropriate seventh-day ceremonies for the dead. If the ritual is performed properly with clear visualization and without distraction, the experience of the dead will be lucid and agreeable, and they will be inclined to remain in place. But if the practitioner's mind is distracted and the performance of the ceremony impure, the minds of the deceased will become agitated, and after a time, as fear mounts, they will be unable to prevent themselves from moving. . . .

. . . It is said in the instructions that if a compassionate teacher performs this profound ritual purely and with clear concentration for a disciple with good samaya, the deceased person (who in the bardo is receptive and easily influenced) will find good support and have a clear consciousness and will attain enlightenment through the teacher's introduction to the nature of the mind. This is the uncommon, swift path of the Vajrayana. Moreover, it is said that if the lama bestows empowerment on nothing so much as a piece of bone of someone long dead, or simply while pronouncing his or her name and reciting dharanis and mantras, the consciousness of the person will be cleansed of karmic obscurations and will be freed from the lower realms. . . .

. . . If the lama dedicates the ceremony and makes pure aspirations for the sake of the dead person, then through the power of the lama's perfect attitude, through the power of the dharmadhatu (which, though it is without absolute existence, is yet all-accomplishing), through the power of the Buddha's compassion and the blessings of the Dharmakaya inseparable from the nature of the deceased person as of every sentient being, and finally through the power of the perfect dedication of merit and aspiration, the person in the bardo will be protected from the fully ripened effect of previous actions. The result of these actions will be attenuated, overlaid by the actions of the lama. As a result, even if the person in question is due to take birth in the states of loss, he or she will be directed to the higher realms, just as someone might change direction on the advice of a friend.

Every seventh day during the seven weeks of the bardo, the deceased will relive the sufferings of the moment of death. The ritual for the dead can protect them from this. If one's visualization is clear and attitude pure, the dead are benefited. But they are harmed if the reverse is the case. . . .

[*Taken from the commentary of* Yönten Gyamtso, *YG I, 223–228*]

The Four Truths

ESSENTIAL DEFINITIONS AND ASPECTS OF THE FOUR TRUTHS

The essence and aspects[263] of the four noble truths (*bden pa bzhi*) are set forth as follows:

1. The truth of suffering, or true sufferings (*sdug bsngal gyi bden pa*), corresponds to all samsaric phenomena, namely, the external universe and the beings that inhabit it. True sufferings display four aspects. Since they are produced and cease at every instant, they are *impermanent (mi rtag pa)*. Since all feelings generated by them are within the range of suffering, they are *unsatisfactory (sdug bsngal ba)*. Although they are appropriated as "one's own," there is in fact no self that owns them. They are therefore *empty (stong pa)* of such a self. Conversely, since there is nothing in them that can be designated as the self, they themselves[264] are *not the self (bdag med pa)*.

2. The truth of origin, or true origins (*kun 'byung gi bden pa*), corresponds to the defiled emotions (attachment, aversion, and ignorance) together with their resulting actions (positive, negative, and unwavering), which propel into samsara. True origins also have four aspects. Since actions and emotions are the continual wellspring of suffering, they are its *source (kun 'byung)*. Since action and emotion are the root of every suffering, they are its *cause (rgyu)*. Since they speedily give rise to powerful suffering, they are *intensely producing (rab skye)*. Finally, since they constitute the environment in which we suffer, they are the *condition (rkyen)*.

3. The truth of cessation, or true cessations (*'gog pa'i bden pa*), is the release from sufferings and origins through following the path. It is also the ground into which these sufferings and origins subside, or ultimate reality. Again, true cessations have four aspects. Since they are the inter-

ruption or stopping of sufferings and future origins, they are *cessation* (*'gog pa*). Since they are the extinction of all delusions, they are *pacification* (*zhi ba*). Since they are the supreme perfection, they are *goodness* (*gya nom*). Finally, since they are an irrevocable liberation from samsara, they are *definitive* (*nges 'byung*).

4. The truth of the path, or true paths (*lam gyi bden pa*), refers to the five paths of accumulation, joining, seeing, meditation, and no more learning (although some schools regard the truth of path as referring only to the paths of seeing and meditation). Once again, true paths have four aspects. Since they lead to ever more elevated levels, they are the *path* (*lam*). Since they are the remedy for the afflictions, they are *pertinent* (*rigs pa*). Since they are the cause of an unmistaken state of mind, they are *effective* (*sgrub pa*). Finally, since they lead to permanent liberation from suffering, they are *conducive to release* (*nges par 'byin pa*).[265]

THE MEANING OF THE TERM "FOUR TRUTHS"

It is said in the teachings that "the four truths are true because they are in harmony with the Doctrine and because the understanding of them is the cause of liberation." The four truths are true since the Buddha's exposition of them corresponds with what is the case. Since the mind is unmistaken when it perceives these truths in the manner in which they were expounded, the four truths are true also from the point of view of the one who understands them. It should be noted, however, that only sublime beings or Aryas are able to understand what these truths really are. By contrast, even though sufferings, origins, and so on, are part of the experience of ordinary beings, the latter fail to recognize them for what they are, and in fact mistake them for their opposites. Therefore, these truths are called noble truths, or "truths for sublime beings." They are not posited as truths for ordinary beings.

A SEQUENTIAL EXPOSITION OF THE FOUR TRUTHS

The four truths are presented in two ways. The presentation of them according to the process of understanding is given in the *Uttaratantra* of Maitreya. "The sickness must be diagnosed. The cause of the sickness must be removed. Good health is to be restored, and to this end medicine should be administered. In the same way, suffering, its causes, cessation, and the path are to be recognized, discarded, achieved, and implemented." Thus, through the recognition of the true character of suffering, the determination to escape from samsara will arise. When the wish is experienced to discard the origins of suffering and realize their cessation, the path will be implemented.

The second way of presenting the four truths is according to a chronological sequence of two sets of cause and result. Thus, the cause of samsara is the truth of origin; its result is the truth of suffering. The cause of nirvana is the truth of path; its result is the truth of cessation.

[Taken from the commentary of Yönten Gyamtso, *YG I, 290–293]*

The Five Aggregates

F orm is defined as something breakable. Feeling is vivid experience. Perception is cognizance of phenomenal characteristics. Conditioning Factors are the causal and conditioning elements not accounted for in the other four aggregates. Finally, Consciousness is defined as the awareness of outer objects and inner mental states.

1. **Form** (*gzugs*). Form in its causal aspect corresponds to the four elements: earth, water, fire, and air. Form in its resultant aspect corresponds to the five sense organs and their five objects, to which is added so-called imperceptible form (*rig byed ma yin pa*). The first ten are easy enough to understand. The last item, which is asserted only by the Vaibhashika school, is described in the *Abhidharmakosha* as follows: "There are three kinds of imperceptible form: vows, nonvows, and others." In this context, "vows" means the binding of oneself to virtuous actions, "nonvows" means a commitment to evil actions, while "others" refers to positive or negative activities performed without conscious intention. This third kind of imperceptible form is termed "intermediate." All such forms originate from the four major elements of the body and speech; even in states of unconsciousness and inattention, they are always present. The Sautrantikas, Chittamatrins, and Madhyamikas, however, make no mention of imperceptible forms.

2. **Feeling** (*tshor ba*) is threefold: pleasant, painful, and neutral.

3. **Perception** (*'du shes*) is differentiated as small, intermediate, and great.*

4. **Conditioning Factors** (*'du byed*). There are "associated conditioning factors" (in other words, associated with the mind) and "nonassociated conditioning factors" (associated with neither mind nor form). The associated conditioning factors comprise forty-nine mental factors

---

* This refers to perceptions in the desire, form, and formless realms.

to which may be added feeling and perception as just mentioned, thus making a total of fifty-one.

These fifty-one associated mental factors are subdivided into six groups:

1. Five omnipresent factors (*kun 'gro lnga*).
2. Five object-ascertaining factors (*yul so sor nges pa lnga*).
3. Eleven wholesome factors (*dge ba'i sa mang bcu gcig*).
4. Six root defilements (*rtsa ba'i nyon mongs drug*).
5. Twenty lesser defilements (*nye ba'i nyon mongs nyi shu*).
6. Four variable factors (*gzhan 'gyur bzhi*).

• The five omnipresent factors are so called because they are present in every mental process and are necessary for every act of cognition. They are:

1. Feeling (*tshor ba*): the experience of pleasure, pain, and neutrality. Feeling is thus the basis of desire and aversion.

2. Perception (*'du shes*): the apprehension of a specific object, as circumscribed and distinct from something else. On the conceptual level, this is the recognition of identities or names, and on the sensory level the discernment of the five objects of sense.[266] (These are *subjective* experiences and are thus the basis of disagreement and controversy.)

3. Intention (*sems pa*): the moving of the mind to a specific object and the clear apprehension of it. This is the basis of all subsequent action and involvement.

4. Contact (*reg pa*): the coming together of object, sense organ, and consciousness. This is the basis of feelings.

5. Attention or mental engagement (*yid la byed pa*): the steady focusing of the mind on its object. This is the basis of concentration.

• The five object-ascertaining factors, which deal with specific aspects of the object, are:

1. Keenness (*'dun pa*), whereby the mind takes a strong interest in an object appearing in one of the six sense fields. It is a nostalgia for past experience, a fascination with present experience, and a desire to experience again in the future. It is the basis for joyful diligence.

2. Appreciation (*mos pa*), whereby the mind savors the qualities of an object, likes that object, and fixes the thought of it in the memory.

3. Recollection (*dran pa*), the factor that prevents the mind from losing or forgetting its object. It is the antithesis of distraction.

4. Concentration (*ting nge 'dzin*), the one-pointed mental stability that focuses on a given object and acts as the basis for accurate knowledge.

5. Intelligence (*shes rab*), the capacity to discern and elucidate phenomena beyond doubt and hesitation.

• The eleven wholesome factors cause the five omnipresent, the five object-ascertaining, and the four variable factors to take on a positive aspect and thus to create happiness in oneself and others. They are:

1. Faith (*dad pa*): in this context, a mental state free from the pollution of the major and minor defilements. It is an attitude of confidence with regard to what is truly pure and authentic, for example, the karmic law of cause and effect and the qualities of the Three Jewels. It is the basis of keenness.

2. Sense of shame (*ngo tsha*): an inner, private sense of right and wrong. This is the impulse to avoid evil on account of Dharma or personal conscience; it is the foundation of self-discipline.

3. Sense of decency (*khrel yod*): a sensitivity to the opinions and feelings of others leading to the restraint from negativity for others' sake. This also is the foundation of pure discipline.

4. Conscientiousness (*bag yod*): a carefulness with regard to virtuous conduct and the avoidance of defilement. It fosters goodness, both relative and ultimate.

5. Flexibility (*shin sbyangs*): an alert aptitude of mind and body that precludes rigidity and opens the way to good and beneficial objectives.

6. Evenness (*btang snyoms*): a calm, clear mental state free from torpor or agitation, which protects against the emotional disturbances of desire, anger, and ignorance.

7. Nonattachment (*ma chags*): the opposite of, and remedy for, craving for existence and worldly possessions.

8. Nonaggression (*mi sdang*): the opposite of, and remedy for, hatred. It is love itself and overwhelms hostility toward sentient beings and painful situations.

9. Nonperplexity (*gti mug med*): the opposite of, and remedy for, ignorance. It is a lucidity and sharpness of mind that removes confusion about objects of knowledge.

10. Nonviolence (*rnam par mi 'tshe ba*): an inability to accept that others should suffer, an attitude of kindness and compassion toward the sorrows of others.

11. Joyful diligence (*brtson 'grus*): an appreciation and joy in relation to positive actions. It should be distinguished sharply from an enthusiasm for nonvirtuous things or things that have nothing to do with the Dharma. Its function is to bring about the achievement of wholesome qualities.

The twenty-six unwholesome factors engender mental turmoil or disturbance. In the case of certain of these factors, such as anger, this is obvious, while anyone who has tried to meditate will have discovered the problems that laziness and dullness can cause. These unwholesome factors, or *klesha*s, are divided into six root defilements and twenty lesser defilements. The root defilements are the cause of all emotional conflicts and mental distortion, and it is because of them that negative actions are performed. These in turn give rise to the sufferings of samsara. The lesser defilements are aspects of the root defilements and accompany them as dependent factors.

• The six root defilements are:
1. Attachment (*'dod chags*): a state of longing for something and the will to possess it. It is a state of delusion in that it arises in relation to objects that only seem to be a source of satisfaction and enjoyment. It is the basis of discontent and, in contrast with love and compassion, which are concerned exclusively with the welfare of others, it is self-centered and geared to the subject's own satisfaction. Technically speaking, attachment also includes the mind's clinging to the five impure aggregates as these occur in the three realms of existence.

2. Anger (*khong khro*): a deluded state arising in relation to objects that appear unpleasant. It is a state of resentment, of being unable to tolerate something or someone, and the wish to remove or damage the

source of irritation in some way. It has a coarsening effect on the mind and is the cause of negative actions.

3. Pride (*nga rgyal*): a strong sense of superiority and infatuation with one's self-image. It is a delusion based on the mistaken concept of "I" and "mine" and gives rise to feelings of self-importance and prominence. It promotes a disrespect for others and renders impossible the attainment of sublime qualities.

4. Ignorance (*ma rig pa*): a state of not knowing, which arises when the mind lacks clarity with regard to the nature of things, such as the law of karma, the four truths, the Three Jewels, and so forth. It is the environment in which all other afflictions arise.

5. Defiled views (*lta ba nyon mongs can*): false opinions entertained in ignorance—for example, of the true status of the ego—and the foundation of all negative mental states. There are five principal defiled views:

a. The view of the transitory composite (*'jig tshogs la lta ba*), whereby the five aggregates (which are transitory and composite) are regarded as a permanent and unitary "I" and "mine." It is the basis of all other wrong views.

b. The view of extremes (*mthar 'dzin pa'i lta ba*). These extremes are: eternalism (the belief in an unchanging personal or phenomenal self) and nihilism (the belief that there is no survival after death).

c. The view of doctrinal superiority (*lta ba mchog 'dzin*), the belief that one's (false) opinion is supreme and universally valid.

d. The view of ethical superiority (*tshul khrims dang brtul zhugs mchog 'dzin*), the belief in the superiority of invalid systems of discipline or ethics that do not in fact produce the effects hoped for (liberation). This includes the practice of extreme and useless asceticism, the sacrificing of animals, and even a proud attachment to Buddhist disciplines, which effectively obstructs spiritual progress.

e. Wrong views (*log lta*), the holding of opinions that are contrary to the facts, for example, to deny the existence of what exists, as in saying that there is no such thing as the karmic law of cause and effect; or to ascribe existence to what does not exist, as in the case of a belief in a divine Creator.

6. Doubt (*the tshom*): A state of vacillation that tends to wrong view and hinders the cultivation of wholesome states.

• The twenty lesser defilements derive from the six root defilements and are often present in the mind without the subject's being aware of them. They are, however, distinct functions and behave in specific ways.

1. Carelessness (*bag med pa*): the opposite of conscientiousness. This is a negligent, unrestrained impulse, indulged in irrespective of the need to do good and refrain from evil. It is the occasion more of nonvirtue than of virtue and is a factor that dissipates positive qualities.

2. Laziness (*le lo*): the opposite of endeavor, the grasping at the comforts of the moment and the failure to strive in virtuous ways.

3. Lack of faith (*ma dad pa*): the absence of belief in or respect toward a worthy object. It is the occasion of laziness.

4. Dullness (*rmugs pa*): a lapse of the mind into a state of insensitivity so that its object is not clearly apprehended. It leads to a condition of mental and physical heaviness and sleepiness.

5. Excitement (*rgod pa*): a state of agitation or scattering, due to attachment, in which the mind strays from its point of concentration and is distracted to other objects.

6. Shamelessness (*ngo tsha med pa*): the suspension of an inner sense of morality. It is the support and precursor of all root and lesser defilements.

7. Disregard (*khrel med*): the absence of self-restraint through neglect, and a contemptuous disregard for the opinions and feelings of others.

8. Aggressive anger (*khro ba*): the desire to inflict harm and retaliate for injuries received.

9. Rancor (*'khon 'dzin*): the harboring of grudges on account of past injuries, the memory of which lingers in the mind—a constant occasion of anger and resentment.

10. Dishonesty (*g yo*): an attitude of dissimulation and cheating in the interests of personal wealth or advantage.

11. Spitefulness (*'tshig pa*): a mental state that prompts malevolent verbal outbursts. It is caused by anger and rancor and is a precursor of harsh speech. It destroys one's own and others' happiness.

12. Envy (*phrag dog*): the inability to tolerate the good fortune of

others, a state motivated by attachment to one's own reputation and material gain. Envy partakes of both anger and resentment.

13. Dissimulation (*'chab pa*): an attitude of refusing to admit one's faults and a refusal to deal with them when they are pointed out or spoken of by another.

14. Miserliness (*ser sna*): possessiveness, the attitude of holding on to things and refusing to let them go. This can refer not only to material things but even to the Teachings.

15. Pretension (*sgyu*): the imagination and flaunting of qualities that one does not possess, motivated by a desire for possessions and reputation. It leads to wrong livelihood and hypocrisy.

16. Self-satisfaction (*rgyags pa*): an arrogance or complacency with regard to one's good fortune, good looks, and so forth. It produces a hollow sense of confidence and is the gateway to the major and minor defilements.

17. Cruelty (*rnam par 'tshe ba*): a malevolent attitude that intentionally inflicts suffering on another.

18. Forgetfulness (*brjes nges*): not just a lapse of memory, but also the losing from sight of virtuous objects and the careless allowing of the mind to drift into unwholesome directions. Forgetfulness is the basis of distraction.

19. Distraction (*rnam par g yeng*): the scattering of the mind to objects other than the positive point of focus.

20. Inattention (*shes bzhin ma yin*): a negligent lack of awareness of one's physical, verbal, and mental conduct.

• The four variable factors (*gzhan 'gyur bzhi*) are so called because their character changes under the influence of other wholesome or unwholesome factors. Although only four factors are mentioned here, this feature of variability is shared also by the omnipresent and object-ascertaining factors.

1. Sleep (*gnyid*): this is a state in which the sense consciousnesses are withdrawn inward and the mind no longer apprehends the body. Sleep is affected by the waking activities of mind and body and will be wholesome or restful, agitated or defiled, accordingly.

2. Regret (*'gyod pa*): an attitude of sorrow or anxiety with regard to

past actions. If the action was negative, regret is a wholesome quality. The reverse is true if the act was positive.

3. Gross discursiveness (*rtog pa*): the mental factor by virtue of which the mind gains an overall impression of objects.

4. Subtle discursiveness (*dpyod pa*): the intense examination of objects with a view to gaining a clear idea of them. Gross discursiveness and subtle discursiveness are wholesome or unwholesome according to their objects.

All these fifty-one mental factors (*sems byung*) are distinct from the main mind (*gtso sems*), but they approximate it in five ways and for this reason are said to be concomitant (*mtshungs ldan*) with it. The main mind and the mental factors thus possess:

1. common basis (*rten*), since they both come into existence in dependence on the same sense organ.
2. common referent (*dmigs pa*), since they always refer to the same object.
3. common aspect (*rnam pa*), since they both perceive the same aspect of an object.
4. common duration (*dus*), since they both occur in the same moment.
5. singularity of occurrence (*rdzes re re bar mnyam*), since in any one moment there is only one main mind and one mental factor.

The relationship between the main mind and the mental factors is subtle. Generally speaking, the main mind is the consciousness that apprehends the fundamental presence of the object, while the mental factors apprehend and react to particular aspects or qualities of that object. In this respect, the relationship of the main mind and the mental factors is similar to that existing between an overseer and the laborers on a building site. The overseer is aware of what each worker is doing without, however, participating in the latter's specific activity. In general, there are innumerable mental factors; in the *Abhidharmasamuccaya*, Asanga (the authority followed here) lists fifty-one of the most important.*

---

* In his *Abhidharmakosha*, Vasubandhu lists forty-seven mental factors.

There are countless nonassociated conditioning factors, of which the twenty-four most important are as follows: acquisition, nonacquisition, similarity of state, absorption without perception (i.e., in the celestial realms), absorption of cessation, nonperception, vital energy, birth, duration, aging, impermanence, names, phrases, letters, the state of an ordinary being (i.e., devoid of the noble qualities of someone on the path), continuity, diversity, rapidity, relatedness, order, temporality, spatiality, countability, and collection.

5. **Consciousness** (*rnam par shes pa*): The Shravakas and most Madhyamikas assert six types of consciousness (the five nonconceptual sense consciousnesses—visual, auditory, olfactory, gustatory, and tactile—and the mental consciousness that identifies specific objects as such and such. The Chittamatrins, the rest of the Madhyamikas, and practitioners of the Secret Mantra teachings assert eight types of consciousness. To the six consciousnesses just mentioned, they add the defiled emotional mind, which, turning inward toward the alaya, constantly conceives of "I," the ego. This emotional mind is absent in the meditation of the Aryas but never ceases in the mindstreams of ordinary beings. Finally, there is the consciousness of the alaya (alayavijnana or *kun gzhi rnam shes*). This is mere knowing, an unspecified apprehension, the object of which is general and uncircumscribed.

Since they are the source of future suffering, the five aggregates illustrate the truth of origin. Insofar as they are the product of past karma, they illustrate the truth of suffering. Because they are the polluted cause, they are origins; because they are the polluted result, they are sufferings. However, while all "origins" are necessarily "sufferings," not all "sufferings" are "origins." The inanimate universe [is the result of polluted karma but] is not the origin [of future suffering].

[Taken from the commentary of Yönten Gyamtso, YG I, 355–358. Khenpo Yönten Gyamtso, however, simply lists the fifty-one mental factors without comment. The definitions have therefore been added, based on Vasubandhu's Abhidharmakosha *and Mipham Rinpoche's* Introduction to Scholarship *(mkhas 'jug).]*

APPENDIX 5 ❧

A Buddha's qualities of realization

Buddhas possess qualities arising from their realization. These are: *The five kinds of eye* (*spyan lnga*), or powers of vision, the fully ripened effect of their positive actions: (1) the eye of flesh, which is the ability to see all forms, gross or subtle, of the three-thousandfold universe; (2) the divine eye, the knowledge of the births and deaths of all beings; (3) the wisdom eye, the understanding of the no-self of persons and phenomena; (4) the Dharma eye, the knowledge of the eighty-four thousand sections of the Doctrine; and (5) the Buddha eye, omniscience.

The six kinds of preternatural knowledge (*mngon shes drug*), accomplished through concentration: (1) the knowledge and ability to perform wonders appropriate to the needs of beings, such as the miraculous multiplication of objects; (2) the clairvoyance of the divine eye (the knowledge of the births and deaths of all beings); (3) the clairaudience of the divine ear (the ability to hear all sounds throughout the three-thousandfold universe; (4) the knowledge of one's own and others' past lives; (5) the knowledge of the minds of others; and (6) the knowledge of the exhaustion of stains, that is, that karma and emotions are exhausted.

The ten powers (*dbang bcu*), due to which no intended action is obstructed: (1) power over life: Buddhas can live for a kalpa or more if they so wish; (2) power over mind: according to the wishes of beings, they can enter or relinquish meditative absorptions; (3) power over material things: they can materialize any kind and any number of physical objects; (4) power over activities: they are proficient in every art and skill; (5) power over birth: they can choose to be born in any of the six realms; (6) power over the aspirations of beings: they can display a three-thousandfold universe filled with Buddhas; (7) power over prayers: they are able to hear and fulfill all the prayers of beings; (8) power of miracles: they can place the entire universe in a mustard seed and so forth; (9) power over wisdom: they have attained omniscience; and (10) power over Dharma: they are able to teach all sections of the Doctrine without any impediment.

The four dharanis (gzungs bzhi), the nature of which is extraordinary memory and supreme intelligence. The first dharani is the power to understand, merely by reflecting on the letter A, that all phenomena are unborn. The second is the mantric dharani, Buddhas have the ability to create a formula and bless it with concentration and wisdom so that it becomes a mantra effective for as long as a kalpa. The third is the word dharani, the ability to hold in unforgetting memory every word of the Doctrine. The fourth is the meaning dharani, the power to remember infallibly the sense of all the teachings.

The ten strengths (stobs bcu). This is defined as an unobstructed cognition of all objects of knowledge: (1) the strength of knowing what is correct (for instance, the idea that virtuous action results in happiness) and what is incorrect (for example, the opinion that virtuous action gives rise to misery); (2) the strength of knowing the fully ripened effects of actions (knowing in detail the entire principle of cause and effect and the specific correlation of actions with results); (3) the strength of knowing the different mental capacities of beings; (4) the strength of knowing different types of beings (their different potential, for example, for shravaka training) and elements (earth, air, fire, water, and space); (5) the strength of knowing the different interests of beings (their aspirations to the vast and profound teachings); (6) the strength of knowing all paths, for instance, the paths of the higher and lower realms and the path of liberation; (7) the strength of knowing all the samadhis and perfect freedoms (knowing every conceivable kind of concentration, that is, the four levels of samadhi and the eight perfect freedoms;* (8) the strength of knowing past lives (the memory of countless past lives of all beings without exception; (9) the strength of knowing the deaths and births of beings (knowing where each and every being will be born after death); and (10) the strength of knowing the exhaustion of stains (knowing that the two veils of emotional and cognitive obscurations have been removed, together with their habitual tendencies).

The four fearlessnesses (mi 'jigs pa bzhi) in the face of all hostility with regard to what Buddhas say about themselves and others. Fearlessness when encountering hostility to (1) the assertion of their own perfect

* See appendix 9, p. 341

realization; (2) the assertion of their own perfect qualities of elimination; (3) the assertion for the sake of others of the noble path that leads to liberation; and (4) the assertion for the sake of others of what causes hindrances on the path.

The four perfect knowledges (*so so yang dag par rig pa bzhi*) of all the ways of helping beings. These are: (1) a perfect knowledge of each and every aspect of the Dharma (knowing all the words of an inconceivable myriad of teachings without confusing them); (2) a perfect knowledge of all the meanings expressed in these words without mixing them up; (3) while teaching the Dharma to others, a perfect knowledge of the way to express it, together with a knowledge of all languages; and (4) a perfect knowledge, through unbounded intelligence and ability, which would not be exhausted, though a single point were to be expounded for an entire kalpa.

The eighteen distinctive qualities (*ma 'dres pa'i chos bco brgyad*), which are not shared by the Shravakas and Arhats. Six of these refer to the way Buddhas behave. (1) Their physical conduct is without delusion. This means that they are unlike the Shravakas, Arhats, and Pratyekabuddhas, whose conduct may exhibit certain defects. For example, the latter may tread on a poisonous snake inadvertently due to the fact that they have not eliminated the obscurations of habitual propensities. In their every movement, down to the opening and closing of their eyes and the stretching of their limbs, Buddhas act solely for the benefit of others. (2) A Buddha's voice is not strident or inconsiderate. The Shravakas may shout when lost in the forest or laugh noisily. Buddhas do not do this; even their sneezing or the clearing of their throats has the nature of benefiting others. (3) Buddhas are never unmindful. Shravakas might forget about something they should do, and since, for their clairvoyance to function, they need to focus specifically on the subject in question, they might be unaware of some approaching danger. On the other hand, the actions of Buddhas are always timely and their knowledge is effortless (and all-inclusive): they know everything in the three times irrespective of conscious intention. (4) A Buddha's mind is always in meditative equipoise. The Shravakas and Pratyekabuddhas are unable to perform actions while still remaining in meditation. By contrast, a Buddha can teach or go for alms, while never stirring from meditation. (5) Buddhas do not impose discriminations on their perceptions. Shravakas differentiate things, regarding some as good and some as bad. For example, they consider nirvana as peaceful and serene, and they feel revulsion toward samsara. Buddhas do not differentiate samsara and nirvana in a dualistic way; all such phenomena subside for them in the expanse of nonduality. (6) The equanimity of Buddhas nevertheless involves full discernment. They know by what means and at what time each and every being may be taught. They act accordingly and at the right moment. The Shravakas and Pratyekabuddhas do not have such discernment even regarding their own disciples, and thus it may happen that, through acting at improper times or through being ignorant of the appropriate method, they fail to benefit them effectively.

There now follow six distinctive qualities of a Buddha's realization. (7) Buddhas have a constant, joyful keenness to act for the sake of beings. (8) They possess a mindfulness that never turns from the welfare of others. (9) They are tireless in endeavor. For the sake of a single being, they are ready to teach for hundreds of kalpas without rest or sustenance. (10) They have a supreme knowledge of all phenomena, (11) a one-pointed concentration, and (12) a complete freedom from the two kinds of obscurations and habitual tendencies, together with a realization of omniscient wisdom.

Then there are three qualities that comprise the three distinctive aspects of primordial wisdom. Buddhas know all objects of knowledge—without impediment (due to the fact that the cognitive veils have been removed) and without attachment (because the emotional veils are also eliminated)—(13) in the past, (14) in the present, and (15) in the future. Arhats possess a like knowledge, but this is limited by "attachment and impediment."

The three distinctive qualities of Buddhas' activities of (16) Body, (17) Speech, and (18) Mind proceed from, and are accompanied by, wisdom. This means that the entire range of their activities is powered by wisdom. On the other hand, Shravakas and Arhats have an impaired vigilance, as we have seen above in the passage about the Buddha's conduct. Taken all together, these are the eighteen qualities peculiar to a Buddha, which are not shared by Shravakas, Pratyekabuddhas, and Arhats.

[Taken from the commentary of Yönten Gyamtso, YG I, 492–498]

*The five paths and the thirty-seven elements leading to
enlightenment*

For people engaged in the path of liberation according to any of the
Three Vehicles,* the qualities of the three trainings may be presented in terms of a sequence of thirty-seven elements that gradually
lead to enlightenment.

While on the path of accumulation, the practitioner mainly receives
and studies the teachings and accumulates merit. On the basic level of
this path, emphasis is placed on the practice of the "four close mindfulnesses" (*dran pa nyer bzhag bzhi*). This means mindfulness of body,† feelings, consciousness, and mental objects. If one practices according to
the Hinayana, one meditates on the impurity of the body, on the feelings of sufferings, on the impermanence of consciousness, and on the
fact that mental objects are "ownerless" (there is no self to which they
belong). If one practices according to the Mahayana, during the meditation session one meditates on the same things as being spacelike, beyond
all conceptual constructs. In the post-meditation period one considers
them as illusory and dreamlike. Between the Hinayana and the Mahayana approach to this meditation, one may observe a threefold distinction. In the Hinayana, the focus is on one's own body, feelings, and so
forth, while in the Mahayana, the focus is also on the bodies, feelings,
and so forth, of others. Again, in the Hinayana, the focus is on the
impurity aspect and so on, while in the Mahayana the meditator con-
centrates on emptiness. Finally, with regard to the purpose of this meditation, in the Hinayana the practice is performed with a view to
liberation from the impure body and so on, while in the Mahayana this
meditation is performed in order to attain the nonabiding nirvana. This
meditation is termed "close mindfulness" because the practitioner dis-

---

* I.e. the Shravakayana, Pratyekabuddhayana, and Bodhisattvayana.
† There are three types of "body." The first refers to the outer universe, the second is one's
own body, while the third refers to the bodies of other sentient beings.

cerns the general and particular characteristics of the body and so forth with uninterrupted attention.

In the middle level of the path of accumulation, the Dharma of realization concerns the practice of the "four genuine restraints" (*yang dag par spong ba bzhi*). The first of these is the preemptive halting of negativities not yet generated. The second is the rejection of negativities already arisen. The third is the solicitation of positive states not yet present, and the fourth is the protection from decline of positive states already generated.

In the greater level of the path of accumulation, the Dharma of realization refers to the practice of the "four bases of miraculous powers" (sometimes known literally as the four miraculous legs, *rdzu 'phrul gyi rkang pa bzhi*). These are like the root or foundation for the subsequent accomplishment of miraculous abilities, such as the five kinds of preternatural knowledge. The first consists in a concentration based on keenness or the power of the will (*'dun pa*). The second is a concentration based on endeavor (*brtson 'grus*). The third is a concentration based on one-pointed mindfulness (*sems*), and the fourth is a concentration based on analysis (*dbyod pa*).

As a result of meditation on the mundane level, nonconceptual wisdom will gradually gain in strength, and this will "join" the practitioner to the path of seeing. This phase is therefore called the path of joining and consists of four stages. According to the Mahayana, the first stage of this path, in which the understanding of phenomena as mere mental projections (*yid kyi snang ba*) acts as an antidote to clinging, is called meditative Warmth. When the wisdom perceptions* increase, the practitioner reaches the stage called Peak. In both these stages, five powers are deployed focusing on the four truths. These are: Confidence with which one embraces the four truths, Diligence whereby one does this with enthusiasm, Mindfulness with which one does not forget the object of focus and the accompanying form or meditative attitude, Concentration with which one embraces the four truths one-pointedly, and finally Wisdom, with which one perfectly discerns them. These are

* I.e., perceptions that penetrate into the nature of phenomena.

called powers (*dbang po*) because they condition the development of enlightened qualities. When clinging to phenomena is eliminated, and the meditator acquires the wisdom of realizing that phenomena are but mind, the stage of Acceptance is reached. Here absolute reality is partially attained. As the meditator progresses, considering that since there is no object of perception there is no subject, but only nondual self-awareness, all clinging to phenomena is overcome, and the meditator is joined, without any hiatus, to the path of seeing. This stage is referred to as the Supreme Mundane Level and refers to the concentration immediately preceding entry into the path of seeing. In these last two stages, five irresistible forces (*stobs*) come into play. They are in fact the same as the previous five powers, but they are so called because they have gained in strength and are able to resist all countering factors.

When the practitioner understands that this nondual awareness is merely a dependent arising, ultimate reality is actualized, beyond all conceptual constructions, and this is called the path of seeing. On this path, seven elements may be discerned leading to enlightenment. They all share the same object of focus (*dmigs pa*), namely, the four truths, but are differentiated according to their form or accompanying attitude (*rnam pa*), as follows. The first of these seven elements is mindfulness (*dran pa*), whereby the four truths are retained and not forgotten. The second is perfect discernment (*chos rab rnam 'byed*), which is a decisive appraisal of the four truths and their nature. The third is diligence (*brtson 'grus*), whereby the meditator embraces the four truths with enthusiasm. The fourth is joy (*dga' ba*), a happiness that the nature of the four truths is now seen. The fifth is flexibility (*shin tu sbyangs*), whereby the body and mind are rendered supple and serviceable in the pursuit of goodness. The sixth is concentration (*ting nge 'dzin*), through which all distraction is eschewed. And the seventh is evenness (*btang snyoms*), which causes the mind to rest in its natural state free from torpor and excitement. The expression "the seven elements that lead to enlightenment" may be paraphrased as follows. "Enlightenment" is a reference to perfect discernment—in other words, the nonconceptual wisdom that realizes the four truths—whereas the six other elements are the means to this discernment.

Through steady familiarity with the wisdom that is a direct vision of ultimate reality, the perceptions of wisdom will continually intensify. This phase is called the path of meditation. Here, the meditator practices what is known as the Eightfold Noble Path. Its object of focus remains the four truths as in the path of seeing. With Right View, the nature of the four truths, which has been previously realized on the path of seeing, is definitively established. By virtue of Right Thought, this realization is understood through evidence and reasoning, and the practitioner is able to establish and nurture this understanding for others. With Right Speech, the realization of ultimate reality is expressed in words, on the relative level, and is taught to others by means of exegesis, debate, and writings, so that people may be inspired with confidence in the right view. Through Right Conduct, all behavior is cleansed of negativity and brought into line with Dharma, thus inspiring others with confidence in pure discipline. Right Livelihood preserves the meditator undefiled by inappropriate and wrong means of subsistence and encourages others to adopt a pure lifestyle. Through Right Effort, the practitioner tirelessly meditates on the ultimate reality already perceived. Right Effort is therefore the remedy to the obscurations eliminated by meditation. Through Right Mindfulness, the object of focus in shamatha and vipashyana meditation is never lost and an antidote is provided for forgetfulness, which is one of the lesser afflictions. By means of Right Concentration, a faultless absorption is accomplished, free from torpor and agitation, and every quality is developed. Right concentration thus acts as the remedy to all adverse conditions. The name "Eightfold Noble Path" may be glossed by saying that the Noble Path is the realization of ultimate reality, while the eight factors just enumerated are the aspects of this realization.

When the wisdom of realization is free from all obscurations, all the qualities of enlightenment are brought to perfect completion. When this happens, the path of no more learning is reached.

This, then, is the manner in which an individual progresses by means of the thirty-seven elements leading to enlightenment, spread out as they are through the five paths.

For the sake of convenience, the thirty-seven elements may be listed as follows:

On the path of accumulation:

a. the four close mindfulnesses
b. the four genuine restraints
c. the four bases of miraculous powers

On the path of joining:

d. the five powers
e. the five irresistible forces

On the path of seeing:

f. the seven elements leading to enlightenment

On the path of meditation:

g. the Eightfold Noble Path
[Extracted from Yönten Gyamtso's presentation, YG I, 508–515]

APPENDIX 7 ⌒
The Two Truths

THE TWO TRUTHS ACCORDING TO THE MADHYAMIKA VIEW

A common ground for the two truths cannot be found, for phenomena are in themselves beyond the conventional designations of true and untrue. They are the same, of equal status, in the absolute sphere beyond characteristics. On the level of ordinary discourse, however, people consider "true" to be the contrary of "false," and it is on the level of the ordinary mind, as the commentary on the *Yuktishastika* says, that the two truths are posited.

Accordingly, the relative truth comprises all the phenomena of samsara, namely, the mind and all phenomena that manifest in relation to it. The *Bodhicharyavatara* says, "Intellect is grounded in the Relative," while the *Madhyamakavatara* declares:

> The vast array of sentient life,
> The varied universe containing it, is formed by mind.
>   (VI, 89)

The absolute truth is the primordial wisdom that transcends the world, all-discerning awareness that has the same flavor as the expanse of ultimate reality. It is said in *Rahula's Praises of the Mother*:

> No name, no thought, no explanation is there for the Wisdom
>   that has Gone Beyond;
> Unceasing and unborn, the very nature of the open sky.
> It is the sphere of the awareness-wisdom all-discerning.
> To this, the mother of the Buddhas, past, present, and to come,
>   I bow.

Because phenomena and this ultimate nature are indissociable; they cannot be independent, existent entities. As the *Madhyamakavatara* says:

> And since inherent nature is in neither truth,
> Phenomena are neither nothing nor unchanging entities.
>   (VI, 38)

THE SPECIFICITY OF THE TWO TRUTHS

The relative, all-concealing truth[267] may be described as what lies within the scope of the intellect. It is unable to withstand logical analysis and appears in the manner of an obscuration. Here "intellect"[268] means the mind and its mental factors; it does not refer to all-discerning primordial wisdom. The *Madhayamakavatara* says:

> The nature of phenomena, enshrouded by our
>   ignorance, is "all-concealed."
> But what this ignorance contrives appears as true.
> Therefore the Buddha spoke of "all-concealing truth,"
> And thus contrived, phenomena are "all-concealing."
>   (VI, 28)

The absolute truth may be described as something beyond all conceptual constructs. It is the purity of phenomena and the equality of their absolute nature. It is free of the ordinary mind and mental ascriptions. As it is said in the *Mulamadhyamika-karika*:

> Not known through other sources, it is peace,
> And not by concepts can it be conceived,
> Unthinkable, beyond diversity,[269]
> This indeed is how it is defined.

THEIR LITERAL, ETYMOLOGICAL MEANING

"All-concealing" or "relative" refers to what appears but lacks inherent existence, like an illusion. The term "truth" is conventionally used because the attributes of phenomena coherently and undeniably appear to what is, for the time being, the deluded (that is, the ordinary) mind. The "absolute truth" is called absolute or supreme because it is the utmost object of attainment. It is truth because it is the infallible quality of the path and result. The *Prajnaparamita-sutra* says: "Transcendent wisdom is to be understood and meditated upon. It is by such thorough meditation that the unsurpassable result is gained. Thus the ultimate truth for Bodhisattvas is Transcendent Wisdom."

THEIR NECESSARILY BINARY CHARACTER

It is clear that the relation between what is to be rejected and what is to be accomplished involves a dichotomy. One is either liberated from conceptual constructs or not liberated from them. There is no third possibility. This is why *two* truths are posited. For even the yogic experiences occurring on the path, being of the relative truth, must be finally purified in the absolute expanse. Another way of distinguishing the two truths is to say that there is the "way things appear" and the "way they really are." Phenomena that appear to the intellect in a dualistic manner and that are reified and assigned a real existence are the relative, or all-veiling, truth. On the other hand, when mind-transcending wisdom "sees" the true mode of being of such phenomena (and here expressions like "seeing" or "not seeing" are used metaphorically), this is the absolute truth. Posited in relation to the subject (namely, the mind), phenomena can only be perceived either correctly or incorrectly, and this again certainly indicates the fact that there are two truths. As the *Madhyamakavatara* says:

> All objects may be seen in truth or in delusion;
> They thus possess a twin identity.
> The Buddha said the absolute is what is seen correctly;
> The wrongly seen is all-concealing truth.
>   (VI, 23)

The conclusion to be drawn from this is that all objects of knowledge are included within the two truths. There is, of necessity, no third possibility. The *Pitaputrasamagama-sutra* says: "The Knower of the world set forth the two truths as his own unique instruction; he was not repeating the teachings of others. These truths are the all-concealing and the absolute. There is no third truth." The four noble truths and the superior relative and absolute truths and their indivisibility,* as expounded in the Mantrayana, are in fact none other than these two truths.

THE KINDS OF COGNITION THAT VALIDLY ASCERTAIN THE TWO TRUTHS

The expanse of ultimate reality, the absolute truth, is beyond the constructions of the intellect. It does not lie within the scope of the referential (dualistic) mind.[270] It can only be experienced by thought-free wisdom that sees it directly in a nonreferential (nondualistic) way. All relative phenomena appear to us conceptually because they are the object of the dualistically functioning mind.

DIVISIONS AND CATEGORIES OF THE TWO TRUTHS[271]

Since the nature of all phenomena is neither single nor multiple, there is no clear-cut division to be made between the two truths. It is said in the *Sandhinirmochana-sutra*: "Compounded phenomena and the absolute truth are neither the same nor are they different. Those who think of them as being identical or different are mistaken." Two sets of unwanted consequences result from thinking that the two truths are different or identical.

If there is no difference between the two truths, the consequence would be as the *Sandhinirmochana-sutra* specifies:

1. When, by means of direct and valid evidence, a relative truth is cognized, the absolute truth would also be realized. That being so, samsaric beings have always been fully enlightened.

2. If the absolute truth, which is free of all distinctions, is not different from its contrary (relative truth), it follows that there are no differences between the elements (forms, etc.) of the relative truth.

---

* See glossary entry *Purity and equality*.

3. When relative truth (phenomena) is the object of reference, defilements proliferate. If the absolute and relative are not distinct, afflictions would develop even when the absolute truth is the object of reference.

4. Since the relative truth has no need of proof (being self-evident), it follows that the absolute truth is also without the need of valid demonstration (it should be immediately cognized).

If, on the other hand, the two truths are held to be different from each other, the same text points out that:

1. The realization of the absolute truth will not result in nirvana.

2. The absolute cannot be the nature of the relative truth, just as a vase cannot be the nature of a cloth.

3. The absolute truth would not be implied by the refutation of inherent existence on the relative level—just as the absence of a vase does not imply the presence of a cloth.

4. Even when nirvana is attained through the direct realization of the absolute truth, it follows that, because relative truth (as distinct from the absolute) is involved with defilements, the mind of the adept would be simultaneously defiled and liberated.

How, therefore, are we to distinguish the two truths? Although in their fundamental nature they have no existence, they have been set forth as though they did, in order to accommodate the understanding of ordinary beings. The *Samadhiraja-sutra* says:

> In the teachings spoken without words,
> Who is it who listens, who explains?
> As impositions upon unchanging nature,
> A hearer and a teacher are assigned.

In the most general terms, when the two truths are distinguished, the multitude of things appearing to the mind (origin and cessation, samsara and nirvana, acceptance and rejection, etc.)—all that cannot be denied by the conventional mind—is the relative truth. On the other hand, the *nature* of these relative phenomena—itself devoid of the fabric of conceptual constructs such as appearance and nonappearance, origination and non-origination, self and no-self—is called the absolute truth. "Freedom from conceptual constructs" is nothing other than this. As it is said in the *Satyadvayavibhanga*:

> The way that things appear, and only this,
> Is relative; the rest is absolute.

More specifically, the two truths themselves may be subdivided in various ways. For instance, phenomena perceived by the mind on the level of the relative truth are either mistaken or unmistaken, following the conventional distinction whereby the deluded perceptions of ordinary people are designated as true and false. Everything that appears to the deluded mind and produces (normal) effects—fire that burns, water that moistens, the moon that sheds light, and so on (together with the consciousnesses that perceive them)—are categorized as the unmistaken relative. They are so called because they are generally perceived in the common consensus. They originate from their respective causes[272] and on examination prove to be empty of inherent existence. By contrast, hallucinations such as a mirage of water, a rope that is taken for a snake, the moon seen as two (through double vision), and all sorts of appearances that manifest within the ambit of the deluded mind but produce no effects (since, respectively, they cannot moisten, deliver a poisonous bite, or dispel the darkness)—all these (together with the consciousnesses that perceive them) are qualified as the mistaken relative. They are so called because they are not perceived by the generality. They are hallucinations of things that do not exist as they appear even on the conventional level, and this is because they do not originate from the causes that are normally ascribed to such appearances. Nevertheless, since they appear when the proper conditions prevail, such hallucinations are not, of course, devoid of causes. Still, because they do not exist "materially" on the relative level (like a seedling, for instance, produced from its proper source), they are referred to as the mistaken relative.

When the Svatantrika Madhyamikas investigate these two kinds of relative truth, analyzing them with absolutist arguments,[273] they affirm their equality in being without true existence though appearing to the appropriate senses through the workings of deluded habitual tendencies. Nevertheless, on the conventional level, they designate these two kinds of relative truth as mistaken or unmistaken depending on whether the phenomena in question exist or otherwise according to their characteristics.* As it is said in the *Satyadvayavibhanga*:

> Though manifesting in a similar way,
> Conventional truths are designated
> As true or false,
> Depending on their power to produce effects.

The Prasangika Madhyamikas, however, consider that to say that things "exist according to their characteristics" is the same as saying that they truly *exist*. But such phenomena have no existence, even on the conventional level.[274] When making a distinction between what is mistaken and what is unmistaken, the Prasangikas, for their part, take their cue from ordinary people, for whom such phenomena are simply either true or false.[275] The *Madhyamakavatara* says:

> Perceptions that derive from faulty faculties,
> Compared with what is known with healthy
>   sense, are held to be mistaken.
>
> And all the six undamaged senses grasp,
> Within the ordinary experience of the world
> Is held as true, according to the world.
> The rest, according to the world, is false.
>   (VI, 24–25)

In this quotation, the first sentence differentiates the two kinds of relative truth from the point of view of the perceiver. The two sentences that follow do the same, but from the point of view of the perceived object.

From another perspective, since the two kinds of relative truth just

---

* *rang mtshan nyid kyis grub pa.*

described appear to the discursive mind, which clings to their true existence, they may both be called the mistaken relative. By contrast, the mind and phenomena that appear, but which are not apprehended as truly existent by those who have attained the wisdom of the Aryas, constitute the unmistaken relative, for in this case they are appearing to minds that are undeluded. . . . This unmistaken relative is again of two kinds. There is an unmistaken relative associated with the path leading to the result, and an unmistaken relative associated with the accomplished result itself. The former refers to the kinds of referential concentration* entered into by Aryas while still on the path of learning, as well as to the dualistic ways† in which they accumulate merit while in post-meditation. In the second case, the unmistaken relative refers to the Rupakaya of the Buddhas and the wisdom that knows phenomena in all their multiplicity.

It might be objected that to speak of an unmistaken relative in this sense contradicts the assertion of the *Madhyamakavatara*, seen earlier, that there are only two truths, the scope of the deluded or undeluded mind, and that there is no third truth. The answer to this is that in the post-meditation of Aryas who are still on the path of learning, a perception of objects separate from the perceiver‡ still persists, and this veils the ground nature. This could be qualified as mistaken, but since the perception in question is in the process of refinement, evolving toward the level of the fundamental nature, and since there is freedom from the apprehension of true existence, it is said to be unmistaken. Furthermore, the kayas, wisdoms, and so forth, on the level of buddhahood, are referred to as unmistaken relative truth only from the standpoint of their mere appearance. Strictly speaking, they are not relative truth at all, for they occur only when the view of absolute truth is perfected. Nevertheless, given that it is not inappropriate to speak in conventional terms of the union of the two kayas, the union of the enlightened body and mind, the union of appearance and emptiness and, in the Mantrayana, the superior relative truth§ and so on, it is likewise permissible to refer to the kayas and wisdoms as the unmistaken relative.

---

* *rnam dang bcas pa.*
† *snang ba dang bcas pa.*
‡ *gnyis snang.*
§ *lhag pa'i kun rdzob.*

In itself, the absolute truth is the fundamental mode or state of things, and it cannot be divided into aspects. However, for the purposes of discussion, certain (progressive) divisions may be made. Thus, after analyzing phenomena and finding that they are without origin, one meditates on non-origination and the absence of conceptual construction and so forth. This activity lies within the scope of the ordinary consciousness and therefore falls within the relative truth. But since this is the authentic way of realizing the absolute truth and is in accord with it, it is called an "approximate" or "concordant" absolute.* It is said in the *Satyadvayavibhanga*:

> Since origin and so forth have no real existence,
> Non-origination likewise is not real.

And also:

> Disproving all origination is
> Concordant with the perfect truth.
> The stilling of all thought of non-origination
> Is referred to by the name of absolute.

The absolute truth in itself† implies that the mind has reached the nature of the fundamental ground—when all concepts of origination and non-origination have subsided in the absolute expanse. This refers to the primordial wisdom present in the meditation of the Aryas who are on the bodhisattva grounds, as well as to the wisdom of buddhahood, in which perception and percept are blended in a single taste. This in turn corresponds to the fact that all phenomena of samsara and nirvana are primordially without inherent existence; they are not separable, nor do they fall into opposing categories. They elude the constructions of thought. The absolute truth is beyond the discursive intellect; it exceeds all verbal expression. For one who realizes it, it cannot be said to exist. For one who does not realize it, it cannot be

---

* Respectively, *rnam grangs pa'i don dam* and *mthun pa'i don dam*.
† *rnam grangs ma yin pa'i don dam*.

said not to exist. Realized or not realized, it is simply the ultimate, unchanging nature of phenomena. As Maitreya, the unvanquished protector, has said:

> As it was before, so will it always be:
> The ultimate beyond all change.

And as it is said in the *Samadhiraja-sutra*:

> All lacks entity and is beyond all speech,
> Empty, peaceful, pure from the beginning.
> Whoever knows the dharmas to be so,
> O Kumara, shall be proclaimed a Buddha.

The Buddha, skillful in methods, made a distinction between the two truths. He did this for the sake of benefiting others. But the two truths are not separate and distinct like a buffalo's horns. From time without beginning, they mingle in a single taste, appearance and emptiness inseparably united. When one sees the moon reflected in a clear pool, one distinguishes the fact that it appears there from the fact that it is not (located) there. But in the water of the pool, these two aspects, of appearance and "nonpresence," are united indissociably. In just the same way, phenomena that arise through interdependence are not wholly nonexistent (like a rabbit's horns). Their mere appearance *is* their relative truth. However, from the very moment they arise, they are utterly lacking in true existence: *this* is their absolute truth. Thus, although a distinction is made between the two truths, they are not distinct in each possessing a separate inherent reality. As the *Madhyamakavatara* says:

> And since inherent nature is in neither truth,
> Phenomena are neither nothing nor unchanging entities.
> (VI, 38)

Once the nature and characteristics of each of the two truths are understood, the inseparability of the latter is necessarily established. But

this is not simply a question of joining appearance and emptiness, existence and nonexistence, together. By their very nature, the two are intermingled. One should thus banish all doubts about the profound
meaning of the ultimate mode of being of phenomena, which is beyond
the reach of our ordinary mental functions. In the *Panchakrama* it is said:

> When relative and absolute are seen as each
> The aspect of the other,
> They blend together perfectly
> And thus are said to be united.

As to how, on the relative level, the two truths are differentiated, the
Omniscient Master, Longchenpa, says in his commentary on the *Mind
at Rest* and elsewhere, "They have one nature that has different aspects."
The *Bodhichittavivarana* says:

> "The relative is stated to be emptiness,
> And emptiness itself is but the relative.
> As with fabrication and impermanence,
> Without the first, the second is not present."

On the basis of such quotations, Longchenpa affirms that the mere
negation of one truth does not amount to the affirmation of the other
truth. For they are not different in nature, and any distinction between
them is made in relation to their common basis.

On the other hand, my kind teacher Patrul Rinpoche, in his general
outline of the *Prajnaparamita-sutra*, said that to negate one truth is to
assert the other, just as to deny existence is the same as affirming nonexistence. He said that it was incorrect to hold that the two truths have
the same nature but different aspects and that this was not the sense of
the quotation from the *Bodhichittavivarana*. He also said that, as a way of
showing that one truth presupposes the other, Longchenpa takes the
example of fabrication and impermanence. This proves that the two
truths are neither identical nor different. On this occasion, Patrul Rinpoche seems to be adopting the Svatantrika approach. However, I think

that both he and Longchenpa are driving at the same key point. The latter considers that the absolute mode of being of phenomena, beginning with the ground and continuing through the path and on to the fruit, is the same: the indivisible unity of appearance and emptiness. Patrul Rinpoche's (real) view is in accordance with the *Madhyamakavatara*, which says:

> The nature of phenomena, enshrouded by our
>   ignorance, is "all-concealed."
> But what this ignorance contrives appears as true.
> Therefore the Buddha spoke of "all-concealing truth,"
> And thus contrived, phenomena are "all-concealing."
>   (VI, 28)

Likewise, Longchenpa himself says in *The Treasure of Wish-Fulfilling Jewels*, "Two truths (the relative referring to the phenomena of samsara, and the absolute referring to the phenomena of nirvana) are taught as a means of leading beings to the great, indivisible, definitive, truth. Even though it is possible to talk of the indivisibility of the two truths, in point of fact the phenomena of samsara, which might be described as indivisible from the phenomena of nirvana, are wholly without existence." In my opinion, Longchenpa is here referring to the relative truth as being the appearing mode of samsaric phenomena only (given that from the ultimate point of view, nothing can be said to exist).

This is a profound point; it is difficult to sound its depth, let alone understand it fully. I have written this just as an investigative outline for intelligent students who are new to the subject. It is important not to approach the various exegeses of sutra and mantra in a spirit of faction. Rather, by considering that they all have the same intention, one should apply oneself to the key points of the practice so that learning and study will achieve their purpose. This is something to which we should devote a good deal of reflection.

The way to understand the nonconceptual indivisibility of the two truths is as follows. For the time being, while one is on the path of aspirational practice, phenomena, the objects of sense, form, sound, and so forth, present themselves distinctly to the five sense consciousnesses.

They are clearly discernible like the colors of a rainbow. The mere appearance of the five sense objects is not, however, what entangles us. It is when dualistic—subject-object—perception arises with regard to them, and when the perceiver identifies percepts (form, for instance) as things to be enjoyed, that the delusions of the mind and mental events arise continually. Undesirable things are rejected; desirable things are indulged in. But if they are examined, these appearances are found to have no real existence; they are beyond the eight conceptual extremes. One should reflect on them and investigate them according to the eight examples of illusion. Like appearances in a dream, phenomena have no origin; like an illusion, they are not subject to destruction, like a mirage, they have no permanence; like a reflection of the moon in water, they are not completely nonexistent; like an optical illusion, they come from nowhere; like an echo, they go nowhere; like a castle in the clouds, there is nothing distinct in them; like magical displays, they are not the same.[276] We must generate certainty in the inseparability of appearance and emptiness and, having done so, rest one-pointedly in it. Those who understand and meditate in this way are said to hold the path to liberation in their very hands. Even so, we should not be satisfied with this alone. We should not practice merely for our own trivial sake, like the Shravakas; rather, we should be like the Bodhisattvas, whose interest is the welfare of others as well as of themselves. Therefore, with minds saturated with bodhichitta, we should accumulate merit by exerting ourselves in the practice of generosity and the other paramitas. Then, having distinguished the two truths, we should train ourselves in their indivisibility, and in accordance with the eight similes of illusion, we should understand that phenomena lack inherent existence and are beyond the eight ontological extremes. This should be the substance of our meditation. The mere fact of understanding all this, however, does not mean that we have attained the ultimate nature of things. And why? Because whatever can be the object of intellectual definition is not the absolute truth. The absolute truth is to be realized by thought-transcending primordial wisdom, wherein there is no duality of subject and object. The dualistic mind, which veils this state of nonduality, pertains to the relative truth.

Furthermore, all phenomena that the mind may refer to are conceived as being, by nature, singular or plural. But even if one thinks of them as beyond the scope of oneness and multiplicity, one inevitably conceives of them as "things."[277] But *spros bral*, the absence of conceptual constructs, excludes the concepts of one and many, existence and nonexistence. The true, ultimate nature, primordial wisdom, can never be the object of the intellect. For as Shantideva says in the *Bodhicharyavatara*, "The absolute is not within the reach of intellect."

THE NECESSITY AND BENEFITS OF ESTABLISHING THE TWO TRUTHS

By relying on the relative truth, the absolute truth is established—in order to dispel the delusions of ignorance that obscure the Real. On the level of dependent arising, the accumulation of merit, far from being repudiated, is linked with the wisdom that perceives ultimate reality—the knowledge that the three spheres of agent, action, and object of action are without inherent existence. Thus, the two accumulations of wisdom and merit are accomplished simultaneously and the utterly pure absolute truth of phenomena is realized fully and perfectly. All this is the reason for establishing the two truths. As the *Madhyamakavatara* says:

> Conventional truth therefore becomes the means;
> And by this means the absolute is reached.
> Those who do not know how these two differ
> Err in thought and take mistaken paths.
> (VI, 80)

And in the *Satyadvayavibhanga* it is said:

> Those who differentiate two truths,
> Are not confused about the Buddha's word.
> Fulfilling both accumulations,
> They win perfection and the other shore.

And in the *Madhyamakagarbha* it is said:

> Those who spurn the ladders of conventionality
> But try to scale the pinnacles,
> The roofs and gables of the palace
> Of the ultimate, are fools indeed!

[Taken from the commentary of Yönten Gyamtso, YG II, 445–464]

APPENDIX 8 ✆

The Madhyamika School

Those who uphold the Madhyamika tenets of the Mahayana understand that both subject and object are devoid of absolute reality. They therefore refrain from attributing true existence either to external phenomena or to the self-knowing mind.* The Madhyamika school is divided into two subschools: the Svatantrika Madhyamikas and the Prasangika Madhyamikas. The former refute the true existence of phenomena and do this on the basis of correct signs and premises according to the three modes of reasoning.[278] By contrast, the Prasangikas induce an inferential understanding of the absence of true existence in the minds of their adversaries simply by exposing the consequences of their assertions.

THE SVATANTRIKA MADHYAMIKAS

The Svatantrika Madhyamikas say that all things, forms and so on, appearing to the six undamaged consciousnesses, exist on the level of the relative truth "according to their characteristics," and their reality is demonstrated by the kind of reasoning that confines itself to the level of conventional existence. Although they are devoid of true existence, such phenomena are real "from their own side," "on their own level," "according to their characteristics," and "as substantial entities."† All these expressions are synonyms for the Svatantrikas. Existence of this kind is not denied by the sort of arguments that seek to establish the absolute truth. It is clear that when the Madhyamika texts declare phenomena to be without inherent existence, the Svatantrikas say that one should add that this refers exclusively to the level of absolute truth. They say that phenomena existing according to their characteristics are

---

* The lower tenet systems all do this in one way or another.

† Real from their own side: *rang ngo nas grub pa*; on their own level: *rang bzhin gyis grub pa*; according to their characteristics: *rang gi mtshan nyid kyi grub pa*; substantial entities: *rdzas su grub pa*.

like illusions, for they arise merely through interdependence. But granting this, it is nevertheless possible to discourse (meaningfully) about specific phenomena such as causation, despite the fact that when such phenomena are investigated with arguments aiming at absolute truth, they are found to be devoid of existence and to be utterly pure and empty like space. In the latter context, expressions like "true existence," "existence on the absolute level," "perfect existence," and "existence on the ultimate level"* all have the same meaning and refer to the ultimate object of refutation at which absolutist arguments are aiming.

As regards the twofold *apprehension* of, or clinging to, the self (by which is meant the self of the person and the self of phenomena), the Svatantrikas distinguish these, not from the standpoint of the referent but from that of the mode of apprehension. When in a moment of personal introspection one detects a self-sufficient and autonomous entity, this is the apprehension of the personal self. When one apprehends (other) people and things as truly existing, this is the apprehension of the self of phenomena. This is the general position of the Svatantrikas; they are, however, divided into two subschools, higher and lower. The so-called lower school is in turn divided into two subgroups, the first of which emphasizes the illusoriness of all phenomena of samsara and nirvana (for which reason Tibetan scholarship refers to them as pan-illusionists).† Thus, masters like Acharya Sagaramegha hold that phenomena have no existence in themselves. They exemplify the two truths in being like illusions. Conventional appearance is unreal, for it is like a mirage. But though empty on the absolute level, this appearance nonetheless occurs unobstructedly through dependent arising. Accordingly, by completing the two miragelike accumulations, practitioners attain the miragelike result of enlightenment. Abiding constantly and evenly in the nature of illusion, Buddhas work for miragelike beings by implementing miragelike activities. Due to the interdependence of causes and conditions, all appearances are like illusions. Delusory appearances are illusions, and even the display of unobstructed luminosity—that is, un-

---

* True existence: *bden par grub pa*; existence on the absolute level: *don dam par grub pa*; perfect existence: *yang dag par grub pa*; existence on the ultimate level: *de kho na nyid du grub pa*.
† *sgyu ma rigs kyis grub pa*.

deluded wisdom wherein all conceptual constructs have subsided—is illusionlike. In short, Sagaramegha and others affirm that the ground, path, and fruit are all like illusions.

The second branch of the lower school are "those who distinguish between Appearance and Voidness."* Thus, the master Shrigupta and others say that, on the absolute level, objects like vases have no existence and are like mirages. Ultimately there is nothing there. On the conventional level, however, vases and so forth are not empty (of existence), for they appear to function and are therefore real. If one investigates them on the absolute level, they are empty, for nothing is discovered. Consequently, they say that relative truth, which cannot withstand analysis, and absolute truth, which does withstand analysis (in other words phenomena and their ultimate nature), do not coincide on the same ground, that is, in the same phenomen or thing. Otherwise it would follow (absurdly) that the absolute is impermanent like the relative truth, or that the relative truth is as unoriginated and unceasing as the absolute truth. They therefore say that the phenomenal appearances of the relative truth and the emptiness nature of the absolute truth exist merely in relation to each other. Both branches of the lower schools are like the higher Svatantrikas in accepting the distinction between mistaken and unmistaken relative truth.

The higher Svatantrika school is represented by such masters as Jnanagarbha, Shantarakshita, and Kamalashila. For them, the absolute truth, taken either as illusion or emptiness (as stated in the previous two points of view), is itself incapable of withstanding analysis.[279] For the absolute truth in itself is the ultimate nature of all phenomena and transcends all conceptual construction. Nevertheless, relative phenomena, at their own level, retain their characteristics and are incontrovertible. It is only when they are analyzed by (absolutist) reasoning that they are found to lack even the slightest degree of existence. What is found is an emptiness that is an approximation of the absolute truth. The Svatantrikas consider these two (the actual absolute truth and the approximate absolute truth) to be on an equal footing and affirm, sub-

* snang stong tha dad pa.

stantiate, and defend their position by using "autonomous" or "positive" reasoning. For example, in order to refute the belief in permanence, they say, "The subject, an existent thing, is impermanent because it is fabricated, like a vase." And they follow this with the "autonomous" proposition, in other words, the independent statement: "The subject, an existent thing, is impermanent because it is fabricated, arising from causes and conditions."[280]

In this school, as in all the lesser tenet systems, production from an extraneous cause is accepted. The relative truth is subdivided into unmistaken and mistaken relative truth in the manner already explained in the section on the two truths. This relative truth, deceptive as it is, manifests irresistibly until the pure grounds are attained, for in their post-meditation experience, Aryas still perceive what are known as "pure" worldly appearances. The proponents of the higher Svatantrika school affirm that they gather the two accumulations and attain the two bodies through the understanding that the two truths are not mutually exclusive.

Depending on whether external objects, separate from the mind, are asserted or denied, the higher Svatantrikas are divided into two camps. First there are the "Svatantrika Madhyamikas who act like Sautrantikas."* These are exemplified by Bhavaviveka in his commentary on the *Mulamadhyamika-karika* entitled the *Prajnapradipa*, and his follower Jnanagarbha in his treatise *Satyadvayavibhanga* and its autocommentary. These masters assert the existence of external objects on the relative level, but deny the existence of the self-knowing mind. Second, there are the *Svatantrika Madhyamikas who act like Yogacharas,*† as represented by Shantarakshita in his *Madhyamakalankara* and his disciple Kamalashila in his *Madhyamakaloka*. On the level of relative truth, Shantarakshita and Kamalashila affirm the existence of the self-knowing mind and deny the existence of objects separate from it.[281] Arya Vimuktasena, who predated Shantarakshita, was also a Yogachara Svatantrika Madhyamika, although he is not credited as being the founder of this school. This kind of situation occurs also in other contexts.[282]

* *mdo sde spyod pa'i dbu ma rang rgyud pa.*
† *rnal 'byor spyod pa'i dbu ma rang rgyud pa.* Yogachara is another name for Chittamatra (the Mind-Only school).

By adopting the Svatantrika method for establishing the two truths, one can gain conviction that phenomena are without true existence on the absolute level, even though, through dependent arising, they manifest unobstructedly. Such certainty is the point of entry to the Great Madhyamika, which is utterly beyond ontological extremes. On the other hand, if, while failing to undermine the powerful conceptual propensity to apprehend true existence, ingrained from beginningless time, one contemptuously dismisses other views and simply snatches at the highest (i.e., Prasangika), the only result will be the fault of disparaging the lower schools and abandoning the Dharma. And the realization of the higher teachings will be rendered even more difficult. By contrast, if the pith instructions of our teachers, sharp and penetrating, strike upon the hard terrain of *our own minds*, it is said that the entire textual tradition (of both Svatantrika and Prasangika) will have the effect of teachings that directly elicit experience.[283]

The Svatantrikas refute the extreme views of permanent existence and nothingness by using the same great logical arguments as propounded in the Madhyamika texts. And as these are not dissimilar from those of the Prasangikas, they will be set forth in due course. . . .

THE PRASANGIKA MADHYAMIKAS

Establishing the ground Madhyamika

The Prasangikas consider that all phenomena, arising through interdependence and appearing in the manner of mirages or dream visions, are relative truth. They do not analyze phenomena as to their existential status but regard them as being of relative validity, seeing them as a means of getting at something else, namely, the absolute. In his autocommentary on the *Madhyamakavatara*, Chandrakirti says, "The relative truth is an avenue of approach to the absolute truth. No analysis is made of relative phenomena to see whether they are self-generated or produced from extraneous causes. On the contrary, phenomena are simply accepted on an empirical basis and as they appear to the common man." Moreover, Lord Buddha himself is quoted in one of the sutras as saying, "People argue with me, but I do not argue with them. What they believe to exist in the world, I also affirm. What they disbelieve, I also disallow."

This appeal to "empirical reality" is not just a sop to general opinion. It means that the Prasangikas accept all interdependently produced phenomena, which appear as undeniably to them as to anyone else. They accept them just as they arise, *without investigating their existential status.* The true reality of these phenomena, however—in other words, their ultimate nature inseparable from them—has from the very beginning been emptiness, *shunyata*, beyond the four extremes of existence, nonexistence, and so on. This is what is referred to as the absolute truth of phenomena, and it is of course no more than a mere label on the relative level. Indeed, the two values (of relative and absolute) are not two separate categories, with phenomena on the one side and emptiness on the other. No, the very nature of phenomena *is* emptiness. The very nature of phenomena is to be groundless and rootless. Phenomena in fact elude every position that the intellect can take in their regard.

By contrast, some people refute only what they call the "true existence" of things, regarded as somehow separate from their conventional existence (which is not itself negated). They may refer to this as the absence of conceptual construction (*spros bral*), but it resembles it only in name and is something quite different. The inseparable union of appearance and emptiness in the authentic *spros bral* disallows both extremes of existence and nonexistence. To deny the true existence of an object and at the same time affirm its conventional existence is to dissociate existence from nonexistence. And in any case, even if someone were to succeed in recognizing this "absence of true existence," such a recognition would be useless as a means of removing attachment. However much one were to meditate on such an emptiness (i.e., an emptiness of "true existence"), it would do nothing to dissipate the perception of conventional phenomena as existing in their own right. And if such an apprehension is not dissipated, how can aversion and attachment to it be overcome?[284] In *The Treasure of Wish-Fulfilling Jewels*, in the section dealing with the refutation of the system of the lower Svatantrika school, according to which the appearance of a thing is different from its emptiness, the omniscient Longchen Rabjam says, "Emptiness that is other than appearance is an impossibility, whether on the relative or absolute level. Such an emptiness is unrealizable, and since it is other than phenomena it would be powerless as an antidote to them. When anger against an attacker arises, merely knowing that it is empty is of no help. In the same way, the simple assurance that desired objects are lacking in some 'true existence' separate from them will likewise be of no avail." As the *Samadhiraja-sutra* says:

> As long as man a "woman" apprehends,
> Desire for her will powerfully arise,
> But let such apprehension be destroyed
> And lust's defilements will depart as well.

The objection might be raised that without perception it would be impossible to meditate on love and so forth, because the true existence of the referent must be apprehended as a basis of such a meditation—given that one must have both a referent and the perception of it. To this we answer that that which apprehends objects as desirable or hateful is dualistic thought. It is this that brings forth the defilement, and it is this that must therefore be removed. Aside from dualistic thought, there is no such thing as the so-called true existence of phenomena—somehow standing apart from them as a possible object of refutation. In his *Songs of Realization*, Jangya Rolpa'i Dorje himself says:

> Our great intellects these days,
> Leave things appearing clearly on one side
> And look for hares with horns as something to refute.
> Old grandmother* will run away from them!

Therefore, even though, as a help for beginners, it is possible to speak of "relative phenomena" as being devoid of true existence, on the ultimate level, nothing of the kind can be found. As far as meditation on love is concerned, this can be explained as follows. Suppose a man is having a nightmare. He is suffering because he is dreaming that he is being chased by a frightful enemy or a wild beast, and he looks every-

---

* A humorous reference to the Prajnaparamita, sometimes referred to as the Great Mother.

where for somewhere to hide. A clairvoyant person (able to see what the man is dreaming about) knows perfectly well that the dreamer has no such enemy and that he is not being chased. Such a person will conclude that in order to comfort the sleeper and remove his fear it would be best to wake him.[285] In the same way, it is said that one must understand that whereas on the absolute level no phenomena are to be found, on the conventional level such phenomena are indeed present. These two modes, relative and absolute, are not mutually exclusive. Thus, phenomena, the objects of the six consciousnesses, *seem* to arise and subside, come and go, and so on. They do so in the manner of reflected images or mirages. In themselves, however, they do not in fact pass through these four processes—for the simple reason that, in themselves, they lack all existence. From this point of view, in accordance with which, phenomena, dependently produced, are primordially "unborn," it is said that appearance and emptiness are essentially one and the same thing. It is as when the four modes of emptiness are proclaimed in the text of the *Hridaya-sutra*: "Form is emptiness; emptiness is form. Emptiness is none other than form; form is none other than emptiness."

The Chittamatrins claim that in absolute terms, the nature of the "dependent reality," namely, the self-knowing mind, is not empty. The Svatantrika Madhyamikas say that phenomena dependent on causes and conditions have a conventional existence on the relative level. By contrast, the Prasangikas refrain from making assertions about the existence of phenomena even on the relative level, let alone on the absolute level. As Nagarjuna has said, "If I assert anything, then I am at fault. But since I assert nothing, I alone am faultless!" And Aryadeva said, "One who refrains from asserting inherent existence or nonexistence, or the two combined, is beyond dispute." And finally, Chandrakirti said in the *Madhyamakavatara*:

Unlike you, who think dependent nature is a true existent,
Even for the all-concealing relative we make no claims.
And yet, to gain the fruit, we speak in harmony with worldly folk,
And grant that things exist (though they do not).
(VI, 81)

Identifying the object of refutation: the two selves

The difference between the "self" and "apprehension of (or clinging to) self"

Although the object of refutation, namely, a concretely existent self, has no reality, unless the conceived object (*zhen yul*) of ego-clinging (or ego-apprehension) is dissipated, this clinging itself cannot be neutralized. We can see this in the example of the rope and the snake.[286] When a distinction is made between persons and phenomena, a person is the subjective individual, such as "Devadatta," imputed upon his own collection of aggregates, which are the basis of such a labeling.[287] By contrast, phenomena are Devadatta's aggregates, his eyes, for example, which act as the ground on which the person "Devadatta" is imputed. The term "phenomena" refers to all other things, in addition to the personal aggregates.

The "personal self," or ego, is the name given to what is assumed to be our inherently existing person; the "phenomenal self" is what is assumed to be the inherently existing phenomenon. These are the conceived objects apprehended in the two kinds of self-clinging. In the example of the rope mistakenly apprehended as a snake, they correspond to the snake. They are as nonexistent as horned rabbits, even on the relative level.[288]

In addition to this, there is self-apprehension, or self-clinging. To cling to the personal self means to believe that one's self is truly existent. To cling to the phenomenal self means to believe that phenomena are truly existent. The person and phenomena[289] are thus the referents of these two self-clingings. In the example given, they are like the colored rope that acts as the basis for the mistaken perception of the snake.

The "personal no-self" is the absence of inherent existence in the person. The "phenomenal no-self" is the absence of inherent existence in phenomena. This is understood by the "wisdom of realizing no-self." Persons and phenomena are, of course, said to exist on the conventional level. The roots of the two veils, which are to be dispelled, are thus the two kinds of self-clinging,[290] the conceived objects of which are the two kinds of self. These are thus the objects of refutation. The conceived object assumed by deluded thought, which takes for real what is utterly without existence, may be dissipated by the analysis that demonstrates its nonexistence. Thus a firm understanding of the two kinds of no-self may be cultivated. One should again and again strive to maintain the continuity of this illuminating conviction that counteracts the two kinds of self-clinging, and one should exert oneself in the techniques that remedy the mental darkness created by mistaken discursive thoughts. If this conviction weakens, it should be reinforced by repeated analysis. On the other hand, it is said that, when it is stable, one should lay aside analytical investigation and simply rest in that state of insight. In the early stages, beginners should meditate by concentrating on the nonexistence of self. But when, thanks to the meditation just mentioned, conviction is gained, there is no need to focus on the "nonexistence of the self" as such. And at length, when one is free from all false assertions, it will be possible to meditate on the great emptiness that is conceptually ungraspable. . . .

Analysis through the application of reason

This method consists of four or five great arguments that establish the fact that phenomena are without inherent existence. The specific explanation of these arguments is preceded by a general exposition of how such assessments are made.

To begin with, the prasangika approach is unlike that of the Svatan-trikas. The Svatantrikas disprove true existence on the relative level but then assert an illusory existence. Likewise they disprove conceptual construction on the absolute level, but then go on to assert (positively) that this absolute is beyond conceptual construction. The prasangika method is simply to demolish the defective propositions of their opponents by directly refuting every assertion to which the mind might cling. But they do not accompany this with any kind of independent pronouncement. In order to eliminate clinging to real existence,[291] it is essential to eradicate the conceived object of such clinging. Therefore, as we have said before, it is necessary to analyze and achieve certainty about the true nature of the two selves which are the object of refutation. Otherwise it is like shooting arrows without seeing the target, and it is impossible to eliminate the assumption of the real existence of a self.

When one uses the madhyamika arguments to search for the meaning of suchness, the idea that "the opponent is wrong" is enough to cause one to stray off the point. Therefore, from the outset, do not refute only the assertion of an opponent, but work to eradicate completely all the innate discursive thoughts in *your own mind*, which have been left unexamined from beginningless time and which deviate from the Truth or Suchness. Likewise, eradicate all clinging to positions or theories, which are imputations arising from philosophical inquiry and which are found in all tenet systems whether Buddhist or non-Buddhist. Subsequently, when you meditate, simply rest without clinging to anything, in the sense of having an object of meditation. This, however, is not to say that you should remain in a state of blankness, a "foolish meditation," so to speak. On the contrary, through the certain knowledge deriving from the realization of the absence of inherent existence, your vipashyana will be rendered extraordinary and you will be able to rest in the union of shamatha and vipashyana. And you will have no doubts. All this is the sign that your analysis has hit the mark.

Generally speaking, at the present time, all the great beings who uphold the Madhayamika declare that the way the phenomena of samsara or nirvana appear is as the mere imputation of thought; they are without real existence. Emptiness consists in dependent arising; emptiness and dependent arising are indissociably united. Everyone is in agreement about this. In our tradition, however, we do not consider that the expression "imputed existence" implies the presence of a "something" that lacks true existence and to which true existence could be ascribed. We say that the object referred to is a kind of empty form, an originless display of the mind's creative power.* Consequently, when emptiness is said to be inseparable from dependent arising, this is not meant to imply that there is a validly established appearance from which emptiness is inseparable. On the contrary, we understand that phenomena are

---

* *rtsal snang.*

themselves ungrounded and rootless. There is no way in which they could exist. And yet they arise freely, produced in interdependence.

Therefore, once the object of refutation, which is to be identified as the two really existing selves, has been eliminated, its place is not still occupied by some (residual) basis of refutation—a so-called person or phenomenon. There is simply nothing left at all. Persons and phenomena are empty of *themselves*. For one cannot say that they are empty of true existence while holding that phenomena themselves (the basis of emptiness) are not empty of themselves on the relative level.[292] It is rather that form, for example, is empty of form and so forth. Therefore, because all phenomena are devoid of real existence, there is no "concrete" object of refutation. All that is refuted is the false imputation that ascribes existence to what does not exist. Nagarjuna says in his *Vigrahavyavartani*:

> Since no object of negation can be found,
> I myself have nothing to negate.
> And so, by saying "I refute,"
> You're the ones who falsely testify.

It might be objected that there is a contradiction in saying, as we have just done, that the two selves are devoid of true existence, while at the same time affirming that persons and phenomena exist on the relative level. All we mean is that as long as there is the tendency to delusion, relative appearances arise constantly and unhindered. But this does not mean that they exist inherently.

The four arguments

Four separate arguments are employed. The first is the so-called Diamond Splinters argument and addresses the question of causes. This is followed by an argument dealing with effects, which shows that no effects, whether existent or nonexistent, can be said to be produced. Then comes the refutation of the idea of production from any of the four alternatives (as will be explained), which is an examination of both cause and effect together. Finally, there is the great argument that investigates the nature of phenomena. This is subdivided into two separate arguments: (1) the argument of dependent arising and (2) the argument of "neither one nor many."

AN INVESTIGATION OF CAUSES: THE DIAMOND SPLINTERS ARGUMENT

Phenomenal appearances are unborn. This is so because it is impossible for appearances to arise either (a) produced from themselves; (b) produced from something else; (c) produced from both self and other; or (d) produced causelessly through sheer randomness.[293]

Self-production. The thesis that phenomena are self-produced is untenable. This is so because in the process of production from self, the product must arise from what is either present (at the time of production) or not present. In the first case, arising cannot be explained because (a) there is no difference between the producer and the produced; (b) since the product is already present, there is no time when it is not actually produced; and (c) there is no end to the process of production. If the product arises subsequently, then given that the cause is itself not present, it cannot properly be so labeled, and this amounts to saying that the product has arisen causelessly.[294]

Production from other. So-called production from other is also impossible. It is unacceptable to say that phenomena are produced from something other than themselves because (a) if the product has not yet been produced, no extraneous object can be qualified as being its producer and (b) if that were the case, anything could arise from anything.[295]

Production from self and production from other combined. This too is impossible since production from self and production from other are mutually exclusive and because both kinds of production have already been refuted.

Causeless origination. It is impossible to say that things are produced causelessly, since (a) this contradicts the evident experience of causality; (b) it would necessarily follow that lotuses could grow from thin air; and (c) all action would be rendered pointless.[296]

The *Mulamadhyamika-karika* says:

Neither from themselves, nor from another cause,
Not from both, nor yet without a cause—
Phenomena indeed of any kind
Are never born.

AN INVESTIGATION OF RESULTS: NO EFFECTS, WHETHER EXISTENT OR NONEXISTENT, CAN BE SAID TO BE PRODUCED

Objects that appear to be different kinds of product are in fact unproduced. The reason for this is that a product, whether regarded as truly existent or truly nonexistent, is empty of origination. No origin can be ascribed to a truly existent product for the simple reason that it is already possessed of existence. Likewise, no origin can be ascribed to a truly nonexistent effect since, in this case, there is nothing that might receive the ascription of origin (like the rabbit's horns). The *Mulamadhyamika-karika* says:

Contributive causes cannot be ascribed
To things existing or without existence.
If things do not exist, what contribution can such causes make?
And if things "are," what is the cause accomplishing?

AN INVESTIGATION OF THE CAUSAL PROCESS ITSELF: A REFUTATION OF ORIGINATION RELATED TO FOUR POSSIBLE ALTERNATIVES

The apparent production of effects from causes cannot be accounted for in rational terms. (1) A single cause cannot be shown to give rise to a single result; (2) a plurality of causes cannot be shown to give rise to a plurality of results; (3) a single cause cannot be shown to give rise to a plurality of results; and (4) a plurality of causes cannot be shown to give rise to a single result. Since neither the cause nor the result is an indivisible discrete entity, they are devoid of both singularity and plurality. To speak of production is therefore as far-fetched as saying that space is solid. The *Introduction to the Two Truths* says:

By many things a single thing is not produced,
And many things do not bring forth plurality;
A single thing does not give rise to many things,
And from a single thing, a single thing is not produced.

AN INVESTIGATION INTO THE NATURE OF PHENOMENA

1. The Great Interdependence argument, which constitutes an affirming negative: mere appearances are not discrete, existent entities, because—being interdependently produced—they are beyond the eight extremes of arising, cessation, and so forth, and are thus empty of inherent reality, like the reflection of the moon in water. As it is said in the sutra:

> Whatever has arisen from conditions is indeed unborn.
> No true origin can be ascribed to it.

And it is said in the *Mulamadhyamika-karika*:

> But for what originates dependently,
> There are no phenomena;
> Therefore without voidness,
> There are no phenomena.*

2. The argument of "Neither One nor Many," which constitutes a nonaffirming negative: all external and internal phenomena are devoid of real existence, because that which is neither a single truly existent thing nor a plurality of existent things must of necessity be empty of true existence. Aryadeva has said:

> See how an instant has an end,
> And likewise a beginning and a middle.
> Because an instant is in turn three instants,
> Momentariness is not the nature of the world.

The above techniques of rational analysis are used when debating philosophical tenets and also when, while practicing on the path, one tries to free oneself (from defilement) through the application of intelligence. Because the proponents of Madhyamika make no assertions, they have no need to prove a position nor to extricate themselves from difficulties. They merely point out the flaws in the propositions of substan-

---

* In other words, emptiness is not different from phenomena.

tialist thinkers and thereby uproot the assumption of true existence. While on the path, when one is engaged in the process of freeing oneself through the application of wisdom, it is important to investigate any assertion or position taken with regard to objects of perception whether in the outer world or in the inner forum. It is necessary to investigate thoughts, the thought-free mind, the absorptions and meditative experiences, and so forth. Similarly, one should examine one's practice of Dharma, oneself and others in all manner of activities, and such matters as samsara and nirvana, existence and nonexistence, happiness and suffering, rejection and acceptance; one should ask oneself what is virtuous and what is not virtuous. One should subject all these matters to analysis, scrutinizing their most elementary constituents. And one should settle in a state devoid of any fixation and clinging, in a spaciousness that is free from conceptual construction. It is said that the Sevenfold Reasoning[297] (based on the image of a chariot) proves that there is no such thing as a personal self. In fact, these same arguments disprove the existence of both types of self (personal and phenomenal).

Why the Madhyamika dialectic is superior to all other tenet systems

Because the Prasangika Madhyamikas make no assertions that presuppose the reality of phenomena, they are without fault and utterly pure. According to their own understanding, the three lower tenet systems take up a position with regard to the nature of phenomena and proceed to investigate that to which wisdom is applied: no-self, non-origination, emptiness, and the absence of ontological extremes. They go some way to dispelling false notions, but each of them assumes true existence in one way or other. In addition, the Svatantrika Madhyamikas assert existence on the relative level. The Prasangikas contend with all of these schools and demolish their extreme positions. They themselves, however, are invulnerable to attack, and thus the Prasangika approach is regarded as faultless, the culmination of all tenet systems.

Consequently, the view of Madhyamika is nothing other than the mind's certainty with regard to the ground nature, a certainty gained through the application of the four arguments. The view itself, however, cannot be regarded as the *object* of this certainty, in the sense of being "emptiness beyond all ontological extremes." This is because if you take this *emptiness* for your view, you have failed to distinguish between the four extremes and the apprehension of these same extremes. If you entertain such a view, you have in fact become embroiled in these four extremes. Therefore, it is important to refrain even from asserting, "The view is beyond all ontological extremes."

In the words of Aryadeva:

> Not existence and not nonexistence,
> Not these two conjoined nor the opposite of this:
> Freed from four extremes, the truly wise
> Are those who keep within the middle way.

[Taken from the commentary of Yönten Gyamtso, YG II, 479–526]

The twenty-one qualities of Dharmakaya wisdom

It is written in the *Abhisamayalankara*:

> Factors leading to enlightenment, the four unmeasured attitudes,
> Perfect freedoms and, arising in succession,
> Nine absorptions, then the ayatanas—
> Ten all-penetrating,
> Eight that overpower and dominate,
> The nonarising of defilement, and the knowledge
> Of all wishes, clairvoyance and fourfold perfect knowledge,
> Four perfect purities, ten powers and ten strengths,
> Fourfold fearlessness, and threefold lack of reticence,
> Three limpidities and unforgetting memory,
> The ending of habitual tendencies,
> And great compassion shown to all that lives,
> The eighteen qualities that only Buddhas have,
> And finally, omniscience, the knowledge of all things:
> All this is said to be the Dharmakaya.[298]

The thirty-seven elements leading to enlightenment (byang chub yan lag so bdun).
See appendix 6.

The four boundless attitudes (tshad med bzhi). See chapter 7.

The eight perfect freedoms[299] *(rnam thar brgyad).* Of these, three concern the powers of miraculous manifestation and transformation, four refer to the formless states, and one to cessation.

(1) Perceiving themselves as embodied, Buddhas can transform material forms and also call them into physical manifestation. This is the perfect freedom of "form beholding form." (2) Perceiving themselves as disembodied, they can transform material forms and call them into manifestation. This is the perfect freedom of "nonform beholding

form." (3) Now, if, allied to such powers of miraculous manifestation, there occurred the urge to produce pleasant things rather than the contrary, this power of miraculous production would be limited and imperfect. But Buddhas see all forms, fair or ugly, as equal and merely interdependent phenomena relative to each other; they are just conceptual imputations, nonexistent in themselves. This is called the perfect freedom of "beholding beauty."

The four perfect freedoms with regard to the formless states concern the four extremely subtle mental perceptions of infinite space, infinite consciousness, utter nothingness, and neither existence nor nonexistence.

The eighth perfect freedom is the freedom of cessation, an experience possible for Aryas who have attained the four samadhis of the form realm, together with the four formless absorptions, and who have arrested the seven consciousnesses together with all mental factors. For such beings, only the alaya is manifest. They can now abide in the absorption wherein there is neither perception nor feeling. Thus they abide in the absorption of cessation. . . .

4. *The nine successive absorptions or "abidings in equipoise" (mthar gyis gnas pa'i snyoms 'jug dgu).* These are the four samadhis, the four formless absorptions, and the absorption of cessation. The difference between these and the perfect freedoms just described is one of emphasis. For one speaks of "perfect freedom" from the standpoint of freedom from obscurations in relation to a certain level of realization, whereas "absorption," or abiding in equipoise, is used from the point of view of the equilibrium of the elements of the physical body, as also of the mind and mental factors. The absorptions are said to be "successive" because they occur gradually, in the course of the meditation through which they are achieved. It is impossible for the higher absorptions to occur before the lower ones.

5. *The ten limitless ayatanas (zad par gyi skye mched bcu).* These comprise four limitless elements, four limitless colors, limitless space, and limitless consciousness. This means that through one-pointed concentration upon one or other of the elements, the specific quality of that element can be transferred to other phenomena (so that, for example, water or air can be given the solidity of earth so that it can be walked upon). . . .

Whereas Aryas can acquire this power only through training, it is the natural ability of Buddhas and is available at their mere wish.

6. *The eight dominant ayatanas (zil gyis gnon pa'i skye mched brgyad).* Of these there are four ayatanas that are so called because they control and dominate "shapes." (1) Perceiving themselves as embodied, Buddhas have power over all larger physical forms. They know them and see them. (2) Perceiving themselves as physically embodied, Buddhas have power over smaller physical forms. They know them and see them. (3) Perceiving themselves as being disembodied, they have power over larger forms. (4) Perceiving themselves as disembodied, they have power over smaller forms.

Likewise, there are four ayatanas that control color. Perceiving themselves as disembodied, Buddhas have power over the four colors of outer phenomena, knowing them and seeing them. These four ayatanas are related to the (primary) colors of (5) blue, (6) yellow, (7) white, and (8) red. What is the meaning of these ayatanas? By perceiving themselves as disembodied or as being of indestructible form, Buddhas perceive things that (to us) appear fair or ugly, wholesome or unwholesome—but without subscribing to the reality of such qualitative differences. Thus Buddhas can change big into small and so forth, performing wonders of transformation and production. It is through shamatha that they control and know, and it is through vipashyana that they control and see.

When it is said that the Buddhas perceive themselves as embodied or otherwise, this refers to whether, in the performance of the above mentioned wonders, the Buddhas are visible or invisible to others. . . .

7. *The nonarising of defilement (nyon mongs med).* . . . When Shravakas are on their way to a village to beg for alms, they first examine clairvoyantly whether their appearance will be an occasion of anger or attachment for the people there. If so, they proceed no further. By contrast, the perfect Buddha goes to such places on purpose and benefits the people by teaching the Dharma and displaying miracles, using every skillful method to prevent afflictions from arising in the minds of the people, both then and subsequently.

8. *The knowledge of wishes and aspirations (smon gnas mkhyen pa).* When Shravakas desire to know something, they focus their minds on it and

enter the fourth samadhi, and subsequently they understand. A Buddha's knowledge is different and has five special features. First, Buddhas know spontaneously and without effort. Second, they are free of the emotional veil, and thus they know without attachment. Third, they are free of the cognitive veil, and thus they know without impediment. Fourth, they know everything uninterruptedly and all the time. Fifth, they are able to answer simultaneously all the questions of every being in the three realms, even though they are all asked at the same moment and in different languages.

9. *The five preternatural knowledges (mngon shes lnga).* See appendix 5.

10. *The four perfect knowledges (so so yang dag par rig pa bzhi).* See appendix 5.

11. *The four complete purities (rnam pa thams cad dag pa bzhi).* Buddhas possess the "purity of bodily existence." That is, they have perfect mastery over the three stages of assuming a body, abiding with it, and relinquishing it. They have the "purity of objects and possessions," in other words, mastery in the transformation and manifestation of the five sense objects, forms, sounds, and so forth. They have the "purity of the mind and of primordial wisdom." The first means that they have mastery over concentration, and the second means that they have mastery in the supreme knowledge of emptiness.

12. *The ten powers (dbang bcu).* See appendix 5.

13. *The ten strengths (stobs bcu).* See appendix 5.

14. *The four fearlessnesses (mi 'jigs pa bzhi).* See appendix 5.

15. *The threefold absence of secretiveness (bsrung ba med pa rnam pa gsum).* The Buddha's every thought, word, and deed is naturally virtuous. Buddhas have therefore no reticence about their actions or fear that others might know of them. They have no need to hide anything.

16. *The threefold limpidity (dran pa nyer bzhag rnam gsum).* (1) Buddhas experience no elation when people listen to them respectfully, worshipfully, and undistractedly. (2) Neither are they irritated when the opposite occurs. (3) And when both situations occur together, they are troubled by neither of these emotions.

17. *The absence of forgetfulness (bsnyel ba mi mnga' ba).* Buddhas never forget anything, even things occurring countless kalpas in the past. They remember everything as if it had just happened.

18. *The complete destruction of habitual propensities (bag chags yang dag par bcom pa).* Although the Shravakas and Arhats have eliminated all afflictions, they are still under the power of habitual tendencies and as a result are still slightly under the power of delusion. Buddhas, by contrast, have exhausted all such propensities, and therefore their conduct is free of even the slightest fault.

19. *Great compassion for all that lives (skye la thugs rje chen po).* With immense compassion, Buddhas consider all beings at all times and in all situations. They know who is progressing on the path, who is declining, who is being led from the sorrows of the lower realms and set upon the blissful path of liberation and the higher realms. They know those whom they can free from the fetters of the afflictions.

20. *The eighteen distinctive qualities (ma 'dres pa'i chos bco brgyad).* See appendix 5.

21. *Omniscience (rnam pa thams cad mkhyen nyid).* The omniscience of Buddhas is threefold. First, Buddhas have a clear and distinct knowledge of each and every phenomenon. (This is true of Buddhas alone.) Second, although the three paths of the Shravakas, Pratyekabuddhas, and Bodhisattvas are ultimately without origin, Buddhas know their respective cause, essential nature, and result on the relative level. (This knowledge is shared by the Bodhisattvas.) Third, Buddhas know that phenomena belonging to the ground (the five aggregates, eighteen elements, and twelve ayatanas) are void of personal self. (This knowledge is shared also by the Shravakas.)

Of these twenty-one kinds of Dharmakaya wisdom, the ten strengths, four fearlessnesses, eighteen distinctive qualities, threefold limpidity, threefold absence of secretiveness, complete destruction of habitual propensities, and great compassion are qualities possessed only by Buddhas. The ten powers and four perfect knowledges are also shared by Bodhisattvas. All the rest are the qualities commonly shared by all, Buddhas, Bodhisattvas, and Shravakas.

[Taken from the commentary of Yönten Gyamtso, YG II, 578–588]

APPENDIX 10 ❧

The three doors of perfect liberation

It is said that implicit in all phenomena there are three ways of approach to ultimate reality. They are known as the three doors of perfect liberation and are: emptiness, absence of attributes, and absence of expectancy.

1. Emptiness is defined as "absence of reference" or "unfindability" (*dmigs med*). This is another way of saying that phenomena have no inherent existence. Phenomena, from form to omniscience, are totally devoid of even the slightest degree of intrinsic being. Their true status in fact lies outside the range of discursive knowledge, and it is precisely mental construction that veils it. As long as thoughts occur (namely, the ordinary mind and its mental factors), phenomena, the objects of thought, appear.* For in themselves such phenomena are without true (autonomous) existence, not only on the absolute level but even on that of relative truth.

2. Absence of attributes or featurelessness is defined as "pacification" or "subsiding" (*zhi ba*). Phenomena arise in interdependence as the natural display of emptiness. Thus, from the very outset, the conceptual ascriptions of existence and nonexistence, good and bad, causes and conditions (beneficial or otherwise) cannot properly be applied to them. What militates against this absence of attributes is the dividing-up of the phenomenal field into self and other, clean and unclean, and so on. For the fact is that phenomena do not exist in this way in the nature of emptiness, the dharmadhatu, the domain of nonconceptual wisdom.

3. Absence of expectancy is defined as "absence of suffering and ignorance." Because phenomena included within the truths of suffering and origin ("true sufferings," namely, the universe and its inhabitants; "true origins," namely, karma and emotions born of ignorance) have never existed, "nirvana" is not different from them.

---

* In other words, apparent objects, whether mental experiences or things in the "extramental world," which will seem solid and existent.

The *Bodhicharyavatara* says:

> Something such as this does not exist, not even slightly,
> Beings have nirvana by their nature.
> (IX, 103)

What militates against this is our tendency to consider samsara and nirvana as distinct realities and to imagine that nirvana is a goal to be attained, whereas in the nature of the mind itself, samsara and nirvana are indistinguishable. The *Madhyamakavatara* affirms:

> The character of emptiness
> Is absence of a real, existent referent.
>
> The absence of all attributes is peace.
> And third (the absence of expectancy)
>   has been defined as non-existence
> Of all suffering and ignorance. . . .
>   (VI, 208, 209)

The three doors of perfect liberation are also associated with the ground, path, and fruit. Emptiness refers to the ground because the true status of phenomena lies beyond the extremes of existence and nonexistence. The absence of attributes refers to the path because even at the present moment, phenomena as such are without existence. The absence of expectancy refers to the fruit, because no hope is placed in some future attainment. As the *Madhyamakavatara* says:

> The present instant does not stay;
> The past and future have no being.
> Because these three cannot be pointed out,
> They are referred to as "the unobservable." [300]
>   (VI, 216)

[Taken from the commentary of Yönten Gyamtso, YG III, 517f]

Notes ❧

ABBREVIATIONS USED IN NOTES

DKR	Kyabje Dilgo Khyentse Rinpoche, notes to the commentary by Kyabje Kangyur Rinpoche
DS	*sdom gsum*, The Three Vows, by Kyabje Dudjom Rinpoche
KJ	*mkhas 'jug*, Introduction to Scholarship, by Ju Mipham Rinpoche
YG I	*Yönten Gyamtso: zla ba'i 'od zer*, vol. 1 of the Great Commentary on the Treasury of Precious Qualities
YG II	*Yönten Gyamtso: zla ba'i 'od zer*, vol. 2 of the Great Commentary on the Treasury of Precious Qualities
YG III	*Yönten Gyamtso: nyi ma'i 'od zer*, vol. 3 of the Great Commentary on the Treasury of Precious Qualities

1   The reference is to Longchen Rabjam and Jigme Lingpa. The expressions "Infinite Expanse" and "rays of Love and Knowledge" in the previous lines are in fact translations of their names (*klong chen rab 'byams* and *mkhyen brtse 'od zer*).

2   *legs bshad*, "well-explained." This expression is traditionally used to describe a discourse, the aim of which is to set forth the principles of virtuous conduct.

3   *rdo rje snying po*, a synonym for the innermost teachings of the Great Perfection.

4   *chings chen po lnga: dgos pa, mtshams sbyor, tshig don, bsdus don, 'gal lan*, a five-element structure around which, according to Vasubandhu, treatises should be composed. See Vasubandhu's *Vyakhyayukti*. Here the system is being applied specifically to the title. The second element, connection (*mtshams sbyor*), relates to the proper arrangement of the subject. It has not been translated here, for it simply indicates the correct position for the explanation of the title, following the mention of its purpose.

5   The three kinds of beings are: (1) those who aspire to happiness in the higher states of samsaric existence; (2) those who aspire to liberation from samsara altogether (Shravakas and Pratyekabuddhas); and (3) those who aspire to the attainment of buddhahood for the sake of all beings (Bodhisattvas).

6   *phun sum tshogs pa lnga*. The five excellences of place, teacher, retinue, time, and

teaching. According to the Shravakayana, this refers to the Buddha Shakyamuni and the various moments and geographical locations in which he expounded the Dharma to his disciples. According to the Mahayana, this refers to the Sambhogakaya Buddhas, such as Vairochana, expounding the teachings of the Great Vehicle in various buddhafields, in the eternal present beyond time, to a vast retinue of Bodhisattvas residing on the tenth ground. In the Mahayana context, the five excellences are also called the "five certainties" (*nges pa lnga*).

7 *dgos 'brel yan lag bzhi*. "The fourfold interrelated purpose refers to a subject (*brjod bya*), its immediate purpose (*dgos pa*), its ultimate finality (*nying dgos*), and the connection between these three factors (*'brel ba*). These four elements are considered essential for meaningful communication to take place. In this context, the subject is the practice of the gradual paths of the three kinds of beings. The immediate purpose is to provide an understanding of the path of liberation through a study of the text. The ultimate objective is the practitioner's attainment of the final goal. The connection refers to the fact that the previous three elements must be consistent with each other." [YG I, 179]

8 These are: realization of the ultimate nature, the vision of the yidam (and, possibly, the reception of authorization), and a knowledge of the five sciences. The possession of one of these qualifications authorizes a person to compose shastras, or commentaries.

9 "Asanga's *Yogacharabhumi-shastra* says: The three qualities of Buddhist compositions are that they are meaningful, are conducive to practice, and lead away from suffering. The six defects of non-Buddhist writings are that they are meaningless, false, of purely academic import, sophistical, misleading, and lacking in compassion." [YG I, 176]

10 *rtsis mgo yan lag lnga*, five important headings: *mdzad pa po, lung gang nas btus, phyogs gang du gtogs, bsdus don, dgos ched*. This is how treatises were traditionally explained by the panditas of the ancient Indian university of Nalanda.

11 Buddhist teachings speak of four types of birth: from the womb, from an egg, spontaneous generation from warmth and moisture, and miraculous manifestation.

12 "Generally speaking, there are three types of human existence: 'merely human' (*mi lus tsam po pa*), as described in the text; 'special human existence' (*mi lus khyad par can*), i.e., in which actions and attitudes oscillate between virtue and negativity; and 'precious human existence' (*mi lus rin po che*), as explained here." [YG I, 182]

13 *mi g yo ba'i las*. Mipham Rinpoche defines unwavering action as: "A positive action, such as a profound state of absorption devoid of bodhichitta, which infallibly, or 'unwaveringly' produces rebirth in the form or formless realms. Other actions are not unwavering in the sense that their result may, depending

on circumstances, ripen in states that are not normally expected from the action in question." [KJ, 80]

14   Beings are described as superior or noble when they have progressed beyond the path of seeing, in other words, when they have realized the absence of self or ego. All beings who have not done so (including the gods of the desire, form, and formless realms) are described as ordinary. The four samadhis of the form realm are subdivided into different levels. There are three such divisions in the first, second, and third samadhis. All of these are inhabited by "ordinary" beings. The fourth samadhi also has three levels of ordinary beings. In addition, however, it possesses five levels on which superior beings are said to dwell. On the last of these levels or, according to some authorities, on a yet higher, ninth, level (i.e., the seventeenth or eighteenth of the subdivisions of the entire form realm) are to be found the Bodhisattvas who are on the brink of full attainment. This is the realm of Akanishta the Fair, the dimension in which the Bodhisattvas spend their last life before achieving buddhahood. The insensate gods belong to the form realm but are different from the other gods of that dimension in being without perception. They are said to be "located" in the vicinity of the Great Fruit, the third level of the fourth samadhi, which is the highest attainment possible to ordinary beings in the form realm. In the case of the formless gods, no locations, even subtle ones, are spoken of. Only the formless gods and insensate gods are said to lack the freedom to practice Dharma. This is not so in the case of the gods of the form and desire realms, since it is said that Shravakas and Pratyekabuddhas may manifest there.

"The absorption of the insensate and the formless gods and that of the cessation enjoyed by Shravakas and Pratyekabuddhas are similar in that both are characterized by a halting of the sense consciousnesses in the alaya, the fundamental level of the mind. They are, however, different in that the absorption of the insensate gods does not involve the cessation of the defiled emotional consciousness (*nyon yid*), whereas the cessation of the Shravakas and Pratyekabuddhas does. For this reason, ordinary beings can only enter the absorption of nonperception, while the absorption of cessation is the preserve of Shravakas and Pratyekabuddhas, practitioners of the Hinayana. Moreover, non-Buddhist traditions mistakenly regard the formless absorptions as liberation and train in them as their spiritual path. The Shravakas and Pratyekabuddhas enter the absorption of cessation for the sake of contentment during their present lifetime. Sublime Bodhisattvas, by contrast, may enter it as an expedient, simply as a means of training in concentration." [YG I, 188]

15   This traditional scheme of eight freedoms (*dal ba brgyad*) and ten advantages (*rang gzhan 'byor bcu*) is supplemented in the writings of Longchenpa by two further lists of hindering factors (each containing eight items) which must be absent if human existence is to be considered truly precious. They are taken

up and commented on by Patrul Rinpoche in *The Words of My Perfect Teacher*, pp. 30–31. First, there are *eight obstructive circumstances* (*'phral byung rkyen gyi mi khom rnam pa brgyad*) that prevent true practice of the Dharma. These are: great strength of the five negative emotions; great stupidity; the following of a false teacher; great indolence; strong obscurations arising from past negativity; a lack of independence; embracing Dharma for the sake of protection from worldly fears; and attempting to acquire wealth and prestige from a show of Dharma practice. Second, there are eight incompatible tendencies (*ris chad blo yi mi khom rnam pa brgyad*). These are: being caught up in worldly activities; a lack of basic humanity; complacency with regard to the ills of samsara; a lack of faith in the teacher and the teachings; finding entertainment in what are negative actions; a lack of interest in spiritual values; the transgression of the pratimoksha vows (monastic ordination, etc.) and the bodhisattva vows; and the breach of tantric samaya. If any of these factors is present, the level of precious human existence has not been fully attained.

16   The body is said to be composed of the elements of earth, air, fire, and water, corresponding to the principles of solidity, movement, warmth, and liquidity. To these is added space, without which the others could not exist. When equilibrium between the elements is lost, a disease occurs.

17   *bsod nams cha mthun.* This means virtuous actions performed in conjunction with a belief in the real existence of the self, both of persons and phenomena. Such actions are productive of happiness in samsara but do not lead beyond it. They are therefore to be contrasted with "virtuous action tending to liberation" (*thar pa cha mthun*), which produce liberation from samsara.

18   The thirty-two divine kings are the lesser gods of this heaven of which Indra is the ruler.

19   A full discussion of the primal substance prakriti and the doctrine of divine creation will be found in Khenchen Kunzang Pelden, *Wisdom: Two Buddhist Commentaries*, pp. 105–115.

20   "In the case of ordinary beings, it is hardly necessary to mention that ignorance is the root of the three poisons. But it is said that until the 'defiled consciousness' is transmuted, the acquisition of higher qualities will also be hindered. By higher qualities is meant, for instance, the ability to visit pure buddhafields and the effortless arising of thought-transcending wisdom. And this is true even among those who are residing on the sublime Bodhisattva grounds." [DKR]

21   See Patrul Rinpoche, *The Words of my Perfect Teacher*, p. 73.

22   Vasubandhu, the author of the *Abhidharmakosha*, is normally considered to have been a Sautrantika in his Hinayana period. However, his *Abhidharmakosha* was composed from the Vaibhashika point of view.

23   In other words, "performed" (*byas*) refers simply to the action as such;

"stored" (*bsags*) refers to intentionality, satisfaction, and so on, which ingrains the effect on the mindstream. H. H. the Dalai Lama says that the four permutations of the performed and stored aspects reveal whether the effect of an action will definitely be experienced. The first and third permutations indicate an action the effect of which is certain to be experienced. The other two permutations are not attended by the same degree of certainty. See *The Dalai Lama at Harvard*, p. 60.

24 The logic behind this is that the Three Jewels are the object of confession, whereby one may purify even the most heinous of negative actions. The gravity of reviling or repudiating the Three Jewels consists in the fact that one abandons the very object whereby purification is possible.

25 The three types of feeling are pleasant, unpleasant, and neutral. The three types of perception mentioned here are associated with the three realms (desire, form, and formless); they are: small, intermediate, and great. See appendix 4.

26 These are: to kill one's father, to kill one's mother, to kill an Arhat, to attack and injure a Buddha so as to draw blood, and to cause a schism in the Sangha. These actions are of immediate effect because they are so grave that their effect overrides any other karma, and at death the person concerned falls directly into hell without even passing through the bardo state.

27 All together, these five are: destroying a stupa, killing a Bodhisattva, killing a practitioner on the noble path, robbing the Sangha, and raping a female Arhat.

28 "In this context, mention is also made of sixteen grave actions and eight wrong actions:

"Four gravely wrong actions (*log pa'i lci ba*): sitting above a learned person, accepting prostrations from a fully ordained monk, stealing the provisions of a meditator, and stealing the ritual implements of a mantrika.

"Four gravely impairing actions (*nyams pa'i lci ba*): to swear coarsely by using the name of the Three Jewels, for ordained persons to act against shravaka discipline, for practitioners of the Mahayana to violate the precepts of the Bodhisattvas, and for practitioners of the Mantrayana to violate the samayas, or sacramental commitments.

"Four gravely disrespectful actions (*smad pa'i lci ba*): out of ignorance to have contempt for the physical form of a Buddha, out of pride to have contempt for the qualities of learned people, out of jealousy to show contempt for what is truthfully said, and out of partiality to discriminate between religious schools.

"Four gravely scornful actions (*skur pa'i lci ba*): cynically to condone wrong views, to condone the shedding of a Buddha's blood, arbitrarily to condemn one among equals and to make false and unfounded accusations.

"Eight wrong actions (*log pa brgyad*): (1) to despise virtue; (2) to praise nonvirtue; (3) to upset a virtuous person; (4) to interrupt the meritorious actions of a faithful person; (5) to abandon one's teacher; (6) to abandon one's yidam deity; (7) to abandon one's spiritual kindred; and (8) to violate the sacred mandala (i.e., the sadhana practice)." [YG I, 276]

29   "The mere failure to commit the ten negative actions, without having a conscious spirit of restraint, is considered indeterminate (in other words, karmically insignificant). Positive behavior is defined as the mind's conscious intention to reject negative practices and to adopt their opposites. These are the active protection of life, the practice of generosity, the perfect observance of the vows, the speaking of the truth, the reconciliation of disputes, peaceful and disciplined speech, speaking what is consonant with Dharma, satisfaction with little, loving attitudes toward others, belief in the doctrine of karma, and so on." [YG I, 283]

30   The Shravakas and Pratyekabuddhas practice all these six virtues but without the complete wisdom of emptiness and the skillful means of bodhichitta. For this reason, the term *paramitas* or "perfections," is not used.

31   A practitioner on the path of joining passes through four stages as the realization of the path of seeing approaches. These are: warmth, peak, acceptance, and supreme mundane level. Until "peak" is gained, the practitioner is still prone to negative action. This is discussed at length in chapter 6.

32   YG I, 296.

33   Sadness (*skyo ba*) in this context is considered a positive quality. Its importance lies in the fact that it gives rise to renunciation, the desire, indeed the decision, to leave samsara.

34   This well-known story, also recounted in *The Words of My Perfect Teacher*, describes the occasion when Arya Katyayana saw a man sitting with his child on his knee. He was in the act of eating some fish, and in order to chase away a dog that was gnawing at the leftovers, he threw a stone at it. Due to the clairvoyance gained as a side effect of his meditative practice, Katyayana perceived that the baby was the rebirth of the man's worst enemy. The man's dead parents had fallen into the lower realms but, due to karmic links, were still drawn to him in his present existence. Thus the fish that he was eating was the rebirth of his father, while the dog had been his mother—who in ignorance was gnawing at the bones of her former husband!

35   "And beings who give up and revile the Doctrine." [DKR]

36   "Fifty human years are equivalent to one day in the heaven of the Four Great Kings. Five hundred years in that state correspond to a single day in the Reviving Hell, and here beings live for five hundred of their own years. The life span of the different hells gradually increases until, in the Hell of Great Heat, it lasts for half an intermediate kalpa and in the Hell of Torment Unsurpassed an entire intermediate kalpa." [YG I, 311]

37 For examples of this last point, see Patrul Rinpoche, *The Words of My Perfect Teacher*, pp. 70 ff.

38 See YG I, 335.

39 It is from the time when the sense organs develop that the fetus starts to experience discomfort.

40 "When the pain of illness manifests in the aggregate of *form, feeling* experiences it, *perception* cognizes it as suffering, *conditioning factors* produce future suffering of the same kind, and *consciousness* is aware of the entire process." [YG I, 343]

41 "The Shravakas and Pratyekabuddhas know that all existents (the universe and creatures) are like the shimmering of a mirage, a flash of lightning, the fiery path of a torch whirled in the air. They are constantly fluctuating, evanescent, and painful by their nature. Shravakas and Pratyekabuddhas understand also that these very "sufferings" are unaccompanied by a self and thereby eradicate the ignorance of wrongly conceiving otherwise. They sever the stream of karma and emotion and reach the state that is beyond all suffering, inwardly relying on the wisdom that realizes no-self, which is itself the truth of path. The *Suhrllekha* says:

> Birth is suffering, and the cause of this
> Is craving. The abolition of this cause
> Is freedom or cessation—gained
> By following the Eightfold Noble Path.

"In the same way that people riding in a chariot progress to their destination, by recognizing (suffering), discarding (its origins), realizing (cessation), and implementing (the path), practitioners practice and gradually progress through the five paths of the Hinayana. This way of proceeding occurs also in the Mahayana, and it is vital to understand it. Vasubandhu advises us to bind our minds with the vows of Pratimoksha, to hear and study the general instructions and the special teachings on no-self, and to meditate on this until deep conviction is attained. To this end, we should destroy the twenty wrong views associated with identifying the perishable aggregates as the 'I,' pondering well the sense of Nagarjuna's *Suhrllekha*:

> Form is not the 'I,' the Lord has said, and 'I'
> Is not possessed of form. Within the 'I,' the form
> Does not inhere, and form is not the dwelling place of 'I.'
> The other aggregates, please understand, are likewise void.

"Firmly convinced of this, the Shravakas and Pratyekabuddhas follow the Eightfold Noble Path. This comprises Right View, a stainless wisdom free from the afflictions; Right Livelihood, the abandonment of all evil ways of making a living; Right Effort, the four genuine restraints; Right Mindfulness, which is not to forget the object of concentration and its accompanying attitudes, in other words, the four close mindfulnesses; Right Concentration,

the four samadhis and so forth, the foundation of the Noble Path; Right
Speech, the four positive verbal actions; Right Conduct, the repudiation of
the three negative actions of the body; and Right Thought, virtuous states of
mind such as benevolence. . . .

"The attainment of liberation depends exclusively upon one's own efforts. In
the *Suhrllekha*, Nagarjuna says:

> Freedom thus depends upon yourself,
> No friend can help you to accomplish it.
> Work hard in learning, concentration, discipline,
> And in the four truths train yourself." [YG I, 358]

42 Nirvana with remainder occurs when cessation takes place in the course of
the practitioner's life. The skandhas of that life (the remainder) continue
until the karmic seeds that are the cause of its existence are exhausted. The
Arhat then dies, at which point nirvana without remainder occurs. All karma
is exhausted and the impure psychophysical continuum terminates.

43 See Khenchen Kunzang Pelden, *Wisdom: Two Buddhist Commentaries*, p. 67.
"Shravakas, on their own admission, have a non-emotional ignorance which
prevents them from knowing objects removed in time and space. In addition,
they fail to understand the no-self of phenomena and are attached to concepts
such as 'samsara is to be abandoned and nirvana is to be realised.' "

44 See YG I, 362.

45 The principle of dependent arising (*rten 'brel bcu gnyis*), also referred to as the
law of interdependence, is one of the most important and profound of the
Buddha's teachings. It describes twelve factors, linked interdependently, in
the form of a cycle that revolves without beginning or ending. The fact that
ignorance is posited as the first link does not mean that it is a permanently
existent first cause. It is, however, the main factor, together with craving and
grasping. If this is eliminated, the entire cycle is interrupted. The twelve links
of dependent arising do not imply causality in a strictly chronological sequence. In the production of a plant, for instance, the principal factor is the
seed, but many other conditions, such as soil, moisture, and warmth, must
also coexist and be present. Likewise certain links in the cycle must coincide
(chronologically). There are many traditional ways of explaining this principle, both from the standpoint of the Theravada, such as in Buddhaghosha's
Visuddhimagga or *Sammohavinodani*, and also from the Mahayana perspective,
such as Asanga's *Abhidharmasamuccaya*. This is only the bare outline of a profound and difficult subject.

46 In other words, Buddhism denies the existence of a Creator in the biblical
sense, as well as that of the unmoved mover of Aristotelian philosophy. In
fact, the belief in a creator god, or first cause, arises from an incorrect understanding of the nature of phenomena. For a more extensive treatment of this
subject, see Khenchen Kunzang Pelden, *Wisdom: Two Buddhist Commentaries*, pp.
105–116.

47 Mipham Rinpoche explains: "It is possible to conceive of the cycle of twelve links unfolding within the time period required for the completion of a single action (*bya ba rdzogs pa'i skad cig.*) In the case of killing, for instance, it is through *Ignorance* that one becomes involved in the action. *Conditioning Factors* are the action itself. *Consciousness* is the awareness in the moment of the action. *Name and Form* and the (six) *Senses* of that instant produce *Contact* with the weapon etc. *Feeling* is the experience of one's own satisfaction and the suffering of the other. *Craving* is represented by the willful engagement in the satisfaction and suffering just mentioned. This leads to *Grasping*, i.e. an enthusiasm for similar events in the future. *Becoming* refers to the aggregates of the entire instant of the action, and this leads to the *Birth* of the present and future aspects of the experience, which in turn passes through a period of transformation (*Aging*) and conclusion (*Death*)." [KJ, 52–53]

48 See the remarks on Maudgalyayana and Kubja the Small in Khenchen Kunzang Pelden, *Wisdom: Two Buddhist Commentaries*, p. 66.

49 "Indeed, the entire range of teachings, from the vehicle of the Shravakas to those of the Natural Great Perfection, have one meaning only, that of dependent arising. And at all times, the meaning remains the same, the only difference lying in the manner in which it is imparted and explained to beings." [DKR]

50 "The Shravakas and Pratyekabuddhas exhibit strong partiality in adopting the truths of path and cessation and in rejecting the truths of suffering and origin. While engaged in uprooting ignorance, the root of existence, they do not fully realize the nature of dependent arising. It is said in the *Kashyapa-paripriccha-sutra*, 'The emptiness that they realize is like the hole left by a worm in a mustard seed.' Thus the Hinayana is simply a support for the path of the Mahayana. The ultimate result transcends all discrimination, that is, adoption or rejection in respect of the karmic law of cause and effect, which is itself an imputation of beings of lesser capacity. The ultimate result transcends the mind, mental factors, and their objects, all of which characterize such imputation. It is a nirvana that does not abide in either extreme, whether of samsara or the peace of cessation. The principal goal to be attained is thus the absolute truth, the ultimate nature of phenomena. This result manifests when the all-discerning wisdom directly and fully understands the primordial "unbornness" of phenomena, phenomena artificially asserted or reified as the four truths, and the twelvefold chain of dependent arising, in other words, when it realizes their ultimate nature that lies beyond existence. All-discerning wisdom understands this in a manner that transcends the intellect, where all concepts of subject and object subside. In what way are phenomena nonexistent? Given that phenomena produced through interdependence have no absolute existence, suffering itself is also without ultimate existence. The *Mulamadhyamika-karika* says: 'How could there be a suffering that does not arise through interdependence? What is impermanent is said to be suffering.

Suffering has no inherent existence.' Since an effect does not occur, there is no cause (for it). The *Mulamadhyamika-karika* (xxiv, 22) says: 'If suffering exists inherently, how could it be produced?' And it is illogical to attribute the possibility of cessation to what inherently exists. 'Cessation of an inherently existent suffering is absurd.' Since things to be abandoned and their antidote cannot meet, there cannot be a path. It is said (xxiv, 23), 'If the past and future instants meet, the indivisible instant must have two parts. If these two parts are simultaneous, it follows that one kalpa and one instant become the same.' Even the four truths do not have inherent existence. It is said in the *Lankavatara-sutra*:

> The unborn is the only truth
> While 'Four truths' is the talk of mere children.
> For those abiding in the essence of enlightenment,
> Not one is found, why speak of four?

Phenomena arising in interdependence are merely our mistaken perceptions, nothing more. Their nature is utterly pure (empty). Knowing this, it is a mistake to cling to phenomena, preferring some and rejecting others." [YG I, 376]

51 Of the "three purities," the first is the fact that the alms gift does not derive from wrong livelihood. The second is that the act of giving itself should be done openly without wrong intention. The third is that the donor is happy with the act and without regret.

52 This is a summary translation of the quotation. The sense of the Tibetan terms *ma brtag, ma bslangs, ma bskul* is difficult to interpret. For meat to be considered pure, three criteria are necessary: (1) the consumers must have seen that the animal in question was not killed specially for them; (2) they must have heard it from a trustworthy source that the animal was not slaughtered for food for their specific consumption; and (3) they must have no doubt that this is so. Subject to these conditions, one is allowed to eat meat. Another, more stringent, oral tradition stipulates the following criteria. The consumer must: (1) see that the animal has died a natural death; (2) have it on trustworthy report that this is the case; or (3) have no suspicion that the animal was intentionally slaughtered.

53 According to a tradition going back to the Buddha himself, the seat of a forest hermit is made of kusha grass.

54 The historical duration of the Buddha's teaching is said to consist of four major periods. First there is the "period of fruit" immediately following the promulgation of the Doctrine by the Buddha, when people who practiced it attained realization with great speed. There then follows the "period of practice," when people have to practice in order to gain the result. In the third "period of transmission," the Dharma is merely transmitted. At this time, only a few people practice it, and those who gain the result are extremely

rare. Finally, in the residual fourth "period of signs," the Dharma is maintained only in its external signs.

55 Approach, accomplishment, and activation are different phases of the sadhana practice. See glossary.

56 There was once an old frog who lived in well. One day, he was visited by another frog who lived by the sea. The two frogs fell into conversation and began to compare their different dwelling places. Unable to comprehend that there could exist something more vast and grand than his humble well, which for him was the summit of excellence and comfort, the old frog was persuaded to make the journey to see the ocean for himself. When he arrived there, the immensity of the sea terrified him so much that his head split open with shock!

57 "People belonging to the first category are disciples who are able to benefit themselves and others. The teacher should instruct them unreservedly. As for those belonging to the other categories, the teacher should use every possible skillful means to draw them onto the authentic path. And, even if the attempt fails, the teacher must continue to care for them lovingly, by means of prayers of aspiration, so that they might become disciples in the future, by virtue of their connection." [YG I, 426]

58 "Even though the teacher has no need or desire for offerings, you should offer him or her everything that you like most. It is said in the *spyi mdo*, 'My kingdom and my body, my children, spouse and wealth, my best possessions that I cherish most, I offer to the holy one.' Limitless merit accrues from this, for it is the teacher who introduces you to the Dharmakaya of the Buddhas. The *dgongs pa 'dus pa* says that offerings made for thousands of kalpas to thousands of Buddhas cannot match a thousandth part of a single drop of sandalwood oil offered for the anointing of a single pore of the teacher's body. If you are poor, a small offering made with a perfect and sincere attitude will equally perfect the accumulation of merit. It is important to make an offering proportionate with what you have." [YG I, 431]

59 "The reason that practice is considered the best kind of service is that it fulfills the true purpose of the teacher's presence. All teachers, from Buddha Shakyamuni onward, have expounded the Dharma for one reason only: that beings might be liberated. Failure to practice their teachings frustrates this end." [YG I, 433]

60 Infinite purity of phenomena refers to a vajrayana realization that appearances, sound, and thoughts are the mandalas of the deities, mantras, and wisdom.

61 "What we call 'time' is an imputation relating to the sequence of moments as perceived by every being individually and posited in relation to a point that is actually being experienced. This is labelled 'the present,' and the past and future are the names given to preceding and subsequent events respec-

tively. Time in itself has no intrinsic existence of its own. Just as when dreaming, the mind arranges temporal sequences of different length, in the same way it assigns events to the past, present and future in the waking state. On the ultimate level, however, in the fundamental state of things, no phenomena terminate in the 'past,' no phenomena occur in the 'present' and no events supervene in the 'future.' To be 'learned in the three times' means to understand their 'equality.' With this in mind, one can then go on to posit the so-called 'inconceivable fourth time' in addition to the past, present and future. For one understands that the temporary and spatial categories are mere imputations and one integrates the ultimate reality, the equality of everything." [KJ, 67]

62 One should perhaps be aware of a tendency to interpret refuge in a "theistic" sense, involving a reliance on a kind of supernatural power. The idea of taking refuge in the Buddha naturally involves an expectancy that the Buddha will bestow protection. He does indeed. But this is not some sort of ready-made liberation, handed down as a reward. The Buddha does not grant salvation. He explains suffering and the causes of suffering and expounds the path to freedom. It is for the disciples to follow. They in turn are liberated from suffering by understanding its nature and themselves uprooting its causes. Thus, rather than being an appeal to divine grace, the true taking of refuge is the commitment to undertake the path whereby the disciples liberate themselves.

63 Obviously, the English word "faith" has connotations deriving from the Judeo-Christian tradition. It is used here to translate the Tibetan word *dad pa*, which certainly shares some of these connotations but extends beyond them, as is explained in the text.

64 *'phags pa'i rigs.* This is a reference to the Arya lineage. According to the Hinayana, it indicates persons who have few desires; who are content with what they have in the way of food, clothing, and dwelling places; and who persevere in purifying negativities and gaining realization. This lineage (or proclivity) is so called because it brings beings to the level of the Aryas.

65 Shuracharya, otherwise known as Ashvaghosha, was an Indian Brahmin very much opposed to the Buddhadharma. He challenged the great pandita Aryadeva in debate, the stakes being that the loser would embrace the tradition of the winner. Ashvaghosha was summarily defeated and was so ashamed that he decided to commit suicide by throwing himself into the Ganges. Aryadeva discovered this and, sending some monks to capture him, had him locked up in the monastery library. Eventually, Ashvaghosha calmed down, and becoming a trifle bored, set about reading the texts. After a time, he was so impressed and moved by the expositions of the Dharma that he underwent a wholehearted conversion. In the course of his reading, he discovered a prophecy about himself, to the effect that he was to write a life story of the Buddha. Ashvaghosha was in fact an important poet in the history of Sanskrit

literature, and the *Buddhacharita*, a biography of the Buddha in verse, was composed by him.

66   It is easy for Western readers to interpret this kind of formulation as an "exhortation to martyrdom," which is in fact quite at odds with the Buddhist spirit. The notion of orthodoxy, in the sense of an ideology commanding notional assent, is of no importance in Buddhism, where all the emphasis is placed on inner conviction as the motivating force of genuine spiritual transformation. Thus, the meaning of irreversible faith is to be found not in expressions of belief adhered to doggedly in a confessional sense, but in an inner conviction that is so profound as to be ineradicable, irrespective of whatever verbal formulations might be wrung from unwilling lips. This point is best illustrated by the story, quoted in *The Words of My Perfect Teacher* (pp. 185–186), of an Indian lay practitioner who was threatened with death if he did not repudiate his refuge in the Three Jewels. "I can only renounce taking refuge with my mouth. I am incapable of doing so with my heart." The man was executed and accepted death willingly, even though "dying for the faith" was not his principal objective.

67   In this context, the four truths must be understood not as general principles but as classes of phenomena. Thus, one speaks not of the truth of suffering but rather of true sufferings, true origins, and so on, referring thereby to the phenomenal world. In this particular instance, the focus is on the five aggregates. See appendix 3.

68   It is, however, enough to understand the points just explained, which apply mainly to the first two truths of suffering and origins. According to Khenpo Pema Sherab, some authorities maintain that these ten factors cannot truly militate against the truth of path, because the latter is the wisdom of no-self and therefore the very antidote to the ten factors.

69   "There are innumerable kinds of thought that veil the essential nature of the mind. All, however, can be grouped under two general headings: (1) misconceptions superimposed on 'what is the case' (*sgro btags*) and (2) innate or coemergent thought patterns (*lhan skyes*) of clinging to a supposed 'I' and 'mine.' The conceived objects (*zhen yul*) of both these ways of thinking (i.e., superimpositions and innate thought patterns) are the two 'selves': the 'self' of persons and the 'self' of phenomena. These two selves are apprehended and clung to by these two kinds of thought. All artificially imputed conceptions of self are eliminated by the wisdom of the path of seeing, the direct understanding of reality. The conceptions of self that are the object of the innate thought patterns are eliminated by the wisdom of the path of meditation, which is the sustained training and familiarization of the mind in the wisdom gained on the path of seeing. The wisdom of the Mahayana paths of seeing and meditation destroys emotional obscurations such as avarice, as well as the cognitive obscurations, which are the notions of a truly existent subject, object, and action, together with their connected tendencies. This,

then, is how the qualities of elimination are perfected. Thus, the term *spangs pa* in the root verse may be interpreted as referring to both the superimpositions and the innate thought patterns that are eliminated. Alternatively, the *spangs pa* may be understood not as what is to be eliminated but as the eliminator, namely, wisdom. Just as the banishing of the miseries of samsara can be understood as the positive state of deliverance, liberation, or nirvana, in the same way, the wisdoms of seeing and meditation may be understood not merely as antidotes to their corresponding defects, but as the wisdom or freedom in which such defects have no place. It is therefore correct to interpret the root verse by saying that emotional and cognitive obscurations are destroyed by two kinds of wisdom." [YG I, 482]

70   Care should be taken with the word "innate," the translation of *lhan skyes*. It is used here to refer to contents, or rather proclivities, that are already present in the mind at birth and which are to be distinguished from the false imputations or ideas that are freshly made or entertained in each new lifetime (under the influence of false tenet systems). Both artificial imputations (*kun brtags*) and innate thought patterns (*lhan skyes*) are kinds of emotional obscuration (*nyon sgrib*). Artificial imputations are relatively shallow. They arise conceptually and are comparatively easy to remove. On the other hand, innate thought patterns are much stronger, being a conditioning from previous existences (an example would be an aggressive tendency already deep-rooted in the temperament of a small child). The cognitive obscurations (*shes sgrib*) also consist of artificial imputations and innate thought patterns, but in this context they are usually referred to as gross and subtle obscurations, respectively. The former are eliminated on the path of seeing, while the latter disappear only in the course of the path of meditation.

71   The Hinayana path of meditation consists of the progressive stages of the development of meditative absorption. Obviously, these absorptions, which correspond to the form and formless realms, can be cultivated before the (supramundane) path of seeing is reached. For they can be attained by non-Buddhist meditators, although in their case, since the wisdom of emptiness (i.e., the path of seeing) is absent, such accomplishments do not result in liberation from samsara. This is why it is said in the Hinayana that practitioners may cultivate the higher absorptions while at the same time working toward the path of seeing and before they achieve this. Those who do this are said to be on the path of "leap over," the implication being that, when they attain the path of seeing, they leap over the stages of the path of meditation that they have already accomplished. Those on the path of "leap over" are either Once Returners or Nonreturners. Thus it can be said that the second and third Hinayana levels can be attained by the worldly path, while the first and fourth are attained only by the transmundane path.

72   "This is the 'Path without obstacles.'" [DKR]

73   "This is the 'Path of liberation.'" [DKR]

74 "This is the 'Path without obstacles.'" [DKR]

75 In the early phase of Buddhism in India, distinct communities had developed in culturally diverse regions. At the time of the king Ashoka there were four main traditions: Sarvastivada, Mahasanghika, Sthavira, and Sammitiya (see note 179). These further divided into eighteen schools, which were asserted as valid Dharma traditions by the council held under the king Kanishka's patronage. For a detailed treatment of the subject, see Tarthang Tulku, *Light of Liberation, Crystal Mirror*, vol. 8.

76 The term "instant" may be understood in two senses. It may refer to the smallest unit of time (*dus mtha'i skad cig*) or to the period of time required for the accomplishment of a given action (*bya ba rdzogs pa'i skad cig*). The latter is necessarily variable. It may correspond to something as brief as a finger-snap, or it may encompass the period extending from the first generation of bodhichitta to the full attainment of buddhahood. In the *grub mtha' mdzod*, the omniscient Longchenpa says that the four truths are realized in sixteen in-stants of the second kind. In other words, they are realized in the course of sixteen successive occasions (of varying length). In this context, "instants of discernment" (*so sor rtog pa'i skad cig*) are the instants necessary for the cognition of each of the sixteen aspects of the four truths. The "instant of absolute reality" (*de kho na nyid kyi skad cig*) is the moment in which absolute reality is realized.

77 "Nagarjuna's tradition states that the system of sixteen instants is used to describe how wisdom arises in meditation, while Asanga's tradition uses it to show how incontrovertible knowledge arises in the post-meditation period. These two ways do not in fact contradict each other; both should be upheld by the followers of the Mahayana." [DKR]

78 "As reported by practitioners of meditation." [DKR]

79 This potential is, of course, innate. It is on the basis of innate thought tenden-cies that false imputations can develop. Indeed, there is something predictable about false tenet systems in the sense that they exhibit certain common fea-tures, which are in turn coordinated with the inveterate self-clinging of the ordinary mind.

80 "Namely, the assertions of mistaken tenets regarding the causal relationships that underpin samsara and nirvana." [DKR]

81 "All other thoughts (i.e., other than the tenets of mistaken systems) derive from the misapprehension of sense data." [DKR]

82 "There are ten meanings of the word 'dharma' (*chos*). Six apply to phenomena; four apply to the sacred Doctrine. The first six are: (1) phenomenon or knowledge object; (2) mental object; (3) life span; (4) future time; (5) cer-tainty; and (6) religion (religious tradition). The four that apply to the sacred tradition are: (1) scriptures, or the Dharma of transmission; (2) meritorious

action or skillful means, such as generosity; (3) the path or wisdom of understanding emptiness; and (4) nirvana, or freedom of all that is to be abandoned." [YG I, 503]

83 "One should know that the truth of cessation has three aspects: it cannot be conceived by the conventional mind; it is the arresting of karma and emotions; and it is the absence of mistaken mental processes. The truth of path also has three aspects: it is free from obscurations; it is clear wisdom; and it acts as a remedy for all opposing forces." [YG I, 504]

84 "The twelve branches (*gsung rab yan lag bcu gnyis*) of the scriptures are:
   1. *mdo sde*: sutra, discourses on a single topic.
   2. *dbyangs bsnyad*: poetic epitome or summaries in verse of teachings existing at greater length in prose.
   3. *lung bstan*: prophecies.
   4. *tshigs bcad*: discourses in verse.
   5. *ched du brjod pa*: teachings not requested by anyone but spoken intentionally by the Buddha in order to propagate the Dharma.
   6. *gleng gzhi*: instructions given in the context of specific events (as often happened with the Vinaya).
   7. *rtogs brjod*: life stories of certain contemporaries of the Buddha.
   8. *de lta bu byung ba*: historical accounts.
   9. *skyes rabs*: previous lives of the Buddha.
   10. *shin tu rgyas pa*: long expositions of the vast and profound teachings.
   11. *rmad byung*: extraordinary unprecedented expositions of the profound teachings.
   12. *gtan dbab*: topics of specific knowledge that clinch the meaning of all the Vinaya and the sutras; the classification of samsaric phenomena, such as aggregates, dhatus, ayatanas; the outline of the phenomena of the path: grounds and paths of realization, concentrations; and the enumeration of the phenomena of the result: kayas, wisdoms, etc."
   [YG I, 505]

85 "The presentation of the four pitakas is asserted also by Aryadeva, Longchenpa, Terdag Lingpa, and others. Some consider that this collection of the Mantrayana is included in the Abhidharma." [YG I, 507]

86 It is for this reason that in the Buddhist tradition the greatest respect is paid to books and manuscripts. Books are never placed on the ground but always in a clean and elevated place. In the same spirit, practitioners take care not to step on texts or walk over them, and when necessary dispose of them by burning, ideally accompanying such actions with the recitation of mantra.

87 "Generally speaking, the Dharma of realization refers to the three trainings of the path. There is not a single Dharma of realization in the traditions of the sutras or the mantras that is not included in one of the three trainings. It is wrong to think that if one's view is high, one does not need discipline, or

on the other hand that the practices of union and liberation of the Mantrayana are in conflict with the discipline. It is also wrong to think that the phases of generation and perfection are different from the trainings in concentration and wisdom. If one regards the three vehicles and the path of the Mantrayana as being in conflict, and if one does not know that all the realizations of the grounds and paths are included within the three trainings, one is lost in ignorance." [YG I, 508]

88   The mandala of the three seats (*gdan gsum tshang ba'i dkyil 'khor*) is: (1) the aggregates and elements, which are the seat of the male and female dhyani Buddhas; (2) the sense organs and their objects, which are the seat of the male and female Bodhisattvas; and (3) the bodily members, which are the seat of the wrathful male and female deities.

89   See appendix 9.

90   These are called *mthar gyis gnas pa'i snyoms 'jug dgu*. These consist of four samadhis for the form realm, four absorptions for the formless realm, and the absorption of cessation.

91   See YG I, 519–527.

92   See note 266.

93   "The various systems of the enumerations of the grounds of the resultant vehicle are simply ways of labeling the different aspects of the three kayas or the qualities of the Buddha. They do not imply progression as in the case of the expository vehicle of causality (i.e., the bodhisattva grounds on the paths of seeing and meditation)." [YG I, 527]

94   "Indeed, that which is commonly referred to as 'Dharma' is not some truly existent entity; it is merely the qualities of realization in the minds of individuals on the paths of learning and no more learning." [YG I, 528]

95   "The noble Shravakas rid themselves of the erroneous idea that the aggregates and other phenomena are permanent and discrete entities. They understand that they are momentary and mere gatherings of elements. Ridding themselves of the personal self, which is nothing more than a merely conceived object (*zhen yul*), they free themselves of the obscurations of the emotions. In addition to this, the Pratyekabuddhas realize the emptiness of the percept, but not that of the perceiving consciousness. Noble Bodhisattvas understand that all phenomena included within samsara and nirvana are like space, primordially beyond all conceptual constructions. They know that not even the names of these two conceived objects, namely, the two types of self (personal and phenomenal) exist. In this way, they have an unhindered capacity for dispelling the two types of obscurations." [YG I, 528]

96   See YG I, 529.

97   "1. On the (Hinayana) path of joining, the practitioner definitively acquires

the character of Shravaka. This ground is therefore called the Ground of the Shravaka Character (*rigs kyi sa*).

"2. The stage of 'Candidates for the Degree of Stream Enterer' is called the Eighth Ground (*brgyad pa'i sa*). (Note that this refers to the Eighth Ground of the Aryas).

"3. The stage of 'Stream Enterer Abiding by the Result' is called the Ground of Seeing (*mthong ba'i sa*), because the practitioner has for the first time penetrated the significance of the four truths.

"4. The stage of 'Once Returner Abiding by the Result' is called the Ground of Fineness (*srab pa'i sa*), for the beings residing on it have abandoned every degree of desire except the three most subtle ones.

"5. The stage of 'Nonreturner Abiding by the Result' is the Ground Free from Desire (*'dod chags dang bral ba'i sa*), for the practitioner has abandoned all nine degrees of desire.

"6. Arhats reside upon the Ground of Realization of the Work (*byas pa rtogs pa'i sa*), for all labors for the accomplishment of the goal have now been completed. There arises the wisdom of knowing that the obscurations related to the three realms are exhausted and that samsaric birth is henceforth impossible.

"7. Candidates for the levels of Once Returner, Nonreturner and arhatship abide on the Shravaka Ground (*nyan thos kyi sa*).

"8. Finally, in addition to the above, the eight levels of candidate and abiders by the result, as attained on the Pratyekabuddha path, are counted as a single ground: the Ground of Pratyekabuddhas (*rang sangs rgyas kyi sa*)." [YG I, 532]

98 These are referred to as the "Outer Sangha." The "Inner Sangha" comprises the dakinis, dakas, and wisdom Dharma protectors.

99 "The Dharma of transmission has to be abandoned in the same way as a boat is left behind when the far shore is reached. All the compounded aspects of the truth of the path are changing and ultimately false, while the cessation as described in the Shravakayana is a state of extinction. Finally, the three types of Sangha still have certain obscurations to discard (and are thus not immune from fears). Thus the sole and ultimate refuge is buddhahood (i.e., our own buddhahood)." [YG I, 537]

100 "In addition to the Three Jewels as identified previously, the main deity of the mandala is considered as Buddha; the four or six classes of tantra, together with the generation and perfection-stage practices, are the Dharma; while the dakinis, dakas, and protectors living in the twenty-four sacred places, thirty-two lands, and eight charnel grounds are the Sangha." [YG I, 539]

101 "These five pathways are mentioned in the *bden gnyis shing rta*, Jigme Lingpa's autocommentary to the *Treasury of Precious Qualities*, but I have not found them discussed anywhere else. According to the explanations I received from my own teachers, the *path of dream* refers to the period after deep sleep when, in a

state of deluded nonconceptual consciousness, various perceptions of places, mental states, and other beings follow each other in quick succession. The *path of habitual tendencies* refers to the instinctual traces left behind by actions that have already yielded their fully ripened effect. They linger behind, manifesting as the recollection of places, mental states, and beings in any of the six realms, high or low, where one has once taken birth. The *path of karma* refers to the propelling positive, negative, or unwavering actions performed in the corporeal form one has assumed. The *path of uncertain feelings* refers to various types of suffering in the bardo of becoming, due to the six uncertainties. The *path of uncertain effects of causes* means that, though positive and negative actions are never wasted and always ripen into their respective results due to the infallibility of dependent arising, nevertheless, some variety may appear in their ripened effect, for the simple reason that they are compounded phenomena. For example, if an evildoer makes a proper confession or implements some other strong antidote, the full effect of the action committed will be attenuated. Conversely, a positive action (i.e., one that is conditioned by the impure view of inherent existence) may be overwhelmed by anger, with the result that its effect will not ripen." [YG I, 544]

102   This means that refuge is the basis of the path by means of which negativities will be successively purified. It does not mean the automatic and sudden removal of evil karma by the act of taking refuge.

103   "Given that this is true, one might wonder whether the so-called seventy protectors and others of that kind should be admitted as protectors of the Dharma. It is incorrect to place one's trust in them without placing reliance also in the Three Jewels, or to consider them as superior to the Three Jewels. On the other hand, if one makes offerings to them as though to friends who help in the performance of spiritual activities, considering them as the agents of enlightened action, not only is there no fault, but it is highly beneficial." [YG I, 558]

104   "Just as the carcass of an elephant contains within it the precious *bezoar*, and the carcass of the musk deer contains the musk, even ordained people who have no discipline are on a higher level than those who have no vows. The reason for this is that their former merit (generated when they took their vows) will give a good result. In the future, they will attain the level of Nonreturner in one of the three vehicles. This happens thanks to the past aspirations of the Buddha." [YG I, 560]

105   "At the moment of death, whatever habits one has acquired in the course of one's life will arise. To remember the Three Jewels at the time of death, even if one has done no other practice, is extremely important. It is said in the *Samadhiraja-sutra*: 'Constantly praise the Buddhas with pure thought, word, and deed. If you become used to this, you will see the Protector of the World, during the day and even at night. And when, one day, after illness and pain,

the suffering of death comes to you, your recollection of the Buddha will not weaken. The feelings of pain will not overwhelm it.' " [YG I, 563]

106 "Even if one does not abandon the Three Jewels, if in comparing them with non-Buddhist teachers and teachings one has some hesitations, or if one thinks that there is only a slight difference between them, this is very close to giving up the refuge." [YG I, 565]

107 *go la'i rlung*. According to traditional Buddhist cosmology, this is a belt of wind energy around Mount Meru which supports the celestial mansions of the sun and moon.

108 "The Chittamatra tradition speaks of the Shravakayana, Pratyekabuddhayana, and Bodhisattvayana as three final vehicles. It asserts that those who *by their type* belong to the Hinayana are, as it were, 'predestined' to the definitive and irreversible attainment of the result of their path. Those, however, whose type is *uncertain* will first engage in the Hinayana and then enter the Mahayana. However, the Madhyamika tradition asserts that, though practitioners who belong to the Hinayana are temporarily alienated from the Mahayana, and though there are specific character types corresponding to each of the three vehicles, nevertheless all beings without exception will ultimately attain enlightenment through the path of the Mahayana. Some beings are able to train in the Mahayana from the first because their attitude is vast and they are drawn to the teachings on emptiness. Others can enter the Mahayana after training in the Hinayana. Finally, there are those beings who will do so only after attaining the final result of their original path. The *Chandrapradipa-sutra* says: 'All beings without exception have the buddha-seed. There is no being who is an improper vessel for it.' " [YG II, 9]

The "buddha-seed," or potential or essence of buddhahood, is a concept central to the *Tathagatagarbha-sutras* of the third turning of the Dharma wheel, Maitreya's *Uttaratantra-shastra*, as well as to Nagarjuna's *Stotras* of the second turning of the wheel. Just as butter is potentially present in milk, so too is buddhahood present in beings. The *Gandavyuha-sutra* says: "Children of the Conquerors! The seed of the Bodhisattva is the dharmadhatu, vast as space and naturally luminous. The Bodhisattvas who recognized this in the past, those who will recognize it in the future, and those who recognize it now, take birth in the family of the Buddhas." And the *Uttaratantra-shastra* says: "The luminous nature of the mind is unchanging like space." Commenting on this in his *grub mtha' mdzod* (pp. 161–162), omniscient Longchenpa says, "This naturally pure expanse is the absolute truth, self-arising wisdom. In its contaminated or veiled condition, it is referred to as 'lineage' (*rigs*), 'seed,' 'element' (*khams*), or 'tathagatagarbha or buddha-potential' (*de bzhin gshegs pa'i nying po*). When it is unveiled, it is called the 'fully enlightened mind' (*byang chub kyi sems*) or 'Tathagata' (*de bzhin gshegs pa*)."

The buddha nature of all beings is unchanging and free from defect. Not only is it untainted throughout the entire process of samsara, but it is also possessed of all qualities of wisdom, and these are inalienable from it, just as light is indissociable from the sun. For these qualities to manifest, the veils that obscure the buddha nature must be removed, just as the clouds have to be blown away for the sun to appear. It is possible for these veils to be removed because they lack intrinsic existence. They are by nature empty, "self-empty," or *rang stong*. Once they are dispelled, however, the ultimate reality, or buddha nature, will shine forth. This nature is replete with every quality of wisdom and is by nature free from every stain, from everything extrinsic to it. As such, it is empty of other, or *gzhan stong*. (Note: the stains are *rang stong*, a nonaffirming negative; the nature of the mind is *gzhan stong*, an affirming negative.) The fact that the mind is in its nature utterly immaculate implies that there is essentially no difference between Buddhas and ordinary beings. In the Buddhas, the mind subsists immaculate and unstained; in beings, the mind is clouded with adventitious veils. For further discussion about the buddha-potential, see Gyalwa Longchenpa's *grub mtha' mdzod* and S. K. Hookham, *The Buddha Within*.

109 On account of great compassion for all beings without exception, the practitioner escapes the extreme of nirvana. Due to the wisdom of realizing the emptiness of all phenomena, the practitioner escapes the extreme of samsara. Authentic bodhichitta, the wisdom of emptiness endowed with the essence of compassion, is possessed only from the first bodhisattva ground onward.

110 "According to the master Buddhagupta, these four attitudes are called boundless because their referent is the boundless aggregate of beings, because they bring forth the boundless accumulation of merit and wisdom, the boundless qualities of buddhahood, and the boundless wisdom of nonduality." [YG II, 11]

111 "The Tibetan word *btang snyoms* has three possible meanings: a neutral feeling (*tshor ba btang snyoms*), the conditioning factor of evenness ('*du byed btang snyoms*); and boundless impartiality (*tshad med btang snyoms*). In this context, the third sense is intended." [YG II, 20]

112 *tshangs pa'i gnas bzhi*, the four divine abidings or attitudes in which the great Brahma is said eternally to dwell. Ostensibly, they are the same as the four boundless attitudes just described, with the crucial difference that they are oriented toward the subject rather than the object. This gives rise to unwarranted distinctions made between beings according to one's own point of view rather than theirs. Thus the tendency is to love what is close and pleasing to oneself, to be compassionate but in a self-interested way, and so on.

113 They are beyond the four ontological extremes: it cannot be said that they exist, that they do not exist, that they both exist and do not exist, and that they neither exist nor do not exist.

114 "There are four conditions for the appearance of the four boundless attitudes: (1) the causal condition, namely, the tathagatagarbha (*rgyu'i rkyen*); (2) the

dominant condition, namely, the spiritual friend who teaches the four bound-less attitudes (*bdag po'i rkyen*); (3) the objective condition, which is the object of the meditator's focus (*dmigs pa'i rkyen*); and (4) the immediately preceding condition, namely, the knowledge of the benefits of this meditation and the defects of the opposite (*de ma thag pa'i rkyen*)." [YG I, 27]

115 The two paths are identical in that they bring about the realization of "empti-ness endowed with the heart of compassion." The same can be said about the final result: the fruit of the Sutrayana and Tantrayana paths is likewise one and the same.

116 Up to and including the seventh ground, the defiled emotional mind (*nyon yid*) continues to manifest in the form of thoughts during the post-meditation experience of the Bodhisattva. It is, however, powerless to produce karma and is likened to a snake that has been cut in half, which continues to wriggle but is unable to attack. On the eighth ground, this is completely arrested. On the ninth ground, the five ordinary sense consciousnesses are completely arrested, but the mental consciousness is only partially so. As a result of this, the four perfect knowledges are realized. At the same time, the whole expanse of phenomenal appearance arises as a buddhafield. On the tenth ground, the mental consciousness is completely transformed into a kind of wisdom that is able to engage in all sense fields simultaneously. It is only at the end of the tenth ground, however, when the level of buddhahood is perfectly attained, that the last traces of duality are transcended.

117 "Bodhichitta associated with a keen aspiration toward enlightenment is lik-ened to the *earth*, for it is the foundation of all qualities. The bodhichitta associated with the wish to practice the six paramitas for others' sake is immutable like *gold*. Concomitant with a sublime disposition of the mind, it is like the waxing *moon*, because wholesome qualities develop from it. Associ-ated with active engagement in the paramitas, it is like *fire*, for it spreads like a forest blaze. Associated with the paramita of generosity, it is like a *treasure*, for it inexhaustibly satisfies all wishes. Associated with the paramita of disci-pline, it is like a *mine of jewels*, a source of precious qualities. Associated with the paramita of patience, it is like the *ocean*, unaffected by assaults of fire and sword. Associated with the paramita of diligence, it is indestructible like a *diamond*. Associated with the paramita of concentration, it is like a *mountain*, unshaken by the gale of thoughts. Associated with the paramita of wisdom, it is like *medicine*, healing the ills of the emotions. The bodhichitta associated with the paramita of skillful means is like a *spiritual teacher*, a constant source of benefit for beings. Associated with the paramita of aspiration, it is like a *magical gem* that grants all wishes. Associated with the paramita of strength, it is like the *sun* that brings the harvest's increase. Associated with the paramita of primordial wisdom, it is like a *song*, teaching the doctrine in harmony with the disposition of each and every being. The bodhichitta connected with preternatural knowledge is like a *king*, with all activities beneath its sway.

Connected with the twofold accumulation, it is like a *treasure house* containing numerous deposits of merit and wisdom. The bodhichitta associated with the thirty-seven factors leading to enlightenment is like a *highway*, trodden by the Buddhas of the past, present, and future. Associated with shamatha and vipashyana, it is the perfect *conveyance*, for it keeps to the center of the path and does not veer off into the two extremes. The bodhichitta associated with dharani and intelligence is like a *spring*, endlessly spilling forth the words and meaning of the Doctrine and revealing them to others. Associated with the feast of Dharma, it is like *music*, an inspiration to beings. Associated with the one and only path, it is like a *river* flowing naturally into the ocean of omniscience. Associated with the Dharmakaya, it is like a *cloud*, showing forth the Buddha's twelve deeds, beginning with his dwelling in Tushita, the Joyous Realm. The above mentioned qualities of keen aspiration and so forth are the supports—emphasized at different moments of the path—of bodhichitta, the attitude of aiming at enlightenment for the sake of others." [YG II, 59]

The Buddha's twelve deeds are recorded in the *Uttaratantra-shastra:*

The Knower of Worlds, the Great Compassionate One, sees the universe, and without stirring from the state of Dharmakaya, he appears in manifold Nirmanakaya forms. Every supreme Nirmanakaya displays twelve deeds perceptible to unenlightened beings, and this until the end of samsara. (1) He descends from Tushita; (2) enters the womb of his mother; (3) takes birth; (4) learns all sciences and arts; (5) takes delight in the company of his queens; (6) renounces worldly life; (7) practices austerities; (8) goes to Vajrasana; (9) vanquishes the hosts of maras; (10) achieves perfect enlightenment; (11) turns the wheel of Dharma; and (12) passes into nirvana.

118 "This is the general approach. More specifically, however, in beings whose general attitude militates against the bodhichitta training (for instance, persons who are incapable of taking the vow to refrain from killing), bodhichitta cannot arise. Even if they go through the motions of receiving the vow, they accumulate nothing but downfalls." [YG II, 77]

119 This accounts for the importance attached to the making of offerings at the moment of taking the vow. When Atisha was at a certain place in Tibet, he twice refused to give the bodhisattva vow because the offerings made were meager and insufficient. He said that because the offerings (in the sense of the preparation of the place and so on as described in the text) were poor, it would be difficult for bodhichitta to develop. At the third request, this time accompanied by more extensive preparations, he announced that the offerings were just sufficient and consented to give the vow.

120 *ba 'byung,* literally "deriving from the cow." This term refers to a substance prepared, in accordance with ancient Indian tradition, from various ingredients derived from cows. It is not easy to come by since the ingredients must be taken only on the full moon and at the moment immediately after the cow has calved for the first time. Moreover, the animal in question must be red, without the slightest trace of white.

121 *rgyal srid sna bdun.* "The seven attributes of royalty, that is, the seven possessions of a Chakravartin, are: the precious golden wheel, the precious wish-
fulfilling jewel, the precious queen, the precious minister, the precious elephant, the precious horse, and the precious general. These symbolize the
seven sublime riches. Ashvaghosha says: 'The precious wheel, rolling day and
night along the path of virtue, symbolizes faith. The precious queen, arrayed
in beautiful ornaments and garlands, symbolizes discipline. The precious
minister symbolizes generosity that brings forth merit and wisdom on a vast
scale. The precious general symbolizes learning that vanquishes the enemies
of wrong thoughts. The supreme horse symbolizes the sense of shame which
buries the defiled emotions in egolessness. The mighty elephant symbolizes
consideration of others, discarding all incorrect conduct. The precious jewel
symbolizes aspirations for oneself and others. These constitute sublime riches
endowed with limitless excellence. All other kinds of wealth bring forth suffering.' " [YG II, 149]

122 *bkras shis rtags brgyad.* The eight auspicious symbols are the eight symbols referring to eight aspects of the Buddha's Body, Speech, and Mind. They are: the
eternal knot, the lotus, the canopy, the conch, the wheel, the banner, the vase,
and the golden fishes.

123 *rdzas brgyad.* The eight substances that were offered to the Buddha after his
enlightenment. They are: white mustard, curd, a mirror, a white conch shell
turning in a clockwise direction, bezoar, orange-colored powder, durwa grass,
and kusha grass.

124 "Generosity and the other paramitas should be practiced in a way that is free
from the following faults, namely, seven types of attachment: (1) attachment
to objects, beginning with material possession and extending to wrong views;
(2) procrastination; (3) self-satisfaction; (4) expectation of recompense; (5)
expectation of karmic result; (6) dormant opposing factors (from avarice to
distorted understanding); and (7) distraction through interest in the Hinayana and belief in the true existence of object, subject, and action." [YG II,
218]

125 "The four special qualities which define the six paramitas are: (1) the fact
that the paramitas eliminate all relevant adverse factors; (2) they are combined
with the wisdom that sees through the false notions of action, agent, and
object; (3) they fulfill the desires and aspirations of others; and (4) they lead
beings to one of the three types of enlightenment according to their capacity
(i.e., that of Shravakas, Pratyekabuddhas, or Bodhisattvas)." [YG II, 185]

126 "These three pure elements mean that the intention is pure because the practice is done in order to cultivate bodhichitta. The substance of offering is
pure since it is untainted by wrongdoing, such as killing, trafficking, or some
other sort of evil livelihood. The object of offering is also pure, for it is the
Three Jewels themselves." [DKR]

127 *stobs bzhi: sun 'byin pa'i stobs, kun tu spyod pa'i stobs, sor chud pa'i stobs, rten kyi stobs.* (See Patrul Rinpoche, *The Words of My Perfect Teacher*, pp. 265, 266)

128 "Rejoicing is the antidote to jealousy. Jealousy is a feeling of displeasure at the prospect of another person's good qualities and actions, and a feeling of satisfaction when others are seen to act wrongly or break their discipline. Such thoughts, besides being utterly futile, are highly reprehensible. Jealous people are an embarrassment to holy beings and an object of contempt for the powers of good. However good a practitioner a jealous person might seem, he or she will not escape the lower realms." [YG II, 110]

129 "The symbolism of the Dharma wheel is explained in different ways. The Vaibhashikas consider that it represents the path of seeing. Others consider that it symbolizes the Eightfold Noble Path. According to the latter perspective, Right Speech, Right Conduct, and Right Livelihood, which belong to the training in discipline, are the center of the wheel. Right View and Right Thought, which belong to the training of wisdom, are the sharp spokes of the wheel. The remaining three elements (Right Effort, Right Mindfulness, and Right Concentration), belonging to the training of concentration, are the rim of the wheel. In the Mahayana, the wheel symbolizes the Dharma of transmission and realization, because, from the time of the perfect Buddha until the disciples of the present time, it has been passed down 'revolving constantly from mind to mind.'" [YG II, 114]

130 "An essential point concerning the dedication is that it should be expressed in the words of someone who has attained the sublime grounds (i.e., the path of seeing or above) so that the formula is thus composed of words of truth. It should be noted also that there is a difference between dedication prayers and prayers of aspiration. The former is focused on merit while the latter expresses a wish of some kind. Dedication necessarily includes aspiration, but the reverse is not always the case." [YG II, 119]

131 See appendix 4, p. 290

132 The Mahayana level of Nonreturner should not be confused with the Nonreturner level of the Shravakayana. Beings belonging to the latter category do not return to the desire realm. In a Mahayana context, it is understood that a Bodhisattva abiding on the grounds willingly returns to lead beings on the path. Bodhisattvas are referred to as Nonreturners because their minds never revert to the samsaric state with all its negativities and limitations.

133 See *The Way of the Bodhisattva*, III, 23–24:

> Just as all the Buddhas of the past
> Embraced the awakened attitude of mind,
> And in the precepts of the Bodhisattvas
> Step by step abode and trained,

Just so, and for the benefit of beings,
I will also have this attitude of mind,
And in those precepts, step by step,
I will abide and train myself.

134 "According to Atisha, they are as follows: not to have a natural proclivity toward the Mahayana; to have little compassion; not to fear the miseries of samsara; to keep bad company; to dismiss buddhahood as something remote; to be overwhelmed by evil forces; to be the follower of a Hinayana practitioner; to practice with the Hinayana attitude; to turn away from any being whatsoever; to have evil intentions toward and speak maliciously to a Bodhisattva; to fail to relinquish what militates against bodhichitta; to be lacking in knowledge, careful attention, and respect; and to be prey to many emotions." [YG II, 145]

135 "This does not mean that on the supreme level, coemergent or innate defilements no longer arise. However, since at that point they are not harmful in the sense of impelling actions leading to samsara (as they are in the case of ordinary beings), the antidotes to them do not need to be so forcefully applied." [YG II, 148] See also YG II, 149: "As a support for the observance of the precepts, it is important to rely on the 'seven sublime riches.'" See note 121.

136 The followers of Nagarjuna's tradition of the Profound View keep to the teachings of the *Akashagarbha-sutra,* the *Mahaguhyaupayakaushalya-sutra,* and the *Shiksasamuccaya* of Shantideva. Followers of Asanga's tradition of Vast Activities keep to his *Bodhisattvabhumi-shastra* and the *Samvaravimshaka* of Chandragomin.

137 *rgyal po'i ltung ba lnga.* "The root downfalls of a king are so called because people in positions of power are liable to commit them. But of course they are downfalls for anyone who has taken the bodhisattva vow. They cause beings to fall from the higher, happy state of gods and humans to the lower realms, destroying all the cultivated roots of merit that empower or 'crown' the royal lineage. The downfalls are:

1. With an evil intention, to take the property of the Three Jewels or to induce others to do the same. This covers the theft of images, books, articles pertaining to a stupa, the goods belonging to the Sangha or the Spiritual Master, and so on.
2. To repudiate any of the three vehicles or to lead someone into the belief that they do not constitute the path to liberation.
3. To rob, beat, imprison, or kill wearers of the monastic robe (regardless of whether they have taken vows or not and, if they have, regardless of the quality of their discipline) or to force them to return to the lay status, or to induce another to do the same.
4. To commit any of the five sins of immediate effect.

5. To hold wrong views (such as that there is no such thing as karma)."
[YG II, 152] See also DS, 239.

138 *blon po'i ltung ba lnga.* "The first downfall is to destroy aggressively a homestead, a village of four castes, a small town or a large town, or an entire region such as Champaka (the area of the Ganges delta). The other four downfalls correspond to the first four downfalls of a king." [YG II, 153]

139 *phal pa'i ltung ba brgyad.*
"1. To teach the doctrine of emptiness to persons who are unprepared for it or who are liable to be alarmed, since they will as a result relinquish bodhichitta and aspire to the teachings of the Hinayana.

2. Consciously to direct people of Mahayana disposition away from the Mahayana path, and lead them to the practice of the Hinayana (insinuating that they are incapable of the attainment of full enlightenment and that they should confine their aspirations merely to freedom from samsara).

3. By an injudicious praise of the Mahayana, to lead people of Hinayana disposition to give up their vows of Pratimoksha, and thereby to leave them without any vows.

4. To hold, or teach another to hold, that the following of the Hinayana path does not eradicate the defilements, and to say that the Shravakas do not have an authentic path to liberation.

5. For reasons of jealousy, to criticize other Bodhisattvas openly and to praise oneself.

6. Falsely to claim realization of the profound view, wishing thereby to receive gifts and respect.

7. To consort with powerful people, encourage them to persecute practitioners, and secretly appropriate the religious offerings for oneself.

8. To disrupt the practice of meditators by appropriating their goods and distributing them to those who merely study or perform rituals. To disturb those engaged in shamatha meditation through the imposition of bad rules and regulations." [YG II, 154] See also DS, 241.

140 "Although eighteen downfalls are enumerated, they in fact amount to fourteen, since four of the downfalls of a king and four of the downfalls of a minister coincide. These acts, moreover, are referred to as belonging to kings, ministers, or ordinary people, because these are the classes of people most liable to perpetrate them. But of course it is possible for any individual to commit them." [YG II, 155]

141 In addition, *Yönten Gyamtso* says that there are eighty faults enumerated in the *Shiksasamuccaya*. In brief, these are: (1) twenty-four faults in connection with happiness and suffering (i.e., the faults of not dispelling the suffering or nurturing the happiness of others when one is in a position to do so); and

(2) sixteen faults connected with the giving-up of the practice (i.e., the failure to contrive remedies to the sufferings of others). These two groups together make forty faults. Further categorized according to whether they are temporary or permanent faults, they come to eighty faults. [YG II, 156]

142 See YG II, 158; DS, 279; Dudjom Rinpoche, *Perfect Conduct*, p. 96, for an exposition of the method of repairing faults according to the tradition of Nagarjuna.

143 "If aspirational bodhichitta is lost, the bodhichitta vow is itself instantly annihilated, without any consideration of the time periods concerned, as when a fresco collapses simultaneously with the wall on which it is painted. The same applies when the bodhichitta precepts are given back. This is in contrast with the four permutations of returning or damaging the vow, as spoken of in the Pratimoksha, according to which vows may indeed be given back if one is unable to keep them. These four permutations are: (1) not giving back the vows and not damaging them; (2) not giving them back but damaging them; (3) not damaging them but giving them back; and (4) damaging them and giving them back. By contrast, the vow of bodhichitta may under no circumstances be returned, on pain of incurring an extremely grievous fault. This is because to return the vow amounts to breaking the promise to help all sentient beings until they attain enlightenment. . . . If, on the other hand, a root downfall is committed, the confession of it, done or not done in the requisite period of time, is the factor that determines whether the continuity of the training has been broken." [YG II, 158]

144 "People of superior capacity realize that downfalls are primordially without true existence. For such people, these arise in the sphere of discursiveness and, like a design traced on the surface of the water, they are unable to leave behind either habitual tendency or residual effect. But people who are still at the stage where meditation is alternated with post-meditation experience must act according to the prescriptions of the *Mahamoksha-sutra*." [YG II, 162]

145 Another, more formal way of confession is described in the tradition of Vast Activities of Asanga. See DS, 283; Dudjom Rinpoche, *Perfect Conduct*, p. 98.

146 For an extensive treatment of this subject, see *The Way of the Bodhisattva*, VIII, 90–98; 141–154; and the commentary of Khenchen Kunzang Pelden translated in the same volume, pp. 180 ff.

147 The demon in Indian mythology who by periodically swallowing the sun and the moon is responsible for eclipses.

148 According to Asanga's *Bodhisattvabhumi-shastra*, there are four root downfalls to be avoided: (1) out of desire for reputation and honor, to praise oneself and belittle others; (2) to refrain from giving, whether materially or spiritually, through a sense of miserliness; (3) to harm others out of anger; and (4) ignorantly to criticize the Mahayana as not being the Buddha's word and to concoct one's own teaching, proclaiming it to be the authentic doctrine. [DS,

252] In addition, there are forty-six minor infractions of the precepts of bodhichitta in action. These are explained in the *Samvaravimshaka* of Chandragomin. See DS, 254; Dudjom Rinpoche, *Perfect Conduct*, p. 84.

149 "The transcendent perfection of generosity and the rest are defined by four special qualities (*khyad chos bzhi*): (1) they eliminate their contraries; (2) they are associated with the wisdom transcending the three spheres, or notions of subject, object, and action; (3) they fulfill the wishes of others; and (4) they lead beings, subject to their karmic lot, to maturation in any of the three types of enlightenment. They are called *paramita* (literally, *param* = other shore, *ita* = gone) because they transcend the corresponding worldly virtues and those of the Shravakas and Pratyekabuddhas and reach beyond samsara." [YG II, 185]

150 This distinction is made according to whether the practice is undertaken in relation to conceptual reference. While the accumulation of merit implies the presence of dualistic concepts of subject and object, the accumulation of wisdom implies their absence.

151 Paramitas seven to ten are not so much separate perfections as qualities accompanying the previous six paramitas.

152 "If a person is able to relinquish attachment to possessions, this is considered to be supreme generosity. For generosity consists in a mind that has no craving for possessions." [YG II, 200]

153 "As for great generosity, we should reflect as follows and make the resolution: 'At the moment I am deeply attached to my family and dear ones; I want to be with them forever, and for their sake I get angry and possessive and this is an evil. We will, in any case, be separated sooner or later, and so I must rid myself of this kind of clinging. I will train myself so that I will one day be able to relinquish them, like the great Bodhisattvas.' " [YG II, 203]

154 "The physical body is a mass of filthy substances, and life is rushing by like a powerful gale. Both these things follow karma and are dependent on it. Even though at all times, people do everything to protect their bodies and their lives, both are liable to be destroyed by fire, water, precipices, political powers, wild animals, robbers, and so on. And even if they do not meet with such a fate, when death comes, their bodies will be cremated or thrown into the water, scattered for the vultures, or buried in the earth. In the end, nothing will be left of them, not even the slightest particle of dust. Yet while in life, people cherish their bodies, considering them their dearest possession. They do everything to protect them, and for their sake they inflict harm on others, whether in thought or deed. For us who are disciples of the compassionate Buddha, all this is a serious mistake. Therefore, we should repeatedly repudiate attachment to our bodies and offer them to other beings. Far from using our bodies as an instrument for harming others, we should use them directly for their help, and indirectly so in the practice of Dharma—for this itself

must be animated by an altruistic attitude. To practice religion for one's own sake is quite incorrect. And even though, at the moment, we are not actually able to make a gift of our bodies and lives, it is important to be aware of the need to train ourselves with a view to emulating the great Bodhisattvas who could indeed give up their bodies, freely and at will. For we will never acquire such a capacity unless we train ourselves over and over again. This truth is set forth in the *Shiksasamuccaya*, and it is important to begin the training now." [YG II, 204]

155 There is a story that a pigeon used to listen to Vasubandhu reciting the sutras. This had the effect of purifying the karma of its previous existences. When it died it was reborn a human being and became the master Sthiramati. [YG II, 214]

156 "How is it that it is sometimes taught nevertheless that, aside from wrong views, the other two negative acts of mind are occasionally permitted? If the motive is analyzed in detail, one can see that it is possible to covet the wealth of a person of low merit in order to make offerings on that person's behalf. Or again one might wish to reduce the power and influence of someone who is destroying the teachings and injuring others. Mental actions such as these do not have the complete characteristics of a negativity. They are therefore admissible. However, it is never taught that truly negative actions of the mind are permissible." [YG II, 227]

157 "Ordination into the monastic life of homelessness is praised as the best condition for progress toward enlightenment, and it remains so until the supreme ground of realization is attained. Thus, monastic ordination is the best situation for beginners, whose principal training is in the discipline of avoiding negativities. Wearing the robes will remind them to observe the discipline, and they will be easily recognized by both gods and humans as a suitable object of offering. In this way, they will receive sustenance without needing to involve themselves in wearisome activities and will not be defiled by the need to involve themselves in unethical situations. Thus, free from distractions and a troubled conscience, they will have the principal living condition for the development of concentration. The holder of the bodhisattva vow who at the same time has the pratimoksha vows is said to observe the 'Pratimoksha of the Bodhisattvas.'" [YG II, 233]

158 "Once upon a time, Indrabodhi, the king of Oddiyana, caught sight of some red objects flying in the sky. They were too far away for him to see what they were. 'What are those strange birds?' he asked. His courtiers informed him that they were Shravakas, the followers of the Buddha. Thereupon the king conceived the desire to see the Buddha and prayed to him, and sure enough, the Buddha miraculously appeared in the company of five hundred Arhats. Indrabodhi paid homage to him and asked him to teach him the path to enlightenment. The Buddha said that the king should go forth into homelessness and embrace the life of a monk, practising the three trainings.

But to this Indrabodhi replied, 'O Gautama, I do not want liberation if it means giving up all that is a delight to my senses! Indeed, I would prefer to be a fox in the pleasant garden of the world!' In that very instant, the retinue of Shravakas vanished and a voice was heard from the sky proclaiming that they had been but the miraculous display of the Bodhisattvas. The Buddha then opened the wisdom mandala of the *Guhyasamaja-tantra*, and in that very instant, the king attained buddhahood, the union of Dharmakaya and Rupakaya." [DS 294]

159 "The monastic discipline should possess eight qualities. It should be (1) unimpaired, that is, not transgressed even once. It should therefore be (2) faultless because free it is of any defect. It should be (3) unadulterated through not being mixed with any unwholesome factors. It should be (4) unsullied by motivations aiming at prosperity or the concerns of this life. It should be (5) uncontaminated by inconstancy. It should be (6) powerful, through possessing the five foregoing qualities, and (7) praised by the learned and the Aryas. Finally, it should (8) favor the practice of concentration. Concentration renders the mind serviceable, so that wisdom and the other qualities of the path may develop. Therefore, discipline is the ground in which all qualities can grow." [YG II, 243]

160 The vows of shramanera or *getsul* are sometimes referred to in English as novice vows. This is incorrect. The term "novice" in this context has been mistakenly borrowed from Christian monasticism where it denotes a monk in training prior to profession or the taking of vows. The novitiate is necessarily a temporary condition (usually lasting between one and two years). In Buddhism, by contrast, the shramanera or getsul ordination embodies a complete monastic grade in itself, and many monks keep this ordination throughout their lives. Moreover, given that the lineage of bhikshuni or *gelongma* vows has been interrupted (and may never have existed) in Tibet, the vast majority of Tibetan Buddhist nuns are permanent *getsulmas*.

161 The basic idea here is that a lie is only completely accumulated (and the vow broken) when a falsehood is spoken to a human being with the above mentioned qualifications. Hermaphrodites and so on are presumably mentioned here in the sense of their not being in possession of the entire range of human attributes. The preoccupation is one of scholastic precision in stipulating the criteria for the loss of the vow. It does not mean that lying to eunuchs is admissible.

162 In addition to touching a man, these are: traveling alone, swimming, sitting close to a man, arranging marriages, and concealing the faults of another woman novice in training for full ordination. [DS, 108]

163 Ibid. In addition to the fault mentioned, these are: shaving the pubic hair, digging the earth, hoarding uneaten food, eating food that has not been offered, and cutting green grass. [DS 108]

164 See also DS, 109.

165 "When a root defeat is committed (*phas pham pa*), the monk's ordination is completely destroyed." [YG II, 249]

166 "These faults are termed residual (*lhag ma*) because after their commission, only a residue of the ordination remains. And before such faults are repaired, the monk in question is demoted and required to take last place in the Sangha, eating only the food that is left over from the communal meal." [YG II, 251]

167 "Downfalls requiring rejection (*spang ba'i ltung byed*) are so called because they can only be repaired by the repudiation of the object through which the downfall has occurred. And they are called downfalls because, if they are not repaired, they create the cause for falling into the lower realms. There are ten such downfalls related separately to monastic robes, seats, and begging bowls (thus thirty all together)." [YG II, 252] See also DS, 119 and Dudjom Rinpoche, *Perfect Conduct*, pp. 34–36.

168 These are called downfalls (*ltung byed 'ba 'zhig*), because, as with the previous thirty, their commission leads to the lower realms, but their reparation does not involve the repudiation of the objects. For more information, see Dudjom Rinpoche, *Perfect Conduct*, pp. 37–44.

169 "These four faults (*sor bshags sde bzhi*)—mainly related to the taking of food— are purified by a specific and contrite confession made while standing outside the monastery precincts." [YG II, 256] See also Dudjom Rinpoche, *Perfect Conduct*, pp. 44–45.

170 These are minor faults (*nyes byas*) of general deportment. In the Theravada tradition, they are less numerous. See DS, 153 and Dudjom Rinpoche, *Perfect Conduct*, pp. 45–50.

171 *sbom po*, lit. gross. This refers to the radical defeats and residual faults the commission of which does not involve all the elements necessary for the full accomplishment of the act. See chapter 3, p. 48ff.

172 The four doors that lead to transgression are: ignorance of the precepts, lack of respect for them, negligence, and an excess of defiled emotions. It is obviously impossible to respect and observe what one is ignorant of.

173 See DS, 163 and Dudjom Rinpoche, *Perfect Conduct*, pp. 51–53.

174 *gso sbyong*, Skt. *uposatha*. "The ritual of confession refreshes the remedial force of virtue and cleanses all faults. This ritual is of two kinds. The first, which is called 'calm abiding' (*zhi gnas kyi gso sbyong*), purifies the obscurations accumulated in the past and perfects the superior trainings in concentration and wisdom. The second is called 'concordant' (*mthun pa'i gso sbyong*), whereby wrongdoing is avoided in the present life and the training in discipline is kept pure. The former refers to the practice of shamatha and vipashyana meditation, while the latter consists of the ritual of formal confession. This again is

of two kinds: first, the ritual performed regularly on the fourteenth or fifteenth of the lunar month, and second, the private confession performed,
when and as necessary, as a means of receiving blessing and in order to avert
calamities and foster harmony in the Sangha." [YG II, 270]

175 *dbyar gnas.* "The traditional summer retreat begins either on the fifteenth day
of the sixth lunar month and finishes three months later, on the fifteenth day
of the ninth month, or else it lasts from the fifteenth day of the seventh
month till the fifteenth of the tenth month." [YG II, 272] See also DS, 168.

176 *dgag dbye.* The ritual that concludes the summer retreat must be performed
even when the retreat is interrupted by external circumstances. It marks the
lifting of all the restrictions imposed during the summer retreat.

177 The seventeen regulations referred to here cover: (1) ordination; (2) confession ritual; (3) summer retreat and (4) its concluding ritual; (5) the prohibi-
tion of the use of fur and leather; (6) the rules for nourishment and the
practice of medicine; (7) the proper color and style of the robes; (8) the
practice of leaving an article of clothing in the monastery, in case of absence,
as a sign of stability and the intention to return; (9) the practice of "kaushambi," or the smooth pacification of divisions; (10) other prescribed activities (of which there are more than a hundred); (11) the imposition of the red
and yellow discipline, in other words, the forceful settling of problems and
the imposition of punishments for indiscipline; (12) the dealing with cases of
indiscipline on the individual level (the problems of how to deal with
breaches of conduct, penances given for faults confessed, and excommunica-
tion for faults upheld); (13) the demotion in monastic rank for serious infractions, and failure to attend the confession ritual (*gso sbyong*); (14) regulations
regarding the nonattendance at confession ritual; (15) rules connected with
dwelling places; and finally (16) the settling of quarrels and (17) the healing
of divisions.

178 This is an allusion to the fact that the inhabitants of the Northern Continent have all that they could possibly wish. They are therefore free of craving
(*chags pa*).
    "In general, there are four types of discipline: naturally infused discipline,
the discipline of one who has realized ultimate reality, the discipline of observing a vow, and the discipline of the one who is in samadhi in which all
faults are discarded." [YG II, 286]

179   1. *thams cad yod par smra ba,* the Sarvastivadins: those who "hold that every-
        thing exists." This does not mean that they accepted the reality of
        everything, but only of seventy-five dharmas which they recognized as
        ultimate and having permanent existence.
        2. *phal chen sde pa,* the Mahasanghikas: the Great Assembly (from which
        the Mahayana is said to have developed).
        3. *gnas brten pa,* the Sthaviras, the Elders (the Theravada, the only shravaka
        school still existent as such, mainly found in southern Asia).

4. *mang bos bkur ba*, the Sammitiya: the followers of Sammita. An important subdivision of this school was known as the Vatsiputriyas, *gnas
ma bu ba*, whose distinctive tenet was the assertion of a quasi-permanent
self, neither different from nor identical with the skandhas. This
school seems to have been very successful, although no original works
have survived the test of time.

180 With regard to the spread of the Sarvastivada in Tibet, Kyabje Dudjom
Rinpoche says: "The Vinaya tradition practiced in Tibetan Buddhism is that
of the Sarvastivada school introduced to Tibet by Shantarakshita. This lineage began with the Buddha and was passed down through Shariputra, Rahula (or Saraha), Nagarjuna, Bhavaviveka, and others. Following the
persecution of Langdarma, this Vinaya lineage revived and spread again from
the lowlands of Kham and is for this reason called the Eastern or Lowland
Lineage of the Vinaya (*smad 'dul*). This lineage continues to this day and is
the system into which all Nyingmapas and most Gelugpas are ordained.

"At a later date, the master Dharmapala, a pandit from eastern India, went
to Ngari in western Tibet (so-called Upper Tibet) and introduced another
ordination lineage, referred to as the Western or Upland Lineage of the
Vinaya (*stod 'dul*). This is also known as the 'lineage of the three Pala brothers'
(referring to Dharmapala's three main disciples: Saddhupala, Gunapala, and
Prajñapala).

"At a still later date, the Kashmiri pandit Shakya Shri came to Tibet and
ordained Sakya Pandita and others, thus inaugurating the tradition known as
the Middle Lineage of Vinaya (*bar 'dul*), into which most Sakyapas and Kagyupas are ordained. Note that since the original 'Upland Lineage' is normally
considered extinct, the 'Middle Lineage' is now often referred to as the 'Upland Lineage of Vinaya.'" [DS, 77]

181 See the text *chos kyi rnam grangs* in the Tengyur, the Tibetan collection of
shastras. Krikin was a contemporary of the Buddha Kashyapa. According to
the story, he had a dream in which he saw a large piece of cloth divided into
eighteen pieces, each of which, when measured, proved to be the same size as
the original piece. It was interpreted as a sign of the propagation of the
eighteen shravaka schools.

182 See also DS, 381.

183 "Some say that the following two root verses are not by Jigme Lingpa."
[DKR]

184 "The spontaneous display of wisdom." [DKR]

185 "The *aspirational deity*, on the path of accumulation, is the deity contrived by
thought at the generation stage only. It is, however, linked with the wisdom
of the perfection stage. By contrast, on the path of joining, the *deity of the
energy-mind* is not contrived by thought. It is a deity manifesting in the manner
of an illusion from the strength of familiarity with the conceptual phase of

the perfection stage. On the path of seeing, the *deity of luminosity* is the spontaneous radiance of absolute wisdom actualized during the nonconceptual phase of the perfection stage. On the path of meditation, one speaks of the *deity of the united level of the path of learning*, while at the level of buddhahood, the union of the Dharmakaya and Rupakaya is called the *deity of the united level of no more learning*." [YG II, 297]

186 "This wisdom may be either 'example wisdom' or 'absolute wisdom.' These are identical in their nature and form; they are different in that 'example wisdom' is accompanied by conceptual movement." [DKR]

187 "There are four additional impediments to the taking of the pratimoksha vows of shramanera and full ordination. These are: (1) *skye ba'i bar chad*, a congenital obstacle, that is, to be born without the capacity for sexual activity, and therefore to be without the basis of the vow; (2) *gnas pa'i bar chad*, an environmental obstacle, namely, the lack of permission on the part of one's family or secular authorities, thereby running the risk of being compelled to repudiate the vow; (3) *khyad par bar chad*, individual and private obstacles, that is, to be so young as to be incapable of scaring crows away, or to be infirm or seriously handicapped to the point where keeping the vows becomes an intolerable burden, with the result that it is impossible to develop the qualities that observance of the vows is meant to produce; (4) *mdzes pa'i bar chad*, to be of deformed physical appearance (as to color and shape) and to follow an evil profession, such as butchery, thereby creating a scandal which weakens the faith of people in the Buddhadharma." It should be noted that these last two obstacles are not insurmountable. [DS, 87]

188 "In the course of the empowerment, the teacher uses symbols, implied meanings, and signs to introduce the wisdom that has dwelt within the mind from the very beginning, thus holding in check the inveterate habit of viewing phenomena as ordinary." [DKR]

189 In other words, the practitioner is beyond observance of the vows and also beyond violation of them.

190 In this context, the term "transformation" is used only approximately. In fact, the wisdom in question is ever-present in the very depths of the ordinary mind, though veiled by adventitious factors. When these veils are removed, the innate wisdom shines forth. This is consequently referred to as *bral 'bras*, "a result occuring through removal" (of obstructions).

191 "For example, the sexual yoga performed with the three specific attitudes may appear to be an ordinary sexual act. But since the yogic practitioner has transmuted his or her ordinary perception of male and female into the perception of male and female deities, the first element, the ordinary object of desire, is absent. Since actual physical union is a practice performed in accordance with the skillful methods of the vow, the second element of ordinary physical union is absent. Finally, since the yogi or yogini transmutes the sensation of

climax into primordial wisdom and does not lose the essence, the third element, pleasure, is absent." [DS 389]

192 According to the *ri chos* of Karma Chagmé, this somewhat shadowy figure was an Indian master who visited Tibet on three occasions (after the persecution of Langdarma), each time assuming a different identity. During his first visit, he was known as Shardakara and transmitted teachings, the nature of which Karma Chagmé does not describe. On the second occasion, he appeared in the province of Ngari and was known as Atsara Marpo (the Red Teacher). It was then that he propagated the ideas on tantric practice described here. At the time of his third visit, he was known, it seems, as Gayadhara and translated the Thirteen Golden Teachings much valued in the Sakya tradition.

193 "I.e., they are superimposed." [DKR]

194 "Scholars who believe that the essence of the three vows is different take exception to the Nyingma standpoint. They say that the notions of transformation and single essence are mutually exclusive. They argue that if one can talk about iron being transmuted into gold, the implication is that the two metals are different and do not have the same nature. Also, in view of the fact that the consciousness of the alaya is transformed into mirrorlike wisdom, the assertion that the two must have the same nature leads, they say, to the absurd consequence that mirrorlike wisdom is the basis of deluded propensities. Once again, the notion of the same nature clashes with the idea of transformation. For if iron and gold have the same nature, what need is there for transformation? Of course one could argue that before transformation, the two metals lack the same nature but afterward, they acquire it. But in anticipation of this objection, they say that if that were the case, the nature of gold is compromised and regarded as changeable. It is therefore incorrect, they say, to claim that gold has the same nature as iron. For if it had, it would follow that gold is a base metal like iron, while iron, even before transmutation, must be precious and as valuable as gold. If this argument is examined, it is evident that it is merely by pointing out the flaws in the example that they are trying to discredit the meaning that the example is intended to express. I do not think this is a valid procedure. In ordinary terms, when iron is transmuted into gold, one would not normally say that (at the end of the process) the gold is something completely different from the iron, but rather that the iron has "changed into gold"—they are one and the same (i.e., a single mass that remains the subject of the transformation). Likewise, the pratimoksha and bodhichitta vows are transformed into the mantrayana vow. The earlier mental stream that had the nature of renunciation and altruism is now enhanced by the pure perception of the Mantrayana. It is in this sense that one can talk about the vows having the same nature. And not only is this not inadmissible, it is, on the contrary, highly acceptable! For it is the *mind* of the person that is gradually transformed, starting from entry into the path and going right up to the attainment of the result. It is in this sense that

it is possible to speak of the single nature." [YG II, 319] According to Karma Chagmé, this is the view of Karmapa Chödrak Gyamtso.

195 According to Karma Chagmé, this is the view of Khedrup-Je, although according to Patrul Rinpoche it is the view of Je Tsongkhapa himself.

196 This sounds like the incorrect opinion cited earlier (with the example of earth, water, and boat). However, here the emphasis is being placed on the enhancement of qualities, due to which a certain transformation is seen to occur.

197 "When hearing about the teachings of the Mantrayana, some people entertain wrong views and reject it, and thereby create the cause for falling into the lower realms. In order to prevent this from happening, one should introduce them to the tantric teachings only at a later time." [DKR]

198 "I.e., the means and wisdom that come from the stages of generation and perfection." [DKR]

199 Uncompounded discipline is the discipline of one who has realized the equality of all things. For such a person there is no observer and nothing to be observed. This is the authentic paramita of discipline.

200 "The Madhyamikas define a vow as a 'consciousness concomitant with a mental factor that is the intention' (*spongs sems mtshungs ldan dang bcas pa*) to refrain from wrong actions. They are not obliged to say that this is an autonomous continuum, because of their general assertion that everything is dependent arising. . . . As long as benefit and harm result from positive and negative thoughts, one should, on the relative level, observe and not neglect the precepts concerning what is to be done and what is to be avoided." [YG II, 331]

201 See note 88.

202 "Their own bodies, the body of a partner, or phenomena in general." [DKR]

203 "Generally speaking, there is nothing definite about what should be cultivated and what should be prohibited. Words and deeds in themselves are neutral (their goodness or badness derives from motive)." [YG II, 333] (It should be noted that, as already shown, the operative attitude is that of bodhichitta. Motive here should not be confused with moral conscience of the kind referred to in certain Western moral theories.)

204 "It is said in the *Avatamsaka-sutra*: 'When Bodhisattvas enter a house, they generate bodhichitta wishing that all beings reach the city of Liberation. When they lie down to rest, they wish that all beings attain the Dharmakaya. When they rise, they wish that all beings attain the Rupakaya, and so forth. . . .'" [YG II, 342]

205 "Free of all self-concern, we should *give* beings our bodies (indeed all the five aggregates), the possessions that we need for our subsistence, and all our merits of the past, present, and future. Because we should *protect* what has

been given for the enjoyment of beings, we must strive in conformity with the Dharma to avoid things that are hazardous for our present and future lives and that endanger the very basis for altruistic activity. Thus the text says: 'Protecting one's body means to stop inflicting harm.' With regard to wealth, the best protection is the practice of virtue and a sense of contentment with what one has. Thus: 'Act correctly. By training in this way, you will protect your wealth without difficulty.' To dedicate the fruits of merit to the enlightenment of all instead of nourishing the improper hope of getting them for oneself is the best way to protect one's merit. 'Abandon the selfish wish for results, thus you will protect all your merits. Have no regret and do not talk about what you have done but rather have a horror of wealth and renown, abandoning all pride. Have faith in the Bodhisattvas and rid yourself of doubt in the Dharma.' It is not enough just to protect one's body, possessions and merits. One must *purify* them of all adverse factors. The body is purified by cleansing negative actions and cultivating the antidotes to defiled emotion. 'To purify the body means to cleanse away all negative actions and emotions.' To give up a wrong kind of livelihood and to cultivate virtue, in which skillful means and wisdom are conjoined, is what is meant by the purification of possessions, and merits. 'It should be understood that one's possessions are pure insofar as one's livelihood is pure. Merits are made pure by cultivating emptiness endowed with the essence of compassion.' However, even though the 'body, possessions, and merit' are purified, if one fails to *increase* them, it will be impossible to fulfill the wishes of beings. It is necessary therefore to develop them further. The increase of strength and endeavor corresponds to the development of the body: 'The development of the body means to banish laziness and train in strength.' Likewise, to give in charity in a way that unites skillful means and wisdom is to increase one's possessions. 'To give emptiness endowed with the essence of compassion means to increase one's wealth.' To increase merit means to train oneself to act in the manner of Bodhisattva Samantabhadra." [YG II, 344]

206 See Dilgo Khyentse Rinpoche in *Enlightened Courage*, p. 61: "When an angry pig rears up at us, if we hit it on the nose with a stick it will immediately turn round and run away, unable to bear the pain. If we clean the butter-lamp while it is still warm, the job is very easily done."

207 "Whichever path one wishes to practice, it is not sufficient simply to speak and act; it is important to pledge oneself with a powerful resolve. People who truly intend the benefit of others are in effect at war with four demons that hinder them from their goal. They must therefore acquire great fortitude, which is a powerful armor, impervious to the weapons of adversaries. In order to vanquish the Demon of the Defilements (a single one of the eighty-four thousand defilements is enough to prevent the attainment of liberation), they must stick to their pledge even if they have to persevere in it, beset by hundreds of difficulties, for measureless kalpas. As for the Demon 'Child of the

Gods,' the dissipater of concentration, when practitioners endure the hardships of the path, they take a pledge not to relinquish their diligence and to strive for virtue, even if they gain the power, reputation, society, and affluence of a Chakravartin king. This pledge is naturally accompanied by the armor that vanquishes the Demon of Death, the creator of obstacles to life, and also the Demon of the Aggregates, which is a hindrance to the gaining of nirvana without remainder. Finally, it is necessary to strive to integrate and bring into experience all the profound and vast teachings that are revealed in the pitaka of the Mahayana." [YG II, 369]

208 "Beginners should most of all avoid negative actions. Those on the level of the path of aspiration must gather virtue while those on the supreme bodhisattva grounds should devote themselves to the benefit of others." [YG II, 371]

209 It is said in the teachings on the intermediary state that the recently dead possess a certain clairvoyance and are able to perceive their former habitat and companions and are aware of the latter's thoughts and actions.

210 These are the Ganges, Indus, Oxus, and Tarim, four rivers rising in the Himalayas and flowing into India.

211 A reference to the traditional classification of diseases according to the four medical tantras.

212 I.e., with the feet resting on the thighs or, in the case of half-vajra, with one foot resting on the thigh of the other leg, the other foot being tucked underneath.

213 In the present context of shamatha meditation, "form" refers to visible objects such as a pebble or an image or visualization of the Buddha, and so on; "formless" refers to the breath, emptiness, the mind, and so on.

214 "At the outset, the beginners devote themselves to the practice of calm abiding or shamatha, concentrating one-pointedly on an image, for example, of the Buddha adorned with all the major and minor marks. As it is said in the *Samadhiraja-sutra*:

> "Those who rest their minds upon
> The beauteous golden form of Buddha,
> Guardian of the world, are called
> Bodhisattvas who repose in evenness.

"The mind is fixed for a lengthy period of time on this object, remaining concentrated on it to the exclusion of all else. Then, in order to accomplish profound insight or vipashyana, the meditator must first examine the object of concentration. The body of the Tathagata, adorned with the major and minor marks, which appears as the mind's object, has no existence whatever separate from the mind, not even to the slightest extent. The object of concentration is but an appearance within the mind. And yet, at the same time, there is nothing that could be pointed out as being 'the mind.' What cannot be pointed out or found does not exist, has never existed, and will never exist. Convinced that this is the inconceivable ultimate reality, the meditator rests in equipoise, free of thoughts." [YG II, 397]

215 "The *Samadhiraja-sutra* says:

> Concentration is the even ground,
> Peaceful, subtle, not to be observed.
> Since all perceptions are subdued,
> It is the holding of the very depths."
> [YG II, 398]

To "hold the depths" is the literal of translation the Tibetan term for concentration (*ting nge 'dzin*).

216 "The expression 'enjoyment concentration' refers to the fact that this kind of concentration results in the enjoyment of the higher realms." [YG II, 400]

217 *shin sbyangs*. This refers to virtuosity in training in the course of which all negative aspects of body and mind are eliminated.

218 *zil gyis gnon pa'i skye mched brgyad*. See appendix 9.

219 *yid la byed pa drug*. "This refers to the six types of attention. (The mental factor of attention or mental engagement, *yid la byed pa*, means that the mind focuses steadily on its object.) The six types of attention are: (1) *mtshan nyid rab tu rig pa yid la byed pa*, attention with regard to a correct understanding of the character of the lower and higher realms. This means to focus alternately, through reflecting on the peaceful character of the higher realms and the harsh character of the lower realms. (2) *mos pa yid la byed pa*, attention with regard to the appreciation of the qualities of the higher realms. This means that the earlier study deepens into shamatha and vipashyana. (3) *dben pa yid la byed pa*, attention with regard to the discarding of the afflictions. It occurs when one is in the process of eliminating the three greatest degrees of the emotions of the desire realm. (4) *dga' ba sdud pa yid la byed pa*, attention with regard to the accumulation of joy. It means that through the absence of affliction one enjoys a lesser kind of bliss. It is now that the medium degrees of the emotions of the desire realm are eliminated. (5) *dbyod pa yid la byed pa*, attention in which the mind focuses steadily on the investigation. It means to examine whether one possesses subtle afflictions, thereby eliminating the lesser degrees of affliction in the desire realm. (6) *sbyor ba'i mtha' yid la byed pa*, attention that focuses on the fruit of the practice." [YG II, 408]

220 I.e., the four samadhis of the form realm, the four absorptions of the formless realm, together with the absorption of cessation. This makes nine. Instead of the aborption of cessation, the Abhidharma speaks of the "preparatory stage, *nyer bsdogs*, of the first samadhi," i.e., *'dod sems rtse gcig*, the "one-pointed mind of the desire realm."

221 "The practice of shamatha renders the mind immovable and impervious to the wind of thoughts. It is, however, unable to uproot defilements. It is vipashyana that eradicates the obscurations of ignorance and the belief in self. The Shravakas have more concentration than wisdom, whereas the Bodhisattvas have more wisdom than concentration. By contrast, the Tathagatas have both in equal measure." [YG II, 410]

222 "When mastery is gained in this meditation, in which all "nonexistent" phenomena of relative truth appear as an illusion, practitioners acquire the power in post-meditation to produce magical apparitions according to their wish. For this reason, they are is said to possess 'miragelike concentration' (sgyu ma lta bu'i ting nge 'dzin). When their concentration is perfect and able to overcome all adversity, and when it is accompanied by all the elements leading to enlightenment and displays the vast activities of buddhahood and is, in addition, immune to the fear of falling into a nirvana without remainder, it is called 'fearless or heroic concentration' (dpa' bar 'gro ba'i ting nge 'dzin). . . . Finally, they attain the 'diamondlike concentration' (rdo rje it a bu'i ting nge), so called because it is able to vanquish all obscurations, just as a diamond can break all other stones. The first concentration is experienced while the Bodhisattva is on the first to the seventh (i.e., the impure) grounds. The second concentration occurs while the Bodhisattva is on the pure grounds, i.e., the eighth to the tenth. Only at the end of the tenth ground is the third concentration attained." [YG II, 413]

223 This complex subject is discussed at length in the *Prajnaparamita sutras*. The distinction between "percept-thought" and "perceiver-thought" may perhaps be compared with the distinction made by Bertrand Russell between "sense-data" and sensation. See *The Problems of Philosophy*, p. 4.

224 "The four reliances are as follows:
 1. Knowledge of the Dharma comes from following a spiritual friend. However, the object of reliance is not the person of the teacher but the doctrine that he or she expounds. One should follow a teacher only after examining what he or she says.
 2. Since the teaching is to be implemented, one should rely on its meaning, not on its mode of expression.
 3. The meaning has two aspects: expedient and ultimate. One must rely on the ultimate meaning, and though one follows the expedient teaching for the time being, one should always do so with a view to the ultimate meaning.
 4. The ultimate meaning is comprehended by the mind. However, since intellectual assessment, however excellent, does not extend beyond the relative truth, it should not be relied upon. Reliance should be placed in thought-free wisdom that sees the absolute truth directly."
 [YG II, 425]

225 See the *Akshayamatinirdesha-sutra*. "What are the sutras of absolute meaning and what are the sutras of expedient meaning? The sutras taught with the purpose

of introducing people to the path are the sutras of the expedient meaning. The sutras taught in order that they penetrate the result are the sutras of the absolute meaning." [YG II, 428]

226 The three natures or realities (*rang bzhin gsum*) are characteristic of the third turning of the Dharma wheel, as discussed in scriptures such as the *Sandhinir-mochana-sutra*. These texts are interpreted differently by the Chittamatra school and the Madhyamika school.

"The following is a general exposition:

1. Imputed reality (*kun brtags*). This consists in the mind's reification of what does not exist in and by itself. An illustration of this is the idea of a 'self,' which in fact has no existence. Imputed reality also refers to all mistaken tenets and to all things of which the mind assumes a real existence but which lack this in any objective, concrete sense.

2. Dependent reality (*gzhan dbang*). This has two aspects: (i) impure and (ii) pure:

   i. Our experience of the environment, the outer world and its inhabitants, is a product of deluded perceptions which are deeply ingrained. These perceptions are deluded precisely on account of the mind's tendency to reify, as previously mentioned. This kind of perception may be likened to a situation in which a man falls victim to a magical trick and sees an illusory horse which he then assumes to exist. All such appearances are classified as impure dependent reality.

   ii. Pure dependent reality refers to the perceptions of the outer world experienced by the Aryas in the times when they are not absorbed in meditation. They are 'pure' because uncontaminated by the tendency to reify, on account of which they are apprehended as existing in and by themselves. They could be also illustrated in terms of the previous example as being like the state of mind of the magician, who also sees the illusory horse that he has magically created but does not assent to its real, concrete existence.

3. Completely existent reality (*yongs grub*) Again, this is twofold: (i) unchanging and (ii) unmistaken.

   i. This is emptiness itself, the ultimate reality of all phenomena, their unchanging nature regardless of whether or not beings understand it.

   ii. This refers to the wisdom that directly and fully understands the ultimate reality of phenomena." [YG I, 281]

227 Mipham Rinpoche said that here the Buddha was speaking from the point of view of ultimate reality, not from the point of view of relative existence. [KJ, 316]

228 Mipham Rinpoche: "The Buddha did not mean that they would be born in Sukhavati immediately after their deaths." [KJ, 316]

229 Mipham Rinpoche: "The expression 'existing in the manner of a dream' means that things exist only on the conventional level." [KJ, 316]

230 In the root verses, Jigme Lingpa adopts the wording of the *Sandhinirmochana-sutra.*

231 These correspond to the incorrect theories of causality (as viewed from the Madhyamika perspective) typified by four schools of Indian philosophy. (1) Phenomena arise from themselves (Samkhya); (2) phenomena arise from extrinsic causes (the lower schools of Buddhist philosophy); (3) phenomena arise both from themselves and from other causes (Jaina); (4) phenomena have no cause (Charvaka). See also Khenchen Kunzang Pelden, *Wisdom: Two Buddhist Commentaries,* pp. 105–115, 227. Cf. the dictum of Nagarjuna: "There is never production anywhere of anything, whether from itself, from other, from both, or causelessly."

232 "For some were saying that his teachings were too elementary." [KJ, 318]

233 I.e., two of the twelve links of dependent arisings. See chapter 4.

234 "Here 'father' and 'mother' are to be construed as the interdependent links of Craving and Grasping, respectively. The king is to be understood as the alaya, while the 'two of pure life' refer to the Brahmins, who represent the view of 'I' (the transitory composite), and to the virtuous ascetics, who represent the wrong view of ethical and doctrinal superiority. The 'country and the royal court' refer to the senses and the eight dualistic consciousnesses." [DKR]

235 "This is the position of the Svatantrika Madhyamikas. From the standpoint of the absolute truth, they argue that, if one assesses the two kinds of relative truth, both 'mistaken' and 'unmistaken' are on a level; they are the same in being produced by deluded propensities. Both appear to the senses and neither has true existence. In conventional terms, however, some phenomena function (i.e., are efficient) and some do not. And this is called unmistaken and mistaken relative truth." [YG II, 452]

236 "For the Vaibhashikas, relative truth (*kun rdzob bden pa*) and imputed existence (*btags yod*) have the same meaning, and likewise absolute truth (*don dam*) means the same thing as substantial existence (*rdzas yod*)." [YG II, 466]

237 "The Sautrantikas are divided into two groups. The 'Sautrantikas following scripture' regard the seven sections of the Abhidharma as the shastras of the seven Arhats (Shariputra, etc.) but nonetheless regard them as authoritative (the Vaibhashikas regard them as Buddha-word). The 'Sautrantikas following reasoning' do not consider these shastras as scriptural authority (i.e., as providing *lung gi tshad ma,* or incontrovertible knowledge deriving from scripture) and have recourse to the sutras." [YG II, 469,5]

238 It is important to bear in mind that the "Sautrantikas following scripture" and the "Sautrantikas following reasoning" (see previous note) have different

ways of distinguishing between the relative and absolute truths. To all intents and purposes, the Sautrantikas following scripture share the same view as the Vaibhashikas in holding that the absolute truth consists in the indivisible particles, while gross extended objects constitute the relative truth. The doctrine of the Sautrantikas following reasoning is more complex and involves an elaborate epistemological theory that in some respects resembles the representationist ideas of certain Western philosophers. Here, a distinction is made between the nonconceptual, direct perception of the sense consciousnesses and the conceptual, indirect perception of the mental consciousness. Whereas the sense consciousnesses actually contact external things, technically referred to as *specifically characterized (rang mtshan)*, and which are no more than agglomerations of atoms, the mental consciousness identifies and knows objects only by virtue of a mental image which is described as *generally characterized (spyi mtshan)*. The mental consciousness does not know external objects but only mental images. Given that the Sautrantikas distinguish absolute and relative truths according to efficiency, that is, the ability to perform functions, it stands to reason that absoluteness is attributed to the external objects and relativeness to the corresponding mental image whereby recognition and knowledge take place. It is obviously only external objects that perform functions and not the mental image that the mind has of them. It is worth reflecting that for the Sautrantikas the division between the two truths does not occupy the same importance as it does for the Madhyamikas. This is because for the Sautrantikas the realization of the absolute truth (as defined by them) does not correspond to spiritual realization. This is natural since, as Hinayanists, they are aiming at the realization of the personal no-self. For them, the ultimate nature of phenomena does not have the same importance as it does in the Mahayana.

239 For a description of the Chittamatra view, see Khenchen Kunzang Pelden, *Wisdom: Two Buddhist Commentaries*, pp. 40–41 and 49–55. See also S. K. Hookham, *The Buddha Within*, pp. 19–20.

240 The absolute is (1) the mind itself, the stuff of which objects, wrongly imagined to be external entities, are "composed." It is absolute because, according to the Chittamatrins, the mind is an ultimate and irreducibly existent reality. The absolute truth consists (2) not only in the mind itself but in the fact that *there is nothing but the mind* and that any phenomena (*kun brtags*) only seem to be separate from it.

241 It seems that for the Svatantrikas, it is theoretically possible to confine oneself exclusively to the relative level and to discourse meaningfully about phenomena—the way they are and the way they function—without reference to the absolute truth. The absolute truth thus becomes a kind of overarching proviso to the effect that phenomena are completely without true existence, but it does not interfere with science and philosophy, which can continue on the relative level. It is still possible to philosophize. There is an obvious, and

probably indispensable, pedagogical advantage in the Svatantrika approach in that it provides space in which a teaching about the nature of phenomena can be elaborated in terms accessible to the ordinary intellect and which can thus help people to progress on the path. At the same time, the critique of the Prasangikas is understandable and inevitable. To say that phenomena have a natural existence of their own on the relative level amounts to attributing true existence to them. It is, so to speak, a ratification of the relative truth as being independently valid. The two truths are divided and their union is in practice abandoned. On the other hand, the purpose of Madhyamika is precisely to undermine the tyranny of clinging to phenomena. It must compromise the status of phenomena radically, even on the relative level.

242 Compare T. R. V. Murti, *The Central Philosophy of Buddhism*, p. 87: "The Madhyamika system seems to have been perfected at one stroke by the genius of its founder—Nagarjuna."

243 Perhaps a reference to Nagarjuna's legendary alchemical accomplishments.

244 According to Butön, Nagarjuna's six treatises on reasoning are: (1) *Mulamadhyamika-karika, dbu ma rtsa ba'i shes rab* (preserved in Sanskrit); (2) *Shunyatasaptati, stong nyid bdun bcu pa* (lost in Sanskrit but preserved in Tibetan); (3) *Yuktishastika, rigs pa drug bcu pa* (lost in Sanskrit but preserved in Tibetan and Chinese); (4) *Vigrahavyavartani, rtsod zlog;* (5) *Vaidalyasutra and Prakarana, zhib mo rnam 'thag* (lost in Sanskrit but preserved in Tibetan); and (6) *Vyavaharasiddhi, tha snyad grub.*

245 The *Madhyamakavatara* is a general commentary on the meaning (*don 'grel*) of the *Karikas*, while the *Prasannapada* is a word-for-word commentary (*tshig 'grel*).

246 Chandrakirti says: "When a state of mind attuned to emptiness becomes manifest, this is referred to as the realization of emptiness. But it does not mean that emptiness is realized as an object." [see YG II, 531]

247 They do not originate, they do not dwell, and they do not cease.

248 See the *Samadhiraja-sutra*:

> Intellectuals asserting being and nonbeing,
> Who thus investigate, will find no peace from suffering.
> Is and is not, pure-impure,
> Are both extreme positions.
> But even in the middle the wise forebear to dwell.
>   [reference given in YG II, 537]

249 Emphasis here is placed on interdependence rather than on the number twelve. It is a statement about evolutionary causality arranged in a symmetrical formula, parallel to the twelvefold cycle of dependent causation as occurring in the existence of sentient beings. See DS, 28, where Dudjom Rinpoche says that outer, dependent arising can be understood by analyzing from where phenomenal results have arisen.

250 "The notion of interdependence can also be applied to nirvana. For even though nirvana is not a product newly contrived on the basis of compounded phenomena, it is through the accomplishment of the path that adventitious obscurations are removed, that nirvana is actualized, and the creative virtuosity of uncompounded wisdom manifests unhindered." [YG II, 543]

251 *gnyis snang*. The lingering appearance of phenomena as separate from the perceiver, even after the belief in their true existence has been abandoned.

252 "Some people object that if a sharp analyzing intellect is not operative at all times in the main meditation, and if there is not a certain apprehension of, and (intellectual) conviction in, the absence of the personal and phenomenal self, the all-discerning wisdom which is the nature of vipashyana cannot occur. But if this were true it would imply that an analyzing intellect must also be present in the meditation of the Aryas—and even at the level of buddhahood. For those who make this objection say that without it there can be no wisdom of vipashyana. In answer, it may be argued that this does not necessarily follow, since, in the context of the present objection, the meditators are ordinary beings and not like the Aryas who have vipashyana due to their direct seeing of ultimate reality. Our answer to this is that, even if there is a certain distinction, according to a given situation, the mind must be attuned to the wisdom that sees the ultimate directly, and it must remain in this state. For a mind caught in ontological extremes cannot bring forth the wisdom that transcends these extremes." [YG II, 549]

253 The formless realm has four spheres. Starting from the lowest one, these are: (1) *nam mkha' mtha' yas*, Infinite Space; (2) *rnam shes mtha' yas*, Infinite Consciousness; (3) *ci yang med pa*, Utter Nothingness; and (4) *yod min med min*, Neither Existence nor Nonexistence (also referred to as the Peak of Existence, *srid pa'i rtse mo*).

254 This means that they gradually spread downward, from the lowest level of the formless realm, through all the levels of the form realm, to the highest divine abode of the desire realm.

255 The six divine spheres of the realm of desire are in ascending order: (1) *rgyal chen rigs bzhi*, heaven of the Four Great Kings; (2) *sum bcu rtsa gsum*, heaven of the Thirty-three; (3) *'thab bral*, Free of Conflict; (4) *dga' ldan*, the Joyous Realm; (5) *'phrul dga'*, Enjoying Magical Creations; and (6) *gzhan 'phrul dbang byed*, Mastery over Magical Creations of Others.

256 Reference is normally made to four periods: (1) *rdzogs ldan* (perfect endowment), when beings are characterized by four features: infinite life, luminous body, miraculous abilities, and sustenance on amrita; (2) *gsum ldan* (threefold endowment), when beings have only three of these qualities; (3) *gnyis ldan* (twofold endowment), when they have only two qualities; and (4) *rtsod ldan*, when all four qualities have declined and beings live in a state of conflict.

257 *rigs bzhi*. The four social classes or castes correspond to four psychological

types as they originally developed when beings began to live in organized society and support themselves by their work. Insofar as it existed within the context of Indian society, Buddhism recognized the existence of the caste system. But in contrast to Hinduism, which is grounded in the Vedic scriptures and therefore assigned rigid ritual functions to the castes, Buddhism advocated spiritual practice for all members of society indifferently. The four castes are *bram ze rigs*, brahmins; *rgyal rigs*, kshatriyas; *rje 'u rigs*, vaishyas; and *dmangs rigs*, sudras.

258 According to the Abhidharma, the actual sense faculties are subtle physical objects, variously shaped and located in their bodily supports. Thus, the faculty of sight is positioned in the eye and shaped like a blue flower, the faculty of hearing is in the ear and shaped like a roll of birch bark, and so on.

259 It is not certain which of these two events—*light-appearance* (*snang ba*) with the arresting of the thirty-three types of thought produced by anger, or *light-increase* (*mched pa*) with the halting of the forty types of thoughts of attachment—will appear first at the time of death. In this text, the dissolution of the red element is mentioned first, whereas it is often preceded by the white element.

260 *mi mjed 'jig rten.* Our universe is so called because its inhabitants endure defiled emotion and suffering in great measure and Bodhisattvas endure hardships and practice with courage. The term *mi mjed* can also be interpreted as "fearless," in which case it is said to apply to our world because the beings therein show no fear of indulging in defilements. Yet another tradition interprets *mi mjed* as "undivided" because in our world, the mind cannot be dissociated from defiled emotions.

261 *bdun tshigs.* Every week, in the course of the forty-nine days of the bardo period, on the day of the person's death, the consciousness "relives" the painful experience of the moment of death. The performance of the weekly ceremonies for the dead has the effect of alleviating this suffering.

262 Here the sun and the moon of the bodhichitta refer respectively to the male and female essences.

263 In the *Abhidharmakosha*, Vasubandhu explains each of the sixteen aspects in terms of an incorrect philosophical view to which it constitutes a remedy (see Roger Jackson, *Is Enlightenment Possible?*, pp. 50, 344).

264 These last two aspects are to be understood as referring to the five aggregates of an individual. The third aspect, namely, that of their being without a "self that owns them," may also be understood as a denial of the existence of a universal Creator.

265 "Are all phenomena accounted for within the four truths? The answer to this is no, for it is asserted that certain things are not included, such as space

and nonanalytical cessation. How then are phenomena categorized? They are accounted for in the aggregate of form, the ayatana of the mind (the six types of consciousness), and mental objects (feelings, perceptions, conditioning factors, imperceptible forms and uncompounded phenomena). [According to the *Abhidharmakosha*, there are three uncompounded phenomena: space, cessation through analysis, and cessation without analysis.] Are all the realizations of the Noble Path included within the four truths? Yes, and necessarily so. It should be understood that when cessation is spoken of in the context of the four noble truths, this refers only to cessation through analysis. Cessation without analysis and the absorption of cessation are not included. . . ." [YG I, 361] For more information on the absorption of cessation, see note 14.

266 According to the Abhidharma (see Mipham Rinpoche's *mkhas 'jug*), perception is defined as "that which grasps or identifies characteristics" (*mtshan par 'dzin pa*). Perception is related to the six senses: the five physical senses, which are nonconceptual, and the mind or "mental sense," which functions by means of concepts. These two categories of conceptual and nonconceptual perceptions are themselves divided into two categories according to whether, in the course of their activity, they succeed in discerning the characteristics of their objects. If they do so, they are referred to as *mtshan bcas* (discerning); if they fail to do so, they are called *mtshan med* (non discerning). The five (nonconceptual) sense perceptions are regarded as discerning (*mtshan bcas*) when they are operating normally and perceiving their proper objects: colors, sounds, smells, and so forth. Mental perception (which, as we have said, functions by means of concepts) is said to be discerning when it distinguishes identities or names. This happens (1) when the mind recognizes an object and correlates it with its name and (2) when the mind knows what is referred to when a name is given.

Perception is nondiscerning (*mtshan med*) when the sense organ in question is fully functional but there is no object. This occurs in states of profound absorption, whether of the Aryas or beings in the state known as the Peak of Existence. It occurs also when the mind is unable to identify and name objects, as in situations where something is encountered but is not recognized because the mind has no prior knowledge of it. This is the common experience of children, who are gradually building up a knowledge of their environment. Conversely, mental perception is also nondiscerning when (again, through lack of experience) it does not know what is referred to when names are given, as, for example, when an unknown language is heard. (It should be noted that nondiscerning perception does not refer to the mere privation of sensory stimulus, as, for example, when one is in a dark place with one's eyes open or in a soundproof room. In these cases, the senses do in fact have objects—darkness and silence, respectively.) [see KJ, 9–10]

267 For the Prasangikas, the *kun rdzob bden pa* has three aspects: (1) *yid rtog spyod kyi shes pa*, discursive mind; (2) *ngag gi brjod pa*, verbal expression; and (3) *lus ngag gi 'jug pa*, speech and physical acts.

268 In this (Abhidharma) context, the Tibetan terms *blo*, *yid*, and *rigs pa* are all synonyms (whereas in Dzogchen they have different meanings).

269 The absolute nature is one and indivisible. One cannot speak, for example, of a table and a chair having different absolute natures.

270 If the absolute is beyond the intellect, how can it be realized by beings? In answer to this, Mipham Rinpoche says that the absolute truth can be approximately understood by the (ordinary) mind. It can be the object of intellect, as it were, on a provisional and temporary basis. In this case, the absolute truth is described negatively (apophatically) as a nonaffirming negation (*med dgag*). This refers to *rnam gcod*, a process of exclusion, a logical analysis in which the existence of an object is searched for and found to be absent, so that absence or "nonfinding" (regarded as its ultimate condition) is the object of the intellect. It is only in this sense that the absolute can be understood by the ordinary mind. However, in the terms of the yogic experience of genuine realization of the absolute, which is utterly beyond the division into subject and object, the intellect is transcended with the result that the absolute cannot be said to be its object. This discovered state (*yongs gcod*) is an experience of the absolute that can only be described as an affirming negative (*ma yin dgag*). It is not a mere nothingness, a mere "nonfinding"; it is the manifestation of the fundamental nature of the mind, even though this is totally beyond conception and description. To deny this last point would be tantamount to saying that ultimate realization, buddhahood, is itself a mere vacuity.

271 See Khenchen Kunzang Pelden, *Wisdom: Two Buddhist Commentaries*, p. 35.

272 In other words, fire arises from the presence of fuel and the act of ignition, water is the combination of hydrogen and oxygen, and so on.

273 In other words, arguments that are driving at the ultimate nature of the object.

274 Existence cannot be ascribed to them simply on the grounds that they function according to conventional expectations.

275 In other words, they refrain from propounding a theory about conventional phenomena.

276 Of these eight, the first six are nonaffirming negatives (*med dgag*); the last two are affirming negatives (*ma yin dgag*).

277 In other words, as long as one is thinking of them at all (with the ordinary intellect), one cannot but think of them as things separate from the mind; one cannot but be imprisoned in duality.

278 The three modes (*tshul gsum*) are three criteria that establish the correctness of a syllogism as used in traditional Indian logic. See Daniel Perdue, *Debate in Tibetan Buddhism*. p. 38ff.

279 When relative phenomena are subjected to analysis, they are found to be devoid of inherent existence. Their emptiness is established and this is their absolute truth. When, however, emptiness is itself subjected to inquiry, it too becomes a conventionality and is itself found to be empty of inherent existence. Nothing that is made the object of intellectual analysis can be found to have absolute reality.

280 This is the traditional form of the syllogism in Indian logic.

281 Of course, on the absolute level, they deny that the mind exists in an ultimate sense, and the view is thus different from that of the Chittamatra or Yogachara school. The position of Shantarakshita and Kamalashila is a synthesis of the Madhyamika and Chittamatra approaches and as such is regarded as the last great development in the history of Buddhist philosophy in India.

282 As in the case of Buddhapalita and Chandrakirti among the Prasangika Madhyamikas. The founder of a school (*shing rta srol 'byed*, the maker of the chariot way) is considered to be not the master who first expressed a given idea, but the one who elaborated it into a fully fledged system. Thus, although Buddhapalita was the first to identify the Consequence (*prasanga*) as the method best expressive of Nagarjuna's intention, it was Chandrakirti who brought this insight into focus and organized it into a complete philosophical statement.

283 The point is that, while Prasangika is acknowledged as the supreme view, the Svatantrika approach is important as a preparation and propaedeutic and is therefore extremely valuable. This appreciation of Svatantrika is characteristic of the Nyingmapa school, for Shantarakshita was one of the founding fathers of the Tibetan tradition.

284 The meaning of this is that if, having refuted "true existence," we are left with phenomena untouched, as it were, we have not got very far in dealing with our cravings.

285 This would surely be more effective than trying to enter the dreamer's dream in order either to save him from what he is dreaming about or telling him, "You are only dreaming."

286 Unless and until we are made to see that self (ego) is unreal and purely imagined, the apprehension of, or clinging to, self cannot be dissipated. The only way that the man in the example can overcome his fear of the snake is to be shown that there is no snake there, but only a heap of rope. Without this, it is impossible for him simply to stop being afraid.

287 It is important to realize that the person in the sense of a sentient (e.g., human) being is not the same thing as the "personal self," which here corresponds to the subjective experience of "ego," of being "I." It is from the point of view of this subjective self that all other things, including other people as well as one's own psychophysical constituents, are regarded as phenomena.

288 The *inherently existent* ego and phenomena are purely imaginary. On the relative level, there is only a "person" and "phenomena," which are nothing but imputations projected onto the appropriate constituents, and the latter are, of course, transitory phenomena. In other words, although "clinging to self" is real enough, the object of clinging (an inherently existent self) is a mere figment, as nonexistent as the apparent snake.

289 That is, the person and phenomena simply as they appear in common experience, but which are not inherently existent.

290 Clinging to the personal self constitutes the "emotional veil," so called because all the defiled emotions arise from attachment to "I" and "mine." Clinging to the phenomenal self constitutes the "cognitive veil." This refers to clinging to the real existence of subject, object, and action, which thus obscures omniscience.

291 Real existence, *dngos po*: all that appears as having origin, duration, and cessation. See Khenchen Kunzang Pelden, *Wisdom: Two Buddhist Commentaries*, p. 53: "Things are understood here as what is cognized validly by sight, hearing or mental activity. Sight in this context refers to everything that is perceived directly through the senses; hearing refers to what is learned indirectly from other sources, and mental activity refers to what is grasped inferentially."

292 In other words, emptiness is not a predicate. It cannot be ascribed to phenomena, which somehow retain their supposedly independent status irrespective of the ascription.

293 These four alternatives refer to specific positions taken in Indian philosophy with regard to the problem of causality and which the Madhyamika subjects to criticism and explodes. The first, namely, the view that causes and effects are manifestations of a single substance, is the position of the Samkhya school. The second view, that causes and effects are of a different nature, is the position taken by the lower schools of Buddhism (including the Svatantrikas) and which the Prasangikas show to be just as problematic as the first view. The third position, which is an attempt to combine the positions of views one and two, is characteristic of the Jaina school (and of Hegel in the West), while the fourth position, which amounts to a rejection of causality altogether, is the standpoint of the Charvaka or materialist skeptics.

294 The whole language of causality implies difference and cannot be accounted for by a theory of identity in which the effect is merely the self-expression of the cause. In other words, as the text shows, an insistence on the identity of cause and effect cannot be combined with talk about causality, for this necessarily involves distinctions between the two terms of the process. Causality is in effect abandoned.

295 In other words, it is impossible to establish a link between producer and product.

296 To abandon causality altogether amounts to the belief that the universe is in chaos. This being so, there is no way to account for the manifest order visible in the phenomenal world. It also stultifies all human endeavor in which actions are undertaken with a view to obtaining certain results, including the attempt to communicate a theory of causeless origination. Thus, even if a theory of pure randomness is propounded, the fact is that no sane person, including the formulator of such a position, ever lives by it.

297 The Sevenfold Reasoning is expounded at length in the sixth chapter of the *Madhyamakavatara* of Chandrakirti.

298 Some of these qualities may be practiced by Bodhisattvas on the path of learning. They come to full fruition, however, only in the state of buddhahood.

299 In this context, freedom is understood as a state of mind totally divested of the obscurations that block the subsequently listed realizations.

300 See Khenchen Kunzang Pelden, *Wisdom: Two Buddhist Commentaries*, p. 118, "All phenomena appearing to exist according to cause, result and nature are established as the three doors of liberation. This means that, as regards the causal aspect, analysis shows that the cause is beyond all conceptual ascriptions or characteristics; as regards nature, analysis shows that this is emptiness; and as for result, analysis reveals that it is beyond expectancy."

Glossary ∽

ABBOT, *mkhan po.* In general, the transmitter of the monastic vows. This title is also given to a person who has attained a high degree of knowledge of Dharma and is authorized to teach it.

ABHAYAKARA. An outstanding Mahayana master in India (11th–12th century) successively abbot of Vajrasana, Nalanda, and Vikramashila; a prolific author and commentator of Sutrayana and Tantrayana texts. Aware of the imminent decline of Buddhism in India, and in collaboration with his numerous Tibetan disciples, he presided over the translation of many Sanskrit texts into Tibetan.

ABHIDHARMA, Skt., *mngon pa.* The third section of the Tripitaka (the other two sections being the Vinaya and the Sutras). The Abhidharma is the corpus of texts expounding the metaphysical content of the Sutras.

ABSENCE OF CONCEPTUAL CONSTRUCTS, *spros bral.* This expression is used to refer to the fact that phenomena, in their true nature, are "empty," or beyond the four possible ontological positions: they cannot be said to exist; they cannot be said not to exist; they cannot be said both to exist and not to exist; and they cannot be said neither to exist nor not to exist.

ABSOLUTE TRUTH, *don dam bden pa.* The ultimate nature of the mind and the true status of all phenomena, the state beyond all conceptual constructs which can be known only by primordial wisdom and in a manner that transcends duality. Thus defined, this is the absolute truth "in-itself" (*rnam grangs ma yin pa'i don dam*), which is ineffable. This is different from the likeness or similitude of the absolute truth that is experienced or known as one approaches it through the avenues of rational analysis and meditation on the absence of origin and so on. For here one is still within the sphere of the relative truth. Nevertheless, since this is the authentic method of progressing toward a direct realization of the absolute and is in accord with it, it is called the "approximate" absolute (*rnam grangs pa'i don dam*) or "concordant" absolute (*mthun pa'i don dam*).

ABSOLUTE WISDOM, *don gyi ye shes.* Primordial knowledge, divested of the dualistic mental activity characteristic of the ordinary mind, which "sees" (nondualistically) the ultimate reality or absolute truth.

ABSORPTION OF CESSATION, *'gog pa'i snyoms 'jug.* According to the Mahayana presentation, this is the absorption practiced by the Shravakas and Pratyekabuddhas as a means of gaining contentment in the course of their present existence. It involves the cessation of the sense consciousnesses and the defiled emotional consciousness. Bodhisattvas also enter this absorption, not, however, as an end in itself, but as a method of training in concentration.

ABSORPTION OF NONPERCEPTION, *'du shes med pa'i snyoms 'jug.* The absorption experienced by the insensate gods of the form realm and the gods of the formless realms. In this absorption, the sense consciousnesses are arrested although the defiled emotional consciousness (*nyon yid*) continues to function.

ACCOMPLISHMENT, *dngos grub.* Accomplishment is described as either supreme or ordinary. Supreme accomplishment is the attainment of buddhahood. "Common or ordinary accomplishments" are the miraculous powers acquired in the course of spiritual training. The attainment of these powers, which are similar in kind to those acquired by the practitioners of some non-Buddhist traditions, are not regarded as ends in themselves. When they arise, however, they are taken as signs of progress on the path and are employed for the benefit of the teachings and disciples.

ACCUMULATE AN ACTION, *las gsogs pa.* To perform an action or karma. Actions leave traces in the alaya and will subsequently fructify in the sense of bringing forth experiential effects.

ACHARYA, Skt., *slob dpon.* Teacher, the equivalent of spiritual master or lama.

ADVENTITIOUS VEIL OR STAIN, *glo bur gyi dri ma.* Impermanent emotional and cognitive obscurations that afflict the mind but which, not being intrinsic to its nature, can be removed from it. *See* Two obscurations; Twofold purity.

AFFIRMING NEGATIVE, *ma yin dgag.* An affirming negative is a negation in which the possibility of another (positive) value is implied. For example, in the statement "It isn't a cat that is on the roof," the presence of a cat is denied, but in such a way as to suggest that something else is there. Compare this with a nonaffirming negative (*med dgag*), which simply negates without any further implication, for example, in the statement "There is nothing on the roof."

AFFLICTIONS, *nyon mongs pa,* Skt. klesha. Mental factors that produce states of mental torment both immediately and in the long term. The five principal kleshas, which are sometimes called poisons, are attachment, hatred, ignorance, envy, and pride.

AGGREGATES, *phung po. See* Skandhas.

AKANISHTA, Skt., *'og min.* In general, the highest of all buddhafields, the place where, according to Vajrayana, Bodhisattvas attain final buddhahood. There are, in fact, six levels of Akanishta, ranging from the highest heaven of the form realm up to the ultimate pure land of the Dharmakaya.

ALAYA, Skt., *kun gzhi,* lit. the ground-of-all. According to the Mahayana, this is the fundamental and indeterminate level of the mind, in which karmic imprints are stored.

ALL-CONCEALING TRUTH. *See* Relative truth.

AMRITA, Skt., *bdud rtsi*, lit. the ambrosia that overcomes the Demon of Death. The draft of immortality and symbol of wisdom.

ANCIENT TRANSLATION SCHOOL, *gsang sngags snga 'gyur*. Referred to also as the Nyingma or Ancient school, the original tradition of Tibetan Buddhism. Its adherents study and practice the tantras (and their related teachings) that were translated in the first period between the introduction of the Buddhadharma to Tibet in the eighth century and the period of New Translation inaugurated by Rinchen Zangpo (958–1051).

ANUYOGA. The second of the inner tantras, according to the system of nine vehicles used in the Nyingma tradition. Anuyoga emphasizes the perfection stage of tantric practice, which consists of meditation on emptiness, as well as the subtle channels, energies, and essence of the physical body.

APPROACH, ACCOMPLISHMENT, AND ACTIVATION, *bsnyen pa, grub pa, las sbyor.* Three consecutive stages in the practice of a sadhana. In the first stage the practitioner becomes familiar with the figure and mandala of the meditational deity. In the second stage, the deity is "accomplished," and in the third, different enlightened activities are practiced.

ARHAT, Skt., *dgra bcom pa*, lit. "Foe Destroyer." One who has vanquished the enemies of afflictive emotion and realized the nonexistence of the personal self, and who is thus forever free from the sufferings of samsara. Arhatship is the goal of the teachings of the Root Vehicle, the Shravakayana or Hinayana. Etymologically, the Sanskrit term can also be interpreted as "worthy one."

ARYA, Skt., *'phags pa*. Sublime or noble one, one who has transcended samsaric existence. There are four classes of sublime beings: Arhats, Pratyekabuddhas, Bodhisattvas, and Buddhas.

ARYADEVA, *'phags pa lha*. The direct disciple and "heart son" of Nagarjuna. He was a powerful advocate of Nagarjuna's teaching later to be known as the Madhyamika. He probably lived at the turn of the second and third centuries C.E. His most celebrated work is the *Catuhshatakashastra-karika, The Four Hundred Verses on the Middle Way.*

ASANGA, *thog med*, C. 350 C.E., a major figure in Mahayana Buddhism; the cofounder, with his brother Vasubandhu, of the Yogachara philosophy. According to tradition, he received from the Bodhisattva Maitreya the famous Five Teachings (*byams pa'i chos lnga*) in which the views of Madhyamika and Yogachara are both expounded. He is the source of the Mahayana lineage of Vast Activities (*rgya chen spyod pa*), which complements the lineage of the Profound View (*zab mo'i lta ba*) stemming from Nagarjuna and Manjushri.

ASHVAGHOSHA, *rta dbyangs*. Originally a Hindu scholar who converted to Mahayana Buddhism under the influence of Aryadeva. He is sometimes identified with the master Shura (*dpa' bo*). A great poet, as important in the history of Sanskrit literature as in the history of Buddhism, he is celebrated as the author of a celebrated account of the Buddha's life, the *Buddhacharita*.

ASPIRATIONAL PRACTICE, *mos spyod kyi sa*. All practice prior to the attainment of the path of seeing, in which ultimate reality is perceived directly, is regarded as being of the nature of aspiration or interest.

ASURA, Skt., *lha min*, demigod or "Titan." One of six classes of beings in samsara. The asuras are usually considered to be similar to the gods, with whom they are sometimes classified. Their dominant emotional characteristic is envy, and they are constantly at war with the gods, of whom they are jealous.

ATI, ATIYOGA. The last and highest of the inner tantras, the summit of the system of nine vehicles according to the Nyingma classification; a synonym of Dzogchen (*rdzogs pa chen po*), the Great Perfection.

ATISHA, *jo bo rje*. Also known as Dipamkarashrijnana (982–1054), abbot of the Indian monastic university of Vikramashila. Philosophically, he is considered to be Prasangika Madhyamika in the school of Chandrakirti, although he also upheld the teachings of the Yogachara Madhyamika. He came to Tibet at the invitation of the king Yeshe Ö to restore the Buddhadharma after its persecution by Langdarma. He introduced there the Mind Training teachings (*blo 'byongs*), which he received from his teacher Suvarnadvipa Dharmakirti and which are a synthesis of the bodhichitta traditions of Nagarjuna and Asanga. He was also a master of the tantra teachings. His main disciple and successor was the upasaka Dromtön (*'brom ston*), who founded the Kadampa school and built the monastery of Reting (*rwa sgreng*). Atisha died at Nyethang in Tibet in 1054.

ATTACHMENT AND IMPEDIMENT, *chags thogs*. *See* Two obscurations.

AVALOKITESHVARA, Skt., *spyan ras gzigs*. The "Lord who Sees," name of the Bodhisattva who embodies the speech and compassion of all the Buddhas; the Sambhogakaya emanation of the Buddha Amitabha; sometimes referred to as Lokeshvara, the Lord of the World.

AYATANA, Skt., *skye mched*. Sometimes translated as "sense fields." The "six inner ayatanas" refer exclusively to the sense organs; the "twelve ayatanas" comprise these six plus the "six outer ayatanas," which are the corresponding sense objects. (The outer and inner ayatanas of the mind are the mental sense organ and mental objects. Here, the mental "organ" is the moment of consciousness immediately preceding the moment in which the mental object is perceived.) From the interaction of the six sense organs and their six objects, the six consciousnesses are engendered.

BARDO, *bar do*. An intermediary state. This term most often refers to the state between death and subsequent rebirth. In fact, human experience encompasses six types of bardo: the bardo of the present life (*rang bzhin skye gnas bar do*), the bardo of meditation (*bsam gtan gyi bar do*), the bardo of dream (*rmi lam gyi bar do*), the bardo of dying (*'chi ka'i bar do*), the luminous bardo of ultimate reality (*chos nyid bar do*), and the bardo of becoming (*srid pa'i bar do*). The first three bardos unfold in the course of life. The second three refer to the death and rebirth process which terminates at conception at the beginning of the subsequent existence.

BEINGS OF GREAT SCOPE, *skyes bu chen po*. Practitioners of the Mahayana teachings who, out of compassion, aspire to buddhahood in order to help beings in the immediate term and to lead them ultimately to enlightenment.

BEINGS OF LESSER SCOPE, *skyes bu chung ngu*. Beings who aspire to happiness in the human and divine realms and who, in order to gain it, consciously practice pure ethics according to the karmic law of cause and effect.

BEINGS OF MIDDLE SCOPE, *skyes bu 'bring*. Practitioners of the Hinayana teachings who aspire to liberation from the cycle of existences.

BEZOAR, *gi wang*. A concretion found in the stomachs or entrails of certain animals and which is endowed with medicinal properties.

BHAGAVAN, *bcom ldan 'das*. An epithet of the Buddha sometimes translated as the Blessed One or the Blessed Lord. The title can be analyzed etymologically as "the one who has vanquished (*bcom*) the four demons, who possesses (*ldan*) all qualities and who is beyond (*'das*) samsara and nirvana."

BHAVAVIVEKA, *legs ldan byed*. An important fifth-century master of the Madhyamika teachings and initiator of the Svatantrika school. *See also* Svatantrika.

BHIKSHU, Skt., *dge slong*. A fully ordained Buddhist monk.

BHUMI, Skt., *sa*. *See* Ground.

BHUTICHANDRA. Disciple of Shakya Shri (thirteenth century) and exponent of the three vows.

BODHICHARYAVATARA, *spyod 'jug*. Shantideva's famous text, expounding the practice of the Bodhisattva path.

BODHICHITTA, Skt., *byang chub kyi sems*. On the relative level, this is the wish to attain buddhahood for the sake of all sentient beings, together with the practice necessary to accomplish this. On the absolute level, it is nondual wisdom, the ultimate nature of the mind and the true status of all phenomena. In certain tantric contexts, bodhichitta refers to the essential physical substance which is the support of the mind.

BODHISATTVA, Skt., *byang chub sems dpa'*. One who through compassion strives to attain the full enlightenment of buddhahood for the sake of all beings. Bodhisattvas may be "ordinary" or "noble" depending on whether they have attained the path of seeing and are residing on one of the ten bodhisattva grounds.

BODY, *sku*, kaya, Skt. *See* Five Bodies.

BRAHMA, Skt., *tshangs pa*. In the Buddhist tradition, this name refers to the chief divinity residing in the form realm.

BRAHMIN, Skt., *bram ze*. A member of the priestly caste of ancient India; this term often indicates hermits and spiritual practitioners. It should be noted that the Buddha rejected the caste system and proclaimed on several occasions that the true Brahmin is not someone so designated through an accident of birth, but one who has thoroughly overcome defilement and attained freedom. *See also* Four castes.

BUDDHA, *sangs rgyas*. The Fully Awakened One, a being who has removed the emotional and cognitive veils and is endowed with all enlightened qualities of realization.

BUDDHAFIELD, *zhing khams*. From a certain point of view, a buddhafield is a sphere or dimension projected and manifested by a Buddha or great Bodhisattva, in which beings may abide and progress toward enlightenment without ever falling into lower states of existence. However, any place viewed as the pure manifestation of spontaneous wisdom is a buddhafield.

BUDDHAGHOSHA. A celebrated fourth-century master of the Theravada, contemporary of Asanga and Vasubandhu. He was the author of the *Visuddhimagga*, a text greatly revered in Theravada Buddhism as the classic presentation of their tradition.

BUDDHAGUHYA, *sangs rgyas gsang ba*. A master of Mahayoga and teacher of both Guru Padmasambhava and Vimalamitra. He composed the celebrated *Gradual Path of the Magical Net*.

BUDDHAPALITA, *sangs rgyas skyongs*. Fifth-century master of Madhyamika who first explicitly asserted *prasanga* or reductio ad absurdum as the appropriate method for Madhyamika disputation, thereby heralding the Prasangika Madhyamika school as later systematized by Chandrakirti.

BUTÖN, *bu ston*. A renowned scholar (1290–1364) famous for his compilation of the Kangyur and Tengyur, and author of an important *History of Dharma*.

CENTRAL LAND, *yul dbus*. A land in which the Dharma is taught and practiced, as opposed to the peripheral or barbarous lands, so called because the Buddha's teachings are unknown there. From this standpoint, a country devoid of Dharma will still be termed barbarous, even though it may possess a high level of civilization and technology.

CESSATION THROUGH ANALYSIS, *so sor brtags pa'i 'gog pa*. The cessation of afflictive emotion brought about by an analytical understanding, or wisdom, that eliminates the conditions in which such affliction can occur. The cessation itself is a nirvana (the "small nirvana" of Arhats) and is regarded as an "uncompounded phenomenon."

CESSATION WITHOUT ANALYSIS. *See* Nonanalytical cessation.

CHAKRA, *'khor lo*, lit. wheel. These are centers of the psychophysical wind energy located at the different points on the central channel, from which smaller channels radiate to the rest of the body. Depending on the teachings and practice in question, their number varies from four to six.

CHAKRAVARTIN, Skt., *'khor lo sgyur ba'i rgyal po*. A universal monarch, the name given to a special kind of exalted being who has dominion over a greater or lesser part of the three-thousandfold universe. According to traditional cosmology, such beings appear only when the human life span surpasses eighty thousand years. By analogy, the word is also used as a title for a great king.

CHANDRAGOMIN, *zla ba*. An Indian lay scholar and contemporary of Chandrakirti. He was associated with the university of Nalanda and was widely reputed for his immense learning in the Mahayana teachings and all kinds of secular knowledge, being, among other things, a renowned grammarian. He also practiced the tantras and attained high realization.

CHANDRAKIRTI, *zla ba grags pa*. A sixth-century Indian master and author of unparalleled dialectical skill. He followed the Madhayamika tradition of Nagarjuna and reaffirmed the prasangika standpoint of Buddhapalita, against Bhavaviveka, as the supreme philosophical position of the Mahayana. He is thus regarded as the systematizer and founder of the Prasangika Madhyamika school.

CHANNELS, ENERGIES, AND ESSENCE DROPS, *rtsa rlung thig le*, Skt. nadi, prana, bindu. The subtle channels, wind energies, and essences, brought under control in the practice of Anuyoga.

CHARVAKAS, *rgyang 'phen pa*. Members of an ancient Indian philosophical school professing metaphysical nihilism. The Charvakas denied causality, the law of karma, and the existence of past and future lives.

CHITTAMATRINS, *sems tsam pa*, lit. the upholders of "mind-only." Followers of the Chittamatra (also called the Yogachara) philosophy of the Mahayana, which asserts the self-cognizing mind as the ultimate reality and identifies shunyata, or emptiness, as the absence of the subject-object dualism that overspreads and obscures the underlying pure consciousness. The Chittamatra or Yogachara school was founded by Asanga and his brother Vasubandhu (fourth century), who base themselves on the scriptures of the third turning of the Dharma wheel, such as the *Sandhinirmochana-sutra*.

CHÖ, *gcod*, lit. cutting. A meditative and ritual practice, based on the prajnaparamita, involving a visualization in which the physical body is offered as food to evil or dangerous spirits, the purpose being to destroy or "cut" the four demons within. Chö was introduced to Tibet by the Indian master Padampa Sangye and his Tibetan disciple the yogini Machig Labdrön.

CLEAR LIGHT, *'od gsal.* The name of the third level in the second samadhi of the form realm.

COGNITIVE OBSCURATIONS, *shes sgrib.* Dualistic thought processes that apprehend subject, object, and action as being truly existent and which thus act as obstructions to the mind's omniscience.

COMPOUNDED PHENOMENON, *'dus byas.* A phenomenon belonging to the relative level, so called because it appears to arise, abide, and eventually cease.

CONCEIVED OBJECT, *zhen yul.* A technical term in Buddhist logic, used to refer to objects of the conceptual consciousness that identifies and names things. It thus refers to sense objects as apprehended by this consciousness, but also to imaginary objects that are mistakenly assumed to exist (e.g., the "self").

CONQUEROR, *rgyal ba,* Skt. jina. An epithet of the Buddha.

DAKA, Skt., *dpa' bo,* lit. hero. A name given to male Bodhisattvas in the tantras; the male equivalent of a dakini.

DAKINI, Skt., *mkha' 'dro ma,* lit. moving through space. The representation of wisdom in female form. There are several levels of dakini: wisdom dakinis, who have complete realization, and worldly dakinis, who possess various spiritual powers. The word is also used as a title for great women teachers and as a respectful form of address to the wives of spiritual masters.

DEFEAT, *pham pa,* a type of transgression of the precepts, a misdemeanor that brings about a complete destruction of the vow.

DEFILED EMOTIONAL CONSCIOUSNESS, *nyon yid. See* Eight consciousnesses.

DEFILED EMOTIONS, *nyon mongs pa.* Skt. klesha. *See* Afflictions.

DEFILEMENTS, *sgrib pa. See* Obscurations.

DEMON, *bdud,* Skt. mara. This term is used to designate either a malevolent spirit or, symbolically, a negative force or obstacle on the path. The Four Demons *(bdud bzhi)* are of the latter kind. The Demon of the Aggregates refers to the five skandhas (body, feeling, perception, conditioning factors, and consciousness), as described in Buddhist teaching, which form the basis of suffering in samsara. The Demon of the Defilements refers to the afflictive emotions, which provoke suffering. The Demon of Death refers not only to death itself but to the momentary transience of all phenomena, the nature of which is suffering. The Demon Child of the Gods refers to mental wandering and the attachment to phenomena apprehended as truly existent.

DEPENDENT ARISING, *rten 'brel bcu gnyis.* A fundamental element of Buddhist teaching according to which phenomena are understood not as discretely existent entities, but as the coincidence of interdependent conditions. The classic formulation of this doctrine is found in the teaching on the twelve links of dependent arising, which, together with the four noble truths, constitutes the teachings of the first turning of the wheel of Dharma. This fundamental exposition, given by the Buddha at Sarnath shortly after his enlightenment, expresses the doctrines of the Hinayana. The doctrine of interdependence is, however, pervasive and is formulated variously according to different levels of teaching. Most importantly, it was interpreted by Nagarjuna as the essential meaning of shunyata, or emptiness, the ultimate nature of phenomena.

DESIRE REALM, *'dod khams*. The six samsaric states of hell beings, pretas, animals, humans, asuras, and the six classes of the lower gods. The six divine spheres are called: (1) the heaven of the Four Great Kings (*rgyal chen rigs bzhi*); (2) the heaven of the Thirty-three (*sum bcu rtsa gsum*); (3) Free of Conflict (*'thab bral*); (4) Joyous Realm (*dga' ldan*); (5) Enjoying Magical Creations (*'phrul dga'*); and (6) Mastery over Magical Creations of Others (*gzhan 'phrul dbang byed*). The desire realm is so called because the beings inhabiting it are prey to intense emotion and crave happiness based on the pleasures of the senses.

DHARANI, Skt., *gzungs*. A verbal formula, often quite long, blessed by a Buddha or a Bodhisattva, similar to the mantras of the Vajrayana but found also in the sutra tradition. The term is also used to refer to the accomplishment of unfailing memory.

DHARMA, Skt., *chos*. This Sanskrit term is the normal word used to indicate the Doctrine of the Buddha. In fact the term has ten meanings (see note 82). The Dharma of transmission refers to the corpus of verbal teachings, whether oral or written. The Dharma of realization refers to the spiritual qualities resulting from the practice of these teachings.

DHARMADHATU, Skt., *chos dbyings*. The expanse of ultimate reality, emptiness.

DHARMAKAYA, Skt., *chos sku. See* Five Bodies.

DHARMAPALAS, Skt., *chos skyong*. Protectors of the teachings. These are either enlightened beings or spirits and gods who have been subjugated by great masters and bound under oath to guard the teachings. Their task is to protect the Doctrine, its upholders, and its practitioners.

DHARMATA, Skt., *chos nyid*. Suchness, the ultimate nature of phenomena—emptiness.

DHATU, Skt., *khams bco brgyad*. A "sphere" of experience involving a sense power, its object, and the consciousness arising from their conjunction. Although a dhatu in this sense may be considered as a composite of these three elements, in fact each of these elements is referred to as a dhatu in its own right. Thus, the six senses, six objects, and six corresponding consciousnesses may be referred to as the eighteen dhatus, as expounded in the Abhidharma.

DIAMOND VEHICLE. *See* Vajrayana.

DOMINANT CONDITION, *bdag po'i rkyen.* One of the four conditions systematized by Vasubandhu in his *Abhidharmakosha* to explain the functioning of causality. The other three are the causal condition (*rgyu'i rkyen*), the immediately preceding condition (*de ma thag pa'i rkyen*), and the objective condition (*dmigs pa'i rkyen*).

DOWNFALL, *ltung ba.* A transgression of one of the precepts, which, if not properly confessed and repaired, will result in rebirth in the lower realms.

DUALITY, DUALISTIC PERCEPTION, *gnyis 'dzin, gzung 'dzin.* The perception of ordinary beings. The apprehension of phenomena in terms of subject and object, and the belief in their true existence.

EFFECTS SIMILAR TO THE CAUSE, *rgyu mthun gyi 'bras bu.* Karmic effects that in some way resemble the kind of actions that give rise to them. These may be "active," in the sense of being a spontaneous inclination to repeat the former action, or "passive," in the sense of being experiences that mirror the quality of the previous action. The former may be exemplified by children who take a natural pleasure in killing insects—a predisposition acquired through having indulged in such activity in previous existences. An instance of the latter would be the experience of poor health and short life, the passive result of killing.

EIGHT ANCILLARY CONTINENTS, *gling phran brgyad. See* Four continents.

EIGHT CLOSE SONS, *nye ba'i sras brgyad.* The eight main Bodhisattvas in the retinue of Buddha Shakyamuni. They are: Akashagarbha, Avalokiteshvara, Kshitigarbha, Maitreya, Manjushri, Samantabhadra, Sarvanivaranavishkambhin, and Vajrapani. Symbolically they represent the pure state of the eight consciousnesses.

EIGHT CONDITIONS THAT LACK FREEDOM TO PRACTICE THE DHARMA, *mi dal ba brgyad.* Eight existential states in which spiritual growth is either impossible or severely hampered. These are the conditions of hell beings, pretas, animals, long-lived gods without perception, the inhabitants of barbarous lands, people who are severely handicapped physically and mentally, and people who espouse false beliefs or who live in a kalpa in which no Buddha has appeared.

EIGHT CONSCIOUSNESSES, *tshogs brgyad,* lit. eight gatherings. A way of classifying the functions of the mind according to the Chittamatra school, also used in the Vajrayana. The eight types of consciousness are the five sense consciousnesses followed by the mental consciousness, the defiled emotional consciousness of conceiving "I," and the consciousness of the alaya, the fundamental level of the mind.

EIGHT EXTREMES, *mtha' brgyad.* Phenomena are beyond the extremes of cessation and origin; they are not nothing and they are not eternal; they do not come and they do not go; they are not distinct and they are not one. Parallel with this, they are like dreams, illusions, mirages, reflections, optical illusions, echoes, castles in the clouds, and magical displays. These eight similes illustrate the indivisibility of the absolute and relative truths.

EIGHT TYPES OF SUFFERING, *sdug bsngal brgyad*. A classification of sufferings particularly associated with the human condition. These are birth, old age, sickness, death, and the sufferings of encountering enemies, of being separated from loved ones, of not having what one wants, and of having to put up with what one does not want.

EIGHT WORLDLY CONCERNS, *'jig rten chos brgyad*. The habitual preoccupations that continually and inevitably afflict beings until they attain the path of seeing and completely transcend the ego. They are concern for gain and loss, comfort and discomfort, good and evil reputation, and praise and blame.

EIGHTFOLD NOBLE PATH, *'phags pa'i lam gyi yan lag brgyad*. Right View, Right Thought, Right Speech, Right Conduct, Right Livelihood, Right Effort, Right Mindfulness, and Right Concentration. These constitute the scheme of moral and spiritual disciplines leading to enlightenment expounded by the Buddha in the course of his teaching on the four noble truths at Sarnath. As such, they form the backbone of the fundamental practice of Buddhism.

EMPOWERMENT, *dbang*, Skt. abhisheka. Empowerment or initiation. Of these two terms, "initiation," though in many ways unsatisfactory, has the advantage of indicating that it is the point of entry into tantric practice. On the other hand, "empowerment" is closer to the Tibetan word and refers to the transference of wisdom power, from the master to disciples, authorizing and enabling them to engage in the practice and reap its fruit. In general, there are four levels of tantric empowerment. The first is the Vase Empowerment, which purifies the defilements and obscurations associated with the body, grants the blessings of the vajra body, authorizes the disciples to practice the yogas of the generation stage, and enables them to attain the Nirmanakaya. The second is the Secret Empowerment. This purifies the defilements and obscurations of the speech faculty, grants the blessings of vajra speech, authorizes disciples to practice the yogas of the perfection stage, and enables them to attain the Sambhogakaya. The third empowerment is the Wisdom Empowerment. This purifies the defilements and obscurations associated with the mind, grants the blessings of the vajra mind, authorizes disciples to practice the yogas of the "Skillful Path," and enables them to attain the Dharmakaya. The final empowerment, which is often simply referred to as the Fourth Initiation, is the Precious Word Empowerment. This purifies the defilements of body, speech, and mind and all karmic and cognitive obscurations; it grants the blessings of primordial wisdom, authorizes disciples to engage in the practice of Dzogchen, and enables them to attain the Svabhavikakaya.

EMPTINESS, *stong pa nyid*. Skt. shunyata. The ultimate nature of phenomena (namely, their lack of inherent existence) beyond the four ontological extremes.

ENJOYING MAGICAL CREATIONS, *'phrul dga'*, Skt. Nirmanarati. The fifth divine sphere of the desire realm, in which the gods can magically produce whatever they wish.

ENLIGHTENMENT, *byang chub*, Skt. bodhi. *See* Nirvana.

EPHEMERAL HELLS, *nyi tshe ba'i dmyal ba*. Infernal states, of varying duration, in which beings suffer due to the fact that they identify as their bodies physical objects such as logs of wood or stoves and suffer the effects of the use to which these objects are put (logs being burned, stoves being heated, doors being slammed, etc.).

ETERNALISM, *rtag par lta ba*. One of two "extreme" views (the other being nihilism); the belief in eternally existing entities such as a divine creator or the soul.

EVIL FORCE, *bdud*. *See* Demon.

EXAMPLE WISDOM, *dpe'i ye shes*. A foretaste or illustration of the absolute wisdom. Example wisdom is not totally devoid of conceptual mind.

EXPEDIENT MEANING, *drang don*. Teachings, for example on the four noble truths, the aggregates, dhatus, and so forth, which, insofar as they do not express the ultimate truth, are of provisional validity only. They are nevertheless indispensable in that their purpose is to lead unrealized beings gradually along the path, bringing them to greater understanding and final accomplishment.

EXPOSITORY VEHICLE OF CAUSALITY, *rgyu mtshan nyid kyi theg pa*. The paths of the Shravakas, Pratyekabuddhas, and Bodhisattvas. The expository vehicle is so called because (1) it expounds the path that leads to the attainment of the goal and (2) the practitioners of this vehicle work only with the causes that bring forth—in a direct sense—the result of their particular path (e.g., arhatship in the case of Shravakas and Pratyekabuddhas) and, indirectly, the final result of buddhahood. In contrast with the expository vehicle of causality, one speaks also of the resultant vehicle. This is so called because here the result of the path (namely, the empty and luminous nature of the mind) is utilized and practiced as the path. The resultant vehicle is another name for the Vajrayana.

FIELD OF BENEFITS, *phan 'dogs pa'i gzhi*. Beings, such as one's parents, to whom a great debt of gratitude is owed for the kindness they have shown. The field of benefits also includes beings who are natural objects of compassion, such as the sick, the old, and the unprotected. All actions directed to them will bring forth a powerful result.

FIELD OF EXALTED QUALITIES, *yon tan gyi gzhi*. The Three Jewels, spiritual masters, abbots, and so forth, who possess extraordinary spiritual qualities of elimination and realization and in respect of whom actions bring forth powerful karmic effects.

FIELD OF MERIT, *tshogs zhing*. A technical term referring to the Three Jewels, the guru, and so forth, considered as proper objects of reverence and offering, whereby the vast accumulation of merit is generated.

FIVE BODIES, *sku lnga*, Skt. kaya. According to the teachings of the Mahayana, the transcendent reality of perfect buddhahood is described in terms of two, three, four, or five bodies, or kayas. The two bodies, in the first case, are the Dharma-kaya, the Body of Truth, and the Rupakaya, the Body of Form. The Dharma-kaya is the absolute or "emptiness" aspect of buddhahood. The Rupakaya is subdivided (thus giving rise to the three bodies mentioned above) into the Sambhogakaya, the Body of Perfect Enjoyment, and the Nirmanakaya, the Body of Manifestation. The Sambhogakaya, or the spontaneous clarity aspect of buddhahood, is perceptible only to beings of extremely high realization. The Nirmanakaya, the compassionate aspect, is perceptible to ordinary beings and appears in the world most often, though not necessarily, in human form. The system of four bodies consists of the three just referred to together with the Svabhavikakaya, or Body of Suchness, which refers to the union of the previous three. Occasionally there is mention of five bodies: the three kayas together with the immutable Diamond or Vajra Body (the indestructible aspect of buddhahood) and the Body of Complete Enlightenment (representing the aspect of enlightened qualities).

FIVE CERTAINTIES, *nges pa lnga*. *See* Five excellences.

FIVE-ELEMENT STRUCTURE, *chings chen po lnga*. In his *Vyakhyayukti*, Vasubandhu describes a five-element structure around which treatises are to be composed. This comprises the purpose of the treatise (*dgos pa*), the correct arrangement of its parts (*mtshams sbyor*), the explanation itself (*tshig don*), its overall meaning (*bsdus don*), and responses to possible objections (*'gal lan*).

FIVE ELEMENTS, *'byung ba lnga*. Earth, water, fire, and wind or air, as principles of solidity, liquidity, heat and movement, and ether or space.

FIVE EXCELLENCES, *phun sum tshogs pa lnga*. The five perfections of place, teacher, retinue, time, and teaching. According to the Shravakayana, this refers to the Buddha Shakyamuni and the various moments and geographical locations in which he expounded the Dharma to his disciples. According to the Mahayana, this refers to the Sambhogakaya Buddhas such as Vairochana, expounding the teachings of the Great Vehicle in various buddhafields, in the eternal present beyond time, to a vast retinue of Bodhisattvas residing on the tenth ground. In the latter case, the five excellences are also called the "five certainties" (*nges pa lnga*).

FIVE FAMILIES, *rigs lnga*. The five families of Tathagata, vajra, jewel, lotus, and action, representing five aspects of buddhahood. Each of them is presided over by a Dhyani Buddha: Vairochana, Akshobhya, Ratnasambhava, Amitabha, and Amoghasiddhi, respectively.

FIVE IMPORTANT HEADINGS, *rtsis mgo yan lag lnga*. A method of textual analysis adopted by the panditas of Nalanda and used by Tibetan scholars. It consists of a sequence of five topics: the author of the treatise (*mdzad pa po*), its scriptural source (*lung gang nas btus*), its general philosophical tendency (*phyogs gang du gtogs*), its condensed meaning (*bsdus don*), and its purpose (*dgos ched*).

FIVE PATHS, *lam lnga*. Skt. panchamarga. *See* Path.

FIVE SCIENCES, *rig pa'i gnas lnga*. The five disciplines of which a Buddhist master must have mastery. They are medicine, philology, logic, philosophy, and "arts and crafts."

FIVE SINS OF IMMEDIATE EFFECT, *mtshams med lnga*. These are: to kill one's father, to kill one's mother, to kill an Arhat, to attack and injure a Buddha so as to draw blood, and to cause a schism in the Sangha. These actions are of immediate effect because they are so grave that their strength overrides any other karma and at death the person concerned falls directly into hell without even passing through the bardo state.

FIVE SKANDHAS. *See* Skandhas.

FIVE WISDOMS, *ye shes lnga*. The five wisdoms of buddhahood corresponding to the five Dhyani Buddhas or five Buddha families: mirrorlike wisdom (*me long lta bu ye shes*, Vajrasattva: vajra family), wisdom of equality (*mnyam nyid ye shes*, Ratnasambhava: the jewel family), all-discerning wisdom (*so sor rtog pa'i ye shes*, Amitabha: the lotus family), all-accomplishing wisdom (*bya ba sgrub pa'i ye shes*, Amoghasiddhi: the action family), and wisdom of dharmadhatu (*chos dbyings ye shes*, Vairochana: the Tathagata family).

FORM REALM, *gzugs khams*. The second of the three worlds of existence. It is divided into four levels of samadhi which, all together, are again subdivided into seventeen spheres. These are the heavens of: (1) the Pure (*tshangs ris*); (2) Priests of Brahma (*tshangs pa'i mdun na 'don*); (3) Great Pure Ones (*tshangs chen*); (4) Dim Light (*'od chung*); (5) Measureless Light (*tshad med 'od*); (6) Clear Light (*'od gsal*); (7) Lesser Virtue (*dge chung*); (8) Limitless Virtue (*tshad med dge*), (9) Flourishing Virtue (*dge rgyas*); (10) Cloudless (*sprin med*); (11) Merit-Born (*bsod nams skyes*); (12) Great Fruit (*'bras bu che*); (13) Not Greater (*mi che ba*); (14) Without Distress (*mi gdung ba*); (15) Manifest Richness (*gya nom snang ba*); (16) Good Vision (*shin tu mthong ba*); (17) Akanishta (the Unsurpassed, *'og min*). This realm is characterized by the absence of gross afflictive emotions. Beings in the form realm remain in blissful states of meditative concentration.

FORMLESS REALM, *gzugs med khams*. The four highest states of samsaric existence. They correspond to the four formless absorptions, that is, the four meditative absorptions devoid of attributes. They are called: (1) Infinite Space (*nam mkha' mtha' yas*) (2) Infinite Consciousness (*rnam shes mtha' yas*); (3) Utter Nothingness (*ci yang med pa*); and (4) Neither Existence nor Nonexistence (*yod min med min*). They are devoid of location and are characterized by the absence of perception.

FOUR BOUNDLESS ATTITUDES, *tshad med bzhi.* Four highly virtuous states of mind, regarded as immeasurable because they focus on all beings without exception and are productive of boundless merits. They are: love, compassion, sympathetic joy, and impartiality.

FOUR CASTES, *rigs bzhi.* The traditional class distinctions of Indian society associated with different psychological types and the kind of work or social function deemed appropriate to them. Over the centuries the caste system developed and is now extremely complex. Buddhist texts refer only to the original fourfold system and repudiate it in the sense of rejecting the idea, still current in Indian society, that such distinctions are immutable and are dictated by the circumstances of birth. The four types or classes are the royal or ruling class (*kshatriya, rgyal rigs*), the priestly class (*brahmin, bram ze rigs*), the merchant class (*vaishya, rje 'u rigs*), and the menial class (*shudra, dmangs rigs*).

FOUR CLASSES OF TANTRA, *rgyud bzhi.* *See* Tantra.

FOUR CLOSE MINDFULNESSES, *dran pa nyer bzhag bzhi.* Mindfulness of the body, feelings, consciousness, and mental objects, as practiced (with respectively different objects of focus and attitude) in both the Hinayana and the Mahayana.

FOUR CONTINENTS, *gling bzhi.* The four continents located in the four directions around Mount Meru, constituting a universal system. They are: the semicircular *lus 'phags po*, Skt. Videha, in the east; the trapezoidal *'dzam bu gling*, Skt. Jambudvipa, in the south; the circular *ba lang spyod*, Skt. Godaniya, in the west; and the square *sgra mi snyan*, Skt. Uttarakuru, in the north. Respectively, the names of the continents mean: Sublime Body, Land of Rose Apples, Bountiful Cow, and Unpleasant Sound. Each of the four main cosmic continents is accompanied by two subcontinents of the same shape. Human beings inhabit these continents with the exception of Chamara (*rnga yab*), which is populated by rakshasas, a kind of flesh-eating demon.

FOUR DEMONS, *bdud bzhi.* *See* Demon.

FOUR FORMLESS ABSORPTIONS, *snyoms 'jug bzhi.* *See* Formless realm.

FOUR GENUINE RESTRAINTS, *yang dag par spong ba bzhi.* These are: (1) the preemptive halting of negativities not yet generated; (2) the rejection of negativities already arisen; (3) the solicitation of positive states not yet present; and (4) the protection from decline of positive states already generated.

FOUR GREAT KINGS, *rgyal chen rigs bzhi.* These are the gods who are traditionally considered to be the protectors of the four directions. Their realm is the lowest divine sphere of the desire realm situated on the four terraces or "steps" of Mount Meru.

FOUR KAYAS. *See* Five Bodies.

FOUR RELIANCES, *rton pa bzhi.* These are: (1) reliance not on the person of the teacher but on the teaching; (2) reliance not on the mere words of the teaching but on its intended meaning; (3) reliance not on the expedient but on the absolute meaning; and (4) reliance not on intellectual understanding but on nonconceptual wisdom that sees the absolute truth directly.

FOUR SAMADHIS, *bsam gtan bzhi*. Four levels of the form realm. *See* Form realm.

FOUR TRUTHS, *bden pa bzhi*. The truths of suffering, origin, cessation, and path expounded by the Buddha Shakyamuni in his first teaching following his enlightenment. These teachings, referred to as the first turning of the Dharma wheel, are the foundation of the Hinayana and Mahayana teachings.

FOUR WAYS OF ATTRACTING DISCIPLES, *bsdu ba'i dngos po bzhi*. Teachers gather disciples by (1) their generosity; (2) the fact that their teachings are attuned to the minds of their disciples; (3) their ability to introduce disciples to the practice leading to liberation; and (4) the fact that they themselves practice what they preach.

GANACHAKRA FEAST, or SACRED FEAST, *tshogs*. A ritual offering in tantric Buddhism in which oblations of food and drink are blessed as the elixir of wisdom and offered to the yidam deity as well as to the mandala of one's own body.

GANDHARVA, Skt., *dri za*. Lit. smell eater. A member of a class of nonhuman beings, said to be nourished on smells and closely associated with music.

GARUDA, *khyung*. A kind of bird, in both Indian and Tibetan tradition. A creature of great size, it hatches already fledged and is able to fly at once. It is therefore used as a symbol of primordial wisdom.

GELUGPA, *dge lugs pa*. One of the New Translation schools, founded by Je Tsongkhapa (1357–1419), whose head is the Throne-Holder of Ganden and whose most illustrious member is His Holiness the Dalai Lama.

GENERATION AND PERFECTION. The two principal phases of tantric practice. The generation stage (*bskyed rim*), also referred to as creation stage or development stage, involves meditation on appearances, sounds, and thoughts as deities, mantras, and wisdom, respectively. The perfection stage (*rdzogs rim*), also referred to as completion stage, refers to the dissolution of visualized forms into emptiness and the experience of this. It also indicates the meditation on the subtle channels, energies, and essential substances of the body.

GODANIYA, *ba lang spyod*. *See* Four continents.

GODS, *lha*, Skt. deva. According to the Buddhist tradition, a class of beings, superior to humans, who, although not immortal, enjoy immense power, bliss, and longevity. The Tibetan and Sanskrit terms are also used to refer to powerful spirits as well as to the deities visualized in tantric meditation, which are not to be understood as "gods" in the ordinary sense of the word. Occasionally, the term is also used in a technical sense to refer to the Buddha or to the guru, as well as, honorifically, to great and powerful kings. The Tibetan usage reflects that of the Sanskrit term, which is rich and elusive in meaning. Originally it seems to have meant "bright" and, later, the "bright ones who give to man." Accordingly, the range of meaning is wide and covers the sun and moon as universal luminaries, human parents who give life and sustenance, and thence to the learned and to spiritual guides who impart knowledge.

GREAT CHARIOT, *shing rta chen po*. Name of Gyalwa Longchenpa's autocommentary to the *Mind at Rest* (*sems nyid ngal gso*), one of the three treatises of the *Trilogy of Rest* (*ngal gso skor gsum*), a description of the entire path, up to and including the Great Perfection, which is expounded according to the scholarly method ("the great way of the panditas") and according to the experiential method of pith instruction ("the profound way of the yogis").

GREAT FRUIT, *'bras bu chen po*. The twelfth level of the form realm corresponding to the highest, but still mundane (i.e., not beyond samsara), level of the fourth samadhi.

GREAT MADHYAMIKA, *dbu ma chen po*. In the Nyingma and Kagyu traditions, the name given to the fusion of the teachings of the second and third turnings of the Dharma wheel. These two turnings are paralleled, respectively, by the approach of Nagarjuna, the view that ultimate reality is beyond conceptual formulation, and the approach of Asanga, the view that ultimate reality is the buddha nature, the tathagatagarbha, free from all defects and primordially endowed with all enlightened qualities. The Great Madhyamika is also referred to as the Yogachara Madhyamika, for it stresses the role of meditation in the realization of ultimate reality, the nature of the mind. Associated with this system is the expression *gzhan stong*, "emptiness of other," referring to the understanding that ultimate reality is an emptiness which is a freedom from all factors extraneous to itself. In other words, it is a positive value and not a mere negation.

GREAT PERFECTION, *rdzogs pa chen po*, Skt. mahasandhi. The ultimate view of the Nyingma school: the union of primordial purity (*ka dag*) and spontaneous presence (*lhun grub*), in other words, of voidness and awareness. *See also* Ati, Atiyoga.

GREAT VEHICLE, *theg pa chen po*, Skt. Mahayana. *See* Mahayana.

GROUND, *sa*, Skt. bhumi. Ground or level. In the Mahayana, the ten grounds of bodhisattva realization (so described from the point of view of post-meditation experience only) extend from the path of seeing through the path of meditation and culminate in the attainment of the path of no more learning, which is buddhahood. The first seven grounds are termed impure, because the defiled emotional consciousness (which, turning toward the alaya, is what constantly conceives of "I") is still present in the mind of the yogi, and, even though not active, this results in the perception of a distinction between the observing mind and the object observed (*gnyis snang*). On the eighth ground, this defiled consciousness is removed, with the result that the strongest manifestations of this dualistic appearance are dissipated. On the ninth and tenth grounds, even the most subtle traces of this gradually cease. According to the Hinayana, there are eight grounds of realization. According to the Vajrayana, there are thirteen grounds or more.

GROUND OF UTTER JOY. *See* Perfect Joy.

GROUND, PATH, AND FRUIT, *gzhi lam 'bras bu*. Each Buddhist tenet system asserts its own approach to reality in terms of ground, path, and fruit. Generally speaking, the ground refers to a specific view of reality, the path comprises the meditation performed within the framework of that view, and the fruit is the final result of the practice.

GUHYAGARBHA, *gsang ba'i snying po*. The chief Mahayoga tantra of the Nyingma school.

GUNAPRABHA, *yon tan 'od*. A disciple of Vasubandhu and master and exponent of both the Hinayana and Mahayana teachings. He is celebrated as the great authority on the Vinaya and composed the famous *Vinaya-sutra*.

GURU YOGA, Skt., *bla ma'i rnal 'byor*. A practice consisting of the visualization of the guru (in whichever form), prayers and requests for blessing, the visualized reception of these blessings, and the merging of the mind in the guru's enlightened wisdom mind. Guru yoga is the single most important practice of tantric Buddhism.

GYURME DORJE, *'gyur med rdo rje*, name of Minling Terdag Lingpa (1646–1714). A celebrated tertön and founder of the Mindroling monastery in central Tibet. He collected the tantras of the long oral lineage of the Nyingma school and all the earlier terma teachings. He was thus instrumental in the preservation of the Nyingma tradition.

HARIBHADRA, *seng ge bzang po*, a disciple of Shantarakshita and Vairotsana in the late eighth century. He was an exponent of the Yogachara Svatantrika Madhyamika school. He did much to propagate the teachings of the Prajnaparamita and is well known for his commentary on the same sutra. He was the preceptor of the Buddhist king Dharmapala and was closely associated with the monastic university of Vikramashila.

HEAVEN OF THE PURE, *tshangs ris*. The first level of the first samadhi of the form realm.

HERUKA, Skt., A term used to refer to any meditational deity, a symbol of the ultimate nature of the mind.

HINAYANA, *theg dman*. The fundamental system of Buddhist thought and practice deriving from the first turning of the wheel of Dharma and centering around the teachings on the four noble truths and the twelvefold chain of dependent arising. In situations where it might be understood in a pejorative sense, Hinayana (small or low vehicle) is often avoided in favor of Shravakayana (the vehicle of the Shravakas or Hearers). It should in any case be noted that in Tibetan Buddhism, the Hinayana is regarded as an intrinsic part, indeed the foundation, of the teachings and is not disparaged, even though the narrowly "hinayana motivation," of aiming solely for one's own liberation (as contrasted with the universal attitude of bodhichitta), is considered incomplete and insufficient. Altogether there were eighteen hinayana schools, of which only one, the Theravada, still exists today, existing mainly in the countries of south Asia.

HOLDER OF THE VAJRA, *rdo rje 'dzin pa*, a title given to the holder of the three kinds of discipline or vow.

IGNORANCE, *ma rig pa*, Skt. avidya. In a Buddhist context, ignorance is not mere nescience but mistaken apprehension. It is the incorrect understanding of, or failure to recognize, the ultimate nature of the person and phenomena, and falsely ascribing true existence to them.

INDIVIDUAL LIBERATION, *so sor thar pa*. Skt. pratimoksha. *See* Pratimoksha.

INDRA, Skt., *dbang po*. Also known as Shakra (*brgya byin*), the supreme god and king of the heaven of the Thirty-three, which is located in the desire realm. Indra is regarded as a protector of the Buddhist doctrine.

INFINITE PURITY, *dag pa rab 'byams*. A technical term referring to the tantric realization that appearances, sounds, and thoughts are the mandala of the deities, mantras, and primordial wisdom.

JAMBUDVIPA, Skt., *'dzam bu gling*, lit. the land of rose-apples. The southern continent of the four situated around Mount Meru. Jambudvipa is the human world in which we live.

JETSUN MILA (1040–1123). The famous disciple of Marpa the Translator. One of Tibet's most revered yogis and poets, who attained buddhahood in the course of a single life.

JNANAGARBHA, *ye shes snying po*, a master of Nalanda university and the ordaining abbot of Shantarakshita. He was an exponent of the "upper school" of Svatantrika Madhyamika and the author of the celebrated *Two Truths of the Middle Way*.

KAGYUPA, *bka' brgyud pa*. One of the New Translation schools, founded by Marpa the Translator (1012–1099). This school is divided into many subschools, the most well known nowadays being the Karma (or Dhakpo) Kagyu, Drikung Kagyu, Drukpa Kagyu, and Shangpa Kagyu.

KALACHAKRA, *dus kyi 'khor lo*, lit. wheel of time. One of the main tantras practiced by the New Translation schools of Tibetan Buddhism. It is celebrated for the unique cosmological system that it expounds and is closely associated with the hidden realm of Shambhala, the king of which was the first to receive this teaching from the Buddha.

KALPA, *bskal pa.* A great kalpa is the time period corresponding to a cycle of formation, duration, destruction, and vacuity of a universe (each of these four phases comprising twenty intermediate kalpas). There is also a so-called measureless kalpa (*grangs med bskal pa*), which, despite its name, does not refer to an infinite lapse of time but to a specific period defined in the Abhidharma as consisting of 10 kalpas. The present (great) kalpa is usually referred to as the Good or Fortunate Kalpa on account of the fact that a thousand universal Buddhas will appear in the course of it. The Buddha Shakyamuni is the fourth in the series.

KAMALASHILA, (713–763). The principal disciple of Shantarakshita and an exponent with him of the Yogachara Madhyamika school. He was invited to Tibet, where he successfully debated with the Chinese master Hashang Mahayana, thereby definitively establishing the gradual approach of the Indian tradition as normative for Tibetan Buddhism.

KARMA, Skt., *las.* Action, the psychophysical principle of cause and effect according to which all experiences are the result of previous actions, and all actions are the seeds of future existential situations. Actions resulting in the experience of happiness are defined as virtuous; actions which give rise to suffering are described as nonvirtuous.

KATYAYANA. An Indian Arhat, a direct disciple of Buddha Shakyamuni.

KAYA, Skt., *sku. See* Five Bodies.

KINNARA, Skt., *mi 'am ci.* A mythical creature half-man and half-animal.

KRISHNAPA, *nag po pa.* An Indian master and teacher of Atisha (fl. c. eleventh century).

LAMA, *bla ma.* Tibetan term for a highly realized spiritual teacher, the equivalent of the Sanskrit word *guru.* In colloquial language, however, it is sometimes used as a polite way of addressing a monk.

LANGDARMA. Brother of the religious king Ralpachen. When the latter was murdered by his Bönpo ministers in the year 906, Langdarma became king. He persecuted Buddhism and almost succeeded in eradicating it, especially in its monastic form, from Tibet. After six years of rule he was assassinated by a Buddhist yogi.

LEAGUE, *dpag tshad,* Skt. yojana. An ancient Indian measurement of distance which according to the *Abhidharmakosha* corresponds to 4.5 miles or 7.4 kilometers.

LEVELS OF EXISTENCE, THREE, *sa gsum. See* Three dimensions of existence.

LILAVAJRA. Name of a master who transmitted the Mahayoga tantras to Buddhaguhya and Vimalamitra.

LONGCHENPA, *klong chen rab 'byams.* Kunkhyen Longchen Rabjam (1308–1363), regarded as the greatest genius of the Nyingma tradition, an incomparable master and author of over two hundred and fifty treatises. He brought together the two main transmissions of Atiyoga, or Dzogchen: the Khandro Nyingthik of Guru Rinpoche and the Vima Nyingthik descended from Vimalamitra. Longchenpa's wide-ranging commentaries cover the whole field of sutra and mantra, in particular the teachings of Dzogchen, or the Great Perfection, but also such topics as history and literature. Many of his writings are considered to be authentic Mind Termas. Of these the most important are the *Four Sections of Heart Essence* teachings (*snying thig ya bzhi*), the *Seven Treasures* (*mdzod bdun*), and the *Mind at Rest* trilogy (*sems nyid ngal gso*). For more details, see Longchen Rabjam, *The Practice of Dzogchen.*

LOWER REALMS, *ngan song.* The hells, the realms of pretas and animals.

LUMINOSITY, *'od gsal.* The clarity or knowing aspect of the mind. Luminosity means practically the same thing as primordial wisdom.

MADHYAMIKA, Skt., *dbu ma'i lam.* The Middle Way philosophy of shunyata, or emptiness, which avoids the extreme ontological positions of existence and nonexistence. It was first propounded by the Indian master Nagarjuna in the latter half of the second century C.E. and is still upheld in Tibetan Buddhism as the supreme philosophical view.

MAHAYANA, *theg pa chen po.* The Great Vehicle, the tradition of Buddhism practiced mostly in the countries of northern Asia: China, Japan, Korea, Mongolia, Tibet, and the Himalayan regions. The characteristic of Mahayana is the profound view of the emptiness of the ego and of all phenomena, coupled with universal compassion and the desire to deliver all beings from suffering and its causes. To this purpose, the goal of the Mahayana is the attainment of the supreme enlightenment of buddhahood, and the path consists of the practice of the six paramitas. On the philosophical level, the Mahayana comprises two principal schools, Madhyamika and Chittamatra or Yogachara. The Vajrayana is a branch of the Mahayana.

MAIN MIND, *gtso sems.* A technical term in Buddhist epistemology, referring to the consciousness that generally detects the presence of an object, whereas the different types of mental factors (*sems byung*) apprehend, and react to, particular aspects of that object.

MAITREYA, *byams pa.* The "Loving One," one of the eight Close Sons of the Buddha and a tenth-ground Bodhisattva. He resides in the Tushita heaven as the Buddha's regent and will appear on earth as the next Buddha of this Fortunate Kalpa. *See also* Asanga.

MAJOR AND MINOR MARKS OF A BUDDHA, *mtshan dang dpe byad.* Thirty-two major physical marks (e.g., the *ushnisha,* or crown protuberance) and eighty minor characteristics (e.g., copper-colored fingernails) that are typical of a Buddha as signs of his realization.

MANDALA, Skt., *dkyil 'khor*. This word has several levels of meaning. At its most basic level, it may be understood simply as a configuration or intelligible unit of space. The mandala of the deity, for example, is the sacred area or palace of the wisdom deity. The mandala of a lama might be considered as the lama's place of residence and the retinue of disciples. The offering mandala is the entire arrangement of an offering, either in real terms or in the imagination, as when a practitioner offers the entire universe.

MANJUSHRI, *'jam dpal dbyangs*. A tenth-ground Bodhisattva, one of the eight Close Sons of the Buddha. He is the personification of the body aspect and the wisdom of all the Buddhas. *See also* Asanga; Nagarjuna.

MANTRA, Skt., *sngags*. Syllables or formulas which, when recited with appropriate visualizations and so on, protect the mind of the practitioner from ordinary perceptions. They are invocations of, and manifestations of, the yidam deity in the form of sound.

MANTRAYANA, *gsang sngags*. *See* Vajrayana.

MARA, *bdud*. *See* Demon.

MASTER OF ORGYEN. *See* Padmasambhava.

MASTERY OVER MAGICAL CREATIONS OF OTHERS, *gzhan 'phrul dbang byed*, Skt. Paranirmita vashavarttina. The sixth and highest heaven of the desire realm, where gods have power over the enjoyments that other gods have created.

MAUDGALYAPUTRA. One of the two most important disciples of the Buddha Shakyamuni belonging to the Shravaka Sangha (the other being Shariputra). Maudgalyaputra was endowed with many magical powers. In traditional representations of Buddha Shakyamuni, he and Shariputra are often depicted standing to right and left of the Master.

MENTAL FACTORS, *sems byung*. *See* Main mind.

MENTAL IMAGE, *don spyi*, lit. "meaning-generality." The conceptual image experienced by the mental consciousness (*rtog shes*) and resulting from the activity of the senses. The mental image is the means whereby objects are recognized and conceptually known, a process which is necessarily indirect in the sense that the mental image is not identical with, but only representative of, the thing in question. This representation of the object is of the most general kind and functions negatively in being an elimination or exclusion of all that is not the object.

MERIT, *bsod nams*. Positive energy arising from wholesome action or virtue (*dge ba*). There are two kinds of merit: (1) mere "merit tending to happiness" (*bsod nams tsam po pa* or *bsod nams cha mthun*) and (2) "merit tending to liberation" (*thar pa cha mthun*), on the basis of which the mind progresses toward emancipation from samsara. "Stainless merit" (*zag med dge ba*) is merit tending to liberation, accumulated on the five paths. *See also* Virtue tending to happiness; Virtue tending to liberation.

METHOD, *thabs*, Skt. upaya. *See* Skillful means.

MIPHAM RINPOCHE, *'jam dbyang rnam rgyal rgya mtsho* (1846–1912). One of the greatest scholars of the Nyingma tradition, famed for his immense erudition and versatility. He was a close disciple of Jamyang Khyentse Wangpo and thus associated with the Rimé, or nonsectarian movement. Through his learning and realization, he greatly contributed to the reinvigoration of study and practice in nineteenth-century Tibet.

MOUNT MERU, *ri rab*. The name of an immense cosmic mountain, acting as the axis of the universe and around which are located the four continents. Every universal system has its Mount Meru and four continents.

MUDRA, *phyag rgya*. A term with several levels of meaning. Basically, it means a ritual gesture performed with the hands.

NAGA, Skt., *klu*. A powerful creature figuring in the Buddhist and Hindu worldview, closely associated with snakes and endowed with intelligence, magical powers, and great wealth. Nagas are said to live beneath the earth and to inhabit the watery element; in traditional medicine, they are linked with certain diseases, especially those of the skin.

NAGABODHI, *klu'i byang chub*. A disciple of Nagarjuna, famed for his devotion.

NAGARJUNA, *klu grub*. Great second-century master of the Mahayana, responsible for the dissemination of the *Prajnaparamita* sutras, which he is said to have recovered from the land of the nagas, where they had been concealed. He was the founder of the Madhyamika system of thought closely associated with the Bodhisattva Manjushri. The Madhyamika teachings of the Profound View are still regarded in Tibetan Buddhism as the summit of all philosophical systems. *See also* Asanga.

NALANDA. The famous monastic university built at the birthplace of Shariputra some distance north of Bodhgaya in Bihar and near Rajgir or Vulture Peak where Shakyamuni Buddha expounded the sutras of the Prajnaparamita. The place where many of the greatest masters of the Mahayana lived, studied, and taught, Nalanda had a long and illustrious history.

NATURAL DISCIPLINE, *rang bzhin gyi tshul khrims*. Spontaneous discipline arising from a total freedom from attachment. The vow of discipline is possible only against the background of desire (the basic expression of which is ego-clinging), for it is the principal antidote to it. Yogis who are free from desire (and who therefore have no need to take such a vow) possess a discipline that is entirely natural to them. This is also said to be the case for the inhabitants of Uttarakuru, the northern continent.

NEIGHBORING HELLS, *nye 'khor gyi dmyal ba*. Sixteen hells, four in each direction, where suffering is slightly less than in the hot hells around which they are situated.

NIHILISM, *chad par lta ba*. The extreme materialist view of considering the experiences of the physical senses as the only reality and which therefore denies the existence of past and future lives, the karmic principle of cause and effect, and so on.

NINE VEHICLES, *theg pa dgu*. The traditional classification of the Dharma according to the Nyingma school. The first three are known as the three causal vehicles of the Shravakas, Pratyekabuddhas, and Bodhisattvas. Following these are the three vehicles of the outer tantras, namely, Kriyayoga, Upayoga, and Yogatantra. Finally there are the three vehicles of the inner tantras: Mahayoga, Anuyoga, and Atiyoga.

NIRVANA, Skt., *myang ngan 'das*, lit. the state beyond suffering. As a blanket term, this indicates the various levels of enlightenment attainable in both the Shravakayana and Mahayana, namely, the enlightenment of the Shravakas, Pratyekabuddhas, and Buddhas. It should be noted, however, that when nirvana, or enlightenment, is understood simply as emancipation from samsara (the goal, in other words, of the Hinayana), it is not to be understood as buddhahood. As expounded in the Mahayana, buddhahood utterly transcends both the suffering of samsara and the peace of nirvana. Buddhahood is therefore referred to as "nonabiding nirvana" (*mi gnas myang 'das*), in other words, a state that abides neither in the extreme of samsara nor in that of peace.

NONAFFIRMING NEGATIVE, *med dgag*. *See* Affirming negative.

NONANALYTICAL CESSATION or ABSENCE, *brtags min 'gog pa*. Refers to the absence of a phenomenon because the conditions for its presence, or perception, are not operative, whether entirely or in part. This includes, for example, all that is not detected by the senses through being outside the range of the sense organs, or anything else that does not appear due to other disqualifying factors, like the absence of horns on a horse's head which are lacking due to the horse's genetic makeup. A nonanalytical cessation is therefore the absence of a certain object in a specific location.

NONCONCEPTUAL WISDOM, *mi rtog pa'i ye shes*, lit. thought-free wisdom. Primordial knowledge divested of all discursive activity.

NONRETURNER, *phyir mi 'ong ba*. The Shravaka level of realization, the attainment of which implies no further rebirth in the desire realm. This is not to be confused with the Mahayana level of Nonreturner, which indicates that the Bodhisattva in question will not return to the samsaric state of mind, even though he or she will continue to manifest in the world in order to assist others.

No-self, *bdag med*. The absence of inherent existence either of the person or of phenomena.

Nyingma school, *rnying ma*. *See* Ancient Translation school.

Obscurations, *sgrib pa*, Skt. avarana. Mental factors which veil the nature of the mind. *See* Two obscurations.

Oddiyana, Skt., *o rgyan*. Also called Orgyen or Urgyen, a region in ancient India corresponding, according to some authorities, to the valley of Swat between Afganistan and Kashmir. Oddiyana was the birthplace of Guru Padmasambhava and Garab Dorje, the first human master of the Dzogchen tradition.

Once Returner, *lan gcig phyir 'ong ba*. The Shravaka level of attainment, so called because it implies that one more birth in the desire realm is necessary before liberation is attained.

Padmasambhava, *pad ma 'byung gnas*, lit. lotus-born. Referred to by many other titles such as the Master of Orgyen and Guru Rinpoche, Padmasambhava was predicted by the Buddha Shakyamuni as the one who would propagate the teachings of the Vajrayana. Invited to Tibet by King Trisong Detsen in the eighth century, he succeeded in definitively establishing there the Buddhist teachings of sutra and tantra.

Paramita, *pha rol tu phyin pa*. A transcendent perfection or virtue, the practice of which leads to buddhahood and which therefore forms the practice of Bodhisattvas. There are six paramitas: generosity, ethical discipline, patience, diligence, concentration, and wisdom. According to another reckoning there are ten paramitas, these six with the addition of a further four, regarded as aspects of the wisdom paramita. They are: skillful means, strength, aspiration, and primordial wisdom.

Path, *lam*, Skt. marga. Progress toward enlightenment is described, in both the Mahayana and Hinayana, in terms of the five paths of accumulation, joining, seeing, meditation, and no more learning. The first four constitute the path of learning (*slob pa'i lam*); the fifth one, the path of no more learning (*mi slob pa'i lam*), is buddhahood. The paths of seeing and meditation are also termed "noble path."

Patrul Rinpoche, *'jigs med chos kyi dbang po* (1808–1887). A highly accomplished master of the Nyingma tradition, from eastern Tibet. He was famous for his nonsectarian approach and extraordinary simplicity of life. He was a prolific writer and is well known in the West as the author of *The Words of My Perfect Teacher*, an introduction to the practice of the Vajrayana.

Peaceful and wrathful deities, *zhi khro lha*. Meditational deities in peaceful or wrathful forms figuring in the Vajrayana and representing different aspects of the buddha nature.

PEAK OF EXISTENCE, *srid rtse*. The highest level in the formless realm and thus the summit of all possible states in the dimension of wordly experience.

PELGYI YESHE. A great translator and one of the principal disciples of Guru Padmasambhava from whom he received the transmission of the *Matarah mandala*.

PERCEPTION OF MERE APPEARANCE, *gnyis snang*. Despite the fact that they have realized emptiness on attaining the path of seeing, Bodhisattvas traversing the path of meditation, when not absorbed in meditative equipoise, continue to experience the percept and the perceiving mind as two separate entities. This is the residue of dualistic habit, which continues but gradually fades away, until full enlightenment is attained, even though, by virtue of their realization, the Bodhisattvas in question have long abandoned any belief in the reality of the phenomena that continue to appear to them.

PERFECT JOY, *rab tu dga' ba*. The first of the Bodhisattva grounds, corresponding to the path of seeing.

PERSONAL SELF, *gang zag gi bdag*. Innate and conceptual apprehension of an inherently existent "I"; the ego. It is a mere assumption or belief in something that in fact has no existence.

PHENOMENAL SELF, *chos kyi bdag*. Innate and conceptual apprehension of phenomena as inherently existent.

PITAKA, Skt., *snod*, lit. basket. Collection of scriptures.

PRAJNAPARAMITA, Skt., *shes rab kyi pha rol tu phyin pa*. (1) The paramita of transcendent wisdom, the knowledge of emptiness; (2) the collection of sutras belonging to the second turning of the Dharma wheel and expounding the doctrine of shunyata, the emptiness of phenomena.

PRAKRITI, Skt., *gtso bo*. The primal substance; one of the two great principles that account for the manifested universe according to the Hindu Samkhya philosophy. Prakriti comprises the three gunas, or universal qualities, which, when disturbed, give rise to the phenomenal appearances of the world. *See* Purusha.

PRASANGIKA, Skt., *thal 'gyur*. Subdivision of the Madhyamika school of philosophy characterized by the use of prasanga, or consequence (i.e., reduction to absurdity), as the best method of dealing with false assertions in order to establish emptiness beyond the reach of conceptual construction. This particular approach was first explicitly formulated by Buddhapalita and later taken up and confirmed by Chandrakirti.

PRATIMOKSHA, Skt., *so sor thar pa*, lit. individual liberation. This term is used to refer to the eight kinds of Buddhist ordination, together with their connected vows and disciplines. These are: the vows of upavasa, or twenty-four-hour discipline; male and female upasaka (*dge bsnyen*), or lay practitioner; male and female shramanera (*dge tshul*), or aspirant for a full ordination; shiksamana (*dge slob ma*), or female novice; and male and female bhikshu (*dge slong*), or fully ordained monks and nuns. Since these vows are specifically motivated by the determination to free oneself from samsara, they are fundamental to the Hinayana. They are, however, widely taken and practiced in Mahayana Buddhism. The system of Pratimoksha is sometimes referred to as the "seven vows," in which case the temporary vow of upavasa is omitted.

PRATYEKABUDDHA, Skt., *rang sangs rgyas.* A "Solitary Buddha," one who, without relying on a teacher, attains the cessation of suffering by meditating on the twelve links of dependent arising. Pratyekabuddhas realize the emptiness of the person and go halfway to realizing the emptiness of phenomena. In other words, they realize the emptiness of perceived phenomena—but not that of the subject, the perceiving mind.

PRETA, Skt., *yi dvags.* Famished spirits, one of the six classes of beings in samsara.

PRETERNATURAL KNOWLEDGE, *mngon shes.* A kind of clairvoyance. There are six kinds of preternatural knowledge. The first five (knowledge of the past lives, etc.) can occur even in the experience of ordinary beings. The sixth one, the knowledge of the total elimination of obscurations, is the exclusive preserve of a Buddha.

PROFOUND VIEW. *See* Tradition of the Profound View.

PURE LAND, *zhing khams. See* Buddhafield.

PURE PERCEPTION, *dag snang.* The perception of the world as the pure display of the kayas and wisdoms, in other words, as a buddhafield. Tending in this same direction is the contrived pure perception of a practitioner who endeavors to view everything purely, while still on the conceptual level.

PURITY AND EQUALITY, *dag mnyam chen po.* A central principle of the Vajrayana. It is the view of the Mahayoga expounded in the tantra *sgyu 'phrul dra ba* (Fantasmagorical Net). All appearances, in their purity, are the mandala of the kayas and wisdoms. This comprises the superior relative truth. Being pure, they are all equal, wisdom and emptiness united. This is superior absolute truth. The "pure" status of the appearing mode and the "equal" status of the absolute mode of being are present indivisibly in every phenomenon. This is referred to as the great Dharmakaya.

PURUSHA, Skt., *shes rig gi skyes bu.* According to the Hindu Samkhya philosophy, the conscious Self, real and eternal, the counterpart of prakriti, the primal substance. *See also* Prakriti.

QUALITIES OF ELIMINATION AND REALIZATION, *spangs rtogs kyi yon tan.* Spiritual qualities (e.g., the realization of the five kinds of enlightened vision) that shine forth in proportion as the emotional and cognitive veils are removed from the mind's nature.

RADIANT CLARITY, *'od gsal.* *See* Luminosity.

RAHU, *sgra gcan.* A mythical demon believed to cause eclipses by devouring the sun and moon.

REFUGE, *skyabs yul.* The object in which one takes refuge; *skyabs 'gro,* the practice of taking refuge.

REFUGE TREE. The field of refuge, the Three Jewels, and so forth, visualized as seated in the center and on the four great branches of a tree, for the purposes of taking refuge. *See also* Field of merit.

RELATIVE TRUTH, *kun rdzob bden pa,* lit. all-concealing truth. This refers to phenomena in the ordinary sense, which, on the level of ordinary experience, are perceived as real and separate from the mind and which thus conceal their true nature.

RESULTANT VEHICLE, *'bras bu'i theg pa.* *See* Expository vehicle of causality.

RINCHEN ZANGPO, *rin chen bzang po.* A great translator (958–1051) and inaugurator of the second phase of translation of Sanskrit texts into Tibetan, so-called the New Translation period.

RISHI, Skt., *drang srong.* Name given to the great sages of Indian mythology, endowed with great longevity and magical powers, who were instrumental in the creation, or reception, of the Vedas. In the Buddhist context, this word is usually translated as sage, hermit, or saint.

RONGZOM CHÖKYI ZANGPO, *rong zom chos kyi bzang po.* Also known as Rongzom Pandita, an eleventh-century scholar and commentator of the Nyingma school.

RUPAKAYA, Skt., *gzugs sku.* *See* Five Bodies.

SADHANA, Skt., *sgrub thabs.* Method of accomplishment. A tantric meditative practice involving the visualization of deities and the recitation of mantra.

SAGARAMEGHA, *rgya mtsho sprin.* A master belonging to the Lower school of Svatantrika Madhyamika and commentator on the *Bodhisattva Grounds* by Asanga.

SAKYA PANDITA, *kun dga' rgyal mtshan* (1182–1251). Regarded as an emanation of the Bodhisattva Manjushri, one of the most illustrious masters in the history of Tibetan Buddhism. Belonging to the Sakya school, he was a great polymath and Sanskritist. His work on the three types of vow, *The Three Vows Distinguished,* was and is extremely influential.

SAMADHI, Skt., *bsam gtan.* Meditative absorption of different degrees.

SAMANTABHADRA, *kun tu bzang po.* (1) Bodhisattva Samantabhadra, one of the eight Close Sons of the Buddha, renowned for his offerings emanated through the power of his concentration; (2) the primordial Buddha who has never fallen into delusion, the symbol of awareness, the ever-present pure and luminous nature of the mind.

SAMAYA, Skt., *dam tshig.* The sacramental bond and commitment in the Vajrayana established between the master and the disciples on whom empowerment is conferred. The samaya bond exists also between the disciples of the same master and between disciples and their practice.

SAMBHOGAKAYA, Skt., *longs spyod rdzogs pa'i sku. See* Five Bodies.

SAMSARA, Skt., *'khor ba.* The wheel or round of existence; the state of being unenlightened in which the mind, enslaved by the three poisons of desire, anger, and ignorance, evolves uncontrolled from one state to another, passing through an endless stream of psychophysical experiences all of which are characterized by suffering. *See also* World of desire.

SANGHA, Skt., *dge 'dun.* The community of Buddhist practitioners, whether monastic or lay. The term "Noble Sangha" refers to those members of the Buddhist community who have attained the path of seeing and beyond.

SARAHA. Indian yogi of high accomplishment, author of three cycles of *doha*s, or songs of realization.

SAUTRANTIKA, Skt., *mdo sde pa.* One of the four systems of Buddhist tenets. Together with the Vaibhashika school, the Sautrantika is considered as belonging to the Hinayana. The Sautrantika is remarkable for its elaborate psychology and logic and is widely studied and utilized in Tibetan Buddhism.

SECRET MANTRA, *gsang sngags. See* Vajrayana.

SEVEN-BRANCH PRAYER, *yan lag bdun.* A type of prayer (of which there are innumerable examples) comprising the seven elements of homage and refuge, offering, confession, rejoicing in the virtues of others, the request for teachings, the supplication that the enlightened beings should not pass into nirvana, and the dedication of merit.

SEVEN IMPURE GROUNDS, *ma dag pa' i sa bdun. See* Ground.

SEVEN-POINT POSTURE OF VAIROCHANA, *rnam snang chos bdun.* The ideal physical posture for meditation: legs crossed in the vajra posture, back straight, hands in the gesture of meditation, eyes gazing along the line of the nose, chin slightly tucked in, shoulders well apart and even, and the tip of the tongue touching the palate.

SEVEN SUBLIME RICHES, *'phags pa'i nor bdun.* Faith, discipline, generosity, learning, sense of shame, consideration of others, and wisdom.

SEVEN TREASURES, *mdzod bdun.* The most famous work of the Omniscient Longchenpa, consisting of seven treatises expounding the entire Buddhist path up to, and stressing, the Great Perfection (which is here discussed in a scholarly manner, "according to the great way of the panditas").

SHAKYA SHRI. A Kashmiri master, the last abbot of Vikramashila, who visited Tibet in the early thirteenth century. He was the source of the lineage of monastic ordination called the Middle Vinaya lineage (*bar 'dul*) of the Ngor branch of the Sakya school.

SHAKYAMUNI. Historical Buddha Gautama, who attained full enlightenment beneath the Bodhi tree in Bodhgaya, circa 500 B.C.E.

SHAMATHA, Skt., *zhi gnas*. Essentially a concentration in which the mind remains unmoving on an object of focus. It is a state of calm abiding which though of great importance is itself incapable of overcoming ignorance and the conception of a self. *See also* Vipashyana.

SHANTARAKSHITA, *zhi ba mtsho*. Also known as Khenpo Bodhisattva. Associated with the monastic university of Nalanda, Shantarakshita was the great exponent of the upper school of the Yogachara Svatantrika Madhyamika. He visited Tibet in the eighth century at the invitation of King Trisong Detsen and ordained the first seven Tibetan monks. He was thus the source of the so-called *smad 'dul*, the Lowland or Eastern lineage of monastic ordination followed by Nyingmapas and many Gelugpas. Among the previous Indian holders of the lineage of Shantarakshita were Shariputra, Rahula (*sgra gcan 'dzin*, another name for Saraha), and Nagarjuna. It was at the suggestion of Shantarakshita that the king invited Guru Rinpoche to Tibet.

SHANTIDEVA, *zhi ba lha*. A member of Nalanda university and the celebrated author of the *Bodhicharyavatara* (*The Way of the Bodhisattva*). He upheld the view of the Prasangika Madhyamika in the tradition of Chandrakirti. Shantideva was also the author of the *Shiksasamuccaya*, a compendium of citations on discipline, which forms a valuable collection of texts that have otherwise been lost.

SHARIPUTRA. One of the two main Shravaka disciples of the Buddha Shakyamuni, noted for his wisdom. *See also* Maudgalyaputra.

SHASTRA, Skt., *bstan bcos*. A commentary on the words of the Buddha.

SHRAMANERA, *dge tshul*. The first stage in the monastic ordination implying the observance of certain precepts. *See* note 160.

SHRAVAKA, Skt., *nyan thos*. One who hears the teachings of the Buddha, practices them, and transmits them to others with a view to his or her personal liberation from samsara, rather than the perfect enlightenment of buddhahood. Shravakas are practitioners of the Root Vehicle, or Hinayana, which is often for that reason called the Shravakayana.

SHRIGUPTA, *dpal sbas*. A master of the lower school of the Svatantrika Madhyamika.

SHURA, SHURACHARYA, *dpa' bo. See* Ashvaghosha.

SIDDHA, Skt., *grub thob.* One who has gained siddhi or accomplishment through the practice of the Vajrayana.

SIDDHI, *dngos grub. See* Accomplishment.

SIX REALMS OF EXISTENCE, *'gro drug.* Six modes of existence produced by specific karmas and apprehended as real. They are all equal in being merely perceptions of the deluded mind and lacking inherent existence. In ascending order they are the realms of hell, produced by hatred; pretas, brought about by extreme miserliness; of animals, provoked by stupidity; of humans, produced by desire; of asuras, by intense envy; and of gods, due to actions concomitant with pride.

SKANDHAS, Skt., *phung po,* lit. heap or aggregate. The five skandhas are the component elements of form, feeling, perception, conditioning factors, and consciousness. They are the elements into which the person may be analyzed without residue. When they appear together, the illusion of self is produced in the ignorant mind.

SKILLFUL MEANS, *thabs,* Skt. upaya. This refers to compassion, that is, the counterpart of the wisdom of emptiness. By extension, it refers to all kinds of action and training performed with the attitude of bodhichitta.

STHIRAMATI, *blo gros brtan pa* (510–570 C.E.). A follower of Vasubandhu. It is said that he was the rebirth of a pigeon that had spent its life nesting near Vasubhandu's dwelling place, with the result that it heard the master's recitation of scripture so frequently that it was reborn as a human being and became one of his greatest disciples.

STUPA, Skt., *mchod rten,* lit. support of offering. Symbolic representation of the Buddha's enlightenment. Stupas, perhaps the most typical of Buddhist monuments, are to be found in a variety of forms all over the Buddhist world. They often contain the relics of enlightened beings and are objects of great reverence.

SUBTLE CHANNELS, *rtsa,* Skt. nadi. The psychophysical channels located in the body, which act as the paths for the subtle wind energies that transport the essences. There are three main channels and thousands of subsidiary ones. The system of channels, energies, and essences is the basis for yogic practice.

SUGATA, Skt., *bde bar gshegs pa,* lit. "One who has gone to, and proceeds in, bliss." An epithet of the Buddhas.

SUGATAGARBHA, Skt., *bde gshegs snying po.* The essence of buddhahood, the luminous and empty nature of the mind.

SUKHAVATI, Skt., *bde ba can,* lit. the Blissful. The name of the "Western Paradise," the pure land of the Buddha Amitabha.

SUR, BURNT OFFERING, *gsur.* Food burnt on coals and offered in charity to spirits who are able to consume only the smell of burnt food.

SUTRA, Skt., *mdo.* A Buddhist scripture, a transcribed discourse of the Buddha. There are Hinayana sutras and Mahayana sutras (as distinct from the tantras). Of the Mahayana sutras, some are categorized as being of expedient meaning (*drang don*) and their purpose, as the *Akshayamatinirdesha-sutra* explains, is to lead disciples onto the path. Other Mahayana sutras are classified as being of ultimate meaning (*nges don*) and introduce the hearers directly to the Buddha's wisdom.

SUTRAYANA. *See* Mahayana.

SVATANTRIKA, Skt., *rang rgyud pa.* "Autonomists," a subdivision of the Madhyamika school of tenets, distinguished from the Prasangika. Inaugurated by Bhavaviveka (fifth century C.E.), the Svatantrika represents an approach to the relative and absolute truth in which positive reasoning, or "autonomous" syllogisms, are employed, together with arguments and examples, in order to produce a (conceptual) understanding of emptiness in the mind of the opponent and to refute the true existence of phenomena. It is distinguished from the Prasangika approach, which confines itself exclusively to consequences or reductio ad absurdum arguments.

TANTRA, Skt., *rgyud,* lit. continuum. The texts of Vajrayana Buddhism expounding the natural purity of the mind. The Nyingma school classifies the tantras into outer tantras (Kriya, Upa, and Yoga) and inner tantras (Mahayoga, Anuyoga, and Atiyoga). The Sarma, or New Translation, tradition uses another method, dividing the tantras into four classes: Kriya, Upa, Yogatantra, and Anuttaratantra.

TATHAGATA, Skt., *de bzhin gshegs pa,* lit. "One who has gone thus." An epithet of the Buddhas.

TATHAGATAGARBHA, *de gshegs snying po. See* Sugatagarbha.

TEN DIRECTIONS, *phyogs bcu.* The four cardinal and four intermediary directions, together with the zenith and nadir.

TERMA, *gter ma.* Treasures. These are teachings and sacred objects concealed mainly by Guru Padmasambhava, to be revealed later, at a time when they would be more beneficial for the world and its inhabitants. Guru Rinpoche concealed such treasures in the deepest recesses of the minds of his disciples, who were themselves practitioners of great accomplishment. In addition, although not in every case, the bestowal of these treasure teachings was accompanied by the creation of certain physical objects, often scrolls of yellow paper carrying the symbolic letters of the dakinis, or other writing (sometimes a few words, sometimes entire texts). These texts, together with other items, were entrusted for protection to the dakinis or Dharma protectors and were concealed, not in the ordinary sense, but within the very nature of the elements. According to the inconceivable workings of interdependence, when the appropriate historical period arrives, the disciples to whom a specific teaching was bestowed appear in the world and proceed to unfold the treasure teachings. In this they are often prompted by the discovery of the items just referred to, or else they spontaneously recollect the teaching received many centuries before from the mouth of the guru. The collection of terma is enormous and forms one of the main sources of teaching and practice of the Nyingma school.

THIRTY-SEVEN ELEMENTS LEADING TO ENLIGHTENMENT, *byang chub yan lag so bdun*. A system of thirty-seven factors practiced on the paths of accumulation, joining, seeing, and meditation, by means of which progress is made toward enlightenment.

THIRTY-THREE, *sum bcu rtsa gsum*, Skt. Trayastrimsha. The second divine sphere of the desire realm, situated on the summit of Mount Meru, presided over by thirty-three gods of whom Indra is the chief.

THREE COLLECTIONS, *sde snod gsum*. See Tripitaka.

THREE DIMENSIONS OF EXISTENCE, *sa gsum*. The world of humans and animals inhabiting the earth's surface, the realm of the gods and spirits in the heavens above, and the kingdom of the nagas and so on in the subterranean regions.

THREE DOORS OF PERFECT LIBERATION, *rnam thar sgo gsum*. A central notion of the Mahayana teachings of the second turning of the Dharma wheel. They are a means of approach to ultimate reality through an understanding of three qualities implicit in all phenomena. The three doors are: (1) all phenomena are empty; (2) they are beyond all attributes; and (3) they are beyond all aspiration or expectation.

THREE JEWELS, *dkon mchog gsum*. Skt. triratna. The Triple Gem of Buddha, Dharma, and Sangha; the object of Buddhist refuge.

THREE KAYAS, *sku gsum*. See Five Bodies.

THREE KINDS OF WISDOM. The wisdom resulting from hearing (*thos pa'i shes rab*), reflecting on (*bsam pa'i shes rab*), and meditating on the teachings (*sgom pa'i shes rab*).

THREE NATURES, *rang bzhin gsum*. A threefold categorization of phenomena consisting of the imputed reality, dependent reality, and completely existent reality, as presented in the sutras of the third turning of the wheel of Dharma. The interpretation of this threefold distinction varies according to the philosophical outlook of the commentator.

THREE POISONS, *dug gsum*. The three main afflictions of attachment, hatred, and ignorance. See Afflictions.

THREE PURE GROUNDS, *dag pa' i sa gsum*. See Ground.

THREE REALITIES. See Three natures.

THREE SPHERES, *'khor lo gsum*, lit. three wheels. Conceptions of the inherent existence of the object, the subject, and the action itself.

THREE-THOUSANDFOLD UNIVERSE, *stong gsum*. A billionfold cosmic system of universes, each of which comprises a Mount Meru and four cosmic continents.

THREE TRAININGS, *bslabs pa gsum*. Trainings in ethical discipline (*tshul khrims*), concentration (*ting nge 'dzin*), and wisdom (*shes rab*). The three trainings form the basis of the Buddhist path.

THREE TURNINGS OF THE DHARMA WHEEL, *chos kyi 'khor lo gsum*. The Buddha Shakyamuni gave teachings on three different levels, referred to as the three turnings of the Dharma wheel. On the first occasion at Sarnath, he expounded the doctrine of the four noble truths. Later, at Vulture Peak, he set forth the doctrine of emptiness subsequently recorded in the Prajnaparamita sutras. Finally, on various occasions, he gave teachings on the Tathagatagarbha, the buddha nature, such as are recorded in the *Sandhinirmochana* and other sutras.

THREE TYPES OF BEINGS, *skyes bu gsum*. (1) those who aspire to happiness in the higher states of samsaric existence; (2) those who aspire to liberation from samsara altogether; and (3) those who aspire to buddhahood for the sake of all beings.

THREE TYPES OF SUFFERING, *sdug bsngal gsum*. (1) the suffering of suffering—pain as such; (2) the suffering of change—the fact that happiness is impermanent and liable to turn into its opposite; and (3) all-pervading suffering in the making—the fact that all actions grounded in the ignorance of the true nature of things will, sooner or later, bring forth suffering.

THREE VEHICLES, *theg pa gsum*. The vehicles of Shravakas, Pratyekabuddhas, and Bodhisattvas. According to the Hinayana point of view, it is asserted that these three vehicles are final paths and correspond to three definite types of beings. By contrast, the Mahayana teaches that the three vehicles correspond to what is merely a temporary orientation and that in the last analysis there is only one vehicle leading to buddhahood. This means that, after accomplishing the fruit of their path, which is not, as they believe, final, the Shravakas and Pratyekabuddhas are at length roused from the peace of their nirvana and enter the Mahayana. They then follow the bodhisattva path and attain buddhahood.

THREE VOWS, *sdom gsum*. The vows and disciplines of the Hinayana, Mahayana, and Vajrayana.

TORMA, *gtor ma*. A ritual object of varying shape and composed of a variety of substances. Depending on the context, the torma is considered as an offering, a symbolic representation of a yidam deity, a vehicle of blessings, or even a weapon for dispelling obstacles.

TORMENT UNSURPASSED, *mnar med*, Skt. avici. The lowest of the hot hells, according to Buddhist teaching, characterized by the most intense and protracted form of suffering.

TRADITION OF THE PROFOUND VIEW, *lta ba zab mo'i lugs*. The sutras of the second turning of the Dharma wheel, setting forth the profound view of emptiness, were compiled by Manjushri and commented upon by Nagarjuna. In his six treatises on reasoning, the latter established that all phenomena are empty by their nature (*rang stong*), and in his Stotras and so on (commenting upon the meaning of the sutras of the third turning of the wheel), he spoke of "emptiness of other" (*gzhan stong*), namely, that the ultimate nature of the mind is empty of adventitious stains and endowed with inalienable qualities. Nagarjuna is the founder of the tradition of the Profound View. This was subsequently upheld and commented upon by Aryadeva, Buddhapalita, Bhavaviveka, and Chandrakirti, while masters such as Shantideva and Jetari propagated the practice of bodhichitta according to the same tradition. With regard to the *ritual* for taking the bodhichitta vow and its ensuing practice, the Nyingmapas mostly follow the tradition of Nagarjuna. With regard to their *view*, however, they follow both the tradition of the Profound View and the tradition of Vast Activities taught by Asanga.

TRADITION OF VAST ACTIVITIES, *spyod pa rgya che ba'i lugs*. The Bodhisattva Maitreya compiled the sutras of the third turning of the wheel, composed the five treatises named after him (which establish the view of "emptiness of other," *gzhan stong*), and taught them to Asanga. Asanga further wrote *Five Treatises on the Grounds* (*sa de lnga*) and other works, while his brother Vasubandhu, after embracing the Mahayana, composed eight *prakaranas*, or explanatory texts. These are the source of the tradition of Vast Activities, which expounds the teaching on the buddha nature and the Bodhisattva bhumis, and so on. This tradition was upheld and propagated by such masters as Dignaga, Dharmakirti, and Chandragomin. The ritual of the vow, and practice of bodhichitta, according to this tradition was introduced to Tibet by Atisha.

TRANSCENDENT PERFECTION. *See* Paramita.

TRIPITAKA, *sde snod gsum*. The Three Collections of the words of the Buddha (Vinaya, Sutra, and Abhidharma). They were compiled at the first council held shortly after the parinirvana of the Lord Buddha in the Nyagrodha cave at Rajagriha under the aegis of King Ajatashatru. Ananda recited from memory all the Buddha's sutric teachings, Kashyapa all his metaphysical teachings, and Upali all the rules of ethical discipline. The collection was supplemented and completed at the third council held at the behest of King Kanishka.

TRUE EXISTENCE, *yod pa*. According to Buddhist teaching, true existence implies characteristics, such as indivisibility, immutability, and so on.

TUSHITA, *dga' ldan*. The Joyous Realm, the fourth divine sphere of the desire realm, in which Buddha Shakyamuni abode before appearing in our world.

TWO ACCUMULATIONS, *tshogs gnyis*. (1) The accumulation of merit performed on the basis of the discursive mind (*bsod nams kyi tshogs*), in other words, the positive energy arising from wholesome action and (2) the accumulation of wisdom beyond discursive thought (*ye shes kyi tshogs*) arising from the understanding that in all experience, subject, object, and action are devoid of inherent existence.

TWO OBSCURATIONS, *sgrib gnyis.* (1) Emotional obscurations (*nyon sgrib*) such as the afflictions of attachment and anger and (2) cognitive obscuration (*shes sgrib*), that is, dualistic conceptual thinking, which prevents omniscience. These two obscurations are like veils that cover the ultimate nature of the mind and phenomena. They are also respectively referred to as attachment and impediment (*chags thogs*).

TWO TRUTHS, *bden gnyis.* The relative truth and absolute truth, the interpretation of which is pivotal in the establishment of the various system of Buddhist tenets. *See* Relative truth; Absolute truth.

TWO VEILS, *sgrib gnyis. See* Two obscurations.

TWOFOLD AIM, *don gnyis.* (1) Buddhahood for oneself and (2) the temporary and ultimate fulfillment of other beings.

TWOFOLD KNOWLEDGE. (1) The knowledge of the nature of things (*ji lta ba'i mkhyen pa*) and (2) the knowledge of all things in their multiplicity (*ji snyed pa'i mkhyen pa*), both of which are possessed by enlightened beings.

TWOFOLD PURITY, *dag pa gnyis.* (1) The original natural purity of the mind, present in the minds of all sentient beings (*rang bzhin ye dag*), and (2) the purity from all adventitious stains (*bur 'phral dag*), which is the result of the path and is the preserve of Buddhas only.

ULTIMATE EXCELLENCE, *nges legs.* The state of buddhahood.

ULTIMATE MEANING, *nges don.* Teachings which directly express the way things are from the point of view of realized beings.

ULTIMATE REALITY, *chos nyid.* Thatness, the nature of each and every phenomenon, emptiness beyond all conceptual constructions.

ULTIMATE TRUTH. *See* Absolute truth.

UNCOMPOUNDED PHENOMENON, *'dus ma byas.* A phenomenon that is devoid of origin, abiding, and cessation and is therefore totally immutable, for example, space and nirvana. The hinayana and the mahayana tenet systems have different interpretations of this term.

UNWAVERING ACTION, *mi g yo ba'i las.* A positive action, such as a profound state of meditation devoid of the motivation of bodhichitta. The characteristic feature of this kind of action is that it invariably produces rebirth in the form or formless realms of samsara. Other actions lack this unwavering or invariable quality in the sense that, depending on circumstances, their result may ripen in a realm different from the one normally to be expected.

UPASAKA, Skt., *dge bsnyen.* A Buddhist lay practitioner who has taken some or all of the precepts of the upasaka vow.

UPAVASA, Skt., *bsnyen gnas.* The twenty-four-hour pratimoksha vow, consisting of eight precepts and taken by laypeople.

USHNISHA, *gtsug gtor.* The crown protuberance, one of the principal physical signs of complete buddhahood.

UTTARAKURU, *sgra mi snyan.* The northern cosmic continent, where beings possess natural discipline.

VAIBHASHIKA, Skt., *bye brag smra ba.* The first of the hinayana tenet systems, in which the indivisible particle of matter and the indivisible instant of consciousness are regarded as ultimate truth.

VAIROCHANA, *rnam par snang mdzad.* The Dhyani Buddha of the Tathagata family corresponding to the aggregate of form.

VAJRA, *rdo rje.* Diamond or vajra weapon, a symbol of indestructibility, also used to represent skillful means or compassion. The vajra or dorje is frequently employed in tantric rituals in conjunction with a bell (*dril bu*), which in turn symbolizes the wisdom of emptiness.

VAJRA KINDRED, *rdo rje spun.* Spiritual brothers and sisters or fellow practitioners in the Vajrayana. The closest kinship exists between those disciples who receive the empowerment in the same mandala from the same teacher.

VAJRAPANI, Skt., *phyag na rdo rje.* A great Bodhisattva, one of the eight Close Sons. He personifies the power and the Mind of all the Buddhas.

VAJRAYANA, Skt., *rdo rje theg pa.* The corpus of teachings and practices based on the tantras, scriptures that discourse upon the primordial purity of the mind. *See also* Expository vehicle of causality.

VAST ACTIVITIES. *See* Tradition of Vast Activities.

VASUBANDHU, *dbyig gnyen* (280–360 C.E.). The only acharya who enjoys equal prestige as an exponent of both the Hinayana and the Mahayana. During his Sarvastivadin phase he composed the *Abhidharmakoshabhasya*, which is the most systematic and complete exposition of the Abhidharma and marks the summit of hinayana scholarship. Later in life, through his own inner development and under the influence of his elder brother Asanga, Vasubandhu adopted the mahayana yogachara view and composed many works of which the *Trimsikavij-napti-karika* (*Thirty Stanzas on the Mind*) is the most outstanding.

VEHICLE, *theg pa,* Skt. yana. A system of teachings providing the means for traveling the path to enlightenment. There are three main vehicles: Shravakayana, Pratyekabuddhayana, and Bodhisattvayana.

VIDEHA, *lus 'phags po. See* Four continents.

VIDYADHARA, Skt., *rig 'dzin,* lit. awareness holder or knowledge holder. A being of high attainment in the Vajrayana. According to the Nyingma tradition, there are four levels of Vidyadhara corresponding to the ten (sometimes eleven) levels of realization of the Sutrayana. They are: (1) the Vidyadhara with corporal residue (*rnam smin rig 'dzin*); (2) the Vidyadhara with power over life (*tshe dbang rig 'dzin*); (3) the Mahamudra Vidyadhara (*phyag chen rig 'dzin*); and (4) the Vidyadhara of spontaneous presence (*lhun grub rig 'dzin*).

VIKRAMASHILA, Skt., *rnam gnon ngang tshul.* An ancient Indian monastic university founded in the eighth century and second only to Nalanda in importance.

VIMALAMITRA, *dri med bshes gnyen.* One of the greatest masters and scholars of Indian Buddhism. He went to Tibet in the ninth century where he taught and translated numerous Sanskrit texts. He was one of the principal sources, together with Guru Padmasambhava, of the Dzogchen teachings in Tibet.

VIMUKTASENA, *sgrol sde.* A predecessor of Shantarakshita as an exponent of the upper school of the Svatantrika, but not considered its founder.

VINAYA, Skt., *'dul ba.* The name of the Buddhist ethical teachings in general and of the code of monastic discipline in particular.

VIPASHYANA, Skt., *lhag mthong,* lit. enlarged vision or profound insight. Vipashyana is essentially the primordial wisdom that overcomes the ignorant belief in the existence of the self and realizes ultimate reality.

VIRTUE TENDING TO HAPPINESS, *bsod nams cha mthun.* All positive actions performed on the basis of a belief in a truly existent agent, act, and object, and which are productive of samsaric happiness.

VIRTUE TENDING TO LIBERATION, *thar pa cha mthun.* The virtue arising from all trainings, meditations, and positive action, accompanied by the determination to free oneself from samsara and combined with the wisdom that realizes the absence of inherent existence.

WATER TORMA, *chu gtor.* An offering made with water, milk, and grains.

WHEEL OF DHARMA, *chos kyi 'khor lo.* The symbol of the Buddha's teachings. *See also* Three turnings of the Dharma wheel.

WHEEL OF INEXHAUSTIBLE ORNAMENTS, *zad mi shes pa'i rgyan gyi 'khor lo.* The enlightened body, speech, mind, qualities, and activities of the Buddhas.

WIND ENERGY, *rlung,* Skt. prana. A psychophysical component that circulates in the subtle channels of the body and acts as the support of the mind. In ordinary beings the wind energy is impure. It is called karmic energy (*las kyi rlung*) because it is contaminated by karma. When purified, however, it becomes wisdom energy (*ye shes kyi rlung*).

WISDOM. (1) *shes rab*, Skt. prajna, the ability to discern correctly; the understanding of emptiness. (2) *ye shes*, Skt. jnana, the primordial and nondual knowing aspect of the nature of the mind.

WISH-FULFILLING JEWEL, *yid bzhin nor bu*, Skt. chintamani. A fabulous jewel found in the realms of the gods or nagas which fulfills all wishes.

WISH-FULFILLING TREE, *dpag bsam gyi shing*. A magical tree which has its roots in the asura realm but bears its fruit in the divine sphere of the Thirty-three.

WORLD OF DESIRE, *'dod khams*. A general term referring to the six samsaric realms. *See also* Desire realm.

YAMA, *gshin rje*. The Lord of Death, a metaphorical personification of death.

YIDAM, *yi dam*. A tantric deity, in male or female form, representing different aspects of enlightenment. Yidams may be peaceful or wrathful and are meditated upon according to the nature and needs of the individual practitioner.

YOGA, Skt., *rnal 'byor*, lit. joining (*'byor*) or union with the natural state of the mind (*rnal ma*). A term commonly used to refer to spiritual practice.

YOGACHARA. *See* Chittamatrins.

ZUR. Teachers of Zur family lineage. Many Nyingmapa teachers of the tenth to twelfth centuries belonged to this clan. They were renowned for both their knowledge and their attainments.

Bibliography 🌊

WORKS IN ENGLISH

Dalai Lama, H. H. *The Dalai Lama at Harvard: Lectures on the Buddhist Path to Peace.* Ithaca, N.Y.: Snow Lion, 1988.

Dudjom Rinpoche. *Perfect Conduct: Ascertaining the Three Vows.* Boston: Wisdom Publications, 1996.

Hookham, S. K. *The Buddha Within: Tathagatagarbha Doctrine According to the Shentong Interpretation of the Ratnagotravibhaga.* Albany: State University of New York Press, 1991.

Jackson, Roger. *Is Enlightenment Possible? Dharmakirti and rGyal tshab rje on Knowledge, Rebirth, No-Self and Liberation.* Ithaca, N.Y.: Snow Lion, 1993.

Jamgon Kongtrul Lodro Taye. *Myriad Worlds: Buddhist Cosmology in Abhidharma, Kalacakra and Dzog-chen.* Ithaca, N.Y.: Snow Lion, 1995.

Khyentse, Dilgo. *Enlightened Courage: An Explanation of Atisha's Seven Point Mind Training.* Ithaca, N.Y.: Snow Lion, 1994.

———. *The Wish-Fulfilling Jewel: The Practice of Guru Yoga According to the Longchen Nyingthig Tradition.* Boston: Shambhala Publications, 1988.

Mipham Rinpoche. *Gateway to Knowledge.* Hong Kong: Rangjung Yeshe Publications, 1997.

Murti, T. R. V. *The Central Philosophy of Buddhism.* London: George Allen and Unwin, 1960.

Patrul Rinpoche. *The Words of My Perfect Teacher.* New York: HarperCollins, 1994; Altamira 1998; Boston: Shambhala Publications, 1999.

Pelden, Khenchen Kunzang, and Minyak Kunzang Sonam. *Wisdom: Two Buddhist Commentaries.* Translated by the Padmakara Translation Group. Saint Léon-sur-Vézère, France: Editions Padmakara, 1993, 1999.

Perdue, Daniel E. *Debate in Tibetan Buddhism.* Ithaca, N.Y.: Snow Lion, 1992.

Rabjam, Longchen. *The Practice of Dzogchen.* Introduced, translated, and annotated by Tulku Thondup. Ithaca, N.Y.: Snow Lion, 1996.

Russell, Bertrand. *The Problems of Philosophy.* Oxford: Oxford University Press, 1912.

Rangdrol, Tsele Natsok. *The Mirror of Mindfulness: The Cycle of the Four Bardos.* Boston: Shambhala Publications, 1989.

Shantideva. *The Way of the Bodhisattva: A Translation of the Bodhicharyavatara.* Boston: Shambhala Publications, 1997.

Thondup, Tulku. *Masters of Meditation and Miracles: The Longchen Nyingthig Lineage of Tibetan Buddhism.* Boston: Shambhala Publications, 1996.

Tulku, Tarthang. *Light of Liberation.* Berkeley: Dharma Publishing, 1992.

SUTRAS

Ajatashatru-parivarta, The Chapter of Ajatashatru, *ma skyes dgra'i le'u*

Akashagarbha-sutra, The Sutra of Akashagarbha, *nam mkha'i snying po'i mdo*

Akshayamati-paripriccha-sutra, The Sutra Requested by Akshayamati, *blo gros mi zad pas zhus pa'i mdo*

Anityartha parikatha, The Discourse on Impermanence, *mi rtag pa'i gtam*

Arya-Lokadhara-paripriccha-sutra, The Sutra of the Questions of Arya Lokadhara, *'phags pa 'jig rten 'dzin gyis dris pa'i mdo*

Avatamsaka-sutra, The Great Compendium Sutra, *phel po che'i mdo*

Bhadrakalpita-sutra, The Fortunate Kalpa Sutra, *bskal pa bzang po'i mdo*

Bodhisattvapratimoksha-sutra, The Bodhisattva Pratimoksha Sutra, *byang chub sems dpa'i so sor thar pa'i mdo*

Chandrapradipa-sutra, The Lamp of the Moon Sutra, *zla ba'i sgron me'i mdo*

Dashachakrakshitigarbha-sutra, The Ten Wheel Sutra, *'khor lo bcu pa'i mdo*

Dashadharmaka-sutra, The Ten Dharma Sutra, *chos bcu pa*

Gandavyuha sutra, The Tree-Garland Sutra, *sdong bo bkod pa'i mdo*

Hridaya-sutra, The Heart Sutra, *shes rab snying po mdo*

Karmashataka-sutra, The Hundred Actions Sutra, *las brgya pa*

Karmavibhanga, Actions Distinguished, *las rnam par 'byed pa*

Kashyapa-parivarta, The Kashyapa Chapter, *'od srung gi le'u*

Lalitavistara-sutra, The Sutra of Great Play, *rgya cher rol pa*

Lankavatara-sutra, The Visit to Lanka Sutra, *lang kar gshegs pa'i mdo*

Mahabheri-sutra, The Great Drum Sutra, *rnga bo che'i mdo*

Mahaguhyaupayakaushalya-sutra, The Sutra of Skillful Means of the Great Secret, *gsang chen thabs la mkhas pa'i mdo*

Mahamoksha-sutra, The Great Liberation Sutra, *thar pa chen po'i mdo*

Niyataniyatagatimudravatara-sutra, The Sutra of Certain and Uncertain Displacement, *nges pa dang ma nges pa la 'jug pa'i mdo*

Pitaputrasamagama-sutra, The Sutra of the Meeting of the Father with the Son, *yab sras mjal ba'i mdo*

Pratimoksha-sutra, The Individual Liberation Sutra, *so sor thar pa'i mdo*

Rajavavadaka-sutra, The Sutra of Advice for the King, *rgyal po la gdams pa'i mdo*

Ratnakuta, The Jewel Mound Sutra, *dkon mchog brtsegs pa*

Ratnamegha-sutra, The Cloud of Jewels Sutra, *dkon mchog sprin*

Ratnarashi-sutra, The Heap of Jewels Sutra, *rin po che'i phung po'i mdo*

Ratnolka-sutra, The Sutra of the Precious Palm Tree, *dkon mchog ta la la'i mdo*

Saddharmapundarika-sutra, The White Lotus Sutra, *pad ma dkar po'i mdo*

Saddharmasmrityupasthana-sutra, The Close Mindfulness Sutra, *dran pa nyer bzhag mdo*

Sagaramati-paripriccha-sutra, The Sutra Requested by Sagaramati, *blo gros rgya mtshos zhus pa'i mdo*

Samadhiraja-sutra, The King of Concentrations Sutra, *ting 'dzin rgyal po'i mdo*

Sanchayagathaprajnaparamita-sutra, The Condensed Prajnaparamita Sutra, *mdo sdud pa*

Sandhinirmochana-sutra, The Sutra Decisively Revealing the Wisdom Intention, *dgongs pa nges 'grel gyi mdo*

Shrimaladevisimhanada-sutra, The Queen Shrimala Sutra, *dpal phreng gi mdo*

Subahu-paripriccha-sutra, The Sutra Requested by Subahu, *lag bzangs kyis zhus pa'i mdo*

Triskandhaka-sutra, The Three Parts Sutra, *phung po gsum pa tshang ba'i mdo*

Udanavarga, The Intentionally Spoken Chapters, *ched du brjod pa'i tshoms*

Vimalaprabha-sutra, The Sutra of the Immaculate, *dri ma med pa'i mdo*

Vinaya-uttaragrantha, The Unparalleled Text on the Vinaya, *'dul ba gzhung dam pa*

Vinayavastu, The Basis of Vinaya, *lung gzhi*

Vinayavibhanga, The Distinctions Regarding the Vinaya, *lung rnam 'byed*

TIBETAN AND SANSKRIT TREATISES

Abhidharmakosha by Vasubandhu, The Treasury of Abhidharma, *mngon pa mdzod*

Abhidharmasamuccaya by Asanga, The Compendium of Abhidharma, *mngon pa kun btus*

Abhisamayalankara by Maitreya/Asanga, The Ornament for Clear Realization, *mngon rtogs rgyan*

Absorption's Easeful Rest by Longchen Rabjam, *bsam brtan ngal gso*

Bodhicharyavatara by Shantideva, The Way of the Bodhisattva, *spyod 'jug*

Bodhichittavivarana by Smrtijnanakirti, The Commentary on Bodhichitta, *byang chub sems 'grel*

Bodhisattvabhumi-shastra by Asanga, The Bodhisattva Grounds, *byang sa*

Buddhacharita by Ashvaghosha, The Life of Buddha, *sangs rgyas kyi spyod pa*

The Chariot of the Two Truths by Jigme Lingpa, *bden gnyis shing rta*

The Commentary on the Praise of the Grounds, *sa'i stod 'grel*

The Description of the Asuras, *lha min gyi rabs*

The Description of the Hells, *dmyal ba'i rabs*

The Garland of Light by Bhutichandra, *'od phreng*

The Great Chariot by Longchen Rabjam, *shing rta chen po*

The Great Commentary on the Kalachakra by Dawa Zangpo, *dus 'khor 'grel chen*

The Introduction to the Two Truths, *bden gnyis 'jug pa*

The Lamp for the Path by Atisha, *lam gyi sgron me*

Madhyamakalankara by Shantarakshita, The Ornament of the Middle Way, *dbu ma'i rgyan*

Madhyamakaloka by Kamalashila, The Light of the Middle Way, *dbu ma snang ba*

Madhyamakavatarabhasya by Chandrakirti, The Introduction to the Middle Way, *dbu ma la 'jug pa*

Maharajakanishka-lekha by Matriceta, The Letter to King Kanishka, *ka ni ka'i spring yig*

The Mind at Rest by Longchen Rabjam, *sems nyid ngal gso*

Mulamadhyamaka-karika by Nagarjuna, The Treatise of the Middle Way Called Wisdom, *dbu ma rtsa ba'i shes rab*

Mulamadhyamakavrttiprasannapada by Chandrakirti, The Clear Worded, a Commentary on the Treatise on the Middle Way, *tshig gsal*

Munimatalankara by Abhayakaragupta, The Ornament of the Muni's Intended Meaning, *thub dbang dgongs rgyan*

Panchakrama by Nagarjuna, The Five Stages, *rim pa lnga pa*

Prajnapradipa by Bhavaviveka, The Lamp of Wisdom, *shes rab sgron me*

Rahula's Praises of the Mother, *sgra gcan 'dzin gyis yum la bstod pa*

Ratnavali by Nagarjuna, The Jewel Garland, *rin chen phreng ba*

Sammohavinodani by Buddhaghosha.

Samvaravimshaka by Chandragomin, The Bodhisattva's Vow in Twenty Verses, *sdom pa nyi shu pa*

Satyadvayavibhanga by Jnanagarbha, The Two Truths of the Middle Way, *dbu ma bden gnyis rnam 'byed*

The Seven Treasures by Longchen Rabjam, *mdzod bdun*

The Seventy Shlokas on Refuge, *skyabs 'gro bdun bcu pa*

Shiksasamuccaya by Shantideva, The Compendium of Precepts, *bslab btus*

The Songs of Realization by Jangya Rolpai Dorje, *gsung mgur*

Suhrllekha by Nagarjuna, The Letter to a Friend, *bshes springs*

Sutralankara by Maitreya/Asanga, The Ornament of Mahayana Sutras, *mdo sde'i rgyan*

The Three Vows by Jigdral Yeshe Dorje, Dudjom Rinpoche, *sdom gsum*

The Three Vows Distinguished by Sakya Pandita, *sdom gsum rab dbye*

A Treasure of Wish-Fulfilling Jewels by Longchen Rabjam, *yid bzhin rin po che'i mdzod*

The Treasury of Tenets by Longchen Rabjam, *grub mtha' mdzod*

Uttaratantra-shastra by Maitreya/Asanga, The Sublime Continuum, *rgyud bla ma*

Introduction to Scholarship by Mipham Rinpoche, *mkhas 'jug*

Vigrahavyavartani by Nagarjuna, The Commentary on the Refutation of Objections, *rtsod ldog*

Vinaya-sutra by Gunaprabha, The Discourse on Discipline, *'dul ba'i mdo rtsa*

Visuddhimagga by Buddhaghosha, The Path of Purity

Vyakhyayukti by Vasubandhu, The Principles of Elucidation, *rnam par bshad pa'i rigs pa*

Yogacharabhumi-shastra by Asanga, The Treatise on the Grounds of Realization in Five Sections, *sa sde*

TANTRAS

bdud rtsi 'byung ba'i rgyud, The Nectar Spring Tantra

dus 'khor, *Kalachakra-tantra*, The Wheel of Time Tantra

gsang ba 'dus pa, Guhyasamaja-tantra, The Union of Secrets Tantra

gsang ba cod pan, The Secret Diadem

'jam dpal rtsa rgyud, The Root Tantra of Manjushri

'khor lo chub pa'i rol pa, The Play of the Accomplished Mandala

kun byed rgyal po, The All-Creating King Tantra

mdo dgongs pa 'dus pa, The Epitome of Essential Meaning

nam mkha'i klong yangs kyi rgyud, The Vastness of the Sky Tantra

pad ma rtse mo rgyud, The Lotus Tip Tantra

phyag rdor dbang bskur ba'i rgyud, The Empowerment of Vajrapani Tantra

rdo rje sems dpa'i sgyu 'phrul drva ba, Vajrasattva's Phantasmagorical Net Tantra

rgya mtsho'i rgyud, The Tantra of the Ocean

rgyud gsang ba snying po, Guhyagarbha-tantra, The Secret Essence Tantra

rgyud phyi ma, The Later Tantra

rig pa mchog gi rgyud, The Supreme Awareness Tantra

sangs rgyas mnyam sbyor, Sarvabuddhasamayayoga-tantra, The Union of Buddhas Tantra

thal 'gyur rgyud, The "Thalgyur" Tantra

yid bzhin mchog gi rgyud, The Supreme Wish-Fulfilling Tantra

Index

Bhutichandra
  on the three vows, 221
Bodhicharyavatara, 47, 58, 63, 69, 121, 158, 162,
    176, 178, 181, 182, 211, 217, 229, 233,
    255, 307, 320, 348
Bodhichitta
  active, 159, 161, 162, 178, 184, 190
  aspirational, 149, 159, 161, 164, 176, 177,
    178, 184, 185–190, 197, 203
  classifications of, 159–163
  giving and taking, 185–186, 190
  importance of attention, mindfulness
    and introspection, 183
  importance of merit for its arising, 165,
    371 n 119
  in the manner of a ferryman, 191
  in the manner of a king, 191
  in the manner of a shepherd, 191
  loss of aspirational bodhichitta, 184,
    376 n 143
  seven-point instruction, 186–188
  vessels of, 164–165, 371 n 118
  when buddhahood is reached, 191
Bodhichitta downfalls
  causes of, 182, 374 n 134
  confessing, 184–185
  eight of ordinary people, 184, 375 n 139
  eighty faults, 375 n 141
  five of a king, 184, 374 n 137
  five of a minister, 184, 375 n 138
  forty-six minor infractions, 377, n 148
  four root downfalls of active bodhi-
    chitta, 376 n 148
  twenty downfalls, 183–184
Bodhichittavivarana, 317
Bodhisattva
  difference between lay and ordained,
    196–197, 378 n 157
  Nonreturner, 176, 373 n 132
  sixteen, 169
Bodhisattva pratimoksha-sutra, 208
Bodhisattva vow
  four aspects of, 227, 385 n 205
  importance of offering, 171 *See also* Of-
    fering

ritual, 176–179
three recitations of formula, 179
Buddha
  Buddha's twelve deeds, 371 n 117
  definition, 19, 134
  Buddha nature, 63, 160, 368 n 108. *See also*
    Tathagatagarbha
Buddhapalita, 258, 398 n 282
Buddhist composition
  five important headings, 21, 350 n 10
  five-element structure, 17, 20, 349 n 4
  fourfold interrelated purpose, 20,
    350 n 7
  six faults of non-Buddhist writings, 21,
    350 n 9
  three qualifications for, 21, 350 n 8
  three qualities of, 21, 350 n 9

Central land, 31
Cessation, 19, 67, 84, 90, 91, 92, 93, 127,
    135, 149, 224, 246, 261, 265, 283–284,
    285, 311, 337, 341, 342
  absorption of. *See* Absorption of cessa-
    tion
  of Arhats, 84
  through analysis, 395 n 265, 406
  without analysis, 395 n 265, 424
Chakravartin, 36, 47, 76, 273
Chandragomin, 198, 377 n 148
Chandrakirti, 258, 327, 330, 398 n 282
Chandrapradipa-sutra, 165, 167
Chittamatra, 50, 164, 165, 224, 250, 256,
    257, 259, 287, 295, 330
  on the three vehicles, 368 n 108
Clairvoyance, 148, 161, 297, 299, 341. *See
    also* Preternatural knowledge
Conceived object, 331–332
Concentration
  childish, 239–242, 388 n 216
  clearly discerning, 239, 242–243
  diamondlike, 264, 267, 389 n 222
  fearless or heroic, 389 n 222
  four samadhis, 62, 76, 128, 240, 342
  meditation and post-meditation dis-
    tinguished, 244, 266

confession ritual, 201

discipline of avoiding negativities, 194–226

discipline of benefiting others, 228–229

discipline of gathering virtue, 226

eight-branch discipline, 198

ending summer retreat, 201, 381 n 176

four types of discipline, 381 n 178

fully ordained monk, 197, 200

fully ordained nun, 200

natural discipline, 202, 221

ritual of confession, 380 n 174

ritual of the summer retreat, 201, 381 n 175

shramanera, 197, 198–200, 199, 212

ten major precepts of shramaneras, 198–199

uncompounded discipline, 222, 385 n 199

upasaka, 197–198, 212

after the manner of Chandragomin, 143, 198

upavasa discipline, 164, 197, 198

woman novice in training, 200

Expedient teachings, 246–247

implied and indirect teachings distinguished, 252

implied teachings, 247–248, 252

absence of inherent identity in phenomena, 248

equality of all phenomena, 247–248

fulfillment at a future time, 248

humbling of pride and conceit, 248

indirect teachings, 247, 248–252

connected with remedial methods, 249, 250–252

expressed in metaphors, 251

introducing people to the path, 249

threefold nature of phenomena, 249–250

False teachers, 103–105

Feelings. See Five aggregates

Field of benefits, 49

Field of exalted qualities, 49

Fifty-one associated mental factors, 288–294

Five aggregates, 61, 82, 84, 92, 265, 287–295, 345

conditioning factors, 83, 287

eleven wholesome factors, 289–290

fifty-one associated mental factors, 288–294

five object-ascertaining factors, 288–289

five omnipresent factors, 288

four variable factors, 289, 293–294

nonassociated, 287, 295

relationship between the main mind and mental factors, 294

six root defilements, 290–292

twenty lesser defilements, 290, 292–293

consciousness, 287, 295

defiled emotional consciousness, 49, 68, 160, 295, 370 n 116

eight kinds of, 295

feelings, 83, 287

form, 83, 287

imperceptible form, 287

perception, 83, 287, 396 n 266

Five certainties, 134, 268

Five elements, 263, 352 n 16

Five excellences, 20, 349 n 6

Five irresistible forces. See Path of joining

Five kinds of eye, 133, 297

Five object-ascertaining factors, 288–289

Five omnipresent factors, 288

Five paths, 62, 136, 160, 233, 284, 301–305

Five pathways, 143, 366 n 101

Five powers. See Path of joining

Form. See Five aggregates

Form realm, 35, 62, 76, 128, 270, 271, 273, 342, 414

Akanishta, 268, 270, 351 n 14

destruction of four abodes of samadhi, 274

Four Great Kings, 47, 76, 168, 270, 271
Mastery over Magical Creations of
  Others, 180, 271
of Great Fruit, 76
of the Pure, 36, 50, 76
of the Thirty-three, 47, 50, 77, 270, 273
Hells
  cold hells, 74, 269
  ephemeral hells, 75, 270
  hot hells, 71–73, 269, 270
  life span in cold hells, 74
  life span in hot hells, 74, 354 n 36
  neighboring hells, 73, 270
  shalmali tree, 73
  Torment Unsurpassed, 72–73, 112, 144
Human existence
  eight freedoms, 32, 105
  eight incompatible tendencies, 351 n 15
  eight obstructive circumstances, 351 n 15
  eightfold lack of freedom, 30, 120
  five circumstantial advantages, 31
  five individual advantages, 31
  mere human existence, 27
  precious human existence, 31–32
  three types of human existence, 350 n 12

Individual Liberation, 22. See also Pratimoksha
Instant, 130–132, 197
  as time required for completion of an
    action, 363 n 76
  as the shortest unit of time, 363 n 76
  meditative, 132
  of absolute reality, 130, 363 n 76
  of discernment, 130, 363 n 76
  sixteen of the path of seeing, 129–132,
    363 n 77

Jangya Rolpa'i Dorje, 329
Jetsun Mila, 110
Jigme Lingpa, 20, 21–23, 30, 61, 103, 141,
  155, 171, 183, 236, 237
Jnanagarbha, 325–326

Kalachakra-tantra, 218
Kalpa, 29, 73, 191, 237, 272, 276, 297, 298,
  299
  aeon of lengthy increase, 273
  aeon of lengthy reduction, 272–273
  dark kalpa, 30, 276
  Fortunate kalpa, 169, 273
  great kalpa, 35, 36, 276
  intermediary cycles, 273
  intermediate kalpa, 29, 35, 36, 272, 273,
    274
Kamalashila, 325, 326
Karma. See also Actions
  as a mere imputation, 63
  basis of, 49
  crucial role of intention, 52
  in general, 43
  proliferation of consequences, 46–47
Karma Chagmé, 384 n 192, 385 n 195
Karmapa Chödrak Gyamtso, 385 n 194
Karmashataka-sutra, 44, 143
Khedrup-Je, 385 n 195
Krishnapa, 176

Lankavatara-sutra, 85, 100, 131, 258
Licchavi Vimalakirti, 169
Lilavajra, 219
Livelihood
  begging for alms, 70, 99, 358 n 51
  impure ways of finding sustenance, 100
Longchenpa, 22, 209–210, 219, 317–318,
  328–329
Lord of Secrets, 115. See also Vajrapani

Madhyamakagarbha, 321
Madhyamakaloka, 326
Madhyamakavatara, 258, 307, 308, 309, 313,
  314, 316, 318, 320, 327, 330, 348,
  393 n 245, 400 n 297
Madhyamika
  on the three vehicles, 368 n 108
  view of, 338
Mahabheri-sutra, 102
Mahamoksha-sutra, 185, 376 n 144

Mahasanghika, 203
Main mind, 294, 266
  fivefold concomitance with mental
      factors, 294
  in relation to mental factors, 294
Maitreya, 20–21, 191, 253, 284, 316,
      368 n 108. See also Tradition of Vast
      Activities
Mandhata, 46–47
Manjushri, 191, 219
Maudgalyaputra, 75
Meat (consumption of), 100, 358 n 52
Meditation and post-meditation, 239,
      244, 266–267. See also Shamatha and
      vipashyana distinguished
Mental factors. See Five aggregates
Mere appearance, 178, 254, 257, 262, 264,
      314, 316, 319, 337
Merit
  dedication of, 173, 373 n 130
  five signs of its past accumulation, 120
  importance of, 120
  intermediary, 222
  stainless merit, 62
  tending to happiness, 188. See also Ac-
      tions tending to happiness
  tending to liberation, 188. See also Ac-
      tions tending to liberation
Mipham Rinpoche, 295, 390 n 227,
      390 n 228, 391 n 229
Mount Meru, 35, 71, 76, 77, 107, 148, 169,
      176, 187, 269, 270, 271
Mulamadhyamika-karika, 308, 326, 335–336,
      337

Nagabodhi, 110
Nagarjuna, 71, 76, 97, 176, 186, 214, 257–
      259, 263, 330, 334, 398 n 282
  on the sixteen instants of the path of
      seeing, 131–132
  six treatises on reasoning, 393 n 244
Nagas, 18, 29, 174, 180, 194, 197
Negation
  affirming negative, 263, 337
  nonaffirming negative, 262, 263, 337

Nirvana
  with remainder, 84, 356 n 42
  without remainder, 84, 356 n 42
Nonassociated mental factors, 287, 295
Nonreturner (Hinayana), 129, 140

Obscurations
  cognitive obscurations, 19, 84–85, 125–
      134, 176, 177–178, 245, 267, 298, 300,
      344
  emotional obscurations, 134, 177, 300,
      344, 399 n 290
  four hundred and fourteen obscura-
      tions eliminated on the path of
      meditation, 127–129, 132–133,
      304–305
  hundred and twelve obscurations elim-
      inated on the path of seeing, 20,
      125–126, 129–132
  imputed misconceptions, 132–133, 259
  innate thought patterns, 361 n 69,
      362 n 70
Offering
  absence of seven kinds of attachment,
      171, 372 n 124
  contentment, 174
  sur food offering, 280
  three pure elements of, 171, 372 n 126
Once Returner, 129, 140

Paramita, 123, 149, 161, 190, 232, 267, 319
  concentration, 234–244
  diligence, 232–234
  discipline, 194–229.
  See also Ethical discipline
  four special qualities of the paramitas,
      171, 372 n 125, 377 n 149
  generosity, 191–194, 377 n 152. See also
      Gift
  patience, 229–232
  six paramitas, 114, 122, 160, 162, 171, 177,
      190, 227, 267
  six paramitas implicit in a single ac-
      tion, 227

Saraha, 111, 214

Saraprarudita, 169

Sarvabuddhasamayayoga-tantra, 111

Sarvastivada, 203

Satyadvayavibhanga, 312, 313, 315, 320, 326

Sautrantika, 50, 224, 255–256, 259, 287, 326

    two groups of, 391 n 237, 391 n 238

Self

    clinging to personal self, 331, 399 n 290

    clinging to phenomenal self, 331, 399 n 290

    definition of personal self, 331, 399 n 288

    definition of phenomenal self, 331, 399 n 288

    personal and phenomenal selves distinguished, 331

Sense powers in the Abhidharma, 275–276, 395 n 258

Seven attributes of royalty, 372 n 121

Seven-branch prayer, 122, 144, 171–174, 185

Seven elements leading to enlightenment. *See* Path of seeing

Sevenfold reasoning, 338, 400 n 297

Seven Treasures, 22

Seventy Stanzas on Refuge, 123, 134, 141, 176

Shakya Shri, 221

Shamatha, 100, 129, 239, 242–243, 304, 333, 343, 387 n 214

    with or without form, 238, 387 n 213

Shamatha and vipashyana distinguished, 239, 389 n 221

Shantarakshita, 325, 326, 398 n 281

Shantideva, 69, 121, 158, 193, 227, 255, 320

Shiksasamuccaya, 193, 227, 374 n 136, 378 n 154

Shravaka

    eighteen shravaka lineages, 130, 203, 363 n 75, 382 n 181

    four categories of, 140–141

    four shravaka schools, 203, 363 n 75, 381 n 179

    Mahasanghika, 203, 381 n 179

Sammitiya, 203, 382 n 179

Sarvastivada, 203, 381 n 179

    spread of the Sarvastivada in Tibet, 203, 382 n 180

Sthavira, 203, 381 n 179

Shrigupta, 325

Shuracharya, 124, 360 n 65. *See also* Ashvaghosha

Six root defilements, 290–292

Solitude, 29, 97–99, 234, 236–238

Spiritual teacher

    behavior in the presence of, 112–114

    characteristics, 101, 106, 117, 125

    eight characteristics of a Vajrayana master, 102-103

    as embodiment of the Three Jewels, 111, 146

    examination of, 116–117

    false teachers, 103

    four ways of attracting disciples, 102

    guru yoga, 115, 116, 117

    reliance on, 101, 107–108

    reasons for serving, 115–116

    three ways of pleasing, 111

Sthavira, 203

Sthiramati, 378 n 155

Stream Enterer, 140

Suffering

    all-pervading suffering in the making, 68, 69, 78, 79, 158, 235

    desire as its source, 69

    eight complementary, 79

    suffering of change, 68, 78, 235

    suffering of suffering, 68, 78, 235

    three kinds of suffering, 68

Sugatagarbha, 102, 143, 271. *See also* Tathagatagarbha

Suhrllekha, 71, 76, 97

Summer retreat

    ending of, 201, 381 n 175

    ritual for, 201, 381 n 175

Sutralankara, 121, 137, 138, 139, 166, 196, 249

Svatantrika, 256, 257, 259, 312–313, 317, 323–327, 328, 330, 332, 338

autonomous reasoning, 326
higher school, 325–326
lower school, 325

Tantra
ground, path and fruit, 102
Tathagatagarbha, 136, 179, 214. *See also*
Buddha-nature
Ten limitless ayatanas, 137, 342–343
Ten powers, 133, 167, 297, 341, 344, 345
Ten strengths, 133, 267, 298, 341, 344, 345
Terdag Lingpa, 219, 364 n 85
Thirty-seven elements leading to enlight-
enment, 301–305, 341
Three doors of perfect liberation, 112, 145,
246, 249, 265, 347–348
Three Jewels, 18–20, 31, 44, 45, 49, 52,
123–125, 141–148, 164, 166, 170–175,
184, 203, 206, 289, 291
threefold salutation to, 19
Three kinds of beings, 22, 349 n 5
Three kinds of faith, 124–125
Three natures or realities, 248, 249–250,
256, 390 n 226
Three seats of the deities, 137, 365 n 88
Three vows
absence of contradiction, 216
bodhichitta vow defined, 211
change of attitude, 212–214, 225
gradual qualitative enhancement, 215
mantrayana vow defined, 211–212
observance according to Nyingma,
206–218
observance according to other traditions, 218–222
observance appropriate to the moment, 216–218
pratimoksha vow defined, 210–211
transformation of the three vows, 204,
210
Three Vows Distinguished, 210–218
Three-thousandfold universe, 32, 35, 118,
166, 169, 276, 297
destruction of beings, 273–274

destruction of the universe, 274
Endurance (universe), 277, 395 n 260
formation of beings, 270–272
formation of the universe, 269–270
four phases of, 35
four phases in human existence,
275–276
period of voidness, 274
Time, 359 n 61, 363 n 76
the fourth time, 120, 359 n 61
Tradition of the Profound View, 176, 178,
374 n 136, 376 n 142. *See also* Nagarjuna
Tradition of Vast Activities, 176,
376 n 145. *See also* Asanga
Treasure of Wish-Fulfilling Jewels, 318, 328
True existence extraneous to phenomena,
328, 333, 334
Truth of cessation, 84, 135
three aspects of, 364 n 83
Truth of origin, 83, 91, 265, 283, 285, 295
Truth of path, 19, 84, 91, 92, 135, 265, 284,
285
three aspects of, 364 n 83
Truth of suffering, 68, 91, 130, 283, 285,
295
Twelve branches of the scriptures, 135,
246, 364 n 84
Two truths
according to Longchenpa, 317
according to Patrul Rinpoche, 317–318
according to the Chittamatrins, 256
according to the Prasangika, 257
according to the Sautrantikas, 255–256,
391 n 238
according to the Svatantrika Madhyamikas, 256–257
according to the Vaibhashikas, 255
Twenty lesser defilements, 290, 292–293
Twofold knowledge, 21

Udanavarga, 251
Ultimate and expedient teachings distinguished, 246–247, 389 n 225

Ultimate teachings, 106, 143, 246–247, 257, 262, 264
Ultimate truth, 21, 93, 144, 175, 309. *See also* Absolute truth
Uttarakuru, 168, 202, 211, 272, 273
Uttaratantra, 284, 368 n 108, 371 n 117

Vaibhashika, 51, 223–224, 255, 259, 287
Vairochana Gangchen Tso, 276
Vajrapani, 38
Vajrayana master
    characteristics of, 101–103
Vasubandhu, 70, 120, 295, 352 n 22
Views, defiled, 291
    of doctrinal superiority, 126, 127, 291
    of ethical superiority, 126, 127, 291
    of extremes, 126, 128, 291
    of transitory composite, 126, 128, 132, 291

wrong views, 27, 53, 56, 58, 60, 112, 126, 144, 175, 291
Vigrahavyavartani, 334
Vimalamitra, 102, 221
Vimuktasena, 326
Vinayavastu, 201
Vinayavibhanga, 187
Vipashyana, 100, 129, 236, 239, 241, 242, 245, 266, 304, 333, 343. *See also* Shamatha and vipashyana distinguished

Wisdom
    absolute, 213
    example wisdom, 213
    resulting from hearing, 245
    resulting from meditation, 245, 265
    resulting from reflection, 245, 261

Yogachara, 326, 398 n 281
Yogacharabhumi-shastra, 198

The Padmakara Translation Group ~

The Padmakara Translation Group is devoted to the accurate and literate translation of texts and spoken material into Western languages by trained Western translators, under the guidance of authoritative Tibetan scholars, principally Taklung Tsetrul Pema Wangyal Rinpoche and Jigme Khyentse Rinpoche, in a context of sustained study and discussion.

TRANSLATIONS INTO ENGLISH

The Excellent Path of Enlightenment, Dilgo Khyentse, Editions Padmakara, 1987

The Wish-Fulfilling Jewel, Dilgo Khyentse, Shambhala, 1988

Dilgo Khyentse Rinpoche, Editions Padmakara, 1990

Enlightened Courage, Dilgo Khyentse, Ed. Padmakara, 1992 (North American edition: Snow Lion Publications, 1994)

The Heart Treasure of the Enlightened Ones, Dilgo Khyentse and Patrul Rinpoche, Shambhala, 1992

A Flash of Lightning in the Dark of Night, the Dalai Lama, Shambhala, 1993

Wisdom: Two Buddhist Commentaries, Khenchen Kunzang Palden and Minyak Kunzang Sönam, Editions Padmakara, 1993

The Words of My Perfect Teacher, Patrul Rinpoche, International Sacred Literature Trust—HarperCollins, 1994, 2nd edition Sage Altamira, 1998, Shambhala 1999

The Life of Shabkar: Autobiography of a Tibetan Yogi, SUNY Press, 1994

Journey to Enlightenment, Matthieu Ricard, Aperture, 1996

The Way of the Bodhisattva (Bodhicaryāvatāra), Śāntideva, Shambhala, 1997

The Lady of the Lotus-Born, Gyalwa Changchub and Namkhai Nyingpo, Shambhala, 1998